Silvia Montiglio is Basil L. Gildersleeve Professor of Classics at Johns Hopkins University. Her previous books include *Silence in the Land of Logos; Wandering in Ancient Greek Culture; From Villain to Hero: Odysseus in Ancient Thought*; and *Love and Providence: Recognition in the Ancient Novel.*

'Through a series of learned and perceptive close readings, Silvia Montiglio shows how ancient Greek writers drew on the fundamental human experience of sleep to structure their narratives, delineate their characters, and represent the intersections of divine and human activity. Montiglio's deep scholarship is lightly worn, and she maintains a clear focus by concentrating on a distinct tradition of mythological and fictional narratives in the genres of epic, drama, and the novel. Through an understated, associative, accretive mode of exposition, she offers readers the particular pleasure of seeing her argument emerge gradually from a wealth of closely observed examples. This is a subtle, wide-ranging, and illuminating study, from which any student of Greek literature stands to learn a great deal.'

– Sheila Murnaghan, Allen Memorial Professor of Greek,
University of Pennsylvania

'This enthralling and thoroughly enjoyable book helps us to understand how different literary genres deal with the seemingly unremarkable and inactive – but actually deeply nuanced and intriguing – things that happen while the ancients either sleep or wrestle with wakefulness. Silvia Montiglio has written a masterpiece of literary analysis which at the same time discloses a fascinating chapter in the history of Greek culture.'

– Marco Fantuzzi, Professor of Ancient Greek Literature, University of Macerata and Visiting Professor of Greek, Columbia University;
author of *Achilles in Love: Intertextual Studies*

'*The Spell of Hypnos* makes visible the subtle and unexpected play between storytelling and sleep in ancient Greek literature. In a study that is both learned and innovative, Silvia Montiglio points her reader towards the various rhythms, interruptions, and creative possibilities of sleep and wakefulness across a broad range of texts. The chapters are rich and engaging, drawing a series of thematic connections between epic, drama and the novel, which together demonstrate that the time for sleep – far from being a blank space in the structure of a narrative – represents a critical juncture in the formation of both plot and character. Her reading opens up new modes of interpretation and is especially suggestive for its ability to illustrate points of contact between different genres and authors. The sleepscapes revealed here are fascinating for the windows they open onto such fruitful topics as emotion and agency, isolation and belonging, or divine and poetic justice. It is rare to find a study that deals so expertly with such a diverse span of genres, and rare again to find one that does so through such an absorbing topic. This is an important, enjoyable, and illuminating book.'

– Alex Purves, Associate Professor of Ancient Greek Literature,
UCLA, author of *Space and Time in Ancient Greek Narrative*

THE SPELL OF HYPNOS

Sleep and Sleeplessness in Ancient Greek Literature

Silvia Montiglio

I.B. TAURIS
LONDON · NEW YORK

Published in 2016 by
I.B.Tauris & Co. Ltd
London • New York
www.ibtauris.com

Library of Classical Studies 13

ISBN: 978 1 78453 351 9
eISBN: 978 0 85773 983 4

A full CIP record for this book is available from the British Library
A full CIP record is available from the Library of Congress

Library of Congress Catalog Card Number: available

Typeset in Stone Serif by OKS Prepress Services, Chennai, India
Printed and bound by CPI Group (UK) Ltd, Croydon, CR0 4YY

FSC
www.fsc.org
MIX
Paper from responsible sources
FSC® C013604

CONTENTS

LIST OF ILLUSTRATIONS

LIST OF ABBREVIATIONS

CI (*Commentary on Homer's Iliad*): G. S. Kirk (general ed.), *The Iliad: A Commentary* (Cambridge, Cambridge University Press, 1985–93), 6 vols (vol. 1 [*Il.* 1–4] by Kirk; vol. 2 [5–8] by Kirk; vol. 3 [9–12] by B. Hainsworth; vol. 4 [13–16] by R. Janko; vol. 5 [17–20] by M. Edwards; vol. 6 [21–24] by N. Richardson).

DK: H. Diels and W. Kranz (eds), *Die Fragmente der Vorsokratiker*, sixth edition (Zurich, Weidmann, 1996–8), 3 vols.

LSJ: H. G. Liddell and R. Scott (eds), *Greek–English Lexicon*, 1940, Rev. H. S. Jones, ninth edition, *Supplement* (Oxford, Oxford University Press, 1968).

CO (*Commentary on Homer's Odyssey*): Alfred Heubeck, J. B. Hainsworth, and Stephanie West (general eds), *A Commentary on Homer's Odyssey* (Oxford, Oxford University Press, 1988–92), 3 vols (vol. 1 [*Od.* 1–8] by the editors; vol. 2 [9–16] by Alfred Heubeck and Arie Hoekstra; vol. 3 [17–24] by Joseph Russo, Manuel Fernández-Galiano and Alfred Heubeck).

ACKNOWLEDGEMENTS

Like most books, this one has incurred numerous debts. My gratitude goes to Marco Fantuzzi, Don Juedes, Kostas Kapparis, Nicholas Kauffman, Jim Marks, Sheila Murnaghan, Christopher Pelling, Alex Purves and the anonymous readers of I.B.Tauris, one of whom in particular was especially helpful. Audiences at Columbia University and at the University of California, Los Angeles, have provided ideal sounding boards for some of my thoughts. At I.B.Tauris, my editor – Alex Wright – has followed the book's production with patience and competence, while assistant editor Baillie Card has secured permissions for the images. One person, I am afraid, has lost sleep to keep up with the toiling of the author: Gareth Schmeling, whose wit and love never doze off. Thank you.

ACKNOWLEDGEMENTS

[illegible]

INTRODUCTION

Scope and goals

In George Eliot's *Silas Marner*, the estranged and secret wife of the gentleman Godfrey Cass plunges into a drugged sleep by the roadside on New Year's Eve, holding their little child. She is making her way to her husband's mansion, planning to ruin him, but her addiction to opium gets the better of her determination. She sleeps unto death. The child leaves her mother's icy embrace and follows a beam of light, which takes her to a small house, where she lies down before the fireplace and falls into a deep slumber. She is still asleep when Silas, who lives in the house, returns from an errand and finds her wrapped in the glow and warmth of the firelight.

Two occurrences of sleep in close succession set in motion events that will change two lives and constitute the novel's two main developments. Godfrey will be able to marry Nancy, the woman he loves, and Silas will find bliss in his new existence with the god-sent child.

Many more fictional narratives exploit sleep for their movement at crucial junctures. Sleep can mark endings (including the ending of the story, as in Diderot's *Jacques le fataliste*) or beginnings (Dante slumbering and losing his way in the 'dark forest' from which his journey starts, and Alice dozing off and dreaming as she enters Wonderland). It can be invested with profound significance but can also represent an unmarked blank in the development of a plot. Two characteristics of sleep render it useful for multiple

Figure 0.1 Henry Fuseli, *The Sleepwalking Lady Macbeth* (1781–4), Paris, Louvre.

narrative goals: its unknown depth and its quality as a break from activity. Because it cannot be known while it happens, it is a state in which many things can happen: healing (Don Quixote recovering sanity after his first sound sleep at the end of Cervantes' novel) or spiritual ascent (Dante dozing and dreaming before his climb to the Earthly Paradise;[1] the legendary Cretan seer Epimenides awakening to perfect wisdom after a 57-year-long slumber), or the opposite, spiritual error (again, Dante at the beginning of the *Inferno*) or the eruption of a delusional imagination (Don Quixote attacking wineskins while he dreams that he is attacking a giant).[2] On the other hand, its routine occurrence and its perception as a suspension of activity make it an expedient structuring tool, serving to break a story up into smaller units. Sleep can be a thematic equivalent to the white space that typographically separates segments of narrative.

Sleeplessness is just as versatile. Literati will instantly think of Shakespeare's *Macbeth* (II 2), where insomnia and sleep disorders showcase guilt after murder (Figure 0.1), or *Julius Caesar* (II 1), where they bespeak anxiety before murder. Sleeplessness does not lend itself to breaking up a narrative as sleep does, because it is not a cessation of activity. On the contrary, wakeful figures are always hyperactive, and the reader stays anxiously awake with them. But at the same time, their restless condition is perhaps even more versatile and productive than sleep because it has a voice, as it were. Sleep talks only through dreams or when sleepers awaken and comment on their slumber. Sleeplessness talks while it happens, about itself, its causes, the thoughts and feelings that besiege its victims. As Menander puts it, 'insomnia is the most loquacious thing'.[3] This is one reason it has a high dramatic impact and a stage presence, which sleep can have only inasmuch as it looks ahead, to awakening.

Greek authors were fully aware of the narrative and dramatic potential of both states. Plato's *Symposium* ends with its participants dozing off one by one in the house of their host, while Socrates outdoes them all in wakefulness and leaves at dawn to start another day, at the end of which 'he went home to rest'. Homeric epic repeatedly exploits sleep as an ending, of days, episodes and books. A wakeful mastermind, Zeus, sets the core action of the *Iliad* in motion, while Odysseus returns home enwrapped in a magic slumber, which begins a new set of adventures for him and the second half of the *Odyssey* for the audience. The tragic Clytemnestra is possessed by an unsleeping murderous force, then by unsleeping anguish, as is Orestes. Unhappy lovers fill the stage or the page with their restless torments. Sleep and wakefulness play a prominent role in the characterization of individualized personages as well as of types ('the responsible ruler', 'the suffering lover', 'the innocent child'). They also help to define the ways in which characters relate to the narratives in which they are found (passive, 'slumbering', or active, 'wakeful') and reveal their levels of awareness about their own actions and those of other characters. Furthermore, both states are sites of divine intervention.

This study is a close investigation of these and other roles of sleep and sleeplessness in the *Iliad*, the *Odyssey*, tragedy and comedy, Apollonius of Rhodes' *Argonautica* and the Greek novels. I have privileged extended narratives and drama over shorter texts, such as lyric or epigrammatic poetry, because their greater length makes for a richer palette of uses and meanings of sleep. To be sure, more condensed works also feature sleeping characters and abnormally wakeful ones. For instance, Hellenistic epigrams are filled with sleep-deprived lovers and slumbering beauties. But those poems' concentration allows only one image to be shown or one brief episode to be recounted, and this limits the presence of sleep and wakefulness to snapshots. By contrast, in more extended narratives and in drama the two states participate in the construction of entire segments of the plot. Though narrative and dramatic works exhibit different patterns, as dictated by their respective genres, in the deployment of sleep and its disturbances, they make a sustained use of both conditions as formal devices as well as motifs. One of my chief concerns throughout this investigation is to appreciate not only the thematic significance of sleep and sleeplessness but also their roles in the formal organization of a fictional work.

This study's focus on fictional literature has proportionally limited its treatment of nonfictional texts and nonliterary contexts. Readers will not find comprehensive discussions of Heraclitus' famously cryptic pronouncements on sleep and wakefulness, of Aristotle's treatises on sleeping and dreaming, of sleep and its pathologies in the Hippocratic writings, or of its role in religious practices, for instance ritual incubation or ecstatic frenzy. Some of the questions asked in scientific and philosophical inquiry (such as, what causes sleep? what makes it pleasant?) do find echoes and correspondences in fictional literature, but systematic treatments of those areas would take us too far afield. Moreover, sleep in nonfictional literature, especially in philosophical and medical writings, has been the object of a considerable number of studies.[4]

Since no literary text exists in a vacuum, however, I have taken cultural-historical detours whenever they might shed light on occurrences of sleep or sleeplessness in the works under consideration. For instance, the fact that the Homeric gods are said to rest on a regular basis and occasionally even to suffer from insomnia, just like their human subjects, begs a question of a more theological nature: were not the two conditions perceived to undermine divinity?[5] Likewise, the recurrent epic motif of night-time attacks calls for contextualization within military ethics and practices in archaic and classical Greece.[6] And again, Penelope's appreciation for the dark, dreamless sleep that carries her through the slaughter of the suitors resonates with well-seated and widespread beliefs in the bliss of a sleep without visions.[7] And a novelist's choice to have a wise man's life end with a serene death in slumber can also be better understood in light of the ever-increasing keenness in Greco-Roman philosophy and culture at large to domesticate death by merging it with sleep.[8]

As might be expected of a book on sleep, dreaming makes regular appearances in the chapters that follow. On those occasions, though, my main goal is not to review ancient theories of dreaming or to interpret dreams per se, but to investigate their roles in defining a character's way of sleeping, their relationship to sleep and its troubles in the construction of a plot, as well as their effects on the sleeper. Dreams can agree, enter into conflict or otherwise interfere with wakeful thinking when a character is in a dire predicament or in the grip of a difficult decision: so for instance Penelope's vision of her sister in *Odyssey* 4 dispels the anguish that keeps her long awake and is in continuity with her slumber, which stops her anxious thoughts; or, on the contrary, a novelistic heroine's dream of her husband instructing her to raise their child is in line with her nightlong thinking, which was reaching the same decision.[9] Dreams can also determine the nature and the experience of sleep. In those episodes the narrative focuses as much on sleep as on the vision it carries, by putting emphasis on how the character about to dream dozes off, how the vision awakens her or how it shapes the quality of her sleep. A dream-filled slumber is often a marked happening. It can come after prolonged sleeplessness and be eerie, god-induced.

Chapter sequence and technicalities

The first chapter is devoted to unearthing the multiple narrative implications of the danger and lack of sleep in times of war as are mapped out in the *Iliad*. Sleep's scarcity plays into the very manner in which the epic (almost) begins, with a scene of nocturnal worry resulting in the abrupt awakening of a warrior, and ends, with hurried activity but no rest, with the sun rising day after day but not setting. The substitution of war with travel and domestic life in the *Odyssey*, the subject of the second chapter, turns sleep into a more routine happening, which regulates the rhythm of the day's activity for the characters and of the narrative for the poet. The two epics also exhibit different patterns in the gods' rapport to the sleep of humans: aloof in the *Iliad*, intrusive in the *Odyssey*.

Drama, discussed in Chapter 3, builds on both Homeric epics for its renderings of sleep and sleeplessness: Heracles in *Trachiniae* returns home unconscious, like Odysseus, but to die rather than live, and other characters stay up all night in excruciating deliberation, like Agamemnon, or beset with sorrowful longing, like Penelope. Tragic plays also engage in dialogue with one another in the staging of sleep and sleeplessness both thematically and formally. And comedy distorts the tragic and epic treatments of the two states that had become stereotypical, such as lonely vigils. While I attempt to bring out these and other shared threads, I discuss each play separately, even if this approach inevitably results in a less condensed narrative than would a more overarching treatment. The reason for my choice is that a main goal of this study is to appreciate the functions of sleep and sleeplessness in the composition of individual works, and this can only be achieved by analysing the plays serially.[10]

Apollonius of Rhodes, the subject of Chapter 4, foregrounds the formal aspects of Homer's use of sleep by playing with it in the contexts of beginnings and endings of narrative units and in the pacing of the Argo's journey, which is broken up by sleep much more rarely than are travel or other activities in the *Odyssey*.

Though Apollonius' main interlocutor is Homer, his sleepless Medea conjures up figures of insomniacs closer in time to the author, such as those found in New Comedy, and her central role bears witness to the growing fascination in contemporary literature and culture with sleeplessness as a symptom of love.

Sleep-deprived lovers make repeated and dramatic appearances also in the Greek novels, which are discussed in the final chapter. As with drama, I treat each novel separately, and in this case not only to bring out the functions of sleep and wakefulness in the construction of each of them but also to emphasize their idiosyncrasies. The varied modes of presence of the two states in the novels are one more piece of evidence bearing out their individuality: even the few we have are not written according to one script. We shall see that these texts also demonstrate a strong awareness of, and creative engagement with, treatments of sleep in past and contemporary literature, and occasionally also in philosophy and the visual arts. But ultimately, as the chapter will attempt to show, Homer remains their main source of inspiration for the novelistic episodes of sleep and its disturbances.

The abbreviations for ancient authors and titles generally follow the *Oxford Classical Dictionary* (an exception is the *Palatine Anthology*, abbreviated *AP*, according to common practice). I have also produced customized abbreviations for two commentaries often quoted in this study, one on the *Iliad* and one on the *Odyssey*. In the interest of space, I only cite the original Greek in cases where it is necessary for the development of points of argument. All quotations are translated or closely paraphrased, with an eye to the Greekless reader. With the non-specialist in mind, I have also given more background context for less known texts (especially the novels), and I have kept technical discussion and language to a minimum, in the hope of making the writing more forgiving and palatable. Ancient authors found many clever ways of goading their audiences and readers awake and keeping them riveted to a performance or a narrative the charm of which, they hoped, would be irresistible enough to drive off sleep even in the wee hours. While this book does not aspire to be sleep chasing, I do hope that it will rouse the readers' interest in the creative ways in which Greek literature has exploited two familiar facts of life for fictional purposes.

CHAPTER 1

THE *ILIAD*

Sleep denied, sleep disturbed

'What is more gentle than a wind in summer?/ [...] What, but thee Sleep?' (Keats, *Sleep and Poetry*). The widely shared sentiment expressed in these verses finds a voice already in Homeric epic, which almost always describes sleep as a sweet, soft state.[1] It is one of life's joys, alongside love, song and dance (*Il.* 13. 636). Pleasantness is its formulaic quality. It does not apply selectively as in the Old Testament, where slumber is sweet only when produced under certain circumstances, for instance a hope-filled revelation or a life of wisdom.[2] Homer calls sleep kind regardless of whom it holds, regardless even of its appropriateness or effects.

In the *Iliad*, however, sleep's formulaic sweetness is either in the words of the primary narrator or of an agent other than the sleeper:[3] never of the sleeper himself. The heroes of this epic do not even talk about their slumber, whether pleasant or not. While characters in the *Odyssey* often pause to describe the length, quality and aftermath of theirs, no one in the *Iliad* ever mentions one's own. This absence is consonant with the sleep-depriving urgency that pervades the action. The exhausted, shipwrecked Odysseus is allowed to sleep a 'boundless' slumber, which lasts well into the day (*Od.* 7. 286–8), but warring Agamemnon must remember that a leader should not even sleep all night (*Il.* 2. 24 and 61). Prolonged rest is an indulgence for 'Iliadic managers'.[4] No individual hero is said to sleep all night long, a luxury afforded only to the community at large and to the gods, and even in these cases descriptions of unbroken slumber serve only to provide a foil for scenes of wakefulness.[5] Other references to hosts asleep point to the threat looming over them,[6] while mentions of sleeping individuals tend to privilege those who are about to rise.[7] Characters are abruptly shaken out of their sweet slumber, by a dream, a noise, a god or another warrior. No hero is said to awake naturally. In contrast, many a character in the *Odyssey* gets up with the sun: 'When early-born, rosy-fingered dawn appeared, [he] rose from his bed'.[8]

True, the day of the Iliadic warrior ideally follows an orderly course. Fighting begins at dawn and should end at dusk. This ideal is captured in the phrase, 'Let us obey the night'.[9] But in fact warriors do fight after dark, and they also hold nocturnal gatherings at critical junctures. In the *Odyssey*, Nestor remembers the last assembly before leaving Troy, when strife over the route for the return journey divided the Achaeans into two camps. The assembly started at sundown. Nestor sees this fact, along with the conduct of the warriors, as foreshadowing the strife that unfolded; as he says, they gathered 'recklessly, not in order, near sunset', and drunk (3. 138). This negative picture of an assembly held in the evening hours highlights Nestor's etiquette-driven vision of the events at Troy, which he can maintain now that the war is over and there is no need to summon assemblies after dark.[10] But in the *Iliad* such gatherings happen regularly. Obeying the night is not incompatible with making war decisions, for it means that one should stop fighting and eat a meal, but still keep watch, not sleep.[11]

Even in a night with no fighting, the Homeric warrior does not expect to rest. Both Achilles and Odysseus allegedly 'spent many sleepless nights'.[12] Odysseus rejects the rich bedding Penelope offers him because, he tells her, in the years at Troy he has grown accustomed to lying awake on foul beds (*Od.* 19. 337–42). To be sure, his words are strategic, for he seeks to deflect Penelope's possible suspicions about his identity by faultlessly impersonating a beggar unused to comforts.[13] But his words match Achilles' unquestionably sincere avowal. In another story, one of his made-up tales, Odysseus again pictures the hardship of nights spent on the field (*Od.* 14. 462–502), claiming that he was freezing for lack of proper clothing. Along with his protestation to Penelope, this 'lie similar to the truth' (*Od.* 19. 203) suggests that in his memory the war was fraught with sleep deprivation.[14]

Other warriors would agree with Odysseus' reminiscences, for only two days of the six that cover the fighting in the *Iliad* end in sleep: days three and four, the latter only in the Greek camp.[15] And how do the warriors rest? At the close of day three, while Greeks and Trojans are feasting 'all night', Zeus has been pondering evil 'all night' and thundering loudly (7. 476–8). The repetition of 'all night' sets Zeus' wakefulness and his control of the action off in contrast with the warriors' blind feasting, followed by equally blind sleep (7. 482). Over that sleep there sounds Zeus' thunder, which breaks in more loudly as the next day dawns and the god 'who rejoices in thunder' (8. 2) summons the other Olympians to initiate another day of fighting. This day leads to a wakeful night in the Trojan camp. The victorious and hopeful warriors sit by burning fires 'all night' (8. 554) and communicate their excitement to their horses, which, standing by the chariots, 'waited for Dawn of the beautiful throne', as if eager for the next day of battle; while on the Greek side the same day ends with slumber but only after protracted night activity: 'There they lay down and took the boon of sleep' (9. 713). And again sleep is soon interrupted when Agamemnon, restless at the opening of Book 10, causes the other warriors to be shaken awake. Alternatively, if we leave out Book 10, which may be a later addition,[16] the boon of sleep points ahead to more doom, to Zeus' momentous attack in the morning, when he hurls awful Discord at the Greek ships (11. 3–4). This day, the day of Hector's victory and Patroclus' death and the longest in narrative time (11. 1–18. 241), ends with a wakeful night on both sides (18. 299 and 314–5). And the day of Achilles' superhuman victory, the last day of fighting, does not wind down in restful slumber either,[17] but climaxes in a resonant night of mourning around Patroclus' pyre.

Soft sleep rather belongs to the prewar past. It is inscribed in the Trojan landscape or evoked in a simile. Athena, removing the shaft that has pierced Menelaus' breastplate, evokes a loving mother keeping a fly away from her child, 'when he lies in sweet slumber' (4. 130–1). The simile plays up the incongruity between an image of innocence and peace and the theatre of war, where flies turn into arrows and slumbering children into vulnerable fighters. Another sleeping child, a thing of the past, takes shape in Andromache's memory as she broods over the gloomy future that awaits the orphaned Astyanax: 'Before [...] when slumber seized him and he stopped his childish games, he would lie in a bed, in the arms of his nurse, on a soft couch, his heart full of happy thoughts' (22. 502–4). This portrait will provide the archetype for several images of sleeping children set off against frightful backgrounds.[18]

Trojan adults used to enjoy sleep as well, in their bedchambers, the evocation of which is prompted by Hector's visit to his family's palace:

> There were fifty chambers of polished stone, built next to each other. Priam's sons were accustomed to sleep there next to their wedded wives. And on the opposite side inside the courtyard there were twelve lofty chambers of polished stone, built near each other. Priam's sons-in-law were accustomed to sleep there next to their revered wives.
>
> (6. 244–50)

While Hector and his relatives used to retire to their appointed quarters every night, he now walks by them quickly, only to rush back to the arena of war. The leisurely description of a place of rest in an 'exceedingly beautiful' palace (6. 242) contrasts with Hector's haste in moving through it and away from it and with his repeated refusal to accept the minimal comforts (a seat, a cup of wine) offered by his womenfolk to restore his strength (6. 258–62; 6. 354). Outward and hurried movements prepare for the scene of Hector's farewell to his wife. He does not find her inside the house because she has 'rushed' to the walls like one possessed (6. 388–9). He then goes through the city and returns to the Scaean gates, where the parting takes place: not in the couple's bedroom or in the palace, but at the entrance to the war, by the gates 'which he was about to cross to the plain' (6. 393), soon to meet his death. Hector and Andromache do not part in the intimacy of their home, because they will never again retire to their bedchamber to sleep together.

There is only one episode in the *Iliad* in which an undisturbed, nightlong rest is followed by the resumption of activity on the next morning. After returning Chryseis to her father, Agamemnon's envoys feast and sing, and 'when the sun set and darkness came, they slept by the stern of the ship. But when early-born, rosy-fingered dawn appeared, they put out to sea to return to the great host of the Achaeans, and far-darting Apollo sent them a favourable wind' (1. 475–9). This episode stands nearer to the *Odyssey*, with which it shares language and themes, mood and morals: a feast after a sea journey, the coming of night (couched in words that occur only here in the *Iliad*, but six times in the *Odyssey*), sleep, the rising of 'early born, rosy-fingered dawn' (with a line that appears only twice in the *Iliad*, but 20 times in the *Odyssey*), more sea travel with the help of a god-sent wind[19] and an outcome that is ethically satisfying, with Chryses obtaining his due and Apollo rewarding the Greek envoys with a fair return journey.

Wakeful plotters: Zeus and Agamemnon

The sleep-depriving urgency that pervades the *Iliad* is reflected in the manner in which the core of its plot is launched: from wakeful thinking, which breaks into a landscape of sleep and targets a sleeper. At the end of Book 1, all the gods retire after feasting:

> When the bright light of the sun sank, they went each to their homes to lie down [...] and Olympian Zeus, the lord of lightning, lay down where he used to sleep before, when sweet slumber would come. There he went and lay down, and near him was Hera of the golden throne.
>
> (605–*fin.*)

The retiring scene crowns the reconciliation that ends the strife on Olympus, while down on earth Agamemnon and Achilles are not shown in their sleeping quarters after they part in anger. Though the first line of Book 2 says that 'the men were sleeping all night' along with the gods, and though Agamemnon dreams, there is no record of the human players' going to rest. Such a detail would be at variance with the tensions dividing the leaders. In contrast, the gods' orderly retiring puts the appropriate seal on their peacemaking and points to their serenity, ultimately untroubled as they are by quarrels caused by humans. (We might recall Hephaestus' words to Hera: 'Do not spoil our banquet for the sake of mortals!').

But Zeus, far from enjoying a good night's sleep, plays the wakeful party in the first scene of lonely vigil in western literature: 'The other gods and chariot-marshalling men were sleeping all night, but sweet slumber was not holding Zeus. He was pondering in his heart how to honour Achilles and destroy many by the Greek ships'.[20] Zeus is worried about the politics of Olympus, for he knows that his promise to honour Achilles will create tensions in his family, above all between himself and his wife.

Sleepless pondering, however, does not trouble Zeus for long: it instantly yields the 'best plan', ἀρίστη βουλή (2. 5), which activates the god's βουλή announced in the epic's opening lines. Zeus' power is enhanced by the vulnerability of his victim: a human, and a sleeping one at that. The dream sent by Zeus finds Agamemnon 'asleep in his tent, and ambrosial (ἀμβρόσιος) slumber was poured around him' (2. 19). Though Homer does not say it, Agamemnon's slumber also seems to have come from Zeus.[21] It is ἀμβρόσιος – the only time sleep earns this epithet in the *Iliad* – as is night, the uncanny, awe-inspiring cover of darkness that belongs to the gods and is safe only for them. A mortal should not be out alone 'in the ambrosial night', when others are resting.[22] The very night in which the god-sent dream comes to Agamemnon feels 'ambrosial' to him (2. 57), and in that eerie night he sleeps an eerie slumber. Its divine provenance is further suggested by the identity of its action with the lingering of the god-sent dream: sleep 'was poured around him' (περὶ [. . .] κέχυτο) just as the dream's voice 'was poured around him' (ἀμφέχυτ') when he awoke (2. 41).

As is typical of Homeric dreams, the one sent by Zeus rouses the sleeper. It scolds him: 'You slumber, son of wise Atreus, the tamer of horses? To sleep all night does not become a man who brings counsel, to whom many people turn and so many cares belong' (2. 23–5). If Agamemnon's slumber comes from Zeus, the dream adds insult to injury by denouncing it as irresponsible. The censure, though, fittingly highlights Agamemnon's unreflective self-importance and his unawareness of the crisis he has caused.[23] The action he takes upon awakening is as unseeing as his sleep, and this in spite of dawn rising when he sets out to gather the heroes. For Dawn this time is biased: 'Now the goddess Dawn went to Olympus, announcing light to Zeus and the other immortals' (2. 48–9). Contrary to its normal pattern, the new day brings light to the gods but not to men.[24] Dawn's bias reinforces the opposition between Zeus' seeing wakefulness and Agamemnon's blind slumber, suggesting that the deluded human leader calls the assembly in the dark, as it were.[25] He does not see the light even when daylight comes, while Zeus sees at night and is the first to see the light of day.[26]

At the beginning of Book 10, however, Agamemnon proves that he has learnt the lesson taught him by the dream,[27] for this time it is he who plays the wakeful party in a scene of lonely vigil:

> The other leaders of the Achaean host were sleeping all night by the ships, overcome by soft slumber, but sweet sleep was not holding Atreus' son Agamemnon, the shepherd of the people, who was pondering many things in his heart.
> (1–4)

Audiences are sent back to the opening of Book 2 by the recurrence of words in the same order ('the other' begins both sequences and 'were sleeping all night' the second line), by the status of the wakeful character (the king of the gods and the king of men respectively) and by the emphasis on retiring that prefaces both vigils: just as all the gods 'went each to their homes to lie down' (1. 606), all the Achaeans 'went each to their tents after making libations, and there they lay down and took the boon of sleep' (9. 712–3).

The detailed parallels between the two episodes bring the weakness of Agamemnon as decision maker into stark relief by inviting comparison with Zeus' plot-driving sleeplessness.[28] While Zeus immediately finds 'the best plan', Agamemnon is prey to gnawing agitation. The simile that describes his state further contrasts him with Zeus, the maker of rain, blizzard or war:

> As when the husband of Hera of the fair tresses hurls lightning and produces much rain or unspeakable hail or snow that sprinkles the fields, or the wide mouth of piercing war, thus thickly did Agamemnon groan in his breast

(ἐν στήθεσσιν ἀναστεναχίζε), from the innermost of his heart,
and his mind inside trembled.

(10. 5–10)

Zeus sends storms; Agamemnon is stormy within. The alliteration *st-st* in ἐν στήθεσσιν ἀναστεναχίζε ('he groaned in his breast'), reinforced by the similarly sounding *ê-e* and *en/an*, absorbs one term into the other, conveying the introverted fruitlessness of Agamemnon's groaning with an etymologizing wordplay. Achilles' warning to him, that he will 'lacerate his heart inside' (1. 243), has come true.

At last a 'best plan' dawns on Agamemnon as well (10. 17 = 2. 5), but it consists of nothing better than seeking advice: he will approach Nestor (10. 19). Agamemnon's weak grip on the situation is further brought out by Menelaus' own sleeplessness, shaking (10. 25–6) and fear for his brother's sake (10. 38–9). Agamemnon admits to his distress when he tells Nestor that, 'I wander thus, since sweet slumber does not rest on my eyes' (10. 91–2). His self-portrait conveys even stronger anxiety than the authorial description of his state: 'my mind is not firm, but I wander to and fro, and my heart leaps out of my chest, and my glistening limbs tremble' (10. 93–5). The series of wake-up calls that follows from the consultation with Nestor (10. 108: 'Let us rouse others as well!') dilutes Agamemnon's authority and builds yet another contrast with Zeus. For Zeus comes up with a decision all alone, unbeknownst to his sleeping recipient, whom he causes to awaken to carry out his plan, whereas Agamemnon causes many to rise so that they can form a plan together. The contrast highlights the difficulties that he faces both as a human leader, who has to reach a consensus, and as an incompetent one, who needs the advice of many.

The deadly sleep of Rhesus

The mission decided in that wakeful night culminates with the killing of Rhesus. He is sleeping with his Thracians, likewise sleeping, all around him, overcome by fatigue (10. 471–4), when 'the son of Tydeus came [. . .] [and] him the thirteenth he robbed of his life. He was panting, for a bad dream stood over his head that night, Diomedes, by Athena's device' (10. 494–7). Rhesus' dream of death merges with his death in slumber.[29]

Did the killing of a sleeping foe conjure up military practice to audiences in the late-eighth or early-seventh century (roughly the time of the epic's composition)[30] or did it sound more mythical than real? Scholars are divided as to whether night-time attacks were acceptable in archaic Greek warfare and how frequent they were. According to one view, they are altogether rare: a powerful idea more than an actual fact.[31] Others prefer to see a development in military ethics towards a greater acceptance of deceptive methods, with the turning point coinciding either with the Persian Wars or even later, with the Peloponnesian War.[32] On any of these models, an audience contemporary with *Iliad* 10 (even if the book was added in the sixth century) would find the long nocturnal action in it remarkable, if not extraordinary, in light of their own dominant ethics.[33] According to yet another view, however, deceptive strategies, including attacks at night, were acceptable in military ethics already in the early archaic period.[34] This view finds some support in Homer, where ambushes are considered part and parcel of heroic conduct because of the courage they require (*Il.* 13. 276–87), and even Achilles is not ashamed of capturing enemies at night (*Il.* 21. 35–40).

How frequently nocturnal attacks occurred is another matter. Historical data for the archaic period are scanty. We know that night-time fighting was prescribed to the Spartan youths during their coming-of-age military service,[35] and Herodotus recounts two early instances of attacks on sleeping foes: Pisistratus falling on the Athenians after their lunch, while some of them were napping (1. 63), and Cyrus and his Persians slaughtering the enemy while they were likewise dozing after a meal (1. 211).[36] The record is slightly richer for the fifth and fourth centuries,[37] which might (but need not) suggest a change in military ethics. Xenophon, for one, has no compunction about narrating how his model king and general, Cyrus the Younger, learned to attack men in their sleep (*Cyr.* 1. 6. 35) and remembered the lesson (7. 5. 21). But all in all, night-time fighting was far from common practice, possibly because of the tremendous risks it involved.[38]

Against this background, it is likely that in the seventh century and even later the Trojan saga stood out for featuring extended scenes of night-time combat: in addition to the capture of Dolon and the killing of Rhesus, it also includes the theft of the Palladium and the final sack.[39] There are further references to night-time war activities, and led not only by Odysseus,[40] as one would expect of that embodiment of cunning, with his special talent for stealthy manoeuvring in the dark,[41] but also by that arch defender of openness and directness, Achilles.[42]

This concentration of night-time fighting looks ahead to Troy's last night, when the sleep-unto-death of Rhesus and his Thracians will be replayed by all the Trojans, in the *Iliad* the wakeful protectors of their wives and children, but on that night no longer protecting or protected by their wakefulness. As Diomedes and Odysseus learn from Dolon, while Rhesus is deep in slumber Hector is holding assembly and the Trojans are on guard duty: 'They are awake and urge one another to keep watch. But the allies, called from many lands, sleep. They entrust the Trojans with watching, for their own children or wives are not around them' (10. 419–22). To audiences who knew how the war ended, the vigilance of the Trojans contrasted with the relaxed and death-causing slumber of their allies must have sounded an ominous note.

The 'deadly' sleep of Zeus

Next it is Zeus' turn to be hurt by a deep slumber. To engineer it is Hera, who enlists the help of Hypnos himself (Figure 1.1) to secure the soporific effects of lovemaking: 'Put to sleep the bright eyes of Zeus under his eyelids, straightaway, after I lie with him in love' (14. 236–7). And sleep seizes the god, a deathlike, still slumber, which prompts two descriptions, one in the authorial voice ('He was slumbering, motionlessly [ἀτρέμας εὗδε] [...] overcome [δαμεἱς] by sleep and love, holding his wife in his arms' [14. 352–4]), the other by Hypnos himself ('Zeus still sleeps, since I have enfolded him in a soft, deep slumber [κῶμα]' [14. 358–9]). Zeus awakes 168 lines later, 'on the peaks of Ida next to Hera of the golden throne' (15. 4–5). Ironically, the all-seeing and most vigilant god is tricked into sleeping the eeriest sleep of the epic and the longest in narrative time.

Hypnos emphasizes the depth of Zeus' slumber by calling it κῶμα: a condition in which every mental activity is stopped. The

Figure 1.1 *Bronze head of Hypnos*, Roman copy of a Hellenistic original (first or second century AD), London, The British Museum.

lexicographer Hesychius explains κῶμα as an 'oblivious sleep', and Hippocrates defines it as a state of unconsciousness different from ὕπνος.[43] For modern scholars, κῶμα is either deadness, a 'turning off of the entire consciousness', or 'a deep sleep induced by enchantment or other special or supernatural means'.[44] The possible etymological connection with κωφός ('deaf and dumb')[45] would suggest that κῶμα is a loss of consciousness deeper than even the deepest slumber.[46] On the other hand, a κῶμα can be slept,[47] as is Zeus', and caused by Hypnos himself. Whatever the case, in archaic and classical texts κῶμα comes from the gods or godlike forces. Pindar uses the term for the irresistible slumber induced by the lyre's music, so spell binding that it can assuage even the god of war (*Pyth.* 1. 12).[48] In Homer, Hypnos' privilege of sending κῶμα is shared only by Athena.

Athena forces κῶμα on Penelope to neutralize her resistance and beautify her against her wishes,[49] just as Hera mobilizes sleep to promote her wishes against Zeus. But there is an important difference: while Athena knocks out Penelope in order to activate a plan that ultimately is meant to help her, Hera intends to harm her husband and undermine his power. To force sleep on him she hires, and for the second time (14. 252–3), a god who is hierarchically subjected to him (as Hypnos' reluctance to reoffer his services spells out, 14. 247–8) but whom she honours with a phrase that normally belongs to his superior: 'lord of all gods and men' (14. 233).

Though Hera means to flatter Hypnos by placing him at the top of the divine ladder, the compliment is not hyperbolic. It is true that Hypnos' control even over mortals is limited. While Death 'holds fast whichever human he has once seized', 'all powerful Hypnos releases those he binds, and does not hold them forever once he has seized them'.[50] If Hypnos' grip is not irreversible, however, his empire is larger than Death's, for he can master even the deathless gods.[51] In the Homeric imaginary, Hypnos is indeed lord of every living being: sleep, and only sleep, earns the epithet πανδαμάτωρ, 'subjugating everything'.[52] The *Orphic Hymn to Hypnos* (85) agrees with Homer in celebrating the god's sweeping power – again, his alone: 'Hypnos, lord of all the blessed and of mortal men and of all the animals that the wide earth breeds, you alone rule over everyone and come to everyone, binding bodies in chains not forged of metal'. In later art and poetry, sleep's rule over the gods is brought into bold relief by images of a slumbering Eros (Figure 1.2) in which the god who shares Hypnos' prerogative of 'subjugating [...] the minds of all gods and men' (Hes. *Theog.* 121–2) is overcome by a force stronger than he.[53] Both sleep and love are 'limb loosening';[54] but sleep loosens the limbs of Eros.

Hera's address to Hypnos as lord of all gods and men underscores his power specifically over Zeus, whose title he appropriates right when he is about to prove that he deserves it.[55] In fact, while Zeus slumbers he loses his rule over gods and men and forfeits control over his own plan. And it is Hypnos himself who puts the plan in jeopardy by urging Poseidon to favour the Greeks (14. 354–5), that is, to implement a 'plan of Hera' against Zeus' own.[56]

But why does Hera summon Hypnos, since originally she thought that lovemaking would be enough to produce the deep slumber she needed to carry out her plan (14. 163–5)? As it seems, she secures the god's help because her victim's eyes and mind are

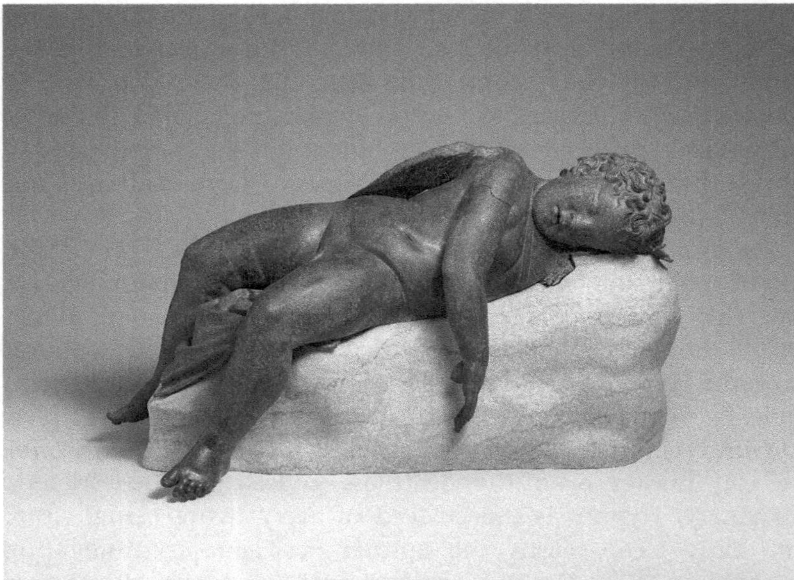

Figure 1.2 *Eros Sleeping*, bronze statue, Greek or Roman (third century BC–first century AD), New York, The Metropolitan Museum of Art.

exceptionally vigilant, requiring more than just natural sleep to be turned off. It is those eyes in particular that she asks Hypnos to neutralize: 'Put to sleep Zeus' bright eyes under his eyelids' (14. 236). The first time Hypnos acted on Zeus, he aimed at his waking mind: 'I put the mind of Zeus to sleep' (14. 252). Likewise Hera was hoping to pour slumber 'over his eyelids and solid mind' (14. 165; see also 160) before she asked Hypnos for help. Zeus' formidable vision causes both Hera and Hypnos to cover themselves in mist so that they can remain unseen while they travel to Ida (14. 282), where he stops 'before Zeus' eyes saw him' and hides in the branches of a pine tree, likening himself to a dark bird (14. 286–91), while she does offer herself to Zeus' eyes (14. 293) but in order to seduce him. Hera's job is to exploit the erotic force of sight to numb her husband's vigilance: 'Zeus saw her. And as he saw her, desire enfolded (ἀμφεκάλυψεν) his solid mind' (14. 293–4), compelling him to make love to her and fall asleep as a result. Hypnos' job is to finish the mind-enfolding work of love by enfolding (περὶ [...] κάλυψα, 14. 359) Zeus further in an eerily deep loss of consciousness, which 'kills' him.

While plunged in his κῶμα Zeus comes as close to death as a god can. The equation of sleep and death is coeval with Greek culture.[57] In Homer, death is 'brazen slumber' (*Il.* 11. 241), and sleep can be 'most similar to death' (*Od.* 13. 80). One warrior boasts that a man he has just killed 'slumbers, overcome by my spear' (*Il.* 14. 482–3). Sleep and Death are called 'brothers' when Hera first approaches Hypnos (*Il.* 14. 231),[58] and 'twins' when they are summoned jointly to carry Sarpedon's dead body home (*Il.* 16. 672–3 and 682–3). (Figures 1.3 and 1.4). Both 'charm' the eyes.[59]

Sleep substitutes for death in one version of the myth of Endymion, to whom Zeus granted 'to slumber for the rest of time and remain immortal and ageless' (Apollod. *Bibl.* 1. 56). Eternal rest removes mortality, characterized by becoming, by the alternation of sleep and wakefulness.[60] But sleep can also 'kill' the deathless gods. In another version of his polymorphic legend,

Figure 1.3 John W. Waterhouse, *Sleep and his Half-Brother Death* (1874), Private Collection.

Figure 1.4 Euphronios Painter, red-figure calyx crater ('Euphronios Vase', late sixth century BC), Rome, Villa Giulia. The dead Sarpedon transported by Hypnos and Thanatos, with Hermes looking on.

Endymion precipitates from the gods' company into an everlasting slumber. The two opposite functions of sleep, as the substitute for death or the qualifier of immortality, appear back to back in this comment: 'Epimenides says that when he [Endymion] consorted with the gods, he fell in love with Hera, for which reason Zeus became angry and caused him to sleep forever. But some say that, because of his great justice, he was made a god and Zeus caused him to sleep forever'.[61] Zeus disposes of Cronus in the same way.[62] A loss of consciousness like Zeus' own in *Iliad* 14, but not as sweet, is the κῶμα that engulfs the perjured gods in Hesiod's *Theogony* (798), 'hiding' them as death hides humans.[63]

In Homer's description Zeus' 'death' is highlighted by more details. He 'was slumbering, motionlessly' (ἀτρέμας εὗδε): the only other instance of this phrase in Homer refers to Odysseus plunged in deathlike sleep as a magic ship takes him to Ithaca (*Od.* 13. 92).

And Zeus is 'overcome' (δαμείς) by sleep, as the warriors are by death.[64] But his 'temporary death'[65] is a travesty of the real death that warriors meet in combat,[66] most poignantly during his long and undisturbed slumber. The sequence of Hera's seduction of Zeus and his forced sleep has rung comical to many readers, who stress the levity and frivolity of the scenes in contrast to the tragedy of the war below, which a deity steers as she pleases while another one deeply slumbers, and which causes many humans to die a real death because a god is put to 'death' by sleep and love. Upon awakening, Zeus instantly and effortlessly reverses the power balance by reactivating his plan with greater impetus and announcing more deaths, 'until the Achaeans will sack steep Ilion' (15. 70–1).[67]

Divine sleep and sleeplessness in Homer and beyond

The sleep patterns of the Homeric gods are noticeably close to those of humans. Did this fact bother ancient audiences? Did they find fault with gods tricked by sleep, unable to control their sleep or simply sleeping?

Predictably, the gods' slumber came under attack for betokening humanlike weakness. Alexander the Great allegedly said, when hailed as a god, that two things made him doubt his divinity: his need for sleep and his need for sex (Plut. *Mor.* 65F). In Quintus of Smyrna's epic (third or fourth century AD), sleep and immortality are at variance: 'The gods, much troubled, went each to their homes and beds and, for all their immortality, slumber the gentle helper was spread over their eyes' (2. 180–2). As immortals, the gods should not need to rest.

Quintus is not the only late author to find sleep at odds with immortality. Commenting on Plato's criticism of Zeus' desire for Hera in *Iliad* 14 (*Resp.* 390b–c), the Neoplatonic philosopher Proclus (fifth century) observes that the Homeric passage includes the problematic view that Zeus could slumber. Was Homer blasphemous in saying that the king of the gods could be wakeful and asleep in turn? Proclus' solution is that the two states depict the twofold relationship of the first principle ('Zeus') to the material world: awake, in its providential intervention, asleep, in its self-sufficiency as mind separated from the world of sense perception.[68] God is unsleeping because he cares for the world, but asleep because he withdraws from it and dwells with himself. From this convoluted allegorizing, we can gauge to which extent Zeus' slumber bothered the Neoplatonic thinker.

An earlier admirer of Plato, Celsus in the second century AD, attacks the God of the Old Testament for resting on the seventh day after completing the world's creation. Celsus is peremptory: this deity is 'a poor artisan' because 'for the supreme god to be tired is against divine law'. Rest is an anthropomorphic feature, and thus un-godlike.[69]

Earlier still, the doxographer Aetius (second century BC) likewise takes issue with the idea that god, as immortal, needed to sleep. He criticizes Anaxagoras and Plato for arguing that god put order in the world, claiming that his meddling in human affairs would detract from his perfect beatitude and that he would not be eternal if the world existed before he put order into it. Otherwise, what would he have done prior to arranging the world? He must have been slumbering since the beginning of time. But this is unacceptable, because it would be tantamount to denying his immortality: 'If god had slept since eternity, he would be dead, for death is an eternal slumber. But god cannot be affected by sleep, for divine immortality and nearness to death are much at variance'.[70] Aetius extends his criticism from the notion of a god sleeping through the immensity of time to that of a god simply sleeping.

No such criticism of divine slumber, however, can be found in classical Greek thought. We can imagine that Xenophanes, who objects to the gods' anthropomorphic shape, objected to their rest as well, but the extant evidence does not prove it. Plato, who admires Zeus' wakeful planning, does not target sleep as its negative counterpart, but rather the effects of desire: we should not admit that Zeus, 'who, while the other gods and men were slumbering, was awake alone and made those decisions, forgot them all easily because of erotic passion and was so struck by the sight of Hera that he did not even want to go to his bedchamber' (*Resp.* 390b–c). Unlike Proclus, Plato passes over Zeus' sleep. He omits Hera's summoning of Hypnos and stops before the sleep scene, reading Zeus' oblivion as the result of mind-numbing desire alone. The erasing of Hypnos from the picture demonstrates that Plato's criticism is aimed at Zeus' sexual appetite and its consequences rather than at sleep's compulsion. And as a matter of fact, Plato does not attack Homeric scenes in which the gods just slumber. Neither does Aristotle. When he claims that the gods must be engaged in some kind of activity because we cannot imagine them to sleep always (*Eth. Nic.* 1178b 19–20), he implies: we can imagine them to do so *sometimes*.

Yet we cannot help asking: why do the gods sleep? And how? How can they demonstrate their divinity if they rest like humans? The gods' eating habits show that they are both close to humans (because they eat) and distinct from them (because they follow a special diet). They mark their difference from mortals by choosing different foods and drinks, nectar and ambrosia (the two diets are contrasted in the scene in which Calypso and Odysseus eat together at *Od.* 5. 196–9). But can they sleep a different sleep? What is it that would mark the difference?

A god's slumber, as it seems, does not shut down his power. This is true for Eros in the representations of the god asleep that populate Hellenistic and Roman art and poetry, where his apparently deep slumber is a deceptive image of innocence and vulnerability. It is the harmless child that is forefront in those representations, his weapons at repose while his body abandons itself to sleep's spell (Figure 1.2). But even so we are not protected from that child, who can still shoot.[71]

Zeus' sleep likewise does not neutralize his powers because it has eyes. The supreme god is vigilant even when he slumbers, and that is why Hera feels the need to reinforce the work of sleep with that of Hypnos to engulf Zeus in a κῶμα and close his eyes shut. Hypnos alone can 'charm even the eyes of Zeus', as Meleager puts it (*AP* 5. 174. 3); for during natural sleep Zeus' eyes are open. While he was napping, Typhon attempted to steal his thunderbolt, but he saw him and struck him with lightning[72] or a 'sleepless shaft', as Aeschylus calls it (*PV* 358). Zeus' power remains untouched: 'Not even sleep takes it away, which makes everything age; not even the inexhaustible months of the gods. Not aged by time, you rule and hold the dazzling brightness of Olympus'.[73]

But why would Zeus and the other Olympians slumber? Do they need to recover from weariness? Apparently Zeus does in *Iliad* 14. The regularity of the gods' sleeping patterns – they retire at night after carrying out their business by day – likewise seems to suggest that they need to rest. This need, though, is not spelled out but remains implied. In Homeric poetry the gods are never said to sleep from tiredness. Terms such as κάμνειν or κάματος ('to be tired', 'tiredness'), which time and again gloss human sleep,[74] never explain a deity's. How could they, since 'the tired ones' (καμόντες) are the dead? To say of gods that they are exhausted is tantamount to qualifying their godhead, as in the tableau at the beginning of *Eumenides*, where the Furies are heavily asleep, worn out by the toil of travelling. Weary slumber lessens the gap between these deities and their human prey, Orestes, also condemned to the wearying toil of travel.[75] Conversely, in the *Homeric Hymn* devoted to him, Apollo stops from travelling not in order to rest but to promote his divinity by spreading his cult.

Rather than sleeping to cure their tiredness, the gods do so to enjoy a languorous pleasure. Just as they eat not to quiet their hunger but to entertain themselves with feasting,[76] they sleep because sleep is blissful. When, in the *Homeric Hymn to Hermes*, Apollo marvels listening to Hermes' music, he adds: 'Truly here are three things to choose from: mirth, love, and sweet slumber' (449). We are reminded of Menelaus' words, 'There is satiety in everything, even in sleep, love, sweet song and the excellent dance, things in which one would rather slake one's pleasure than in war' (*Il.* 13. 636–8). We might also recall Eumaeus' declaration: 'There is satiety also in too much slumber' (*Od.* 15. 394), and add to it the Phaeacians' pronounced taste for 'beds' (*Od.* 8. 249) and Mimnermus' inclusion of the bed among the pleasures that make life worth living (Fr. 1. 3).[77] The gods celebrate the joy of sleep as humans do.

To be sure, Mimnermus combines the luxuriousness of divine slumber with a humanlike need to rest in a charming poem about Helios:

> Helios' lot is to toil day after day. He and his horses take no break once rosy-fingered Dawn leaves Oceanus and goes up to the sky. For a lovely bed, of many colors, a work of metal beaten by Hephaestus' hands, of precious gold, winged, carries him, slumbering pleasantly, across the sea, on the surface of the water, from the country of the Hesperides to

> the land of the Aethiopians, where his swift chariot and his horses stand at repose until early-born Dawn arrives. Then the son of Hyperion goes on another ride.
>
> (Fr. 12)

The god is imagined to sleep in order to restore himself after his toil. The poem, though, is not a serious work of theology but a playful exercise in aetiology: it imaginatively explains why the sun is not in the sky at night by humanizing the 'tireless' Helios of Homer (*Il.* 18. 239 and 484). And the god's tiredness is not what the poem emphasizes. Rather, in describing Helios' sleep Mimnermus puts a premium on the pleasure it offers and on the elaborate craftsmanship, precious material and magical powers of the bed, worthy of the sleeper's divine status.[78]

Mimnermus' poem calls to mind the opening paragraphs of Lucian's *The Double Indictment* (1–3), where Zeus complains that he cannot enjoy sweet slumber as much as he would like because he is too busy: if Selene and Hypnos lose sleep doing their job at night, even more so does he, the king of the gods, who has to supervise the work of his immortal subjects and cannot afford aloofness, lest mortals believe Epicurus and stop sacrificing. Citing *Iliad* 2, Zeus protests that 'while the other gods and chariot-marshalling men sleep all night', 'sweet slumber does not hold me, though I am Zeus': the king of the gods is like the pilot of a ship, who gets no rest but 'ponders in his heart' for the benefit of all. Zeus wishes for a more leisurely lifestyle, with a more generous sleep allowance.

These gods, however, do not oversleep. They retire with the darkness and get up with the sun. They are bound to the same schedule as men: 'The time-limit for natural sleep among both gods and humans is sunset'.[79] The Homeric gods are not as fond of slumber as their Mesopotamian counterparts, who can even default from their duties for its sake and make such a cult of it as to punish humans and other gods for disturbing their peace.[80] Had the Olympians overindulged in sleep, perhaps they would have come under more severe scrutiny (as suggested by Aristotle's assertion that the gods should not be asleep all the time). But instead, their sleeping patterns show them in harmonious concert with humans ('all the other gods and men were slumbering all night') and equally submitted to cosmic law, to the orderly rhythm of day and night. Dawn rises for mortals and immortals alike (*Il.* 11. 2; 19. 2), both of whom have to wait for it;[81] and the sun shines for both (*Od.* 12. 385–6).[82] The gods' sleep belongs in the order of things.

Nevertheless, Homeric literature is noticeably shy about describing individual gods asleep. There are only two in the corpus: Zeus in the *Iliad* and Hera in the *Homeric Hymns*,[83] where it is her turn to suffer injury from her husband. Zeus goes off to Maia's cave to make love to her 'in the dead of night, when sweet slumber held white-armed Hera fast' (*Hymn to Hermes* 7–8). Both Zeus and Hera are shown asleep only to tell a story of deceit at their expense. These pictures of gods made vulnerable by slumber further validate Hera's address to Hypnos as 'lord of all gods and men'.

The story of Hermes' birth and first exploits in the *Homeric Hymn* devoted to him teases out the association of sleep with un-godlike vulnerability. The circumstances of Hermes' conception – on the sly, in the nocturnal recesses of a cave, and away from the other gods – qualify him to 'see at night' (15) and roam around in it even as a newborn babe.[84] He spends no time in his cradle: 'Born at dawn, he played the cithara at noon, and stole Apollo's cattle in the evening' (17–8). His un-childlike deeds quickly succeed one another in the course of one day, at the end of which he pretends to be a somnolent child. As he catches sight of Apollo, he snuggles up in his swaddling clothes 'and squeezed his head, hands and feet in a small space, like a newborn babe seeking sweet slumber. But in fact he was awake' (240–2). Apollo, however, detects him and asks him about the cattle. To no avail, for Hermes sticks to his role as the sleep-loving child, incapable of stealthy deeds: 'I am not a cattle thief [...] This is no work for me, but I rather care for other things: I care for sleep, and the milk of my mother's breast, and swaddling clothes around my shoulders, and warm baths' (265–8). Hermes has just given demonstration of godlike powers when he fakes the opposite, a child's need for warmth, nurture and a cosy slumber. Since he is a god of yet unclear status, however, his game risks becoming real. Indeed, Apollo pays him back by undermining his immortality in the language of sleep:

'Come, lest you sleep your very last slumber' (289), and by calling him 'swaddling baby' (301). Apollo downgrades Hermes to a sleeping mortal child and threatens him with the sleep of death, while Hermes is wide awake and striving to be acknowledged as his brother's equal.

The protagonist of another *Homeric Hymn*, Aphrodite, asserts her divine status by staying awake and forcing sleep on her mortal lover. The *Hymn to Aphrodite* tells the story of a loss of power: the goddess of love is compelled to fall in love with a human. Though she causes Anchises to return her passion (91, 143), she falls prey to erotic desire first, a 'terribly strong desire' (57), which Zeus inflicts on her (45, 53) usurping her own powers. But as soon as the mating is over and evening descends, at 'the hour when the shepherds drive their oxen and fat sheep back to the hut from the flowery pastures', then 'she poured sweet slumber upon Anchises and put on her beautiful clothes' (168–71). This conclusion to their lovemaking enhances their asymmetry in status: instead of dozing off along with her mortal lover and in his arms, the goddess compels him to sleep and gets up to prepare her epiphany. After getting dressed and recovering her divine stature and dazzling beauty, she shakes him out of sleep in the manner of a Homeric dream, forcing him to see her divine self:

> 'Awaken, son of Dardanus! Why do you sleep so deeply? And mark, do I look the same as I did when you first saw me with your eyes?' So she spoke. He instantly awoke and obeyed her, and as he saw the neck and beautiful eyes of Aphrodite, he was afraid and turned his eyes aside another way.
>
> (177–82)

The goddess who averted her eyes upon approaching the couch (155–7), behaving like the virgin she pretended to be (133), is now in full view, and the mortal who led her there averts his gaze in turn, in recognition of her divinity. Aphrodite has wielded sleep as a weapon against her mortal lover to reestablish the balance of power. Her exploitation of slumber to control her mate while she remains awake brings this story near to two Homeric tales: Poseidon's rape of Tyro, over whom 'he poured sleep' after taking her virginity (*Od.* 11. 245), and Hera's seduction of Zeus in *Iliad*

14.[85] Though Hera herself does not wield sleep, as do Aphrodite and Poseidon, she secures it with the help of Hypnos. And although Zeus is next to her when he awakens (*Il.* 15. 5), she is not said to sleep. The Homeric gods do not slumber after making love unless they are forced to.

This can be inferred also from the behaviour of Ares and Aphrodite in the lay sung by Demodocus in *Odyssey* 8. This story bears many resemblances to Hera's seduction of Zeus. Ares and Aphrodite are adulterers; Hera and Zeus behave like adulterers (her extravagant toilette, his listing her amongst his extramarital affairs, his hurry to 'do it' right on the spot rather than in the proper marital setting turn wedded love into an illegitimate consummation). Both stories hinge on deception, and both deceivers, Hera and Hephaestus, count on the irresistible compulsion of sex.[86] A fundamental difference, however, is that Ares and Aphrodite have the same desire and the same intentions. Another is that they remain awake after making love. It is true that Hephaestus summons the other gods to come watch 'where the pair sleeps in love' (313) and predicts that 'soon they will not want to sleep together' (316–7). The spectacle would gain force if the adulterers should be deep in slumber under the public eye. Nevertheless, the meaning of 'sleep' in those phrases seems to be erotic.[87] The lovers are not dozing, for immediately after mating and before the other gods assemble around their bed, they 'realize' (299) that they are trapped in the net of chains that surrounds them, and as soon as the chains are removed, they jump up and flee (361–2). The absence of sleep from this episode bears out its role in the other stories of divine lovemaking: post-coital slumber in them does not express harmony and togetherness, as it does, for instance, in the scene of Odysseus and Penelope dozing off after their reunion, but unequal power or intentions, for only the weaker and human party (Anchises, Tyro) or the party who is being tricked (Zeus) goes to sleep.

Let us now turn briefly to the gods' sleeplessness. Later authors, it seems, were not bothered by it. Divine sleeplessness could easily be salvaged, even admired, because it lent itself to being read as the unceasing activity of a responsible ruler (like the one Plato describes at *Leg.* 808a–c) or as a force that cares and oversees and is stronger than sleep. As we have seen, Plato approved Zeus' wakeful deliberation in *Iliad* 2, and Proclus read in it the first principle's concern for the world. But was the gods' sleeplessness perceived to be identical with its human counterpart? If not, what features marked the difference?

As conceived in the *Iliad*, sleeplessness both brings the gods nearer to and sets them apart from mortals. Unsleeping Agamemnon and unsleeping Zeus are in a similar predicament, equally in need of 'the best plan'. The parallel suggests that the gods cannot suppress or even postpone their worries when they would wish to rest. But on the other hand, their wakefulness does not bear visible marks of anxiety. Agamemnon's disquiet can be seen and heard: it has a voice, a body that shakes and trembles, a heart that also trembles and groans, limbs that cannot stay in place, hands that pull hair from his head by its roots (*Il.* 10. 15). His despair and helplessness are conveyed by his physical agitation, exposed. The same, as we shall see, holds true for Achilles and, in the *Odyssey*, for Odysseus, both of whom move restlessly during their sleepless nights. The narratives about their condition are much longer than those describing wakeful gods and devote a wealth of detail to the character's feelings, postures or words. In sharp contrast, Zeus' insomnia is bodiless and wordless: we neither see his movements nor hear him while he is considering how to reach his goals. The divine protagonist in the last scene of sleeplessness in the *Iliad*, Hermes, is likewise pictured in soundless and invisible mental activity. The only thing both gods do is to ponder (2. 3; 24. 680). Plato might have found it easy to read Zeus' insomnia as responsible, but not agitated, wakefulness because he was not confronted with an image of the god roaming and groaning or debating with himself, but only thinking, and instantly solving his predicament. A god's sleeplessness does not last in narrated or narrative time but quickly turns into effective action.

Achilles' insomnia

After the funeral games in honour of Patroclus,

> The rest thought of supper and of delighting in sweet slumber (ὕπνου γλυκεροῦ ταρπήμεναι), but Achilles wept, remembering his dear friend, and sleep that subjugates

> everything did not seize him, but he tossed this way and that [...] He lay now on his side, now on his back, now on his face. Then, up on his feet, he would wander (δινεύεσκ') distraught, by the seashore [...] And dawn would not miss (λήθεσκεν) him when it shone on the sea and the shore. Then he would yoke his swift horses beneath the chariot and would bind (δησάσκετο) Hector behind it to drag him, and after driving him three times around the grave marker of the dead Patroclus, he would rest (παυέσκετο) again in his tent, and would leave (ἔασκεν) Hector in the dust.
>
> (*Il.* 24. 2–17)

Achilles continues in this state for twelve days (24. 31). His chronic insomnia, highlighted by the oxymoronic phrase, 'sleep that subjugates everything did not seize him',[88] is the farthest removed from the bodiless sleeplessness of the Homeric gods: Achilles' body is forefront as it tosses, turns, wanders, and performs a desperate daily ritual, while his mind is filled not with thinking but with anger and longing.

Achilles' insomnia dramatically reverses the unconcerned slumber in which he indulged prior to Patroclus' death. The *Iliad*'s main hero stands apart from the others also in his sleep patterns, for he rests undisturbed in his tent while the war raging outside deprives his fellows of sleep. After the visit of Agamemnon's envoys,

> Patroclus ordered his companions and the handmaids to spread a thick bed for Phoenix straightaway. They obeyed and spread the bed as he ordered, fleeces and a rug and soft linens. There the old man lay and waited for divine Dawn. But Achilles slept in the innermost part of his well-built tent, and next to him there lay a woman he took from Lesbos, fair-cheeked Diomede, the daughter of Phorbas. And Patroclus lay on the other side, and next to him was fair-girdled Iphis.
>
> (9. 658–67)

Achilles and his friend are the protagonists of a retiring scene in the style of the *Odyssey*, with the guest sleeping in a separate area from the hosts, whose bedchamber lies far inside the house. The careful making of Phoenix's bed is one more feature that conjures up the retiring scenes of the *Odyssey*, where hosts show attentiveness to their guests by providing copious and soft beddings, elaborately described by the narrative. This leisurely enactment of a retiring scene underscores the autonomy of the two friends, their separation from the community of warriors, and gives an impression of calmness that clashes with the hectic climate of the night.[89] In particular Achilles' sleep spells out his indifference to the fate of his fellows. While Phoenix waits for dawn, uneasy about the future, he can rest as in times of peace, because he has created an artificial world of peace around himself.

This retiring scene is nonetheless unique in Homeric epic because the hosts in it are a pair of couples: Achilles and Diomede, Patroclus and Iphis. The parallel sleep of the two friends interlocks them in an interdependent unity, faintly suggesting that the peace Achilles has created around himself will be broken when Patroclus does not return to sleep opposite him the next night, that he cannot retire without his friend doing the same.[90] And in fact Patroclus' death causes him to experience sleep disturbances even prior to his twelve nights of insomnia.

Achilles cannot rest between the death of Patroclus and that of Hector. After the latter, he falls asleep at last, twice in a short interval. The first episode begins as a lonely vigil, with Achilles as the waking party: 'When they had put away their desire for food and drink, they went each to their tents to lie down, but the son of Peleus lay by the shore of the much-sounding sea, groaning heavily' (23. 57–60). The contrast between the restful background and the groaning Achilles is, however, corrected by the onset of a soothing slumber: 'And sleep caught him, freeing his heart from cares, sweet, poured around him, for he was very tired in his glistening limbs' (23. 62–3). Achilles' sleep is fully described, with three verbs for its action. The account, unusually rich by the *Iliad*'s standards, conveys the force with which peace-bringing slumber takes hold of Achilles. But the vision of Patroclus awakens him, reminding him that the job is not done yet.

After the 'all night' burial (23. 217), Achilles dozes off again: 'He lay down tired (κλίνθη κεκμηώς), and sweet slumber leapt on him' (232). Both times sleep overpowers the weary hero, proving that he cannot challenge his human limits, as he was eager to do earlier, when he refused to eat before fighting and killing Hector. At that point, the gods underscored his human weakness by treating him with ambrosia to keep him strong (*Il.* 19. 347–8; 353–4). Now sleep demonstrates his weakness by falling on him suddenly and even violently: 'catching' him, 'leaping on' him.

In the second episode, however, sleep does not catch Achilles unawares, but finds him already disposed to rest. When daylight spreads over the sea, the fire on Patroclus' pyre dies out and the winds that have been feeding it leave. The pacified landscape harmonizes with Achilles' pacified spirit,[91] which relaxes into a deeper acceptance of sleep. In the previous episode, his withdrawal from the other, slumbering, heroes is the dominant note, as signified especially by his choice to lie down on the 'shore of the much-sounding sea'. Furthermore, in that scene Achilles does not lie down in order to sleep, but on account of his misery. He yields to sweet slumber unprepared, from exhaustion.[92] And that sleep carries a dream that shakes him awake and urges him to bury his friend.[93] After the funeral, in contrast, Achilles lies down with the express purpose of relieving his fatigue. The description begins with the weary hero assuming a sleeping position ('he lay down tired'), and with five long syllables (κλίνθη κεκμηώς) to slow him down and lay him to rest. And this time he would have slept soundly, for it is not any uprising in his heart that rouses him but the noise around him (23. 234).

Still, Achilles is far from ready to retire again to the 'innermost part' of his tent. Both times sweet slumber catches him while he is outside. After the games he intermittently enters his tent, even to rest, but only as part of the desperate sequence of actions that fill his restless nights. Achilles loses sleep to an excess of memory.[94] He was able to doze off only when he forgot, as his dead friend protested when he awoke him: 'You slumber, Achilles, and have become forgetful of me' (23. 69). Then, Achilles' memory of Patroclus yielded to a sleep that had the power, uniquely in the *Iliad*, of 'freeing one's heart from cares'. But that oblivious relaxation caused by extreme fatigue was superficial. The burial and the games should have helped Achilles contain and transform his memory permanently. Instead, he is remembering his friend more vividly than ever[95] and longing for him, as loving wives long for their husbands, dead or thought dead. We might think of Penelope's restless nights,[96] or of Aigialeia, who would 'wake her household from sleep with her lament, longing for her wedded husband', should Diomedes die (*Il.* 5. 413–4).

The cause for Achilles' insomnia singles him out from the other sleepless characters in the epic. While Zeus, Agamemnon and, as we shall see, Hermes stay awake to come up with a plan in response to a crisis, Achilles is not seeking a way out of his predicament.[97] The exceptional nature of his insomnia is reflected in its frame, which does not follow the 'habitual pattern', as the Byzantine commentator Eustathius calls the background to the sleeplessness of Zeus, Hermes and (if we leave out the gods) Agamemnon. The pattern runs: 'The other gods and men slept all night, overcome by soft slumber, but sleep did not seize such and such a character, who was pondering in his heart'.[98] Since Achilles is not 'pondering in his heart', his sleeplessness is introduced in markedly different language: 'They thought of supper and of delighting in sweet slumber. But Achilles…'[99]

Because of its purely emotional content, Achilles' insomnia will provide a template for love-induced sleeplessness in later Greek literature. Two frustrated novelistic lovers, Artaxerxes and Arsace, imitate the nocturnal restlessness of the Homeric hero by tossing and turning in their beds.[100] The exploitation of the insomniac Achilles as a model for those lovers, while it might imply an eroticized reading of his longing for Patroclus, must have come naturally to the novelists, because love-induced sleeplessness is not the response to a problem that calls for creative thinking but is the expression of unmanageable inner turmoil.

Achilles' turmoil traps him in a cyclical repetition of destructive and self-destructive gestures, in which he finds no purpose.[101] His imprisonment in his emotions is effectively conveyed by the frequentative verbs that his insomnia breeds (δινεύεσκ', λήθεσκεν, δησάσκετο, παυέσκετο, ἔασκεν), which take him on the same journey over and over again, with no new beginnings. Sunrise, which in the *Odyssey* often marks the launching of a journey and creates anticipation for fresh adventures after a night's sleep,[102] restarts Achilles on an identical path day after day. His insomnia has the same unproductive effects as his angry withdrawal from the war in

Book 1, which was similarly characterized by a setting on the seashore (349–50), by longing and by a description rich in frequentative verbs: 'He would not go (πωλέσκετο) to the assembly or to war, which brings men fame, but would wither (φθινύθεσκε) his heart [. . .] and long (ποθέεσκε) for war and the war cry' (490–2). The insomniac Achilles, though, brings not only himself but also the plot of the *Iliad* to an impasse.[103]

Wakeful plotters: Hermes

The impasse is solved entirely from Olympus.[104] Hermes, who is in charge of the mediation, enters the stage as the master of sleep and waking ('He took his wand, with which he charms the eyes of the men as he wills, and others he wakes out of slumber', 24. 343–4), and activates this double power of his in the present mission by putting the Greek guards to sleep towards the end of Priam's outward journey (24. 445–6) and by rousing him to start his return journey before dawn (24. 683–4). Hermes' call is the result of wakeful thinking: 'The other gods and chariot-marshalling men were sleeping all night, overcome by soft slumber, but sleep did not seize Hermes the helper, who was pondering in his heart how to send king Priam back from the ships, unseen by the trusty sentinels' (24. 677–81). We are reminded of Zeus' sleeplessness in Book 2 by the identical background, the divinity of the wakeful character, the mortality of his slumbering target and the call. Like Zeus' unsleeping thinking, Hermes' gives the plot the decisive thrust, but in the opposite direction, towards its close.[105]

Hermes' sleeplessness, however, reverses the meaning of Zeus' not just in narrative function but also in moral purport, insofar as it demonstrates the god's sympathy for the human whose predicament keeps him awake. Zeus is 'pondering in his heart how to honour Achilles and destroy many by the Greek ships'. The concern that prevents him from resting is political rather than ethical, and his thinking is specifically aimed against the human with whose sleep he interferes. In contrast, to keep Hermes from sleeping is his concern for the safety of the human whom he awakens to help.

The god's caring behaviour brings this episode closer to the thought world of the *Odyssey*. For in that epic, it often happens that a deity intervenes in the sleep patterns of mortals to protect them, restore their strength or assuage their sorrows,[106] while in the *Iliad* gods generally do not provide any such help. Both sleepless humans and exhausted ones are left to their own devices. Zeus does manipulate Agamemnon's slumber, probably by causing it and certainly by ending it; but the god's goal is to harm him. Conversely, Hermes applies his wand to protect his mortal charge, first by casting sleep over the sentinels so as to help him reach Achilles' dwelling unseen, then by rousing him so as to help him leave the enemy camp unseen. The worry underlying Hermes' call is akin to Athena's concern for Odysseus at the beginning of *Odyssey* 6, when, in spite of his desire to keep on slumbering, she causes him to awaken in order to activate her rescuing plan.

In his role as helper, Hermes speaks truthful words to Priam when he rouses him. Likewise, Zeus' message to him, via Iris, is truthful.[107] Her words, '[Zeus] greatly cares for and pities you', are identical to those in Agamemnon's dream (24. 174 = 2. 27), but they are honest rather than, as in the earlier scene, chillingly ironic. Homer confirms the veracity of Iris' message, relating that 'He [Zeus] saw and pitied the old man' and sent Hermes down (24. 332–3). Hermes' sleeplessness fits the new 'plan of Zeus' that initiates the action of Book 24: a plan in which his compassion prevails over personal interests and attachments or Olympian aloofness.[108]

Wakefulness and the end of the *Iliad*

When Hermes rouses him, Priam has yielded to sleep for the first time since Hector's death (24. 637–40). His need to rest conjures up Odysseus' at the end of the storm in *Odyssey* 5. Priam has completed a journey that shares features not only with Odysseus' nightly reconnaissance in *Iliad* 10,[109] but also with two of his more superhuman journeys: his descent to Hades[110] and his navigation from Ogygia to Scheria. The latter journey starts off with Zeus sending Hermes, just as Priam's begins with Zeus dispatching Hermes; both travellers reach their destinations thanks to significant divine guidance and both think of sleep at the end of the journey. Priam rather unceremoniously asks Achilles for a bed:

> Now, quickly, fosterling of Zeus, give me a place to lie down, so that we may now delight in sweet slumber (ὕπνῳ ὕπο γλυκερῷ ταρπώμεθα) and rest. For my eyes have not been shut under my eyelids since my son lost his life at your hands, but I keep groaning and brooding over countless sorrows, rolling in the dung in the feeding place of the courtyard.
>
> (24. 635–40)

To the ears of an attentive audience, the words ὕπνῳ ὕπο γλυκερῷ ταρπώμεθα hark back to ὕπνου γλυκεροῦ ταρπήμεναι ('to delight in sweet slumber'), which appeared earlier in the book (24. 3) to describe what Achilles could not do. The repetition draws attention to the extent of the appeasement reached by the two men at the end of their evening together.[111] Priam is ready to resume the daily routine of civilized life, to replace sleeplessness in the dirt with sleep in a bed, and exhorts Achilles to join him, suggesting that the two can spend a restful night in the same spirit and even close to each other.

Achilles in turn is ready. His memory of Patroclus is no longer solitary, but he has joined Priam as he remembers Hector (τὼ δὲ μνησαμένω, 24. 509). Their identification has drawn Achilles out of his paralysing isolation and back to the simple needs and comforts of life, to eating and sleeping in his tent instead of roaming sleeplessly under the stars. He gives instructions for the beds to be prepared, prompting the most elaborate description of a bed-making ritual in the *Iliad*:

> And Achilles ordered his comrades and the maids to put beds under the portico and throw on them beautiful purple blankets and spread rugs on top and add fleecy cloaks on top for them to wear. And the maids left the hall holding a torch in their hands and quickly and busily they spread two beds.
>
> (24. 643–8)

The scene echoes and amplifies the leisurely retiring scene at the end of Book 9 by emphasizing further the rich bedding and the caring and thorough manner in which the beds are made. The detailed description again evokes retiring scenes in the *Odyssey*, far from the arena of war. And so does the distribution of the sleepers: 'And they slept there under the portico of the house, the herald and Priam, whose minds had wise thoughts, while Achilles slept in the innermost part of his solidly built hut. And next to him Briseis of the beautiful cheeks lay' (24. 673–6). This arrangement calls to mind two episodes in the *Odyssey* in which Telemachus' host and hostess retire inside the palace while he and his friend rest under the portico or in the entryway (3. 396–403; 4. 296–305). Priam impersonates the guest sleeping outside with his travelling companion, while Achilles, cast in the role of the host, slumbers, as in Book 9, in 'the innermost part' of his dwelling, but this time next to the woman whose loss had caused his anger.[112]

Achilles' reply to Priam's request for a bed, however, points up the danger he is in: 'Lie outside, lest one of the Achaean leaders see you and report to Agamemnon' (24. 650–5, summarized). Though it is the norm for Homeric guests to spend the night in the outer parts of the house,[113] the retiring scene in *Iliad* 24 is the only one in both epics in which the guest must do so because he is told that he would not be safe inside. Here, sleeping outside connotes a state of emergency and prepares for Hermes' call, which sets Priam on the road suddenly and before dawn. Contrary to the parallel retiring scenes in the *Odyssey*, this one is marked by asymmetry: only the host takes his fill of slumber, while the guest is warned that his fatigue must not overcome his fear (24. 689).

The permanence of this state of anxiety or, narratologically, the openness of the *Iliad*'s ending[114] is also reflected in the absence of a scene of sleep or nightfall at the conclusion of the epic, after the return of Hector's body, his funeral and the feast that ends it.[115] Though wrapping up the narrative at an indeterminate time of day is a common feature in epic poetry, geared to allow continuation,[116] there is more at stake than just generic patterns in Homer's choice to skip over the coming of night in the account of Hector's funeral and at its conclusion. For night is evoked towards the end of the epic; but rather than being described as setting in, it is used to underscore the urgency with which the ritual of Hector's burial must get underway:

> And all day until sundown they would have mourned Hector in tears, before the gates, if the old man had not

> spoken from his chariot to the folks: 'let me go through with my mules! You will have your fill of wailing, when I have taken him to the house'.
>
> (24. 713–6)

After the body reaches the house, the sun does not set – though dawn has already risen once, when Priam has made it back (24. 695), and rises two more times: to mark the beginning of the tenth day, when Hector's body is burnt (24. 785), and of the eleventh (24. 788), when the fire is quenched, the bones are collected and put in an urn, and a grave marker is heaped. The repeated mention of dawn captures the swiftness with which time passes for the Trojans, who watch the sunrise day after day because they know that they have only so many days to bury Hector before the resumption of the hostilities. The recurrence of dawn also conveys the energetic pace with which the ritual is prepared and performed, the anxious, ceaseless activity dictated by the approaching end of the truce. The last gestures in honour of the dead are indeed hurried (24. 797: αἶψα; 799: ρίμφα).

The final lines of the epic combine details that suggest appeasement with others that imply ongoing tension. The feast after the burial belongs to the former category, the soldiers on guard duty to the latter: 'Quickly they heaped the grave marker, and watchers were sent everywhere around lest the well-greaved Achaeans should attack before the time' (24. 799–800). Sentinels keep watch because the truce might be broken, as the Trojans know firsthand, having themselves betrayed their oaths in Book 4. More important, the lookouts are embodied projections of what is to come: a forward-looking reference to the imminent resumption of war, offering 'a subliminal glimpse of the unfolding future'.[117] They are a reminder that the night watches are not over, that sweet slumber will again have to be resisted. The Trojans and the audience know for certain that the war will resume the next day[118] and will continue until the expansive plan of Zeus is fulfilled.[119] A final note on Priam taking his fill of sleep at last, or even on night falling and bringing rest from toil and sorrow, would clash with that tragic certainty. Instead, the lookouts remind the audience that Troy will fall on a night in which no sentinel will look out for the enemy, but everyone will sleep: unto death.

CHAPTER 2

THE *ODYSSEY*

PART ONE: AT SEA, ON THE ROAD

Following the course of the sun

The *Odyssey*'s characters are freer than the *Iliad*'s to rest at night and resume activity in the morning. They rise naturally to start the day. The narrative takes the time to follow the cycle of sleep and wakefulness and to describe arrangements for the night: the selection of a place to lie down, the making of the beds, the quality of the beddings and the distribution of the sleepers. Retiring scenes, an anomaly in the *Iliad*, belong to the *Odyssey*'s thematic core, Odysseus' recovery of his household and wife. There are also twice as many books ending with sleep.[1]

This fact might be considered insignificant if we dismiss the book divisions as non Homeric. Their origin is a thorny issue. Are they coeval with the epics? And what does 'coeval' mean, considering the nature of oral poetry, which defies fixity? A great number of scholars believe that the book divisions were created as late as the Hellenistic period. What matters, however, is not their authenticity (whatever the term might mean in a context of evolving oral composition), but the fact that the editors who put them in place saw in sleep an appropriate marker of endings.[2] Furthermore, even if we should disregard the book divisions, the *Odyssey*, compared to the *Iliad*, has a far greater number of narrative units that conclude with a mention of sleep.

The sequence, 'they went to sleep, and on the morrow' is almost a refrain, which gives the rhythm to the day and to the narrative by creating a pause between episodes, be they legs of a journey or gatherings in a palace. Illustrations of this pattern are countless. For instance, at end of Book 3 Telemachus and Pisistratus ride 'all day', then, 'when the sun set and all the streets were shadowy', they arrive in Pheres, where they rest that night to leave again at dawn and travel all day until darkness. Earlier in the same book Nestor has a last drink with his people and his guests, then the locals go home to sleep, while Telemachus, Nestor and his family do so in the palace (3. 396–403). At sunrise they get up and assemble (3. 404–14), just as at sunrise Athena departs (3. 366).[3] Likewise Menelaus, in recounting how he and his companions trapped Proteus during his daytime nap, takes care to note that they stopped on the previous night: they prepare a meal and lie by the shore, but 'when early-born rosy-fingered Dawn appeared', they start on their way (4. 429–31). Upon returning that night, he also relates, they prepare another meal and again lie by the shore, but 'when early-born rosy-fingered Dawn appeared', they start on their way (4. 574–6). A night of rest followed by dawn rising also frames the Cyclops episode at both ends (9. 168–70; 558–60).

To appreciate the *Odyssey*'s pattern of regulating activities according to the cycle of the sun, we might compare Athena's words urging Telemachus to action in Book 1 and the dream's exhortation to Agamemnon in *Iliad* 2.[4] The dream just says, 'arm the Achaeans', without specifying, 'tomorrow morning'. It is still night when Agamemnon awakens, gets dressed and starts off. Dawn rises while he is on his way. Conversely, Athena instructs Telemachus to 'summon the Achaean heroes to assembly *tomorrow* and speak to them all' (*Od.* 1. 272–3). He obliges: '*at dawn* let us go to assembly' (1. 372); and though he cannot sleep, he waits for the new day to dress and act (2. 1–7).

We might also compare two scenes, one from each epic, in which a deity visits a mortal by night and speeds him on his way. In *Iliad* 24, Hermes awakens Priam, frightening him and causing him to rise and set out before dawn without saying goodbye to his host. In *Odyssey* 15, by contrast, Telemachus cannot leave at night as he wishes but has to wait. After being counselled by Athena, he kicks his travelling companion awake: 'Up, Pisistratus, [...] yoke the single-hoofed horses under the wagon, so we can take to the road' (*Od.* 15. 46–7). But Pisistratus protests: 'In no way can we drive through the dark night, no matter how eager we are for the journey. And soon it will be dawn' (15. 49–50). Telemachus' desire to leave before sunrise clashes with the travelling protocol. In addition he is a guest, and as such he is expected to wait for his host's rising (see 15. 56–66).

Characters in the *Odyssey* strongly feel that there is a time for sleep, and they pontificate on the subject. Athena is the first to give voice to the sentiment when Nestor finishes his story and night comes: 'Let us mind slumber. For it is time. The light of the sun has already gone under the horizon' (3. 334–5). Odysseus and Alcinous exchange views on the relative appropriateness of sleep and storytelling (11. 330–1, 373–9), while Eumaeus reminds Odysseus that going to bed too early is not right (15. 392–4), and Penelope would not wish to keep Odysseus awake longer than is fitting (19. 591–3). Timeliness, of sleep and activity, is an organizational principle in the epic, where things, from the simplest to the most complex, run according to a schedule.[5] So, in the first place, does Odysseus' *nostos*, which is given impulse only 'when, as time rolled on, the year came' in which it was due (1. 16–8).[6]

Odysseus' slumber at the helm

The section of the epic that is most fraught with sleep disruptions is Odysseus' narrative of his wanderings, which are paired with the war because of the pain they caused him.[7] He spends two sleepless nights in the Cyclops' cave and many more on troubled waters. The storm that hits him after he leaves Calypso forces him to swim two days and two nights (5. 388–9) after seventeen days of uninterrupted sailing (5. 278–9; 5. 271): some twenty days without a nap! Sequences such as 'so many days and nights' or 'so many nights and days' often appear in conjunction with Odysseus' navigation, used to describe either his unrelenting sailing or the long time he spends lying exhausted by the seashore after strenuous sailing.[8]

Nine nights without sleep cause Odysseus to yield to an irresistible, and unfortunate, slumber, just as he is about to arrive in Ithaca thanks to Aeolus' wind-controlled conveyance:

> Nine days we sailed, night and day. On the tenth my native land appeared, and we were so near as to see men tending fires. Then sweet sleep came upon me, for I was tired. I had ever held the sheets of the ship and not given them to anyone else, in order to reach my native land more quickly. But my comrades talked to each other, saying that I was bringing home gold and silver [...] Looking at each other they would say...
>
> (10. 28–37)

Ithaca has just come into view when Odysseus' slumber causes the ship to turn around, preventing the foreclosure of the plot, since he would otherwise have reached home too quickly on account of Aeolus' magic and his own unremitting control of the navigation.[9] His enduring wakefulness at sea prior to dozing off – pointed up by the redundant 'nine days, night and day', which stretches the duration of his sailing[10] – connects this episode to the last storm in his journey, which likewise causes him to sleep from extreme tiredness (5. 493; 6. 2), but after landing. While his rest at that point marks the end of a leg of his journey, his slumbering at the helm on his way to Ithaca reverses the journey's purposefulness by allowing the chaotic winds out. After he is blown back to Aeolus and his prayer for help is rejected, he and his crew start on an aimless navigation: a 'sending from', ἀποπέμπειν (10. 76), which undoes the directionality of Aeolus' conveyance, his πομπή (10. 18, 79). The travellers fall back into the pattern of sailing 'further', with no specification of direction or wind.[11]

In recalling his sleep, Odysseus speaks in the voice of the acting character. For, though he knows how much sorrow it caused him, he calls it 'sweet', reliving his experience of it, whereas later, in explaining to Aeolus what happened, he stresses its disastrous effects by calling it 'dire' (10. 69) and emphatically placing the adjective in enjambment at the beginning of the line.[12] Sleep was sweet when, with Ithaca's silhouette on the horizon, Odysseus thought it safe to give in to his tiredness. The memory of his relaxation informs his account even as far as the rhythm of the line that describes his abandoning himself to Morpheus, ἔνθ' ἐμὲ μὲν γλυκὺς ὕπνος ἐπέλυθε κεκμηῶτα ('Then sweet sleep came upon me, for I was tired'): a brisk succession of dactyls stopped by a spondaic fifth foot coinciding with 'tired'. The rhythm slows down as if Odysseus were re-experiencing his fatigue and his yielding to sleep, heavily.

Though he adopts the perspective of the acting character, Odysseus fills his sleep with his companions' conspiratory words, reported verbatim. In so doing he behaves like the omniscient narrator of Homeric epic, who knows all of his characters' movements, thoughts and speeches. But how could Odysseus know what his comrades said? One commentator attributes this narratological slip to '[Odysseus'] – or the primary narrator's – desire to expose the foolishness of his companions', which 'overruled narrative logic'.[13] Alternatively, the speech can be taken as a reconstruction after the fact, Odysseus' own dramatization of his companions' behaviour, how he imagines them to have acted while he was sleeping. In any case, the effect of the speech is to lengthen the duration of his slumber and make it not just the originator, but also the container, of the baneful action.[14]

Odysseus' isolation: sleeping on Trinacria

Odysseus dozes off inopportunely another time, and with more dire consequences, after a month of forced detention on Trinacria:

> Then I went apart, up the island, in order that I might pray to the gods, if one could show me a way to go. And when I got far from my comrades, walking through the island, I washed my hands in a place sheltered from the wind and prayed to all the gods who hold Olympus. And they poured sweet slumber over my eyelids.
>
> (12. 333–8)

The immediate effect of Odysseus' sleep is once again a mutinous speech, and he again reports its literal words. This time, though, the words have an individual speaker, Eurylochus, who leads the mutiny. His rebelliousness had already confronted Odysseus and forced him to come ashore. As night was approaching and the ship was nearing the island, Odysseus, mindful of Tiresias' and Circe's warnings, had urged his companions to steer clear:

> But Eurylochus instantly replied with a hateful speech: 'you are hard, Odysseus, you have strength beyond other men, your knees do not get tired. All about you is of iron, since you do not let your comrades, worn with fatigue and sleep, set foot on land. There, on the sea-girt island, we could once more prepare a pleasant meal, but you urge us even as we are to wander through the swift night, driven away from the island, on the dark sea. At night dire winds are born, the ruin of ships [...] No, let's now obey black night and prepare a meal by the swift ship. And at dawn we will go aboard and put out into the vast sea'.
>
> (12. 278–87; 291–3)

Eurylochus is the spokesman for the dejected crew, whose fatigue has soared after so many dreadful experiences. At the start of the journey Odysseus' companions are more energetic. The rhythm of their actions on the island near the Cyclopes' is dictated by the rhythm of the sun, not by abnormal tiredness. They reach the island at night, go to sleep (9. 151) and explore the site at dawn; they feast all day, lie down at night (9. 168–9) and the next day at dawn Odysseus calls the assembly (9. 170–1). After they escape from the monster, the sun regulates their actions again: they eat all day, sleep and at dawn resume their journey (9. 556–62). Nonetheless, they depart in utter dejection (9. 565–6).

Fatigue and dejection become palpable in the Circe episode. Upon touching the shore Odysseus and his men 'lay down two nights and two days, eating our hearts from tiredness and suffering' (10. 142–3).[15] This time it takes three days, not one night, for the action to resume. And only Odysseus finds enough strength to get up and go hunting. As Eustathius saw, the tragedy in Polyphemus' cave is to blame for this state of affairs: 'before the happenings at the Cyclopes', hunting was a common business, but now the others lie down from much weariness, while much-enduring Odysseus alone finds food for his friends'

(*Od.* 1. 373. 40–1). When he comes back, he encourages his comrades. Does he find them asleep?

Odysseus says, 'I ἀνέγειρα my companions with honeyed words, standing near each man' (10. 172–3). The verb ἀνέγειρα has been variously read, to mean 'awoke', 'reanimated', 'reassembled' or 'heartened'. However we take it, it is undeniable that Odysseus' companions have run out of steam. And on the morning of their departure from Circe's palace they would have slept well past dawn if Odysseus had not called them: 'I urged on my companions with honeyed words, standing near each man: "now sleep no longer, drowsing in sweet slumber"' (10. 546–8). As the repetition of the phrase 'my companions with honeyed words, standing near each man' suggests, Odysseus behaves here as he did in the earlier episode; but this time he makes it clear that his comrades are asleep and draws attention to their slumber with a redundant phrase. Though shortly beforehand it had fallen on them to shake Odysseus out of his oblivion by reminding him of his journey (10. 472–4), they still seem to be keen on the decadent life of feasting – and sweet sleep – provided by Circe.

By the time they reach Trinacria, Odysseus' men no longer bear up with his endurance but let their tiredness direct the journey. Eurylochus singles Odysseus out as the one who does not need to rest and does not want to respect the orderly sequence, 'stopping for the night, leaving at dawn', which often structures the rhythm of travelling in the *Odyssey*. The taunt resonates with Odysseus' own reproach to Achilles in *Iliad* 19, where he insists that the Greek warriors, who have long been without food, cannot wage war on an empty stomach. The reversal in Odysseus' role from sensible leader to insensitive superman matches the different situations he is in, for eating before fighting would be safe, while stopping on Trinacria, even for one night, could be fatal. As was often the case during the Trojan War, the night cannot be obeyed this time. The reappearance, unique in the *Odyssey*, of the Iliadic phrase 'let us obey the night' highlights the warlike danger of the circumstances. Odysseus alone is ready to disobey the night, as in Book 10 he alone endures nine days and nights of wakeful sailing.

Though Odysseus' endurance both times singles him out, the second episode shows him further apart from his comrades, preparing for his irrecoverable severance from them.[16] While the mutiny that disrupts the navigation from Aeolia is without a leader, and no one makes protestations to Odysseus openly, on Trinacria the crew's riotous inclinations predate his sleep and are stirred up by one fearless individual. Signs that Odysseus is losing his grip on his men can be traced back to the Circe episode, where Eurylochus speaks against him, opposing his request that they go with him to Circe's palace. Eurylochus attacks his foolishness, reminding everyone of the tragedy at the Cyclops' cave (10. 431–7). On this occasion, though, the defiant voice remains isolated and finally even Eurylochus agrees to go along. On Trinacria he gains the crew's approval (12. 294), forcing Odysseus to step ashore on the fateful island.

Sleep patterns reflect the increasing separation between the crew and its leader. The night they land near the Cyclops' territory, they lie together by the shore to rest, and the next morning Odysseus shares his plan (9. 168–71). On Circe's island they behave identically (10. 185–8). But at the end of their stay there, Circe takes Odysseus aside and instructs him all night long until dawn (10. 541) while his companions are slumbering. The separation is strongly marked by means of opposing particles and the emphatic personal pronoun: 'And when the sun sank and darkness came, they, on the one hand (οἱ μέν), went to sleep in the shadowy halls, but I (αὐτὰρ ἐγώ) went up to Circe's beautiful bed' (10. 478–80).

Further enhancing the separation is the echo in these lines of the description of the night's rest in the earlier episodes: 'And when the sun sank and darkness came, we slept by the edge of the sea' (9. 168–9; 10. 185–6).[17] The first line is identical, but in the earlier instances Odysseus is among the sleepers: 'we slept', not 'they slept', as at the end of the Circe episode. At dawn, as we have seen, Odysseus awakens his comrades, quite possibly for the first time in the journey. The pattern is largely repeated when they return from Hades. They sleep together one more time upon landing (12. 7), but soon thereafter, 'when the sun sank and darkness came', Circe takes Odysseus by the hand, *apart* (ἀπονόσφιν) from his companions, to map his journey while they are resting (12. 31–3). Dawn again rises as soon as she has explained everything (12. 142).

After Circe sends her guests on their way the second time, Odysseus and his men no longer sleep simultaneously and in the same spot. Odysseus himself emphasizes their division in his account of the first night on Trinacria:

> We drew the well-built ship in a hollow harbour [...] My companions went off the ship, and then skillfully prepared a meal. But when they were sated with food and drink, they remembered and mourned their friends [...] and [...] sweet slumber came upon them.
>
> (12. 305–11)

Odysseus does not participate in eating, lamenting, or resting.[18] Sleep functions as one of the markers of the crew's distance from its leader, as is further underscored by the reappearance of the inclusive first person plural in the narrative of the resumption of activity on the next day: 'But when early-born, rosy-fingered Dawn appeared, *we* moored the ship' (12. 316–7).

After a month of being detained on the island, Odysseus' comrades do not even share daytime activities with him. They fish, hunt and eat anything they find, worn down by hunger (12. 330–2), while he physically removes himself from them to pray. His behaviour 'is more in the individualistic manner of a Hebrew prophet than typical of the very communal and ceremonial religion of the Homeric hero'.[19] This un-Homeric ritual individualism demonstrates Odysseus' separation from his companions. To be sure, his removal and subsequent sleep are in keeping with a pattern of Homeric narrative: actions happening simultaneously in different settings are presented sequentially, or, to put it a different way, only one action and its protagonists are in the focus of the narrative at any given time, while the other characters sit idle and are meant to step into the background.[20] Odysseus withdraws from the group and falls asleep, and the narrative returns to the group that stays awake. His departure, however, has thematic relevance: it is the culmination of his growing alienation from his men. As happened on the journey from Aeolia, he dozes off in the daytime, but this time he does so in a separate location, which he has deliberately sought. His sleep creates a vacuum of leadership, allowing Eurylochus to take over.

This greater separation is in keeping with the greater seriousness of the fault committed by the crew. While in Book 10 Odysseus' companions show mistrust and envy but do not betray orders, in Book 12 they rise up against his injunctions, tread on their oath and breach divine law. And both the greater separation and the greater seriousness of the fault are in keeping with the more destructive power of sleep in the second episode, as perceived by Odysseus himself. As in Book 10, he describes his daytime slumber according to how he experienced it: sweet when it came, still sweet when it left him (12. 338, 366). But after he smelled the roasted meats it became a νηλέϊ ὕπνῳ, a 'pitiless sleep' (12. 372). Odysseus chooses an epithet unique for sleep[21] but common for the bronze of weapons, which his nap literally replaces by occupying the same metrical position as bronze in the formulaic phrase νηλέϊ χαλκῷ: the last two feet of the line. His sleep is a killing weapon indeed, for it brings about his comrades' death.

Odysseus' claim that the gods caused him to doze likewise underscores the dire consequences of his slumber. The claim sounds like an excuse, a way of denying responsibility.[22] Why indeed would Odysseus seek a windless spot if he were not tempted by a nap? His choice of locale calls to mind his search for a bushy shelter when he lands on Scheria (at the end of Book 5) and Eumaeus' retiring to a protected area to spend a wintry night (at the end of Book 14). But more than just self-exculpation is at stake in Odysseus' emphasis on the divine origin of his slumber. In the parallel episode in Book 10 he blames not the gods but, less dramatically, his tiredness. The supposedly divine provenance of his sleep on Trinacria is in line with its more tragic effects. The skillful narrator suggests the inevitability of the catastrophe it caused by casting it as the gods' immediate response to his prayer.

A covering sleep

When Odysseus reaches Scheria after twenty nights of sailing and swimming, he seeks a place to rest (5. 472). Ruling out the possibility of sleeping near the river and opting instead for 'thick bushes' (5. 471), he chooses two entwined together, through which neither wet wind nor sun nor rain can go (5. 478–80), and he makes a large bed of leaves. He lies in the middle, 'poured' (ἐπεχεύατο) more leaves upon himself and 'covered himself' (καλύψατο) with them. Athena acts in sync, 'covering' (ἀμφικαλύψας) his eyes by 'pouring' (χεῦ') slumber upon them (5. 487–*fin.*). Sleep's enfolding properties demonstrate its corporeality. Like night, which also covers, sleep is a substance.[23]

The book that begins with Odysseus leaving Lady Cover, Calypso, ends with him enwrapped in leaves and sleep: ἀμφικαλύψας is the book's last word.[24] These two movements in counterpoint play up the fundamental ambivalence of covering in Homeric epic:[25] a protective gesture, but only if the cover is eventually lifted, as when gods save their favourite heroes from death in battle by pouring clouds or mist over them just in time to snatch them away. A permanent cover is (like) death.

Odysseus must leave Calypso in order not to disappear; but once his departure is granted, the text emphasizes the warmth and comfort of cover, in a love scene shrouded in darkness at the heart of Calypso's hiding dwelling. Night descends, and the pair retires to the 'innermost part of the hollow cave' to taste the pleasure of love (5. 225–7). Now that Calypso has promised not to hide Odysseus any more, night comes to envelop him in love's embrace and take him far inside the nymph's cave. This sketched retiring scene starkly contrasts with the way Odysseus had been forced to lie by the nymph in the same hollow cave – but, significantly, not in its 'innermost part' – for nights on end, when the cover had not been lifted, and night after night of constrained proximity alternated with day after day of tearful staring at the sea (5. 151–8). The last night with Calypso, and the first of joyful love after many years, is followed by a description of dawn rising to lift the cover of darkness and give impulse to the preparations for the new journey: 'But when early-born, rosy-fingered Dawn appeared' (5. 228). This line, which always marks a fresh start, looks ahead to that journey.

Even the sleep that ends the journey, however, has an engulfing, deathlike quality, pointed up by Odysseus' effort to keep the winds completely out of it[26] and by the simile that compares him, as he covers himself with the leaves poured thickly around him, to someone who seeks to preserve the spark of a firebrand by burying it under embers, since he has no neighbour to ask for help (5. 488–91). The simile casts cover and the absence of wind as a life-saving shield, but also suggests that Odysseus, like the firebrand, might lose his spark – his life – under his blanket in that windless spot.[27] His deathlike slumber is worrisome indeed, for it lasts well into the next afternoon and would have lasted even longer if Athena had not interfered (6. 112–3).

Odysseus' sleep attracts much narrative attention. The detailed descriptions of his preparations, including the choice of the locale and the making of the bed, how he lay down in the middle of it and covered himself, give the narrative a slow tempo. His sleep also seems to last longer in the narrative, because it bridges the end of Book 5 ('Athena poured slumber over his eyes, so that it would quickly end his distressful tiredness, covering his eyelids') and the beginning of Book 6 ('So there he slept, the much-enduring, noble Odysseus, worn by sleep and tiredness'). We mark a pause between the two sentences, but instead of dawn rising in the second to restart the narrative, it is continuing slumber that fulfils this role. The prolonging of sleep in the authorial account matches Odysseus' own recollection, for he dwells on his sleep as expansively as Homer, and calls it 'boundless':

> Ambrosial night came, and I [. . .] lay down in the bushes and gathered leaves around me. And a god poured boundless slumber over me.[28] And there on the leaves I slept, with sorrow in my heart, all night until dawn and midday. The sun was declining [or set] when sweet slumber left me.
>
> (7. 283–9)

We face a textual problem here: the Oxford Classical Text prints δείλετο, which makes the sun 'declining', rather than the transmitted δύσετο, 'set'. The emendation goes back to the Hellenistic scholar Aristarchus, who objected to δύσετο because much happened between Odysseus' awakening and sunset. A modern critic, however, notes that δείλετο would occur only in this instance, and suggests, 'Homer might have been careless here'.[29] According to this interpretation, the reading δύσετο is correct, but Homer did not see that it was the wrong verb. But is it wrong? Could not δύσετο rather be meant to point to the duration of Odysseus' 'boundless slumber'? Thus another commentator: 'The poet's evident desire [...] is to exaggerate the length of Odysseus' exhausted sleep'.[30] Odysseus would have wished it to last longer than Athena allows, as he suggests by calling it 'sweet'. Though 'sweet slumber' is a standard phrase, this time the adjective is marked, because only Odysseus uses it, and not the primary narrator. Already when he is seeking the right spot to make his bed, Odysseus calls sleep 'sweet' in anticipation (5. 472), whereas Homer chooses the unmodified noun, and twice (5. 492; 6. 2). As we shall see, the weary traveller still desires sweet slumber in Alcinous' palace.

Athena's control of sleep and the beginning of the *Odyssey*

When Athena enwraps Odysseus in slumber, she has just reappeared by his side. She enters the stage by administering sleep, first to all the winds except Boreas (5. 384), then to the exhausted victim of shipwreck himself. Athena controls the *Odyssey*'s action largely by manipulating its characters' sleep and wakefulness. Soon after pouring slumber on Odysseus, she rouses Nausicaa by a commanding dream, then rouses Odysseus in turn, to effect his encounter with the princess. In the formulaic phrase, 'but grey-eyed Athena had another thought', which often prefaces an attempt to steer the action away from an unwanted course, the thought is in most cases a decision to send sleep, to work on it or to prepare the conditions for either sleeping or awakening.[31] The goddess' interferences demonstrate the importance of sleep and wakefulness in the development of the *Odyssey*'s plot.

We first meet Athena as a controller of sleep on Ithaca. She pours 'sweet slumber' over Penelope's eyes (1. 362–4) but keeps Telemachus from sleeping. When the suitors retire, he goes to his bed 'pondering many things in his mind' (1. 427), and 'all night long, covered with a sheep's fleece, he considered in his mind the journey that Athena had shown him' (1. 443–*fin.*).

This instance of wakefulness near the epic's beginning recalls the one at the beginning of the *Iliad*, when sleepless Zeus causes Agamemnon to wake up. The two episodes unfold identically: a group (the gods in the *Iliad*, the suitors in the *Odyssey*) retires

(*Il.* 1. 606 = *Od.* 1. 424 except for particles); a character (Zeus, Telemachus) is singled out as he withdraws to his bedchamber (*Il.* 1. 609–11; *Od.* 1. 425–7), where he ends up staying awake, 'deep in thought' (*Il.* 2. 3: μερμήριζε; *Od.* 1. 427: μερμηρίζων); a deity (Zeus, Athena) rouses a human (Agamemnon, Telemachus) to action. Eustathius connects the two scenes, taking Telemachus' sleeplessness as an illustration of the appropriateness of the dream's reproach to Agamemnon ('a man who bears the scepter should not sleep all night').[32]

These detailed correspondences, however, underscore meaningful thematic differences. In the *Iliad* the deity who makes the decision is Zeus, who is himself sleepless, while the deity in the *Odyssey* is Athena, and it is not she who is sleepless, but the human who must implement her decision. The two configurations highlight Zeus' different modes of presence in the two poems and the different relationships between gods and mortals in them. Zeus' launching action is more 'bossy' in the *Iliad* and more mediated in the *Odyssey*, where he remains in the background and acts indirectly. Instead of conceiving his plan upfront in sleepless solitude, he stimulates Athena's intervention.[33] And the goddess intervenes by stirring Telemachus and causing him to think after sharing her plan with him, while Zeus, the *Iliad*'s wakeful thinker, shakes Agamemnon out of sleep to make him carry out a plan about which he knows nothing. This difference reflects Zeus' inscrutability in the *Iliad* as opposed to his, and Athena's, stronger sense of justice in the *Odyssey*, which determines also the treatment of sleep and wakefulness. While the gods in the *Iliad* (with the exception of Hermes in Book 24) do not help humans by interfering in their sleep patterns, in the *Odyssey* Athena repeatedly manipulates them to help Odysseus and his family, or to harm the suitors. A god-sent slumber never hurts a well-deserving character.[34]

Athena's choice to goad Telemachus awake is in keeping with the coming-of-age subplot in the epic. Odysseus' son cannot sleep because he ponders the goddess' exhortation to leave: that is, he is roused to his duties as a man. His night filled with thinking is a *vigilia in armis*;[35] and it is set off against the suitors' irresponsible and unaware relaxation. Just when Telemachus realizes Athena's stirring action (1. 420), they start dancing and singing. And 'black evening came upon them while they were taking their joy, and each of them went home to lie down' (1. 423–4). The evening is markedly black, because the suitors are blind and sleepy even before going to bed.[36]

Wakefulness also distinguishes Telemachus from Penelope. The goddess keeps the son up all night and lulls the mother to sleep, separating the one from the other now that Telemachus must find news of his father, come closer to him, become like him and leave motherly nurture behind.[37] This is vividly signified by the discrepancy between Euryclea's treatment of Telemachus as a spoiled child when she sees him to his bed and his inability to sleep like a spoiled child that night.[38] The account of his retiring sends conflicting messages, for he behaves like an adult and specifically his father, 'pondering' (1. 427: μερμηρίζων), while Euryclea, 'who nursed him as a baby' (1. 435), makes sure that he is safe and comfortable in his childhood bed. She follows him with lighted torches, folds and hangs his clothes, then locks the door of the room. When she leaves, he is all tucked up in his blanket: but his mind has already taken to the road indicated by Athena. Two women are competing for his attention: the caring nurse who locks him in his cosy bedroom and the goddess who sends him out into the world. And the goddess wins. The book (or the episode) ends with her name.

When Telemachus makes the final preparations for his journey, his wakefulness is once again set off against his mother's sleep, which allows him to act unbeknownst to her, to leave her in the dark while she is slumbering. He plans to fetch the provisions for his journey in the evening, 'whenever Penelope shall go up to her quarters and be mindful of sleep' (2. 358–9).

The rousing effect of Athena's action is consistent with her behaviour towards Telemachus throughout the epic: she never puts him to sleep, as she does with his father. While she reappears by Odysseus' side with her hypnotic wand in Book 5 and applies it again on the night before the slaughter in Book 20, she appears by Telemachus' side to prevent him from sleeping in Book 1, and does not use her wand when he lies sleepless on the night before his return journey in Book 15. Athena's penchant for rousing Telemachus reflects the necessity for him to keep steadily at his task of earning his place in the world. He is not, not yet, entitled to the soothing slumber to which Athena treats his much-tried and much-battered father.

The pleasure of sleep, the pleasure of tales: in Menelaus' palace

During his visits in Pylus and Sparta Telemachus sleeps on comfortable beds, carefully made. Offering good bedding is a mark not only of hospitality but also of wealth: 'I am not destitute', protests Nestor when Athena and Telemachus prepare to leave the palace and retire by the ship, 'but I have plenty of covers to make soft beds for my guests' (3. 346–55, summarized). After arranging for Telemachus to rest under the portico on 'an inlaid bedstead' next to his unmarried son, he himself 'slept in the innermost part of the lofty palace, and besides him was the lady his wife, who had made the bed and the couch' (3. 402–3).

This is the first retiring scene in the epic. The second is in Menelaus' mansion, where the hosts again sleep 'in the innermost part of the lofty palace' while Telemachus and Nestor's son Pisistratus do so on the porch (4. 302–5). These orderly arrangements create a stark contrast with the imbalance that upsets Ithaca. During the three years of the suitors' besiegement, Penelope withdraws to her bedroom each night to weep; the suitors leave each night for their homes; Laertes, who has moved to the fields, sleeps outside or in the dust near the fire, without a bed (11. 188–94)[39] and Telemachus supposedly sleeps in his childhood bedroom – though when we first meet him there, he is wide awake. His stays with Nestor and Menelaus lead him to discover something he did not know: a harmonious household, with a married couple retiring together.[40]

In Menelaus' palace, however, sleep is delayed by storytelling. The evening must have already been advanced when he and his guests engage in conversation after a meal. For Pisistratus tries to stop that conversation, which has taken a tearful turn, by telling his host: 'I do not delight in postprandial weeping. And early-born Dawn will come' (4. 193–5). Menelaus' sorrowful reminiscing about Troy has revived in the young man a distressful longing for his dead and never known brother. To counter it, he invokes the late hour.

But Pisistratus' move clashes with his own desire to remember. Right after asking Menelaus to stop, he nonetheless endorses the human need to mourn and speaks of his brother (4. 195–202). It is now Menelaus' turn to stop the concert of tears and adjourn the conversation: 'Let us cease from lamenting [...] and think of supper [...] There will be tales at dawn for Telemachus and me to tell to each other to the full' (4. 212–5).

Like Menelaus' words, the authorial narrative that follows creates an anticipation of sleep: a herald pours water on the diners' hands, and they 'threw their hands on the food laid before them' (4. 218). This formulaic line is normally complemented by another, 'and when they put away their desire for food and drink', which marks the end of the meal and, almost always, the beginning of a conversation or a poetic performance.[41] But in this episode, the first line of the pair stands alone. This anomaly may suggest to a trained audience that there will be no more conversation indeed, that the party is closing down.

The next line, though, defies this expectation, since 'Helen had another thought' (4. 219). Her intervention, like Athena's when she alters the course of the action ('has another thought'), causes an abrupt move.[42] And the move is the unexpected resumption of speeches, with a corrective: the nepenthe, the drug that Helen pours into the wine to remove the pain that the stories were causing for Menelaus and his guests, making them wish for sleep. As soon as the drugged wine is served, she tells her tale. Thus, storytelling takes the place of the suggested rest.

Helen promises her audience 'delight of speeches' (4. 239), confident that the drug will prevent personal memories from marring aesthetic pleasure. Does her nepenthe work? While under its influence, Helen and Menelaus recall Odysseus' exploits at Troy. Menelaus compliments his wife on the exactitude of her narrative (4. 266), which he has apparently enjoyed. But after he tells his story, Telemachus asks for sleep instead. He finds those recollections of Odysseus' heroism 'all the more painful. For those deeds did not ward off mournful death, though he had a heart of iron inside. But please send us to bed, so that we may lie down and delight in sweet slumber' (4. 292–5). Τέρψις ('delight') does not settle on one object during the long night in Menelaus' palace, but shifts from stories to sleep and vice-versa. Sleep wins in the end, and all retire in grand style (4. 296–305).

At dawn Menelaus asks Telemachus the reason for his coming (4. 312). The young man's request for news of his father prompts the long narrative of Menelaus' encounter with Proteus, which leaves Telemachus spellbound: 'I would hold on even for a year, sitting here with you, and feel no longing for home or parents, for I exceedingly delight in listening to your words and stories' (4. 595–8). While on the previous night Telemachus sought the delight of sleep, now he enthusiastically clings to the delight of Menelaus' narrative. Telemachus did not enjoy the stories of the previous night because they did not prove to him that Odysseus was alive. Now he rejoices in hearing a tale that for the first time gives him news of his father in the present tense. At last he is receiving the information he is after.

The inconclusive back-and-forth between the desire for rest and the desire for stories on the night of Telemachus' arrival has the narrative function of delaying the climax.[43] For on that night Menelaus already knows, or should know, that his guest is paying him a visit to hear about Odysseus or receive help. Telemachus does not disclose his identity, but is nonetheless recognized, and the goal of his trip is explained by Pisistratus (4. 162–3). Yet Menelaus ignores his guest's wish until the next day, when he asks him, 'what do you need?' and this time honours his request for information. The leisurely description of Menelaus' rising at dawn, getting dressed and leaving his room to find Telemachus (4. 307–11) gives the new day a strong forward-looking impetus. Sleep erases the painful and pointless conversation of the previous evening to prepare for the hope-inducing revelation.

Telemachus' response provides a model for the audience's. For he listens with true delight to a tale – Menelaus' ambush of Proteus – that does not belong, like the stories told on the previous night, to the Trojan War, to a pre-*Odyssey* past, but to the aftermath of the war: a tale, in other words, that is fully *Odyssey* material.[44] Considered from this angle, the richly described retiring scene that ends the previous night in sleep has the narrative function of turning the page, so to speak, from stories still informed by memories of Troy to stories more directly related to the Odysseus of the *Odyssey*, to his *nostos*.

The pleasure of sleep, the pleasure of tales: in Alcinous' palace

Odysseus arrives at the palace of Alcinous in the evening. It is sunset when he reaches the nearby grove of Athena (6. 321), and bedtime when he appears at the hearth: 'He found [the Phaeacians] pouring libations to sharp-sighted Hermes, to whom they made libation last, when their thoughts turned to sleep' (7. 138). Odysseus' arrival, though, like his son's in Sparta, postpones sleep, by causing Alcinous to offer another libation (7. 164–5; 179–81) and to have a table set and a meal prepared for the suppliant (7. 173–7). After the libation Alcinous dismisses his Phaeacian guests: 'Now that you have dined, go home to lie down' (7. 188). At dawn they will make sacrifices, entertain the stranger and think about his conveyance.

In fact, however, no one leaves until Odysseus rebuffs Alcinous' suggestion that he might be a god, says that his hunger prevents him from narrating his story and renews his request for conveyance. After making more libations, the Phaeacian people finally 'went each to their homes to lie down' (7. 229). But Odysseus cannot go to sleep yet, for he has to answer Arete's question about his clothes. To satisfy her he provides a longer narrative (7. 241–97), whose incipit ('It would be hard, queen, to tell all of my tale of woes, since the gods of heaven have given me many') harks back to the phrase with which he earlier put his need for food upfront: 'I could tell you a longer tale of all the ills I have suffered by the will of the gods. But let me eat, for all my sorrows' (7. 213–5). After quieting his hunger, Odysseus gives his hosts a tantalizing sample of his character, adventures and narrative skills, whetting their appetite for more. Sleep's long deferral foreshadows its downright denial on the next night, when Alcinous, eager to hear Odysseus' story to the full, keeps him awake against his expressed desire.

In the Phaeacian chapter Odysseus is remarkably drowsy. The sailor who can keep his eyes fixed on the stars night after night, is always ready to doze off while on Scheria.[45] His fatigue upon landing sharply contrasts with his hosts' cult of sleep: not so much a necessity as an indulgence. As Odysseus learns from Alcinous, his people cherish 'the feast, music and dance, clothes often changed, warm baths, and the bed' (8. 248–9). These words resonate with Menelaus' in the *Iliad*: sleep, love, song and dance are things of which one would rather take one's fill than of war (13. 636–9). The life of the peace-loving Phaeacians is a permanent party with sweet slumber as one of its attractions. They sleep for pleasure, as they eat for pleasure. Nausicaa and her friends 'delight' in their picnic (6. 99), while starved Odysseus eats with a ferocious hunger (6. 249–50). The Phaeacians are neither hungry nor sleepy, because they live in plenty and are close to the gods. They do not know what it is to labour even when they travel, which they do 'without effort' (7. 325). Poised between gods and men, untried by storms, they have no experience of the 'distressful tiredness' (5. 493) that plunges Odysseus into a deathlike slumber upon arriving on their island.

After Odysseus is offered hospitality and promised conveyance, his somnolence becomes a sign of relaxation, spurred by the confidence that his return to Ithaca is close, and that it will be, as Alcinous says, 'without toil or pain' (7. 192). The ever-wakeful sailor will this time be carried, 'overcome by slumber', on windless waters (7. 318–9). His eagerness to sleep seems reflected in the extended retiring scene that concludes his first evening in Alcinous' palace:

> While they were so talking to each other, white-armed Arete asked the maids to put a bedstead under the portico and throw shining purple blankets on it, spread rugs, and put fleecy coverlets on top for him to wear. And the maids left the hall with torches. When they had busily spread the sturdy bed, they came to Odysseus and called him with these words: 'rise, stranger. A bed is made for you'. So they said, and sleeping seemed welcome to him. So there he slept, the much-enduring, noble Odysseus, on a corded bed under the echoing portico. And Alcinous lay in the innermost part of the lofty palace, and next to him was the lady his wife, who made the bed and the couch.
>
> (7. 334–7)

Odysseus takes part in a formal retiring scene for the first time in the epic. His new role fits his new circumstances: he is no longer in a world in which 'hosts' either issue deadly threats or wish to detain their guests forever, but is back in the civilized world, where guests enjoy proper hospitality and are not kept against their will (7. 315–8; 15. 68–9). For the first time in his journey, Odysseus has his own bed, a comfortable, richly decked-out one, where he is glad to retire. The repetition of the line 'So there he slept, the much-enduring, noble Odysseus', which describes him as he lies in the bushes at the beginning of Book 6, draws the audience's attention to the different conditions and spirit in which he now rests: his bed is no longer made of leaves and he is no longer beaten by extreme fatigue (6. 2), but anticipates sleep's pleasure. The detailed description of the bed's preparation replaces the mention of exhaustion, pointing up Odysseus' reentry into civilization. The leisurely narrative also conveys the extent of his eagerness to make up both for sleep's long postponement on that night and for many past nights he spent in discomfort and danger, whether asleep or awake.

On the next evening Odysseus is reminded that he will 'sleep a sweet slumber' through his homeward journey (8. 445). He must think it imminent, because he has been promised conveyance on that day (7. 318), which is almost over (8. 417), and he has been told that 'the journey will not be delayed, but the ship is launched and the crew is ready' (8. 150–1). Odysseus has received signal after signal that his departure is upcoming, and he is ready to leave. But when the songs of the bard stir him to tears, Alcinous asks not just for his name and the name of his native country, but also for an accurate narrative of his wanderings and losses at Troy (8. 572–86). As he is soon to find out, he will not sleep that night, either on the ship that is supposed to take him home or even in the palace.

Sleep is denied to Odysseus throughout the next four books: the longest night of the epic in narrative time, filled with the account of his adventures. At the end of Book 8, Alcinous asks a question that looks ahead, creating suspense and anticipation: 'Tell me why you weep. Did any of your relatives die at Troy, or one of your friends? For wise friends are as good as brothers' (577–*fin.*, abridged). The audience cannot take a break at the end of the book but is eagerly projected onward, towards the answer to come. Its introduction, moreover, increases this sense of continuation by an atypical use of a common formulaic line: 'And in answer much-cunning Odysseus said' (9. 1). The line normally punctuates a back-and-forth conversation between two speakers in the flow of events, whereas in this instance, and in this instance only, it introduces a book and a sole-authored narrative. Whatever the origin of the book divisions, their author(s) felt that a transition from a speaker ending one book with a question to another starting the next with the answer was appropriate for the expectation of narrative created by Odysseus' protracted reticence.

Odysseus, though, does not give up on his desire for sleep. While he is listing the heroines he saw in Hades, he abruptly interrupts himself, telling his audience that he cannot mention them all, since there would not be enough time: 'immortal night would be gone. But there is also a time to sleep, whether I go to the swift ship to join the crew or stay here. And my conveyance will be your concern and the gods'' (11. 330–2). Odysseus' pronouncement on the late hour recalls Athena's, likewise issued in the expectation of a departure (3. 334–5): goddess and hero are connected even in their shared appreciation of timely sleep.

But what exactly is Odysseus' goal? It could be that his interruption is purely rhetorical, a strategy to frustrate his listeners and pique their curiosity. This reading is supported by his choice to end his story with an anticlimax, a hurried list of heroines, whereas Alcinous wanted to know about the heroes who died in Troy, a request he repeats in response to Odysseus' claim that it is time to sleep (11. 370–2). But Odysseus' decision to end on a bland, low-key note could also suggest that he is indeed getting tired and is rushing to an end.[46]

Unlike his son in Sparta, however, Odysseus does not say, 'let us go to bed', but couches his wish in a maxim ('there is also a time to sleep').[47] This is a tactful move, for should not the hosts decide when to break up the party? Normally it is they who initiate a retiring scene.[48] When Priam urges Achilles to have a bed made for him, he demonstrates his uncontrived candour. Young Telemachus is likewise direct. Conversely, his father hides behind a dictum, as he does again to restate his desire for rest when his host objects that the night is young: 'There is a time for many speeches, but also a time for sleep' (11. 379). This roundabout phrasing also legitimizes Odysseus' desire with the cachet of gnomic wisdom.

In reply to his guest's first protestation, Alcinous rejoins: 'this night is very long, marvellously long. It is not yet time to sleep in the hall. Tell me of your wondrous deeds. And I would hold on even until bright dawn, as long as you are willing to tell me the tale of your woes' (11. 373–6). Alcinous calls the night measureless, colouring it with his eagerness to listen and countering Odysseus' claim that it is fading.[49] His rejoinder emphasizes the enchanting atmosphere, stronger than sleep, that poetry creates[50] and might be directed to the external audience.

According to an attractive theory, the *Iliad* was performed in three nights and the *Odyssey* in two, and mentions of night and sleep marked the end of each stretch of the performance.[51] The *Iliad*'s first part would run to the end of Book 9, when the Achaean leaders fall asleep after the embassy to Achilles, and the second part, which would begin with dawn rising at the opening of Book 11,[52] would end with night at 18. 354. Though dawn does not appear right at the start of Part Three but at 19. 1, it has been announced towards the close of Part Two (18. 136). Part One of the *Odyssey* would conclude with the description of Odysseus slumbering on the Phaeacian ship that carries him to Ithaca in Book 13, and Part Two would begin with the mention of dawn rising on the island.

If we adopt this theory, the comment on Odysseus' sleep-chasing narrative would have come very late in the performance and might have served as an encouragement to stay up for its last stretch: 'Heed my words!' Alcinous would be saying, 'The story is worth the effort of remaining awake an extra hour!'[53] To secure his grip on the audience, the bard praises the performance's magic at a relatively dull point before redirecting the narrative. We hear a second beginning when Alcinous repeats his request for narrative in exactly the same words he used the first time: 'But tell me this, tell everything exactly, whether you saw any of your godlike companions' (11. 370–1), which harks back to, 'But tell me this, tell everything exactly, whither you wandered' (8. 572–3). Like a scene of actual sleep, but more emphatically, this protracted interruption – caused by the tension between the narrator's desire to call it a night and his audience's eagerness to hear more tales – leads to a fresh and revitalized new start.

Sweet slumber at the crossing

At the end of the long night of storytelling, the Phaeacian people go to sleep (13. 17), and perhaps Alcinous, his family and their guest do too; but the narrative is elliptical and moves straightaway to the rising of dawn (13. 18). This lack of a retiring scene to round off Odysseus' poetic feat projects the plot forward to his return, his only desire. Almost nothing happens on the new day, and Odysseus only wishes for it to end: 'He would often turn his head to the bright sun, eager for its setting, for he very much wanted to go home' (13. 29–30). Like a labourer who looks forward to his dinner after a long day of work and welcomes the sunset when he goes home, his knees broken with tiredness, 'thus welcome to Odysseus was the sinking of the sun' (13. 35). The simile conveys the length of his waiting and his weariness with it. Now, evening is longed for as much as sleep was the first night in Alcinous' palace (7. 343).

At last, Odysseus boards the ship:

> And they spread a rug and a linen cover for Odysseus on the deck of the hollow ship, so that he might sleep soundly on the prow. He went on the ship and lay down in silence. And they [the crew] sat each at their benches in order, and loosened the cable from the pierced stone [...] and sweet slumber fell on his eyelids, a sound, most sweet (ἥδιστος) slumber, very much like death [...] Thus the ship swiftly running cut the waves of the sea, carrying a man the equal to the gods in counsel, who before had suffered very many sorrows in his heart, passing through wars of men and grievous waves, and now was sleeping, motionlessly, oblivious of all that he had suffered.
>
> (13. 73–7; 79–80; 88–92)

Sleep is instilled into Odysseus by the soothing, lullaby-like rhythm of the three lines that prepare for departure (13. 75–7):

they all start with a spondee coinciding with one word and have a similar metrical pattern (identical in the last two), which creates a monotonous effect.[54] An ancient audience is likely to have been sensitive to the hypnotic force of the passage, at least if we believe a Byzantine rhetorician's appreciation of an Iliadic line used to wake a sleeper: 'You sleep, son of Tydeus, the fierce breaker of horses?' (Εὕδεις Τυδέος υἱὲ δαΐφρονος ἱπποδάμοιο). He notes that the rhythm of the line, which quickens after the first spondaic word, makes it suitable for its context: 'You see how the verse imitates arousal from sleep: it begins with long sounds, as if with lulling ones'.[55]

Odysseus' transporting slumber is more lavishly described than any other Homeric instance of sleep. It has four epithets, one of which, ἥδιστος, is unique,[56] and the account of its qualities and effects occupies four lines. The episode also invited an array of interpretations in antiquity.[57] Some of these may appear fanciful to us: that Odysseus was naturally somnolent; that he faked sleep to avoid appearing ungrateful to his hosts for not inviting them to his palace, which would have led to his being recognized by his family; that the Phaeacians put him to sleep to prevent him from realizing where Scheria was and exposing it to attacks, or alternatively to show their respect for their guest by making it impossible for them to ask for a ferrying fee! More appealing to modern sensibilities and closer to the text is Eustathius' observation that Odysseus' deep slumber compensates for his long suffering by drowning it in forgetfulness.[58] The man who 'suffered many sorrows in his heart at sea' (1. 5) becomes the man 'who *before* had suffered very many sorrows in his heart'. Poseidon frowns on Odysseus' sleep (13. 134) because it makes his journey painless. While the god thought that his enemy would return home 'suffering many woes' (13. 131), sweet slumber turns suffering from wars and waves into a pluperfect, ἐπεπόνθει (13. 92).[59]

By harking back to the introductory presentation of Odysseus, however, the line 'who before had suffered very many sorrows in his heart' endows sleep with more than just a healing function: it also announces that the first part of the *Odyssey*, as well as the first night of the performance, is over.[60] The audience can go to sleep along with Odysseus and reconvene, energized, the next night to hear the second half. The 'before' that modifies the allusion to the beginning of the *Odyssey* signals the transition to Part Two, in which Odysseus will still suffer, but no longer from the sea or foreign wars. His own silence as he prepares himself for sleep puts an emphatic ending to the Phaeacian chapter, dominated by his storytelling. Both Odysseus' grievous wanderings and his account of them are over.

Yet another narrative marker for this transition is the abruptness with which Odysseus ceases to sleep and breaks into the final episode of the Phaeacians' chapter. We meet them for the last time as they sacrifice to Poseidon, 'standing around the altar. And noble Odysseus awoke' (187: ἑσταότες περὶ βωμόν. ὁ δ'ἔγρετο δῖος Ὀδυσσεύς). Our ears are drawn to ὁ δ'ἔγρετο, 'he awoke', by the position of the phrase: after the pause, which marks it out. Odysseus' aoristic awakening in the middle of a line, with the action suddenly switching from Scheria to Ithaca, represents perhaps the strongest narrative discontinuity in the *Odyssey*. There are two more instances where a character stops sleeping in coincidence with a switch in narrative focus in the course of a line: 'they [Nausicaa's friends] cried aloud. And noble Odysseus woke up' (6. 117), and 'limb loosening [of Odysseus' sleep], but his true-hearted wife woke up' (20. 57).[61] In these instances, though, the subjects who share the line eventually converge, whereas Odysseus' awakening on Ithaca occurs along with the definitive disappearance of the Phaeacians from the narrative.

This emphatically transitional sleep advances the plot *and* Odysseus' wishes, both homeward bound. Thematic parallels conjure up Odysseus' slumber at the helm when he almost reaches Ithaca in Book 10: the magic aid he receives and the real or suspected treasures he carries. But in the earlier episode Odysseus' wishes clash with the plot's design. He 'has' to sleep for the plot to continue, whereas in Book 13 it is time for him to return, both in the gods' scheme and in the scheme of the narrative, which moves on from Odysseus' wanderings to the planning of his revenge, and from fantasy land to humanity and geographical reality.[62] In Book 10 Odysseus' eagerness to return meets with both divine and poetic opposition: the gods are not by his side (he is 'a man hateful to the blessed gods', 74), his return is not yet fated, and it would cut off the fun of more fabulous wanderings. In Book 13, by contrast, Odysseus' wishes are supported by both Athena and the now centripetal movement of the narrative.

Odysseus slumbers at the junction of two worlds and portions of narrative already at the end of Book 5, before his first reentry into human society.[63] The parallel role of sleep as he transitions from the world of wandering to Scheria and from Scheria to Ithaca is pointed up by identical associations, with cover, absence of wind, and death.[64] Just as Odysseus sleeps on Scheria in a wind-blocking shelter, so he is carried to Ithaca on a ship shrouded in mist and clouds (8. 562) and sailing without wind (8. 556–60; 7. 328). His magical slumber on that ship is called 'un-awakening' νήγρετον, and indistinguishable from death.[65] As these two episodes of sleep signify, he comes close to the breathlessness of death both when he enters Scheria and when he leaves it.[66]

Odysseus' deathlike slumber at each crossing back to the human world befits the heroic way he embraces the mortal condition. Odysseus chooses mortality[67] and, with it, the necessity of sleep. In this important respect, he is the opposite of Gilgamesh, with whom he is often compared because both wander to the outer limits of human experience. But Gilgamesh's wanderings are a quest for immortality and are characterized by a horror of sleep, which he identifies with death. Seeing his friend Enkidu dead, he asks, 'What is this slumber that has seized you?' (Tablet 8), and then wanders relentlessly, sleeplessly (Tablet 10). His aspiration to find immortality takes the shape of an ever-wakeful search. Accordingly, the test of immortality he is given consists of seven nights without sleep (Tablet 11). He fails. His failure proves that he is mortal and sends him home to die.[68]

Odysseus does not need to learn this lesson. His extraordinary wakefulness is not dictated by repulsion for sleep but by the urgencies of travelling and survival, just as his wanderings are not a quest but a detour. His greatest feat of wakefulness occurs not along a journey to find immortality but as he sails to reenter the human world after declining an offer of immortality. Odysseus forsakes sleep to survive as a human and return to humankind. And as soon as he lands on Scheria, he falls into a boundless, deathlike slumber: a confirmation, or even a recovery, of mortality.

Back to light and life

The deathlike quality of Odysseus' sleep as he is transported to Ithaca equates his homecoming with a return to life. This identity is further underscored by the timing of the journey from night to the rising of the morning star, which inspires an extended and non-formulaic description: 'When that brightest of stars rose, which more than others comes to announce the light of early-born Dawn, then the sea-cleaving ship approached the island' (13. 93–5).

Arrival at daybreak foreshadows safety, while night-time landings tend to mark journeys particularly fraught with misadventures. The strange night that takes Odysseus to the Cyclops in retrospect foreshadows ill, imprisonment in a cave and death. When he leaves the island, it is dawn. The early-morning departure, though standard in the *Odyssey*, contrasts with the nocturnal arrival and highlights the end of danger. It is again evening when Odysseus catches sight of Trinacria (12. 265), and night when he lands on Calypso's island (12. 447), the island of disappearance. The most dangerous and the darkest realm of all, Hades, is also entered via sunless regions. After sailing 'all day', at the coming of night the crew reaches the limits of Oceanus and the land of the Cimmerians, wrapped in a perennial, dreadful night (11. 9–19). The journey to Hades is a descent from day to night, while the return to Circe is to the dwelling of daybreak, 'the house of early-born Dawn' (12. 3). As one critic puts it, 'Odysseus sails from darkness to light, from night to morning, death to life'.[69]

Dawn rises again to show Odysseus Scheria the first time he hopes he can reach it, after Poseidon has covered land and sea with clouds to make 'night rise from the sky' (5. 294). For 'two nights and two days' Odysseus is adrift and expects death, but 'when fair-tressed Dawn brought the third day to its birth, the wind stopped and a windless calm came to be. And he saw the land nearby' (5. 388–92). The phrase, 'nights and days', highlights the magnitude of the storm and of Odysseus' stamina,[70] and it is also appropriate because daylight ends the night of the storm and of wandering. The first time Scheria appears (5. 279) prior to the storm, no dawn rises. The island's appearance then neither brings salvation nor builds a contrast with darkness: Odysseus has been sailing without sleeping for 'seventeen days' (5. 278), not 'seventeen days and nights'. The mention of the birth of day in combination with the end of the storm in the second instance emphasizes his return to life. (Though the waves resume, the sight of the land in daylight announces deliverance, for the comparison of Odysseus to a child seeing his father unexpectedly recovered from a deadly illness occurs at this point [5. 394–8].) As on his journey to Calypso's island, Odysseus is the victim of shipwreck, is alone, naked and carried on the waves for days on end;[71] but that journey, with its nocturnal landing, takes him to the swallowing night of the nymph's cave, while the journey to Scheria, with dawn appearing on the horizon, advances his return to life and home.[72]

Sleep and disorientation

When Odysseus awakens on Ithaca, dawn has risen, but a mist poured by Athena prevents him from recognizing his native country. His slumber prepares for the disorientation that follows it by effacing his memory and by keeping him in the dark while he is transported from one place to another and when he is landed on Ithacan soil.[73] The verse describing Odysseus' failure to recognize Ithaca points up sleep's responsibility by beginning with 'sleeping' and ending with 'he did not know': εὕδων ἐν γαίῃ πατρωίῃ, οὐδέ μιν ἔγνω (13. 188). εὕδων and ἔγνω are interlocked not only by their symmetrical positions but also by their identical metrical pattern (two spondees). We hear sleep turn into disorientation.[74]

Odysseus' experience of disorientation colours the story he tells Athena just after discovering that the strange land he sees is Ithaca. He casts himself as a wanderer who has lost his way. He was headed to Pylus or Elis, he says, but the Phoenician ship taking him there was hit by a storm, and

> Wandering we came here by night. Eagerly we rowed into the harbour, and none of us was mindful of food, though we

> sorely needed to eat, but we all left the ship just as we were and lay down. Then sweet sleep came upon me, for I was tired. They took my goods from the hollow ship and placed them down where I was lying on the sand. And they went on board and left for the well-peopled land of Sidon. But I was left here, troubled in my heart.
>
> (13. 278–86)

This is the first of Odysseus' 'lies similar to the truth' (19. 203). It is true that he was carried on a foreign ship, that he slumbered and that upon awakening he found himself alone but with his goods safe and next to him. It is not true that he arrived on Ithaca at night or that he was headed elsewhere. But even these lies reflect his real state of confusion when Ithaca appeared to him as an unknown land, shrouded in mist if not in darkness. The real personage, like the fictional one, was headed elsewhere indeed, to Ithaca, not to the unrecognizable land where he found himself. Odysseus' choice of line to describe sleep's onset ('Then sweet sleep came upon me, for I was tired') pushes him back to the world of wandering. The line repeats 10. 31, reminding the audience of Odysseus' unfortunate slumber when he was about to reach Ithaca the first time around and lost his return. The detail that he was stranded on Ithaca at night likewise conveys his experience of disorientation, because nocturnal landings, as we have seen, are associated with perilous crossings. Though he lands at the rise of dawn this time, he does not see its light until Athena, over 160 lines after he awakes, scatters the fog (13. 352).

Odysseus' disorientation is one more feature connecting his return to Ithaca with his arrival on Scheria, where he likewise awakes suddenly from a long and deathlike sleep and in the middle of a line ('they cried aloud, and Odysseus awoke'). There too he realizes that he does not know where he is and asks the same questions, the ones he used to ask during his wanderings: where have I come? Are the people here friendly or violent? (6. 119–21 = 13. 200–2) These questions build up dramatic irony by highlighting Odysseus' ignorance and keeping him from returning, when we know that his homecoming is imminent (on Scheria) or accomplished (on Ithaca).

PART TWO: ON ITHACA

In Eumaeus' hut: sleeping arrangements and sleep-chasing stories

The arrival of Odysseus at Eumaeus' dwelling prompts an account of the swineherd's husbandry. He has set up sleeping quarters for his master's livestock: 'Inside the farmstead he had built twelve sties next to each other, as beds for the swine. And in each of them were kept fifty female swine for breeding, which slept on the ground. But the boars slept outside' (14. 13–6). The care with which Eumaeus tends the animals is reflected in the neat arrangements he has made for their rest. They 'retire' each to their appointed place. Like the members of a well-functioning household, they have regular sleeping habits (14. 411).

The swineherd has his sleeping habits as well. He prefers to remain near the animals rather than in his hut. On the first night of Odysseus' visit, he prepares a bed for him by the fire, then leaves:

> Odysseus lay down there. And he [Eumaeus] threw upon him a thick and large cloak, which he kept at hand to wear whenever a fierce storm would arise. So there Odysseus slept, and next to him the young men slept. But it did not please the swineherd to make his bed there, to sleep far from the swine.
>
> (14. 520–7)

Eumaeus plays the host in a retiring scene by preparing for his guest's night, and himself retiring after him. But this host's arrangements reverse the typical locations of the sleepers in such scenes, for he makes his bed outside. Seizing sword and javelin and wearing a thick cloak, he 'went to lie down where the white-toothed swine slept, beneath a hollow rock, under shelter from the north wind' (14. 532–*fin.*). The reversal displays his devotion, which causes him to put his job before his comfort, to his master's delight (14. 526–7). Spending the night outside is the decisive mark of his good husbandry.[75]

Spending the night outside also isolates Eumaeus from the other swineherds, who stay inside. His physical separation from them betokens the distance between the young servants who can sleep in comfort and the old one who is beset with worries because he knew Odysseus.[76] Eumaeus' worries affect the manner of his departure by keeping him alert and his muscles at attention. For he leaves after performing a combination of two type scenes – a dressing and an arming scene – that normally introduce action.[77] The narrative focuses on his wakeful energy rather than his desire for rest.

A large part of the next night is spent without sleeping. When asked to tell his story, the swineherd prefaces it by exhorting his guest to remain awake:

> Stranger, since you ask and question this of me, now listen in silence and take delight, drink your wine and sit. These nights are marvellously long. There is a time for sleep, and a time for taking delight in listening to tales. And you should not lie down to sleep before the right time. There is distress also in excessive slumber. As for the others, if their heart and spirit so bid them, let them leave and sleep [. . .] But as for us, let us drink and eat in the hut, and take delight in each other's grievous woes, as we remember them. For with time man takes delight even in sorrows, whoever has suffered much and wandered much. I will tell you what you ask and question of me.
>
> (15. 390–402)

Eumaeus' words call to mind those of Alcinous when, to oppose Odysseus' desire to sleep, he claims that the night is 'marvellously long'.[78] Eumaeus' comment, however, does not follow but introduces a narrative, and is made not by an enchanted listener who wants to hear more stories but by a speaker who advertises the delight of prolonged storytelling before narrating his own story. It is offered, moreover, to a listener who needs no such advertisement, because he has given no sign of impatience. On the contrary, he has solicited the story, as Eumaeus himself stresses by framing his exhortation to remain awake with the phrase 'you ask and question of me' at both ends. What is the purpose of this emphasis on the inappropriateness of sleep and the delight of stories, since Odysseus is willing to listen in any case?

When Alcinous urges Odysseus to forsake slumber and continue his tale, he compares him to a poet. Eumaeus, by 'imitating' Alcinous but with reference to his own story, sets himself up as a poet preparing for a performance that will match those of Odysseus, both in Alcinous' palace and in Eumaeus' own hut the night before.[79] Homer endows the swineherd's narrative with poet-like qualities from the outset by putting in his mouth words that an enchanted listener uses earlier to praise a poet-like performance. Eumaeus' request that Odysseus should sit in silence further casts the speaker in the role of the poet, and his guest in that of the audience. For poets ought to be listened to in silence (1. 325–6 and 369–70; 17. 513–4).

Eumaeus, however, isolates Odysseus from the group by addressing his exhortation only to him, and allowing the other men present to retire. If he offers to let them withdraw, it is because they already know his story.[80] But the result of this separate treatment is to create a strong connection between himself and Odysseus, who will stay up late and talk in intimacy. Eumaeus stresses this bond by using dual forms to describe their wakeful entertainment (15. 398–400) after sending the others off to sleep.

There is no such privileged bond between Odysseus and Alcinous in the parallel scene in Book 11. No one is sent to sleep, and Odysseus performs in front of a large audience, composed of Alcinous' family and the Phaeacian nobles. The difference relates to the different expectations attached to the performance by both performer and audience in that scene. As many have noted, Odysseus and the Phaeacians do not live in the same world. While he is the suffering wanderer, they are close to the gods. His performance accordingly charms them but does not stir their hearts.[81] They all appreciate the beauty of the story, but no one has any reason to feel emotionally close to the storyteller, to stay up alone with him. In Eumaeus' hut, by contrast, poetic τέρψις ('delight') hangs on a delicate equilibrium between detachment and identification.[82] Though the passage of time has removed speaker and listener from the narrated events, Eumaeus' story touches Odysseus deep inside: 'You stirred my heart with each thing you said, all that you have suffered in your heart' (15. 486–7). One heart has suffered; the other is moved by the tale. And the movement is reciprocal, for when Odysseus tells 'his' tale to Eumaeus, he responds in exactly the same way (14. 361–2 = 15. 486–7).[83] Stories on Ithaca are no longer pure entertainment, but a means for Odysseus to rebuild solidarity with the members of his household.[84] By inviting his master alone to stay awake and listen, Eumaeus creates an atmosphere of commonality that would be out of place in the Phaeacian episode.

Telemachus' second bout of sleeplessness and the three men's bonding

While Eumaeus and Odysseus tell each other stories through the night, Telemachus is nearing Ithaca. His homeward journey repeats his journey out in a number of features, among which is the rhythm of his travel and sleep patterns. The first leg of his outward journey is nocturnal and profits from the fair wind sent by Athena (2. 420). To start him off on his way back, Athena tells him that he will have to sail all night and that the gods will send a fair wind to speed up the trip (15. 34–5).[85] In the account of both voyages, the line 'the sun set and all the ways grew dark' introduces, not an arrival, which is typical,[86] but a departure (2. 388)[87] or a swift sailing onward (15. 296). The two journeys also follow corresponding sequences of sleep and waking. Telemachus forsakes sleep at both ends, while in the central stretch, from Pylus to Sparta and vice-versa, he stops in the same place to rest until dawn (3. 487–91 = 15. 185–90).

Another feature that connects the two voyages is Telemachus' sleeplessness on the eve of both. When Athena arrives in Sparta to urge him to depart, she finds him deep in thought while Pisistratus is resting: 'The son of Nestor was overcome by soft sleep, but sweet slumber did not hold Telemachus. In his heart thoughts of his father kept him awake through the ambrosial night' (15. 6–8). Pisistratus' sleep smoothes over the change of scene from Ithaca to Sparta at the transition between Books 14 and 15 by repeating the activity performed at the end of the earlier book: just as Odysseus and Eumaeus are resting on Ithaca, Nestor's son is resting in Sparta.[88] The repetition also enhances Telemachus' wakefulness by casting it as a lonely vigil, set off against the sleep not only of his friend near him, but also of his father and his servant far away. We are sent back to the end of Book 1, where Telemachus is deep in thought while everyone is slumbering. In the later episode, though, he is not goaded by Athena but by his own mind. The wakeful man is attuned to the goddess' prompting.

Telemachus cannot wait to leave. He wants to do so in the middle of the night, but Pisistratus stops him (15. 44–50). His impatience further clashes with Menelaus' retentive hospitality. Though he knows that a good host should not detain the guest who wants to depart (15. 68–70), he himself is unable to follow this protocol. Even after offering gifts and a meal, he pours one more libation and greets his guests (15. 147–53). The untypical presence of a greeting scene in conjunction with a departure (rather than an arrival) is owing to 'an amusing tension that has developed between Telemachus' impetuous eagerness to return home and Menelaus' persistent failure to incorporate this in his mind'.[89] Telemachus is wary of being delayed further by Nestor, and for this reason he begs Pisistratus to let him leave Pylus without visiting his palace (15. 199–201).

The journey quickens both in actual speed and in narrative time in its last leg, from Pylus to Ithaca. With the help of Athena, who sends a wind that 'blows strongly', the ship 'runs' through the sea, sails on and on as evening comes (15. 292–9) until ... we enter Eumaeus' hut, where he and Odysseus are having the supper that is followed by their long night of storytelling. At dawn, after servant and master have rested only little, Telemachus lands (15. 494–5). The double switch in locale and actors as day transitions to night and night to day highlights the wakefulness shared by the three men. The day-to-night transition does not bring sleep but action in a different setting (Eumaeus' hut), and the night-to-day transition heralds the return of a traveller who has sailed all night. Telemachus further accelerates his pace towards the book's end: 'His feet bore him swiftly as he walked on, until he reached the farmstead where his thousands of swine were. By them the worthy swineherd used to spend the night (ἐνίαυεν), he who had kind thoughts for his masters' (15. 555–*fin.*).

It is unclear whether Eumaeus is taking the short nap mentioned earlier (15. 494) or whether ἐνίαυεν refers to his habit of spending the night at the sty. I favour the second reading because the next book opens with Eumaeus and Odysseus preparing their breakfast at dawn, and dawn had already risen with Telemachus' arrival on Ithaca (15. 495).[90] Whatever the case, wakefulness is the keynote in the behaviour of the three men, who will soon stay up another night, this time jointly, to kill the somnolent suitors while Penelope sleeps.

Slumbering Penelope

It is Penelope's habit to retire upstairs and weep, and Athena's to put her to sleep. The pattern recurs four times. What is its purpose? Each time, Penelope's sleep rounds off an episode and expedites a scene change: from her room to the halls (1. 362–5; 21. 356–60), the portico (19. 603–20. 1) or Eumaeus' hut (16. 450–3). Her god-induced slumber, though, not only helps narrative shifts but also removes her from the theatre of the action in a more definitive way than would her withdrawal alone. That sleep is not just a means of transitioning from one locale to another emerges especially from the first and the last episodes (in Books 1 and 21), where no true transition occurs. For the narrative follows Penelope upstairs, but as soon as she dozes it returns downstairs, right where it was before she retired. Sleep draws a black curtain around her and prevents her not just from acting, but also from following the actions of others.

This pattern reverses what used to happen in Penelope's pre-*Odyssey* past, the three years in which her nights were spent in unsleeping activity. Like the ever-wakeful herdsman who could earn double wages from the extraordinary length of the day in the land of the Laestrygonians (10. 84–6), Penelope used to work double shifts, weaving her shroud in the day and unweaving it at night. Her wakefulness was a major aspect of her ability to control her plot, woven by her nightly unweaving, during the time when she pretended to be the least active.[91] In contrast, her first appearance in the *Odyssey* ends with her withdrawing to her room not to plot but to weep and finally sleep, while Telemachus makes plans for the morrow. In the *Odyssey*'s prehistory she acts unbeknownst to others during their nightly rest and is formidably capable of pushing sleep away; within the epic, others act unbeknownst to her while she slumbers and she cannot control either her sleep or her wakefulness.

This reversal does not speak in favour of an active Penelope. Her mode of presence in the epic has prompted a lively discussion in the last few decades, spurred especially by feminist readers or readers otherwise sympathetic to her. For them she is more active than she has traditionally been held to be.[92] I cannot fully engage with this question here, but only wish to argue that Penelope's sleep patterns severely limit her presence onstage, even as spectator, and suggest a strong discontinuity between her past weaving and her present weeping.[93] It is true that she weeps for the same reason she used to weave: because she keeps the memory of Odysseus alive. By preserving his memory, her weeping makes his return possible.[94] Her unremitting lamentation is her way of keeping herself for him, as Athena suggests by mentioning it at the crucial juncture in which she sits with him to plan his revenge (13. 336–8). By the time Penelope enters the stage of the *Odyssey*, however, her memory is no longer creative but only painful. And, at least in the lonely hours of the night, she wishes she could find oblivion in sleep (20. 85–6).

Advocates of an active Penelope find support in a simile that describes her as she lies in her chamber,

> Without eating, without touching food or drink. She pondered whether her blameless son would escape from death or be killed by the haughty suitors. As a lion in a throng of men ponders, seized with fear, when they draw a cunning circle around him, thus she pondered, and sweet slumber came upon her. She leaned back and slept, and all her joints were loosened. But Athena had another thought.
> (4. 788–95)

Since 'lion images are typically reserved for heroic men', the simile is taken to suggest that Penelope 'has come remarkably close to enacting the role of a besieged warrior'.[95] Penelope-lion, however, does not actively find a way out of her prison but falls asleep while thinking, and Athena sends her a revealing dream that replaces her thinking and changes her mindset with the good news that Telemachus will survive. Penelope-lion is at an impasse, the resolution of which comes to her unawares, with sweet slumber as the vehicle for an orientating dream. And her earlier sleep, which allows Telemachus to leave on the sly, deprives her of an opportunity for action normally granted to epic mothers and wives, who often attempt to detain their departing sons or husbands.[96] Indeed, Penelope scolds her maids for not rousing her when Telemachus was leaving; otherwise, he would have had either to stay or to see her dead (4. 729–34).

Penelope's sleep patterns set her passivity off against the active wakefulness of Odysseus and Telemachus. Of the four formulaic episodes in which Athena lulls her to sleep, two effect a transition from her inaction to Odysseus' activity, with him replacing her by name immediately after she dozes off. Athena pours sweet slumber over her eyes, 'but in the evening the trusty swineherd went to Odysseus and his son' (16. 452–3); Athena pours sweet slumber over her eyes, 'but noble Odysseus was lying under the portico' (20. 1). The contrast is even starker with Telemachus, who literally sets in motion the other two instances of Penelope's formulaic sleep (1. 360–4 = 21. 354–8) by sending her to her room, where Athena shuts her eyes and mind.

Penelope's 'beauty sleep'

Penelope is about to join the suitors downstairs when Athena 'had another thought' and 'poured sweet slumber over Icarius' daughter. She leaned back and slept, and all her joints were loosened, there on the couch. And meanwhile the goddess gave her immortal gifts, so that the Achaeans might admire her' (18. 187–91). After completing the beauty treatment Athena leaves. Penelope awakes when she hears the maids talking: 'Sweet slumber released her, and she rubbed her cheeks with her hands and said: "in my dire suffering a soft, deep sleep (κῶμ') enfolded me all over"' (18. 199–201).

The episode parallels those in which Athena beautifies Odysseus by reversing the ageing process (for Penelope she uses the lotion of Aphrodite) and increasing his stature (for Penelope, see 18. 195). The goddess, however, always acts on Odysseus while he is conscious, and she even speaks to him before providing the treatment (16. 167–71), whereas Penelope is enwrapped in a magically deep slumber.[97] Sleep clears Odysseus' loyal wife of any suspicion of coquetry.[98] It is also consistent with the way Athena interacts with her, always indirectly and without her noticing.

Penelope's ignorance of the goddess' presence calls to mind Odysseus' unawareness of it before he reaches Ithaca. Athena reappears by his side during the last storm but intervenes unbeknownst to him: she 'puts thoughts' into his mind (5. 427; 5. 437) as she does into Penelope's (18. 158; 21. 1), and she sends him to sleep as she does her. Odysseus, though, becomes aware of Athena's presence when they plan his revenge together. If she hides herself from him while he is still abroad, it is to avoid incensing Poseidon (6. 329). By contrast, the indirectness with which she treats Penelope is her only mode of communicating with her. Athena orients her actions to make her fit the plot, even against her wishes, for her beauty sleep is forced on her and is not even meant to help her deal with her immediate circumstances, to soothe her heart and dry her tears, but rather to remove her resistance.[99]

Though the κῶμα is forced on Penelope, it feels sweet to her nonetheless. When she awakens she seems to regret that it is over, for she calls it 'soft' and asks for a similarly 'soft death' to come quickly (18. 202–3). In the parallel scene in *Iliad* 14 it is Hypnos, the sender of κῶμα, who calls it 'soft'. Its recipient, Zeus, has no fond memory of it, for obvious reasons, and does not comment on it, whereas Penelope dwells on its gentle embrace, foregrounding the pleasure only suggested by the formulaic 'sweet slumber' with which the primary narrator describes her state.

Penelope's appreciation of her κῶμα is in line with her keenness to talk about sleep. Her interest in it is a feature she shares with her husband, one of the many facets of their like-mindedness. Odysseus, we noted, dwells on his 'boundless slumber' and on occasion records his feelings when sleep seized him and left him, or cost him dearly. Penelope comments on her sleep at greater length and even compares her sleep experiences. As we shall see, the eerie slumber that takes her unconscious through the slaughter is, in her words, the best she has had since Odysseus left for Troy.

Closural sleep and mounting wakefulness

Book 16 ends with Eumaeus, Odysseus and Telemachus sleeping at last in the swineherd's hut: 'But when they put away their desire for food and drink, they thought of rest and took the boon of sleep'. The joint slumber of the three men betokens their connivance and their sympathy for one another by building a unity among them. As noted above, simultaneous sleep is a mark of harmony and peace: the orderliness in the households of Nestor, Menelaus, Alcinous and, I will now add, Aeolus (10. 8–12) is mirrored in regular and shared sleep patterns, whereas Odysseus and his companions cease to rest in the same place and at the same time when they drift apart. In Odysseus' besieged estate domestic harmony is relegated to Eumaeus' hut, the only setting of a formal and harmonious retiring scene.

The three men's sleep signals a major transition in the plot: the conclusion of Telemachus' journey, culminating in his recognition of Odysseus, and the transference of the action to the palace, with Odysseus as the main protagonist. The *Odyssey* progressively gravitates towards one centre.[100] Until Book 13 there are three centres: the wanderings of Odysseus, the journey of Telemachus and the happenings on Ithaca. When Odysseus leaves Scheria, he leaves his wanderings behind in his sleep; soon thereafter, the Phaeacians leave the stage; Telemachus returns and he and his father get ready to move to the palace, where the action is concentrated from Book 17 on. This final narrowing of focus is preceded by the three men's slumber with its closural force, enhanced by the formulaic phrase 'they took the boon of sleep', which appears two other times at book endings.[101]

As the slaughter approaches, Odysseus' wakefulness comes to the forefront. His power to push sleep off was a winning weapon already against the Cyclops, in the feat that Odysseus himself deems his highest achievement during his wanderings, just as he deems the nocturnal attack on the slumbering Trojans his highest achievement in the war. Odysseus' ability to forsake sleep is a manifestation of the endurance that his guileful methods demand. He has the stamina characteristic of other embodiments of cunning intelligence, such as fishermen and hunters, who cannot succumb to their tiredness.[102] His unsleeping cunning in the Cyclops' cave exploits his victim's drunken slumber, which Odysseus himself contrives. It is not a god that causes the Cyclops to doze off, as Athena does Alcyoneus when Heracles kills him;[103] and not godlike magical powers, such as those with which Medea lulls the dragon that guards the Golden Fleece to sleep in Apollonius' *Argonautica*.[104] Nor does Odysseus receive divine guidance in his attack on the monster in the manner of Perseus when he beheads the Gorgon[105] or of Menelaus when he ambushes Proteus during his siesta.[106] Odysseus has no god and no godlike helper by his side, but his wakeful mind comes up with the idea to debilitate the enemy through sleep and with another to destroy him. Odysseus also accomplishes a feat of endurance unparalleled in other stories of heroes killing sleeping monsters, for he stays up two nights and one day to conceive and carry out his plan.

The slaughter is likewise an accomplishment of Odysseus' mental and physical stamina over carelessly feasting and drowsy victims. He takes the initiative to ask the maidservants to entertain Penelope, stating that he will tend the lamps for the suitors' party: 'I will offer light to all, even if they should wish to wait for dawn of the beautiful throne, and in no way will they beat me. I am much enduring' (18. 318–9). The offer sends hints of Odysseus' power by suggesting the sudden appearance of light that accompanies divine epiphanies[107] and by foregrounding his wakefulness. The double entendre in 'they will not beat me' both looks to the next night, the night of Odysseus' victory, and puts forward his ability to go without sleep. The maidservant Melantho unwittingly underscores the winning force of his wakefulness by blindly reading it as madness and wishing he would go to bed instead (18. 327–8).

While Odysseus' staying power heralds his victory, the suitors' long-drawn preparations for retiring at the end of the same evening foreshadow their doom. Their sleep carries more and more sinister overtones as their end approaches. The first time their retiring, though surrounded by a gloom that signifies their folly, is unremarkably formulaic: 'They turned to dance and lovely song and took their joy of them, waiting until evening. Black evening came upon them while they were taking their joy, and each of them went home to lie down' (1. 421–4). On the next night, however, their desire for sleep is unnatural and their retiring is described in non-formulaic language: '[Athena] poured sweet slumber over the suitors, made them wander in their drinking and cast the cups from their hands. And they rose to go to sleep throughout the city and no longer sat there, since slumber was falling on their eyelids' (2. 395–8). Athena engulfs the drinking suitors in a heavy and disorientating sleep just before urging wakeful Telemachus on his night journey.

The next and last time the suitors retire, the evening that falls on them while they are feasting is, like the first, black (18. 306). But against its blackness this time shines the light that Odysseus offers for their nightlong revelling. And this time they do not leave as soon as black night comes but linger on until the very end of the book, when at last they retire in an unusual way and at an unusually slow pace. They do not depart of their own accord but following Telemachus' request:

> Good sirs, you are mad and no longer hide in your heart
> that you have eaten and drunk. Some god is moving you.
> But now that you have well feasted, go home and lie down,
> whenever your hearts bid you. I will drive no one out.
> (18. 406–9)

In spite of the corrective 'I will drive no one out', the suitors feel the sting of Telemachus' words (they 'bite their lips', 18. 410). One of them calls for a last drink, 'that we may pour a libation, and then go home and lie down' (18. 419). The drink is served, and they 'drank the sweet wine after offering libation to the blessed gods. But when they made libation and drank to their heart's content, they went each to their home to lie down' (18. 425–*fin.*). The suitors take 28 lines to retire, during which very little happens. This unprecedented emphasis on their preparations for sleep announces that it will be their last. The beginning of the next book further collapses their sleep and their approaching death by picturing Odysseus 'as he pondered the killing of the suitors with the help of Athena' (19. 2). The narrative transitions from the suitors retiring to rest to Odysseus wakefully planning their death. Their dragged-out movement towards sleep sets their unawareness of their fate against Odysseus' heightened vigilance.

Telemachus is as wakeful as his father. After storing away the arms with his help, Odysseus tells him to go up to bed. And the young man

> Went through the hall by the light of glowing torches to lie down in his room, where he used to sleep before, when sweet slumber would come. And even then he lay down there and waited for bright Dawn.
>
> (19. 47–50)

Telemachus does not sleep. The phrases describing his behaviour suggest anxiety. The line 'where he used to sleep before, when sweet slumber would come' is applied to Zeus retiring to his bed only to be unable to stay asleep (*Il.* 1. 610). Likewise, the expression 'waiting for dawn' suggests mental tension and orientation towards the future. It is used for the Trojan horses that stand by the chariots at the end of *Iliad* 8, on the night in which the victorious Trojans cannot wait to resume the fighting; for Phoenix as he lies in Achilles' tent, unsure of his friend's plans for the morrow (*Il.* 9. 662); by Antinous narrating the suitors' nightlong sailing to ambush Telemachus (*Od.* 16. 368); and by Odysseus when he offers to hold the lights for the suitors' nightlong feast (*Od.* 18. 318) and when he recalls the two nights in the Cyclops' cave (*Od.* 9. 306, 436) as well as the many wakeful nights during the war (*Od.* 19. 342). The additional mention of sleep in two other instances (*Od.* 9. 151; 12. 7: 'they slept, waiting for dawn') is further evidence that the phrase does not include it.[108] Telemachus' waiting for dawn in his childhood bed is his second *vigilia in armis*. It harks back to his sleepless night in the same bed on the eve of his journey, but also demonstrates that he has grown up: this time, there is no caring nurse to illumine his way to his room and fold his clothes.

Telemachus, though, however wakeful he may be, has removed himself from the action, which progressively centres on his father, preparing for his long night with Penelope (see 19. 46). Odysseus is 'left behind' on stage, first by the suitors' retiring (19. 1), then by his son's (19. 44), and is isolated in his plotting vigilance. Each time he is left behind he 'ponders the killing of the suitors with the help of Athena' (19. 2 = 19. 52).

Odysseus and Penelope on sleep

As soon as Odysseus is left behind awake, Penelope comes down from her room to meet the stranger. Their conversation touches on sleep and its disturbances. The two reconnect also by dwelling on their similar sleep patterns, for neither has enjoyed restful nights since severed from the other: Odysseus has lain awake on the battlefield, Penelope on a bed of tears. He tells her that he has hated covers since he left Crete for Troy, where he spent many sleepless nights waiting for dawn on a poor bed (19. 336–42). And she, more expansively:

> Soon it will be time for pleasant rest, for him at least to whom sweet slumber should come in spite of his cares. But to me a god has given sorrow beyond measure. In the day I delight in mourning, in weeping and looking to my household tasks and those of the maids, but when night comes, and sleep takes hold of all, I lie in my bed, and thick, sharp cares stir my sorrowing heart, while I mourn.
>
> (19. 510–7)

The stranger's presence and his talk of Odysseus further interfere with Penelope's rest. Though she generalizes in describing her condition (see also 17. 102–4), she experiences more severe sleep disturbances after Odysseus comes back and she receives predictions of his return. While he is still away, her sorrowful waking is ended by Athena's magic wand. That wand works successfully again in Book 16, when Penelope still knows nothing about the stranger's presence near the palace and has heard no announcement about Odysseus' return. But soon thereafter she finds out what Telemachus knows of him (17. 106–50) and hears Theoclymenus' prophecy, Eurynome's loud wish that the suitors would die on that very day (17. 496–7) and Eumaeus' praise of the stranger's charm (17. 514–21). Finally, she herself meets him, entertains him and hears more predictions of Odysseus' return from him. When she retires at the end of that night, the application of Athena's wand (19. 603–4) fails to lull her sorrow, for she is awakened by a dream that upsets her (20. 87–90).

Penelope's sleep-depriving sorrow is fed by and merges with the pleasure of the stranger's conversation, likewise sleep chasing. Penelope mourns Odysseus consciously, and her mourning keeps her awake; she is attracted to the stranger subliminally, and her attraction keeps her awake. Mourning and attraction are in fact the same emotional force: they have the same object, both absent and present, and the same effects.[109] Penelope draws as much pleasure from mourning as from the stranger's stories, which in turn cause renewed mourning with its attendant pleasure (19. 213; 19. 251). She would like to detain him longer than she herself thinks appropriate, countering by her wish the ideal of timely sleep that pervades the *Odyssey* and in which she herself believes. Though she gives directions for the stranger's bed to be made as soon as he finishes answering her questions about Odysseus (19. 317–20), in fact she wishes for 'a little more' conversation – just a little, because 'soon it will be time for pleasant rest' (19. 509–10). After listening to the stranger again, however, she has to force herself not to detain him further. Her guest is delighting her so much that she could stay up all night to hear him talk:

> Stranger, if you should wish to sit in the hall and give me delight, slumber would not be poured over my eyelids. But it is impossible for humans to be without sleep always. The immortals have set for mortals an appointed time for each thing upon the earth, giver of grain.
>
> (19. 589–93)

The emphasis with which Penelope again pontificates on sleep's timeliness betrays the effort it takes her to abide by it and separate from her guest. Her desire to listen to him all night long and longer has drawn her dangerously close to him. To reestablish her distance, to check that desire, she switches from the personal mode ('slumber would not come to me') to an impersonal, gnomic statement ('it is impossible for humans not to sleep'), marking the switch with the adversative particle 'but'. With another 'but' she announces that she will go to rest and invites the stranger to do the same, though emphatically not near her: 'But I (ἐγώ) will go upstairs and lie in my bed', while 'you (σύ) will lie down in the house' (19. 594 and 598). She abruptly severs herself from her guest by cutting their conversation short and by specifying their separate sleeping quarters.[110]

Penelope offers Odysseus the option of lying on the floor or on a bedstead (19. 598–9). She gives him this choice because he had rejected her earlier offer of a soft bed near the fire, 'with a bedstead, covers, and shining rugs' to stay warm until dawn (19. 317–9). By refusing a bed, Odysseus aims to 'keep himself in total opposition to the suitors regarding physical circumstances as if savouring the irony: the usurpers enjoy all the comforts of the palace while the rightful king has no more than a beggar'.[111] Odysseus' refusal demonstrates his ability to wall himself within his role even when he is facing his hardest trial: a warm conversation with his wife, who offers him all-too-warm hospitality.[112]

We might contrast Odysseus' decision to decline Penelope's offer with his wholehearted acceptance of the cosy bed offered by Eumaeus on their first night together. The two nights share patterns: in both, Odysseus and a loyal member of his household exchange personal stories and develop a strong sympathy for each other.[113] However, Odysseus does not feel compelled to play the beggar through and through when treated royally by his loyal servant. He does not decline Eumaeus' offer because he does not need to keep him at a distance. On the contrary, he stresses their common destiny as wanderers and lets his warm feelings out when Eumaeus finishes his narrative. Sharing stories with him on a long night is a pleasure he can control. But on the night with Penelope he plays with fire. By refusing the bed she offers, he protects himself from the temptation of recognition, of getting too close to her to keep his secret.[114]

Odysseus' ascetic hardness, so to speak, starkly contrasts with his sleepy disposition in the land of the Phaeacians. In his own palace he chooses to lie on the floor and does not even express a desire to rest, but as the guest of Alcinous he keeps bringing up his tiredness and is happy to accept the comforts proffered to him. These opposite attitudes reflect the different situations and narrative junctures he is in. On Scheria Odysseus is weary from his wanderings, and the section of the epic concerned with them is drawing to a close. His expressed need for sleep is a need for an ending: for him, an end to his wanderings, and for the poet, to the narrative of them. Both indeed end with Odysseus' deep slumber, as he is carried back home and the narrative moves to Ithaca with him. In his palace Odysseus is recharging for his revenge and the narrative is building towards it. His choice to forsake the comforts of a bed – and, as we shall see presently, his inability to sleep altogether – betokens both his urgency to punish the suitors and the narrative's forward-looking thrust, aimed at the same goal.

Odysseus' sleeplessness on the eve of the slaughter

At the beginning of Book 20,

> Odysseus lay awake, with evil thoughts for the suitors in his heart. And through the hall went the women who before were accustomed to lie with the suitors, laughing and making merry with each other. And his heart was stirred in his chest, and he considered much in his mind and heart, whether he should rush upon them and kill each of them or whether he should let them lie with the suitors for the last time. But his heart was barking within (4–13).

Odysseus succeeds at quieting his heart but not his body, which 'tossed from side to side' (28). The agitation and anxiety that keep him awake are atypical of him. Normally his wakefulness is caused by discomforts, or by situations that demand his active presence, such as storms. We can also imagine that he would forsake sleep for material profit, as is clear from his appreciative comment on the boreal nights in the land of the Laestrygonians (10. 84–6), so short that an ever-wakeful man could have two jobs tending two herds of cattle. Odysseus wished he were such a man.[115] But at the opening of Book 20 there is no emergency or lure of profit to keep him from resting, only inner upheaval. His body participates in his disquiet, reminding us of the sleepless Achilles, tossing and turning for nights on end.[116]

In spite of his Achilles-like restlessness, however, Odysseus is not unproductively drowned in his emotions. While Achilles feeds on his feelings and is not seeking to overcome them, he is grappling with his predicament and trying to plan for his revenge.

He is the protagonist of a *vigilia in armis*, as is pointed up by his recollection of his fortitude in the Cyclops' cave: 'You endured until a cunning trick got you out' (20. 20–1). The dominant note in his sleeplessness is still one of his signature verbs, μερμηρίζειν ('to consider'), which recurs four times (20. 10, 28, 38, 41) in the description of his state. Odysseus is in the grip of intense deliberation.

But μερμηρίζειν this time yields little. Though Odysseus' first effort to make a decision ('kill the maids or not?') implicitly results in self-restraint, in the narrative it evolves into a rebuke to his seething heart: his internal monologue goes from deliberative ('he considered whether') to exhortative ('bear up, my heart!').[117] His second attempt at decision making ('how to kill the suitors? Where to find refuge?') ends when Athena chides him for his lack of confidence: another man would obey even a lesser helper, while she is a goddess and protects him unfailingly (45–8):

> 'But let slumber come over you. There is distress also in staying awake all night, and soon you will come out of your troubles'. Thus she spoke and poured sleep over his eyelids. [...] And sleep caught him, freeing his heart from cares, limb loosening.
>
> (52–7)

While in Book 13 Athena answers Odysseus' question, 'how shall I take revenge?' (386), by giving him instructions, now she only reassures him. And instead of engaging in μερμηρίζειν with him, as she does twice earlier on the same evening (19. 2 and 52), she lulls him to sleep after lecturing him on the painfulness of excessive waking.[118] Why does she turn off the light this time instead of planning the revenge with him?

Athena's main reason seems to be to provide the poet with a means of keeping the audience in suspense over how the revenge will come about.[119] In Book 13 she does not strategize the slaughter but only instructs Odysseus to keep his identity hidden and stay with Eumaeus while she travels to Sparta to urge Telemachus on his journey home. Now that she would have to give more specific instructions in reply to Odysseus' questions, she avoids spoiling the effect of surprise, leaving him and the audience in ignorance and disappearing immediately after sending her protégé to sleep (20. 55).

Athena's intervention is also geared to stress that she has taken control of the action. The goddess' presence is felt more tangibly as the slaughter approaches: in Book 19 she magically illuminates the room where Odysseus and Telemachus store the arms, deliberates with Odysseus and distracts Penelope's attention from Euryclea's recognition of him.[120] When in Book 20 Odysseus lies awake, she reminds him of her power and for the first time in fact decides for him, after his renewed attempts at μερμηρίζειν (38, 41);[121] then she switches off his mind.

This time, and this time alone, Odysseus seems to be aware of Athena's wand. Normally when characters ascribe their sleep to a god it is to Zeus or a generic god. Lacking the omniscience of the primary narrator, they cannot know which deity, if any, caused it.[122] This holds true for Odysseus when he attributes his boundless slumber to 'a god' (7. 286), while the audience knows that the deity is Athena (5. 491–3). In Book 20, though, it is otherwise, for Odysseus *hears* from Athena that he will doze off: 'let slumber come over you'. The goddess is closer to him than when she put him to sleep in Book 5: she now acts openly. But her hypnotic action distances him from her planning by removing him from the scene, just as it removes Penelope. By touching both husband and wife with her wand (see 19. 604–5), Athena diminishes the gap between them. If sleeping Penelope remains unaware of any plan made for revenge, sleeping Odysseus, who was striving to make such a plan in his insomniac pondering, becomes unaware of the goddess' strategy.

Sleep and wakefulness: a duet

The slumber Athena pours over Odysseus' eyes has a marked quality: it loosens the limbs. 'And sleep caught him, freeing his heart from cares, limb loosening'. We are sent back to Achilles' nap shortly before the burial of his friend, except for that marked quality, which takes the place of the unmarked, formulaic pleasantness in the description of Achilles' slumber: 'And sleep caught him, freeing his heart from cares, sweet' (*Il.* 23. 62–3). Odysseus' sleep has the same melting powers as love, which is also limb loosening. The choice of epithet might suggest that he is giving in to longing for Penelope, whose nearness he has just felt but from whom he has forced himself to keep at a distance. Now that he lies alone in the vestibule and is off guard in his slumber, he surrenders to his desire. Sleep reunites him with his wife upstairs.

The two draw nearer in the last hours of that night of forced separation. They experience alternatives of sleep and wakefulness, which connect them as if in a musical duet, but do not yet bring their voices together. Odysseus cannot rest while Penelope dozes; when he succumbs to slumber she stirs (20. 57), and her lamentation in turn rouses him (20. 92). The two suffer similar disruptions in their sleep, but not simultaneously. The 'ping-pong' has a cumulative effect: it builds up tension and suspense by transferring anxiety from one spouse to the other and back. When Odysseus dozes off and Penelope rises from sleep at the same time, the immediate shift of anxiety is conveyed by the coexistence in the same line of his abandoned slumber and her sudden awakening: '... limb loosening [sleep], but his true-hearted wife awoke' (20. 57). One has just relaxed into a sleep filled with sweet longing when the other begins to cry (20. 58).[123]

The ways in which sleep and sleeplessness are transferred from one spouse to the other mark their growing proximity, because the second time the awakening of one spouse affects the other: whereas Penelope ceases to sleep *when* Odysseus dozes off, with no explicit causal connection, Odysseus stirs *because* Penelope has awoken and he hears her voice. He also thinks that she has recognized him, and sees her standing by his head in a dreamlike vision (20. 93–4), as if he were connecting with the dream she has just had of him lying by her side (20. 88–90). This is the closest they have ever come in 20 years, and the closest Odysseus ever comes to dreaming.

Sleeping and dreaming in Odysseus' family

Penelope receives guidance in her slumber. Athena sends a vision from which she learns that Telemachus will survive. The knowledge she acquires in her sleep reverses a pattern in the *Odyssey*, according to which the sleeper is unaware and the wakeful in the know. While Penelope is slumbering, the suitors take their meal and prepare to leave at nightfall (4. 786); they are sailing to their post of attack (4. 842–7) when she awakes comforted (4. 839–40). We have an echoing in reverse of the sequence at the end of Book 2, where Athena pours heavy sleep on the drunken suitors (395–8) but urges Telemachus to sail, and he sails all night (434). In Book 4 she enlightens Penelope in her sleep, whereas the suitors stay up to prepare for an ambush that will not succeed.

Odysseus does not receive any such guidance. Though Athena puts him to sleep, she does not send him visions. On his insomniac night she plays the role of a reassuring dream but appears to him in person while he is fully conscious and reveals her identity.[124] Athena makes it clear that she is replacing a dream by mimicking one. She takes the posture of Homeric dreams by standing above Odysseus' head (20. 22), but spells out that she is no dream by asking him, 'Why are you awake?' (20. 23) and eventually putting him to sleep, whereas dream visions, including the one she sends to Penelope, ask, 'why are you asleep?' (4. 804) and rouse the sleeper.

Athena does not send dreams to Telemachus either. Her decision to speak to him while he lies sleepless at the beginning of Book 15 matches her succoring appearance to his sleepless father at the beginning of Book 20.[125] Though she does not reveal herself quite so openly to Telemachus, and though it is not even clear whether he recognizes her,[126] she helps them both in an up-front manner, while they are awake. Why then does Athena make herself manifest to Odysseus and Telemachus in their waking hours but send a dream to Penelope and never appear to her?

One reason could be that Odysseus and his son are actively in on the goddess' plot, at least to some extent, while Penelope is not. Athena makes plans with Odysseus and instructs Telemachus openly, whereas she inspires Penelope or, when she sends the dream, simply reassures her without asking her to do anything. Athena also brings her closer to the plot that is being played around her and without her knowledge, for the vision enlightens her about a fact, Telemachus' safe return, that is vital not only for her well-being but also for the plot's success.

Athena's choice to send dreams only to Penelope also fits a more general pattern: at no point in the narrative is Odysseus or

Telemachus ever said to dream, be it with or without explicit divine interference. While he sits among the suitors, Telemachus 'sees his noble father in his mind' (1. 115): a reverie perhaps, but not a dream. Though the disguised Odysseus tells a tale in which 'Odysseus' had a 'god-sent dream' (14. 495), he is lying. Conversely, Penelope has two more dream visions, which follow in close succession on the eve of the slaughter and have Odysseus at their centre. In the first he is the interpreter. She sees her pet geese killed by an eagle and is told while she sleeps, by the eagle turned Odysseus – and later, by the stranger in whom she is confiding – that the vision portends Odysseus' revenge (19. 535–58). In the second he is the protagonist: 'This night he lay by me, similar to the man he was when he went on the expedition. And my heart rejoiced, because I thought it was not a dream but a true vision' (20. 88–90). The emotional strain of the last hours bursts into a dream in Penelope's night, but not in Odysseus', whose sleep before the slaughter is as dreamless as usual.

The closest Odysseus comes to Penelope's visions of him is not in a dream but in a fantasy: 'Noble Odysseus heard her voice as she wept, and he considered (μερμήριζε), and it seemed to him in his heart that she knew him and stood by his head' (20. 92–4). Critics debate the exact nature of the vision. An attractive interpretation locates it in the intermediate state between sleeping and waking,[127] of which later poets and thinkers demonstrate awareness.[128] Another reading, however, 'emphatically asserts that it [Odysseus' vision] is a *waking* impression, noting how rich the *Odyssey* is in words expressing strong imagination'.[129] Whatever the case, Odysseus' vision follows, or is simultaneous with, an act of thought and one described by the verb which, more than any other, captures the fervid movement of his mind: μερμηρίζειν.[130] His thinking engages with everything he sees, even a dreamlike fabrication.

Why is it then that Penelope dreams while her husband does not? Is the difference related to their different ways of looking at reality? As is well known, several critics have attributed to Penelope an intuitive cast of mind, contrasting her with the purely rational Odysseus: he sees what is around him and thinks about it, whereas she always walks with a veil before her face, suggesting an 'involuted, indirect perception'.[131] If we embrace this view, it is tempting to read Penelope's susceptibility to dreams as one aspect of her intuitive mind, which can see subconsciously, whereas Odysseus' cannot. While Penelope's sleep has content and orients her thoughts and feelings, sleep for Odysseus is a break from thought and feeling. While he sees reality in the bright light of day, she touches upon it in the twilight of a dream-filled sleep.

The theory of an intuitive Penelope, however, has been challenged on a number of grounds.[132] Here I will consider only issues connected to her dreams. Scholars have read them either as wish fulfilling,[133] or as coming from an outside force, a deity.[134] In favour of the first interpretation are Penelope's own comments: in one case she avows that she would be happy if her dream should indeed portend Odysseus' return and revenge (19. 569), and in another she dwells on the pleasure of the vision while it lasted and seemed real to her (20. 89–90). It is true that the recollection of it upsets her, for she says, 'But upon me a god sends bad [. . .] dreams' (20. 87). This comment, however, does not qualify the joy she had while dreaming. On the contrary, the vision appears bad to her because it contrasts with her waking reality (or so she thinks),[135] because the intense memory kindled by it crushes her,[136] making her long for oblivion in sleep. There can be no doubt that Penelope this time wishes that her dream would come true.

Yet, the dreams might simply be in accordance with Penelope's desire, not fashioned by it. Athena might be the efficient cause of both visions, as she is of the one in Book 4 and of Nausicaa's in Book 6, which also match the dreamer's desires.[137] On this reading, Penelope is not the origin of the dream but its instrument, through which Athena works out her plan. To speak for this interpretation are again Penelope's own words, when she comments on the second vision: 'But upon me a god sends bad dreams'. She does not perceive her erotic dream as her own but as god sent.[138]

According to either interpretation, the dreams are not Penelope's way of predicting the future with subliminal intuition, of sensing the truth. If wish fulfilling, they reveal her state of mind; if god sent, they reveal Athena's action. Indeed, Penelope's stark disbelief in the truth of her first vision (19. 568–9) and her despair about the second one speak strongly against the theory that she is intuitively divining Odysseus' presence in her dreams. Far from anticipating or even hoping for Odysseus' nearness, she wishes for death.

Instead of invoking the theory of an intuitive Penelope to explain her tendency to dream, we might look at what she does in the epic. She lives a confined and static life, a life in which sleeping or trying to sleep is one of her main activities. She spends much of her time in her upstairs quarters, where she is described as she weeps and cannot find rest, as she is lulled to sleep by Athena and as she dreams. Penelope dreams perhaps because sleeping in whatever way – well, badly, not at all – is one of her few modes of presence in the epic. Even her thoughts are hardly known. By dwelling on her dreams, the narrative allows us a glimpse of her inner life.

Things are different for Odysseus, who sleeps but does many more things as well. When he sleeps it is to rest from those things, which take up his time and energy and are the main focus of the narrative. He does not dream because the narrative does not give him the time to do so, not because we are supposed to imagine that he has no experience of dreams or does not care about them. In fact, the one he makes up in a fabricated tale (14. 495) may reflect his actual experience, as do many other features of those tales. The narrative does not spend time on Odysseus' dreams but on his thoughts, directly connected to the plot in which he plays an active role.

By putting a premium on Odysseus' thinking as opposed to his dreaming, Homer casts him as a hero who can fight his tough battles without total reliance on divine help. We might contrast his blank sleep with Aeneas', filled with visions. Virgil's hero dreams at crucial junctures: on the night of Troy's fall, Hector appears to him to urge him to leave with the city's *penates* (*Aen.* 2. 270–301); in Crete the *penates* themselves direct him to Hesperia (3. 147–71) and in Italy the god Tiberinus guides him to his final home (8. 36–65). Whereas Aeneas' journey receives major impulses from dreams, which push him along his destined path, Odysseus is given no guidance on his homeward-bound journey until its last stretch, and when Athena sits by his side to plan his revenge, she treats him more like her mortal peer than like her subject. They 'think together' (13. 373). The dreamlessness (in the narrative) of Odysseus' sleep points up his creative imagination and spirit of initiative.

Long day's journey into night

The title of Eugene O'Neil's drama seems appropriate to capture the length of the hours in Odysseus' palace as the slaughter approaches.[139] The eve of the massacre is slow to end, and it keeps ending. It starts in the first line of Book 17, which closes with the coming of the afternoon and the anticipation of the next day: 'And wise Telemachus answered [Eumaeus]: [...] go take your afternoon meal, but at dawn come and bring good sacrificial victims [...] And they [the suitors] were taking delight in dance and song, for already the afternoon had come' (17. 599–600 and 605–6). This afternoon lasts until 18. 305–6, when 'black evening' sets in. The extended narrative time that separates the beginning of the afternoon from the coming of darkness has the effect of lengthening the declining day. And activity continues through the long evening until the very last line of Book 18. Towards its close the suitors accept Telemachus' exhortation to call it a night and leave, yet they take a long time to retire, further extending the evening hours with their slow movement. Even when they are gone, the scene is further prolonged, as Telemachus and Odysseus store away the arms and then Penelope and Odysseus converse at great length, until both retire at the end of Book 19. The long day comes to an end a second time with this second preparation for sleep, but again it is not over, because Odysseus cannot sleep. The subsequent shifts in narrative focus, from Odysseus slumbering to Penelope awakening to Odysseus stirring again, draw out the transition from sleep to wakefulness and from night to day. When Odysseus hears Penelope's voice, dawn rises (20. 91): 1,128 lines after it was first alluded to (17. 600). The day has taken up 1,728 lines.

The next day, the suitors' last, is almost as long. Evening must be approaching around the middle of Book 21, when the suitors (265) and mockingly Odysseus (280) suggest reconvening the next morning, and Penelope goes to sleep a little later (357–8). Nevertheless, evening is not mentioned at all and night only after the recognition in Book 23 (243). But activity (in the form of storytelling) continues through the night, an immobile night, the course of which is suspended by Athena until Odysseus has had his fill of sleep (23. 347). The day has taken up 1,585 lines.

An almost obsessive emphasis on the rising of characters marks this day's beginning. At dawn Odysseus asks for an omen from 'one of those who are awaking' (20. 100), and the person who delivers it is not even getting up but has not slept at all, while her co-workers are resting:

> And a woman who worked at the mill uttered an omen from a house nearby, where the mills of the shepherd of the people were. Twelve women applied their strength to them, preparing barley and wheat meals, the marrow of men. The other ones were sleeping, since they had ground their wheat, but she alone had not yet stopped, for she was the weakest. And standing by the mill she spoke.
>
> (20. 105–11)

The omen gains resonance from the background of sleepers and the nightlong wakefulness of the figure who utters it. Shortly thereafter Telemachus is reported to get out of bed (20. 124) and, according to a manuscript variant, even the maidservants who kindle the fire are said to be awake.[140] It is tempting to read in this concentrated stress on wakefulness a message to the audience, especially if the *Odyssey* was originally performed in two consecutive nights. The poet would be urging his listeners to push sleep off as the performance reaches the wee hours of the second night and the story its climax.

When the sun goes down (possibly shortly before 21. 258), the day of the slaughter is lengthened further by the absence of formulaic sleep at the end of formulaic eating and drinking. After Eurymachus fails to string the bow, Antinous suggests that they should leave for the night, following a familiar pattern: let's put down the bow, make a libation and go home, and the next day 'at dawn' we will sacrifice to Apollo and resume the contest (21. 259–68). The heralds bring around water for their hands, young servants the cups for the wine. They make the libation and drink, acts that typically mark the end of a day and effect a transition to the evening rest. The suitors expect to go home and sleep as they have done every night for three years. But of course they will not. For the audience, who is in on the plot, Antinous' exhortation to the other suitors to follow the cycle of the sun is laden with dramatic irony.[141]

The irony deepens after the last libation, when Odysseus intervenes with a speech that both agrees with the suitors' wishes to suspend the match and makes it impossible for them to retire: 'Now stop the contest and leave this with the gods, and at dawn a god will give strength to whomever he wishes. But come, give me the polished bow, so that I can try my hands and my strength among you' (21. 279–82). Odysseus purportedly suggests resting for the night with words that chillingly wink at Antinous' on account of their sinister emphasis on next day's dawn; but his request to handle the bow causes a stirring and the resumption of action, preventing the suitors from going to sleep as they were planning and as was the normal pattern.[142]

This disruption in the normal pattern is subtly underscored by an untypical use of the formulaic line, 'after making libations and drinking to their heart's content' at 21. 273, where it applies to the suitors. The line appears five other times to introduce a movement towards retiring.[143] The suitors themselves have lived by this sequence as recently as the previous night, when, 'after making libations and drinking to their heart's content, they went each to their homes to lie down' (18. 427–8). But on their last night the formulaic line is followed by Odysseus' non-formulaic intrusion: 'And much cunning Odysseus spoke to them with crafty thoughts' (21. 274). His sudden interference counters the expectations created by the standard phrase and intimates, even before Odysseus asks for the bow, that the suitors will not sleep.

Odysseus' last words before the slaughter further bring out the exceptionality of that day by suggesting a normal closing activity, a feast: 'Now it is time that a meal too be prepared for the Achaeans, while there is light, and afterwards that they amuse themselves in other ways, with song and the lyre, for those are the accompaniments of a feast' (21. 428–30). This exhortation echoes the narrative of the suitors' feast on the first day we meet them, when they behave just as Odysseus recommends here: they eat their fill, then turn 'to song and dance, for those are the accompaniments of a feast' (1. 152),[144] and they retire to sleep thereafter (1. 421–4). Odysseus' suggestion recalls the pattern of that day by reminding the suitors that the present day is waning, that they 'should' sport while there is light.[145] He also gives voice to the sentiment of timeliness, which he and others invoke elsewhere to regulate the course of a peaceful day, ending with dinner, drink and sleep. This day's dinner is as timely as every day's, but it is in the hands of armed chefs, whose preparations for it turn the fading light of day into the threatening shimmer of weapons, with which Book 21 ends: 'And he [Telemachus] stood by the chair near his father, armed in shining bronze'.

By inscribing the suitors' impending doom into the cyclic rhythm of a day's activities, Odysseus intimates that their punishment naturally and appropriately fits into the course of a well-regulated day, with its timely awaking, eating and sleeping. The punishment of Melanthius is likewise set off against his day's routine and turned into an unexceptional happening. Tied to a pillar for the night, he is reminded of his daily job: 'Now indeed you will keep watch the whole night through, lying on a soft bed, as befits you. And you will not miss the Early-Born rising from the streams of Oceanus on her golden throne, at the time when you bring goats to the suitors to prepare a meal in the house' (22. 195–9). The mention of Melanthius' normal day casts Odysseus' revenge as its appointed substitution.

Penelope's sweetest sleep ever

For a long part of the long day of Odysseus' victory, Penelope has been slumbering in her room (21. 358–23. 5). 'A god' caused her sleep, Euryclea tells Odysseus, as she sets out to awaken his wife (22. 429). And we know from the omniscient narrator that the god was, as always, Athena.

To Penelope, this god-sent slumber is the best that she has been given in twenty years. She rebukes Euryclea for rousing her with the unbelievable news that Odysseus has returned and killed the suitors: 'Why do you tell me this foolish tale and awaken me from sleep, the sweet slumber that has bound me and covered my eyelids? For I have never had such a sleep since Odysseus left' (23. 16–9). Penelope's distress upon awakening is not new,[146] but here it rings ironical to the audience, who knows that her reality this time is even better than the blissful slumber she does not want to relinquish.[147]

This episode of sleep, while consistent with the pattern of removing Penelope from the action at crucial moments, also has a specific narrative function: it postpones the coming recognition and gives it prominence by keeping her offstage during the slaughter.[148] The scene of her awakening creates a smooth shift from the slaughter to the staging of the recognition. For Euryclea tells Penelope, who asks her how Odysseus, being one, could kill the suitors: 'I did not see, I did not ask. I only heard the groaning of men being killed. We sat inside the well-built chambers [...] Then I found Odysseus standing among the bodies of the slain' (23. 40–6). By stating her ignorance of the story we have just heard, Euryclea puts it aside, while by urging Penelope to meet her husband (23. 52–3), she looks ahead to the recognition.

Penelope's slumber, however, is not just a narrative device to get her out of the picture.[149] It has a rich thematic relevance, deeper than the other episodes of sleep, which merely bespeak her passivity and unawareness of the actions around her. This time her sleep is emphatically without dreams. It has 'bound' – the only time in Homer – Penelope, stopping all mental activity, all sense perception. The sleep's dreamlessness is highlighted by the substitution of the real Euryclea for a vision: 'She stood above her head and said: 'awaken, Penelope!'' (23. 4–5). The real thing assumes the position of dreams and, like them, rouses the sleeper. A blank slumber is not an unmarked blackout for Penelope but it is a treat because, in her own account, her nights are normally filled with upsetting dreams. Dreamlessness is part and parcel of this sleep's exceptional delight.

(Dreamlessness is associated with pleasant sleep in other cases, too. The blackness of Penelope's sweetest slumber illustrates a belief shared by Greek authors as well as by Shakespeare's Hamlet: the best sleep carries no visions. Witness for instance Atossa's complaint of having lived 'in the constant company of dreams' since her son's departure to Greece [Aesch. *Pers.* 176–7]; or Socrates in Plato's *Apology*, who argues that if death should be 'like a sleep in which the sleeper does not even dream, it would be a wonderful gain. For anyone, if asked, would say that the night in which he slept a dreamless slumber was one of the most pleasant times of his life'.[150])

Penelope's sleep is dreamless for another reason: it brings her back to Odysseus. It is the equivalent to the deathlike slumber that twice advances his homecoming. Her description of her sleep resonates with Homer's description of Odysseus', both upon arriving on Scheria and on his way to Ithaca. Just as his transporting slumber is not just 'sweet' but 'the sweetest', she underscores the exceptional sweetness of hers by decomposing the formulaic phrase 'sweet sleep'. She markedly separates noun and adjective[151] and has the latter begin a line and occupy the entire first foot, the dactylic rhythm of which further stretches the duration of that sweetness: ἐξ ὕπνου μ' ἀνεγείρεις/ ἡδέος (literally: 'from sleep you awake me/ sweet [sleep]'). Her blissful slumber shares another quality with Odysseus', this time with his sleep on Scheria: it 'covers her eyelids' and with the same phrase (5. 493; 23. 17). The phrase appears only in these two instances for actual sleep, singling out husband and wife and bringing them together by the workings of sleep on them. Penelope has at last obtained the healing slumber she had been praying for night after night, a sleep 'that makes one forget everything [...] when it covers the eyelids' (20. 85–6).

The sweetest slumber brings Penelope home, just as it does Odysseus. As critics have noted, when she recognizes him she also reaches the end of a *nostos*, though not physically but emotionally.[152] Penelope's homecoming is figured in the justly celebrated simile that compares her, as she holds Odysseus after the recognition, to a shipwrecked swimmer finally seeing and reaching the shore. As one scholar puts it, 'The full simile is a capsule description of Odysseus' landing on Scheria, but now the brine-laden, ship-wrecked mariner touching soil is Penelope. Both sailors are at last home from the sea'.[153] In the reading of another critic, while even in her last dream Penelope was attached to the prewar past, she now 'takes on the mature Odysseus' experiences as her own'.[154] Like Odysseus, Penelope has returned, and she has done so, like Odysseus, during a deep, dark sleep. For both, the sweetest slumber marks the end of the 'storm'. And when they awaken, both refuse to believe that they have returned: Odysseus that he is on Ithaca, Penelope that the stranger is Odysseus and that he has killed the suitors.[155] The sleeping Odysseus has not followed the navigation, has not seen where the ship was going. The sleeping Penelope has heard and seen nothing, not even a dream. In both cases the abrupt awakening into a new reality makes that reality appear unreal.[156] A perfectly black slumber adds to the disorientation and destabilization that precede both returns.

The longest night and the first ending of the *Odyssey*

After the climactic recognition there comes the final retiring scene of the epic, towards which the others have been building:[157]

> Meanwhile Eurynome and the nurse made ready the bed with a soft cover, by the light of blazing torches. And they spread the sturdy bedstead, keeping busy; then the old woman went back home to lie down, while Eurynome, the chambermaid, led them [Odysseus and Penelope] as they went to their bed, holding a torch in her hands. She led them to their bedchamber and then went back. And they came gladly to their old rite of the bed.
>
> (23. 289–97)

The couple's first night together after twenty years demands careful preparations. The narrative not only details the making of the bed, but also involves two women in it and accounts for their movements in and out of the bedchamber, the centre of the house towards which the whole *Odyssey* has gravitated and which Odysseus and Penelope now enter as newlyweds, by the light of a ceremonial torch. The focus on the long-travelled-to bedchamber has produced a peculiar retiring scene, one in which the elaborate arrangements for the night are made not for guests, as is the rule in Homer, but for the master and the mistress of the house. The surrounding characters are reported to go to sleep after them and to do so unceremoniously: 'But Telemachus, the herdsman and the swineherd ceased from the dance, stopped the women, and they themselves went to bed in the shadowy hall' (23. 297–9). The security and stability finally achieved are reflected in another anomaly in the sleeping arrangements: Odysseus' servants, who technically do not reside in the palace, sleep there. Their help in the slaughter has brought them inside as full-fledged members of Odysseus' household, or rather family.[158]

The preparations for the retiring scene begin even earlier, when Penelope's lasting embrace of her husband inspires Athena to hold back the sunrise and retain the night, presumably to allow the couple long hours together with no disturbance:[159]

> And rosy-fingered Dawn would have appeared upon them weeping had not Athena, the grey-eyed goddess, had another thought. She held the long night at the end of the heavens and checked Dawn of the golden throne at the streams of Oceanus.
>
> (23. 242–4)

Athena produces the first instance in western literature of the motif that I will call, after a French tune from 1966, '*Retiens la nuit*': the unnaturally long night of love, either enjoyed, as in the *Odyssey* and in Plautus' *Amphitryon* or, far more frequently, prayed for (as in the French song, in Ovid's *Amores*, or in a number of epigrams from the *Palatine Anthology*).[160] In most instances night is only for lovemaking and talk. There is no leisure to sleep, and the lovers curse dawn for forcing them to part.[161] Odysseus and Penelope, in contrast, can take their fill of love, storytelling and finally sleep: 'She took delight in listening to him, and sleep did not fall on her eyelids until he told all the tale' (23. 308–9); 'Thus he ended his tale, when sweet slumber, limb loosening, leapt on him, freeing his heart from cares' (23. 342–3). This emphasis on rest at the end of the longest night points up the legitimacy of the couple's union. Odysseus and Penelope are not lovers who meet on the sly but husband and wife celebrating a second wedding, officially extended by Athena, and enjoying the recovery of marital tranquility.

The couple's togetherness is brought into bold relief by the perfect synchrony of their sleep,[162] in stark contrast to the alternating bouts of sleep and wakefulness at the beginning of Book 20, the night before, a night of growing proximity, but one still marked by separation. On that night Odysseus' slumber is also limb loosening, and it frees his heart from cares (20. 56–7). But it comes only because Athena helps him, and just when he is plunging into it, Penelope awakens and her lament in turn rouses him. Here, by contrast, sleep comes to him naturally and lasts as long as needed for him to enjoy it to his heart's content. Athena makes dawn rise only 'when she thought in her heart that Odysseus had taken his fill of being in bed with his wife and of slumber' (23. 345–6).

Sleep, though, also fixes Odysseus and Penelope in different roles: he as a narrator, she as a listener, and a listener so enchanted that she remains awake until he 'told all the tale'. Penelope fulfils the desire she had expressed the previous night to listen to 'the stranger' indefinitely. On that night she had to check her eagerness and did so by invoking the human need for rest; now she can drink in Odysseus' story to the full. Sleep comes to her only in the negative (not until...) whereas it engulfs him in its limb-loosening embrace.

The emphasis on Odysseus' sleep rather than on Penelope's is meaningful in at least two ways. First, it is nicely attuned to their different roles during the slaughter, for he has fought while she has been unconscious through it. He is exhausted, as is plain from his earlier request: 'Let us go to bed, wife, so that now we may take our joy of rest, lulled by sweet sleep' (23. 254–5). Odysseus' tiredness is conveyed by the sudden manner in which limb-loosening slumber 'leaps' (343) on him, as it does on Achilles after the nightlong funeral of Patroclus (*Il.* 23. 232). Second, and more important, the unequal treatment of the couple's sleep suggests that the story we have just listened to, from Homer and from Odysseus himself, is his more than Penelope's: the protagonist and narrator deservedly plunges into a melting slumber when his story ends.

The two references to sleep that frame the recapitulation of Odysseus' adventures thus give the epic the luster of a narrative that can keep the audience awake for many hours through its delightfulness, and at the end of which the virtuoso performer – as character and as narrator – can rest. Odysseus' dozing off as narrator beautifully merges with his sliding into sleep as acting character: sweet slumber leaps on the raconteur as he is telling how the Phaeacians 'sent him with a ship to his dear native land, giving him bronze, gold and clothes in plenty' (23. 340–1) – right before sleep overcomes him.

Odysseus' relaxing slumber draws the curtain on the stage. Coming as it does after lovemaking and the recapitulation of his adventures, it is strongly closural. It has the quality of a final surrender, the surrender of love or even of death, which also loosens the limbs. The melting effects of sleep on Odysseus replicate the likewise melting and deathlike effects of the recognition on Penelope: 'her knees were loosened' (23. 205).[163] Soft slumber for the hero who has wandered much and told many stories including this last one is the equivalent of the recognition for the heroine who has patiently waited for him: the end of the efforts and of the tensions, the happy ending.

Further enhancing the finality of Odysseus' sleep is the contrast it builds with Telemachus' inability to find rest at the opening of the epic. Athena presides over Odysseus' slumber as over Telemachus' wakefulness; the setting of the two scenes is the same, a bedroom, and the retiring of the protagonists follows a similar script: both Telemachus and his parents have escorts who take them to their rooms by torchlight, and Euryclea assists in both scenes.[164] To plot-launching sleeplessness responds closure-bringing sleep.

Sleep's closural force, however, is qualified by the narrative of future events that precedes even the couple's retiring. As soon as Athena lengthens the night, Odysseus tells Penelope:

> We have not yet come to the end of our trials, but hereafter there will be measureless toil, much and hard [...] But come; let us go to bed, so that now we may take our joy of rest, lulled by sweet sleep.
>
> (23. 248–50 and 254–5)

Odysseus' words upset the a-temporal and immobile equilibrium created by Athena's gesture.[165] Breaking into a night held 'at the end of the heavens', they deny the end to both his suffering and his story and reintroduce indefinitely endless time. Odysseus, though, gives almost no detail and urges sleep instead. For the much-suffering hero, the call of the bed and of slumber is a call to oblivion, of past and future toils, and for the poet telling his story, it is a call for an ending. But Penelope cannot agree to this call, after the future has broken into the immobile night:

> The bed will be ready for you whenever you wish in your heart, since the gods have indeed caused you to come back to your well-built house and native land. But since you have thought of this and a god has put it into your heart, tell me of that trial.
>
> (23. 257–61)

Odysseus starts off by announcing his future destiny, but then steps back and calls for sleep; Penelope begins by engaging with his wish, but then she does not honour it and asks him to tell his tale. Her request postpones the climactic retiring scene by pushing sleep off and replacing it with a story of new trials, when the story being told and the trials hitherto endured are reaching their end.

But even the story told and the trials endured in the *Odyssey* are not quite over with the couple's sleep, because news of the slaughter is going to reach the suitors' relatives. Athena's next intervention is consistent with the openness of the *Odyssey*'s first ending. While her gesture of holding the night works towards closure by creating expectations of the couple's sleep and their renewal of their 'old rite' (expectations, as we have seen, instantly challenged by the couple's concern over post-*Odyssey* events, which delays their retiring), her gesture of making dawn rise reopens the narrative within the timeline of the *Odyssey*, reestablishing the natural cycle of night and day and giving impulse to renewed activity along with the return of the sun. The sun she causes to rise causes Odysseus to rise in the same line (23. 348). He tells Penelope that he is going to the fields to see his father and leaves, armed, to rouse Telemachus and the servants who have slept in the palace (23. 366–8). This chain of wake-up calls gives a strong forward movement to the new day and the activities it brings.

The sunlight will also carry news of the slaughter, which the nocturnal dance had muffled. Odysseus worries: 'quickly the rumour will go out with the rising of the sun' (23. 362–3). We follow this broadcasting light as it grows brighter: from Athena's awakening of it, to Odysseus' anticipation of its spreading, to its actual shining. When Odysseus leaves with the three men, all armed, 'there was light over the earth' (23. 371), a light from which Athena protects them by means of a sudden artificial night (23. 372). Though her gesture harks back to the scene in which she poured mist about Odysseus to prevent the Phaeacians from seeing him (7. 14–5), the cover of night also calls to mind the darkness in which the gods envelop their favourite heroes on the battlefields of the *Iliad*. The book ends with the threatening image of armed men shrouded in night, as they set out for the fight that Athena will abruptly stop at the end of the epic's last book.

CHAPTER 3

DRAMA

PART ONE: CRIME AND WAKEFULNESS IN AESCHYLUS' *ORESTEIA*

Agamemnon

In a painting by Pierre-Narcisse Guérin (Figure 3.1), Agamemnon is slumbering in his room, draped in finery, his left arm relaxingly bent near his head, while Clytemnestra and Aegisthus are shown behind the open door as they hesitantly prepare to kill him. This is not Aeschylus' version of the story, but the painting does not misrepresent the spirit of his trilogy, insofar as the murderers in it awake to kill, and in killing they murder sleep. In the *Oresteia*, as in *Macbeth*, wakefulness and sleep disturbances are centre stage, as is suggested already by the untypical beginning of the first play: a scene of sleeplessness.

We might think of sleeplessness as eminently appropriate for the tragic stage because of the mental strain it conveys and the choreographic possibilities it offers. Greek playwrights did not pass over its strong dramatic impact. Quite the contrary, Eteocles opens *Seven against Thebes* by pointing up his ever-wakeful statesmanship, and Oedipus reassures his subjects, telling them, 'You are not rousing one caught by sleep', but 'I have tried many paths in the wandering of my mind' (Soph. *OT* 65–7). Troubled nights are evoked again near the beginning of *Trachiniae*, where they afflict Deianira. Mentions of sleeplessness fittingly give impetus to plots that grow out of dire predicaments and involve intense emotions.

Figure 3.1 Pierre-Narcisse Guérin, *Clytemnestra hesitating before killing Agamemnon* (1817), Paris, Louvre.

Yet, abnormal wakefulness is shown on the tragic stage only twice, in *Agamemnon* and *Iphigenia in Aulis*. The concentration of the dramatic action, the daytime setting of the tragic performance and the rudimentary decor of the stage are the main reasons that it appears so seldom. Plots normally unfold in the course of one day, from sunrise to sunset.[1] This timeframe makes it difficult to render sleeplessness on stage, because one cannot be sleepless in the daytime. Accordingly, wakeful nights belong to the prequel of the drama, as in *Seven against Thebes*, *Trachiniae* or *Oedipus the King*, or are projected forward, to an indefinite post-dramatic time, as in *Prometheus Bound*, whose protagonist is condemned to 'guard this rock, standing, without sleeping or bending [his] knees' (31–2). The two scenes of sleeplessness that do occur come at the opening of plays that begin, exceptionally, on the nights prior to the unfolding of their plots. We might ask why only two tragedies exploit this possibility. Is it because a night-time setting in an open-air theatre and in the daytime would have demanded too much of the imagination, even for spectators who saw what words told them to see?[2]

The scene in *Agamemnon* is woven into the play's thematic fabric, for sleeplessness is in fact the driving impulse in the trilogy we are just beginning to watch or read. As one critic has shown, the murders of Agamemnon and Clytemnestra are carried out by a force of revenge that is markedly unsleeping.[3] Wakefulness is both metaphorical (the wrath of the dead cannot sleep) and literal (its embodiments cannot, either), but the two levels are inextricably intertwined, for the murderers cannot sleep because they host the wakeful impulse of revenge: because the murdered, or the murders, 'won't lie'.[4] In *Agamemnon* unsleeping revenge rouses three sets of characters: the executioners, through whom it operates; their unwitting helpers, who lose sleep to zeal and fear; and their subjects, sleepless from obscure terror, from vague and anguished presentiments.

When the play begins, one of Clytemnestra's slaves is lying awake[5] at his post, hoping to see the beacon that will announce Agamemnon's victory. In the first line the sentinel prays for 'the end of toils' (ἀπαλλαγὴν πόνων), of his nightlong watches. But a few lines later his work-related lack of sleep takes on sinister overtones:

> Whenever I am on this restless (νυκτίπλαγκτον)[6] couch of mine, drenched with dew, not visited by dreams – for fear stands by me instead of sleep and prevents me from joining my eyes fast in slumber – whenever I decide to sing or hum as a remedy, preparing an antidote of song for my somnolence, I cry, lamenting the calamity of this house, no longer governed in the best way, as in the past. But now may there come a happy ending to my toils (ἀπαλλαγὴν πόνων)!
>
> (12–20)

Fear visits the watchman. It replaces slumber and its attendant dreams, standing by him as dream visions stand by sleepers in Homer. Is it simply the fear of being punished for neglect of duty, if he should doze off? Or a more vague, unsettling fear, caused by the governance of the house? The first interpretation is in the foreground, because the watchman is chronically sleepy and trying to shake off his drowsiness.[7] But his remark on the palace's administration pushes the audience to associate his fear with an object that he cannot, or will not, state clearly (36–9). The verses charge his sleep deprivation with unspoken anguish by leaving the content of his fear unstated. After he mentions his lamentation and its causes, the end of toils which he again prays for is the deliverance of the palace from its current rulers, as well as his own deliverance from his weary task. What would allow him to rest is not just the successful end of the war and Agamemnon's return, but his return to power, which would redress the misfortune that has fallen on the house and caused the watchman's nocturnal weeping.

At the appearance of the beacon he rejoices and cries out: 'Oh! Oh! To Agamemnon's wife I declare: rise quickly from your bed!' (25–6) The watchman transfers wakefulness from himself to Clytemnestra by summoning her as soon as he is able to go to sleep. It is highly significant that the action that provokes the entrance of the murderess-to-be is a wake-up call, which 'forges a direct link between the act of waking and the violent purposes of an avenger'.[8] As is about to become clear, together with Agamemnon's wife there rises the impulse of retaliation that she hosts.

Before Clytemnestra enters, the old men who compose the chorus extend sleep disturbances to a general condition of the guilty. Zeus sets mortals on the way to wisdom through suffering, and 'the toil of painful memory drips before the heart in sleep' (179–80: στάζει δ'ἐν θ'ὕπνῳ πρὸ καρδίας/ μνησιπήμων πόνος).[9] Rather than being a respite from toil, as is traditional, sleep receives it drop by drop.[10] It is the vehicle for inflicting on the criminal a Chinese torture of subliminal remorse. An ancient gloss explains: 'The guilty imagine calamities and toils even in sleep'.[11] This description of the action of remorse harks back to the chorus' earlier evocation of the dreadful, likewise memory-filled Wrath (μνάμων Μῆνις) that guards Agamemnon's house, 'ready to rise again' to avenge Iphigenia (151–5).

In the first episode Clytemnestra, who has just risen, exhibits a disdain for sleep, both literal and metaphorical. She has not trusted dreams, the visions 'of a sleeping mind' (275), but the relay of an ever-wakeful fire, a fire that was never 'overcome by slumber' (290–1), never went out (296), with one runner 'awaking' the next (299) and the flame growing in brilliance (301) and rushing (304) to reach the palace. By pointing up her own and her helpers' wakefulness, Clytemnestra identifies with the unrelenting Wrath that guards the palace.

That Wrath is bound to upset the victors' peaceful rest. Clytemnestra describes the Greek victory at Troy as the end of sleep deprivation: the 'toil that made [the warriors] wander at night (νυκτιπλάγκτους) after the battle' (330) is over, she says, as if answering the watchman's prayer for the end of toil and his complaint of a νυκτίπλαγκτον bed (12–3); 'having got rid of dew' (336), as the watchman wished for himself,[12] the warriors 'will slumber like happy men, without guards, the whole night' (336–7). Clytemnestra produces a rare narrative in Greek and Roman literature, one that focuses on the night *after* the sack of Troy. Typically narrators stress the sleep of the Trojans on the night *of* the sack.[13] While in the standard story the Trojans' unconcerned, drunken slumber is contrasted with the Greeks' killing wakefulness, in Clytemnestra's imagination it is the Greeks who sleep unconcerned: 'without guards' emphasizes their postwar relaxation. The alleged bliss of the warriors' rest is brought out also by the emphatic position of εὐδαίμονες ('happy') at the end of the line, as well as by the assonance of εὐδαίμονες with εὑδήσουσι ('they will sleep') and εὐφρόνην ('night'), which interlocks well-being and nightlong sleep.

The words that follow, however, suggest that Agamemnon's unguarded slumber does not mark the end of toil, for the force of revenge is not going to sleep. Even if the Greeks should leave Troy successfully, 'the suffering of the dead might become awake (ἐγρηγορός), if sudden calamities have not hit yet' (346–7).[14] On the surface the dead could be the Trojans or the Greek warriors who died for Menelaus' private cause, but the vagueness of the formula introduces the possibility that Clytemnestra is thinking of Iphigenia.[15] Over Agamemnon's victorious slumber there looms the awaking offence suffered by his daughter, which had already surfaced in the chorus' evocation of memory-filled Wrath (151–5). Is Agamemnon's sleep then 'without guards' because it is safe, or rather because it is not protected?[16]

The speech of the herald who announces Agamemnon's arrival is linked to Clytemnestra's by the repetition of central words and ideas. Agamemnon, one of the εὐδαίμονες who rested unguarded at Troy, is now the εὐδαίμων who is returning in glory (530);[17] the nocturnal dews reappear (336, 561) and sleep is again centre stage to signify the end of toil. As a participant in the war, the herald knows its hardships, which he expounds by putting special emphasis on sleep discomforts: 'Our beds were near the enemy walls and the dews of the meadow from the sky and the earth were dripping continuously' (559–61). The warriors' distress matches the watchman's, who also lay on a dewy bed night after night. The landscape surrounding the fighters did sleep, but its calmness, when the sea 'fell on its windless bed' in the midday heat (565–6), was a sickening, oppressive condition. This is all past misery, however: 'The toil is over, is over, so that the dead have no more care of ever getting up' (567–9). To the audience the herald's words sound like a rebuttal of Clytemnestra's intimation that the dead might rise. No, he proclaims with an emphatic double negative, they will *not* (μήδ') awaken, *never* (μήποτ'). For the survivors the success of the enterprise does not risk being compromised by the 'suffering of the dead' (346), but amply compensates for 'the suffering of war' (574).

The herald's confidence fits his position: he was a fighter in a war spurred by an impulse to revenge similar to the one that is now driving Clytemnestra to her crime, but that war is over, whereas its successful end marks the awakening of her revenge. For Clytemnestra the dead are rising because she is readying herself to kill; for the herald they lie because he does not wish to be reminded of the Greek losses. Additionally, he does not even remotely suspect what is brewing in Argos. The toil he has suffered, and which has robbed him of sleep, is routine in war. He has no experience of the other sleep-depriving toil, no share in the chorus' anguish.[18]

The herald, however, gives a positive answer to Clytemnestra's intimation that the warriors might have met with disaster on their journey home. The Greeks have indeed suffered a fierce storm, the onset of which is described again in the language of awakening: at night dreadful waves rose (653). Their rising turns the already disturbing sleep of the sea in the midday heat into an ominous happening and the sea itself into an agent of divine retribution, awakening to kill, like Clytemnestra.[19] The herald's narrative of the destruction wrought by the awakened sea qualifies his own confidence that toil belongs to the past and that the dead will never rise.

Clytemnestra, it seems, has not been sleeping well all the while. In greeting Agamemnon she tells him that her tears have dried up from crying for such long hours, that her eyes are

> Sore from going to sleep late, weeping over the firebrands that never appeared, and the light flapping of a buzzing mosquito would awaken me while I was seeing you surrounded by sufferings in greater number than the minutes of my sleep.
>
> (889–94)

Clytemnestra persuades Agamemnon of her loyalty by attributing to herself the restless sleep characteristic of wives longing for their husbands. She fashions herself specifically after Penelope, as is suggested by the metaphor she uses: Agamemnon is the un-hoped-for land that appears to sailors (899–900), just as Odysseus is the land where Penelope the sailor finds safety (*Od.* 23. 233–40). Clytemnestra's story of her troubled nights also recalls Penelope's complaint of sleeplessness to her still unrecognized husband in *Odyssey* 19.[20]

Is Clytemnestra lying through and through? Though of course she has not been losing sleep to longing, the dreadful dreams that have allegedly shaken her awake could be wish fulfilling, like the rumours she allegedly kept receiving about Agamemnon, wounded so many times that he should have more holes than a net, killed so many times that he could boast of three bodies, like Geryon (866–71).[21] Those rumours sound all too predictive to the audience: predictive as a wish-fulfilling fabrication, that is. The manner of Agamemnon's death, caught in a net, struck by three blows, will prove those rumours 'right'. The audience, by now acquainted with the rousing action of the dead Iphigenia, will believe Clytemnestra's complaint of sleeplessness but read into it a masked allusion to her plotting wakefulness, especially because she has pointed up (and honestly, though with a double entendre) her steady watching for the coming of the beacon.

After urging the servants to spread the red carpet on which Agamemnon will tread to 'enter an unexpected dwelling, led by Justice', Clytemnestra reassures him of her vigilant care: 'My solicitude, unconquered by slumber, will set the rest aright, justly, as destined by the gods' (912–3). Her claim is truthful in a sense hidden from Agamemnon but clear to the audience. As was the case with her comment about the 'suffering of the dead', the vagueness of her phrasing here authorizes two readings: 1) I have been thinking day and night of your return and am anxious to welcome you back to your palace, as justice and the gods demand (Agamemnon's reading), and 2) I have been thinking day and night of how to pursue my rightful revenge and am anxious to do so (Clytemnestra's reading and the audience's). The chorus, who has presentiments but no firm knowledge, could be suspended between the two readings, though the song accompanying Agamemnon's entrance, with its heightened anguish (no longer 'sing the song of sorrow but let the good prevail', as in the first ode, but the reverse: 'I have learnt of Agamemnon's return, yet my heart sings the song of the Erinyes') accords with the second.

When the killing is imminent, however, the chorus seems to have a faint hope that it can be avoided if only Cassandra's prophetic voice, which has just announced it unambiguously, will slumber: 'Silence, wretched one, put your mouth to sleep' (1247). The chorus treats Cassandra's words like deeds.[22] It fears that to speak ill-omened utterances is to activate them and wants to believe that to avoid them is enough to ward off the crime of which they speak. Aeschylus expresses this idea, widespread in Greek culture, in an original way, by merging the imagery of silence with that of sleep, in keeping with the thematic prominence of the sleep motif in the play. But sleep and silence are at variance in this tragedy of unspoken terror.[23] Silence does not contain calmness and peace, but fear and anguish: it is the accompaniment or even the equivalent of sleeplessness, not sleep.[24] The chorus' own reticence is filled with obscure forebodings of death, which Cassandra's words spell out as the murder is coming to pass.

While the murder is called – not surprisingly at this point – the work of unsleeping hands (1357), the helplessness of the murdered king and his entourage prompts sleep imagery. Agamemnon lies in disgrace. The precious bathtub in which he has been killed becomes a bed strewn on the ground, evocative of wartime discomforts. 'I wish I had died before seeing you occupy the lowly bed of a silver bathtub', sings the chorus (1539–40), echoing an earlier lament: 'You lie [. . .] on this bed unworthy of a free man' (1492 and 1494, repeated at 1516 and 1518). The chorus itself can only wish for a sleep with no awakening, a death 'that will bring us endless slumber, now that the best-minded watcher has succumbed' (1450–1).

The play began with the watchman's prayer for the sleep-bringing end of toil, and now, towards the end, we find a corresponding prayer for a different kind of rest: eternal slumber. This time, the wish comes from the citizenry – including, we are to imagine, the watchman himself – deprived of its guardian, whose own undignified sleep epitomizes his impotence throughout the play. Agamemnon's unguarded and nightlong slumber in a Trojan home, as imagined by Clytemnestra, did not save him from the wakeful hands of an avenger who plunged him into ignominious sleep. The audience will remember the chorus' lament over the loss of its guardian when, in *Eumenides*, a watchful institution will be appointed to protect the citizens' nightly rest. But the murder that ends *Agamemnon* perpetuates sleep disturbances, as the opening scenes of *Choephoroe* make instantly clear.

Choephoroe

The action onstage receives its impulse from Clytemnestra's sudden awakening, caused by a frightening dream: 'A nocturnal scream – clear, with hair standing up, prophet of the palace, breathing anger from sleep – resounded with fear, from the recesses of the house, heavily falling on the women's chambers' (32–7).[25] The prominence given to Clytemnestra's rising is unique to Aeschylus' tragedy. In the two plays by Sophocles and Euripides on the same subject, her nocturnal fears are evoked much later (Soph. *El.* 400; Eur. *El.* 617), and they do not impact the action with comparable force. This difference demonstrates the thematic relevance of sleep disturbances in Aeschylus' trilogy. In both *Agamemnon* and *Choephoroe,* Clytemnestra's awakening provides the initial dramatic motor.

The interpreters explain Clytemnestra's dream as a consequence of the 'reproach and anger of those under the earth against their killers' (40–2), and this harks back to Agamemnon's imagined sleep at Troy, over which hovered the wakeful suffering of the dead Iphigenia. Now Clytemnestra's sleep is in turn shattered by dreams that evince the wrath of the dead Agamemnon. She takes on the role he filled in the earlier play, but with a difference. His imagined slumber is not broken from within but is threatened from without, by the embodiment of Iphigenia's unsleeping anger. He has no remorse or presentiment either in his waking hours or in his sleep. He does not dream. This is in keeping with the nature of dreams in *Agamemnon*: fleeting, vain and insubstantial (420–6), an image of weak old age (79–80), they provide no insight.[26] Clytemnestra dismisses them as unreliable. In *Choephoroe,* on the other hand, her guilt fashions a veridical dream, which speaks volumes to its interpreters.[27] Remorse bursts into her sleep. Though the anger of the dead remains an outside force that acts unrelentingly (324–8), Clytemnestra internalizes it, whereas Agamemnon was unaware of its workings. The difference is highlighted by contrasting applications in the two plays of the Aeschylean coinage νυκτίπλαγκτος ('night-wandering'). While Agamemnon's and the watchman's nocturnal restlessness was caused by external circumstances, by their jobs, Clytemnestra's comes from within, from 'night-wandering terrors and dreams' (523–4).

In his capacity as one of the offended dead, Agamemnon is not allowed to remain asleep either. Orestes and Electra seek to awaken him: 'Father, unhappy father, with what words or deeds could I reach from afar to the bed that holds you?' (316–9); 'Remember the bath [...] Remember the net [...] Won't you awake at hearing these offences? Won't you raise straight your dearest head?' (491–2; 495–6)

To cast an invocation to the dead as a call to wake up might seem unremarkable. But Aeschylus does not use the same imagery for the evocation of Darius' ghost in *Persians*,[28] though the purpose there is literally to rouse the dead. Orestes does not mean to conjure up the ghost of Agamemnon, but more modestly to excite his anger and obtain his support, yet he asks him to awaken. This call reminds the audience that the same unsleeping force that killed Agamemnon is now driving the murder of his killer. Orestes' exhortations to his father link him to the remembering Wrath that was ready to 'rise again' to avenge Iphigenia (*Ag.* 155).

As the murder of Clytemnestra draws near, the wakefulness of the force of revenge moves to the foreground. Orestes the executioner rises. He has 'got up straight' in his resolve to kill his mother (512), while she is compared to another wakeful murderess, Scylla, who killed her father Nisos in his carefree sleep by plucking the lock of hair that made him immortal; and 'Hermes got hold of him' (619–21).[29] Agamemnon's unawareness of his wife's plot is retrospectively associated with literal sleep: an abandoned, unsuspecting slumber, as in Guérin's painting.

The next episode plays up the incongruity between the prospect of sleep and that of murder. Seeking admission to the royal palace, Orestes urges the servant to call his masters in a hurry because 'the dark chariot of night also hurries, and it is time for travellers to drop anchor in homes welcoming to strangers' (660–2). Orestes wears the mask of the weary traveller in the style of the *Odyssey*, claiming that he longs for rest at the end of the day. And Clytemnestra, who does not recognize the traveller, genuinely behaves like a good hostess: 'Strangers, tell me what you need. The palace offers you what you can expect of it: warm baths and a bed to soothe your toils' (670–1). Orestes ironically endorses her sincere display of hospitality by apologizing for the news of her son's death (700–6). Promising that she will treat him no worse for that, Clytemnestra sends him off to sleep: 'The time has come for guests who have ended their day to find appropriate care after a long journey. Take him to the quarters reserved for guests' (710–2).

The murderer is offered the comfort of a bed and invited to retire and recuperate from the toils of travel. But of course Orestes' journey is driven by another toil, the 'inborn toil of the race' (466). The resonance between this episode and scenes of hospitality in the *Odyssey* brings out the perversion of religious and social norms that stains Agamemnon's house. The situation recalls the last night of the suitors, and the use of sleep to build climactically towards the murder in the play is paralleled in the epic. Both Orestes and Odysseus have returned incognito to claim their rights; in both circumstances the victim, unaware of the stranger's plans, urges retiring for the nightly rest,[30] and both avenging heroes are markedly wakeful.

Orestes' wakefulness is brought into stark relief by the evocation of his sleep patterns as a child, presented to the audience while the adult Orestes is readying himself to kill. His nurse, on learning of his alleged death, remembers with despair 'dear Orestes, the care of my life, whom I received from his mother and nurtured, and those screams that called me and made me go about at night (νυκτιπλάγκτων)' (749–51). The picture is one of innocence and blissful normality for the woman who remembers happier days, but the appearance of νυκτιπλάγκτων links the description of the infant's nocturnal screaming to episodes in which the term is applied to sleep-depriving situations fraught with abnormal strain. Thus, the overtly innocent vignette 'points to his [Orestes'] role as a waking adult avenger'.[31]

A second image of the child Orestes is fashioned by Clytemnestra when, to deter her son from striking, she bares her breast and reminds him of 'how often, sleeping, you drew nutritious milk with your lips' (897–8). Her gesture repeats Hecuba's when she tries to hold Hector back.[32] Audiences ancient and modern will recognize the allusion and mark the detail of the child's slumber, added by Aeschylus.

Images of peacefully sleeping children set off against dire circumstances appear elsewhere in Greek poetry: Astyanax, orphaned, who used to doze in luxury when Hector was alive;[33] Perseus, blissfully asleep while his mother, who holds him as she is borne on the surge of the sea and her sorrows, prays: 'sleep, my child, and you, sea, sleep; sleep, my endless woe'; and Astyanax again, this time dead, with 'those slumbers, gone'.[34] Clytemnestra, however, evokes the guileless image of a sleeping child guilefully: not with affection, but to disarm her killer with a picture of motherly love, which the spectators may even take as a fabrication by the un-motherly woman because they know (from Orestes' nurse) that Clytemnestra did not hold her baby to her breast, at least not often, as she claims.[35] She did not take much pain to tend her child, but now counts on the emotional power of the made-up image to lull the killing hands of her adult son to sleep. Her appeal both enhances the murderer's wakefulness and strengthens the association of sleep with helplessness, pursued in *Agamemnon* and also, shortly before Clytemnestra's plea, in *Choephoroe*. For at hearing Aegisthus' death cry, a servant speaks agitatedly to the inhabitants of the palace: 'Am I shouting to deaf men? Is it sleepers I am calling, in vain, for nothing?' (881–2) The servant's words are to be read not literally but as a reminder of a metaphor: sleep equals impotence. They match the chorus' feeling of impotence in *Agamemnon*, also phrased in the language of sleep (1357).

After Clytemnestra's murder Orestes becomes the guilty person who suffers the dripping of remorse invoked by the chorus of *Agamemnon*, now materialized in the Furies who 'drip foul blood from their eyes' (1058). His predicament is even more dreadful, for remorse does not creep into his slumber as it does into the guilty person's; nor does it fashion a frightening dream as it does for Clytemnestra. Instead, it takes the even more frightening shape of a waking vision, which drives the murderer away from Argos and off the stage (1061–2).

The chorus, however, nurtures greater hopes than the one in *Agamemnon*. While the old men of Argos wished only for the eternal sleep of death, the slave women who watch Orestes become the prey of terror present the sleep of the forces of destruction as a possibility, albeit in the form of an unanswered question: 'When will it complete its work, when will the rage (μένος) of Ate, lulled back to sleep, stop?' (1075–6) These are the play's last words. Together with the chorus' prior reassurance to Orestes that Apollo will free him from his sufferings (1059–60), the question that ends *Choephoroe* sets the stage for *Eumenides*, where it will be answered.

Eumenides

The last play of the trilogy seems to engage with this question instantly, for the Erinyes are sound asleep when they appear onstage (Figure 3.2).[36] Apollo has knocked them out: 'You see them caught, those furies, fallen into sleep' (67–8). He undermines the Erinyes' divinity by pointing up their heavy, unnatural slumber, which they have suffered at his hands, the hands of a younger god who makes naught of their powers.[37] And their repulsive snore (54) 'communicates the unwholesome nature of their prerogative'.[38]

Enter Clytemnestra, a dream vision. Like a Homeric dream she shakes the sleepers reproachfully: 'You slumber, eh? What need is there of sleepers?' (94) In Homer, though, reproachful dreams are sent either by a god to a mortal or by one mortal to another,[39] whereas Clytemnestra is a mortal who forces herself into the sleep of goddesses. This reversal further undercuts the Furies' divine status. The mere fact that they dream assimilates them to mortals, for in classical Greek literature deities do not.[40]

Orestes, however, cannot find rest while the weary and ungodlike Erinyes are snoring. Apollo urges him on: 'Flee, do not be

Figure 3.2 Eumenides Painter, red-figured crater (*c*.380 BC), Paris, Louvre. Clytemnestra tries to wake the Furies while Apollo purifies Orestes with the blood of a piglet.

faint hearted. For, as you keep going over the earth trodden by wanderers, they will chase you through the vast mainland, beyond the sea and the islands' cities. Do not grow weary of working at your toil' (74–9). Apollo can keep the Furies asleep only temporarily;[41] he cannot make real the wish expressed at the end of *Choephoroe*. Clytemnestra instantly proves this by rousing them with words that hark back to the end of that play but cast her as the willing perpetuator of the working of anger: 'Sleep and toil, masterly conspirators, have enfeebled the rage (μένος) of the terrible snake' (126–7). She expresses her keenness to keep the μένος awake and urges the Furies not to be overwhelmed by toil (see also 133), further adding to her instigating action: 'Do not ignore my suffering (πῆμα), softened by slumber' (134), she says, harking back to her veiled threat in *Agamemnon*: 'The suffering (πῆμα) of the dead might awake' (346–7). She rouses the Erinyes because her suffering has not been lulled to sleep, though they have 'lost their prey, overcome by slumber' (148).

In sum, the play that opens with the Furies asleep soon begins to repeat the message of *Agamemnon*: the murdered won't lie. The awakening of the Furies' μένος visibly and dramatically denies the possibility, expressed in abstract terms at the end of *Choephoroe*, that μένος might be permanently put to rest.[42] Orestes' claim that the blood on his hands already 'slumbers and fades' (280) is instantly challenged by the Erinyes' threat of an endless pursuit, to the netherworld and even beyond (338–9).

Nonetheless, Apollo has already announced the end of the pursuit. When he urges Orestes to flee, he also reassures him that his flight will come to a definitive stop in Athens: 'And there, with judges and enchanting speeches, we shall find a way of setting you free from your toils forever' (81–4). In fact, it is only the enchanting speeches that save Orestes and Athens by mollifying the Erinyes and warding off their threats,[43] and those speeches belong exclusively to Athena. While Apollo handles the Erinyes confrontationally, knocking them out, Athena appreciates their temper (848) and does not seek to neutralize them by wielding sleep as a weapon. Instead, she exhorts them to 'lull to rest (κοίμα) the black surge of bitter anger' (832), promising them honours. The patience (881) with which she applies the 'sweetness and charm' (886) of her tongue to their anger eventually pays off, for they say, 'It seems that you will charm me: I am giving up my anger' (900). While in the two earlier plays persuasion led to crime, it now leads to peace,[44] and the peace worked out by Athena's persuasiveness is the sleep of black anger, which the goddess has soothed by a hypnotic charm.[45] The wish expressed at the end of *Choephoroe* comes true at last.

With their black anger forever at rest, the Erinyes will become the honoured members of a community who will look after everyone's slumber. When Athena sets up the court on the Areopagus, she calls it 'a wakeful sentry of the land, to protect those who sleep' (705–6). For the first time in the trilogy sleepers are not threatened or harmed; for the first time sleep is not an enfeebling condition or a mark of impotence, but betokens civic harmony. The guardian of the citizens' rest is a rampart (701) that avails itself of 'fear' and 'reverence' to restrain them from crimes 'day and night' (690–2) – a pregnant emphasis in a trilogy filled with anguished nocturnal awakenings and murderous plotting[46] – and is itself restrained by fear and respect for the people it guards.[47]

While in *Agamemnon* and *Choephoroe* fear prevents sleep, the fear enthroned on the Areopagus will make it possible. This is because that fear is not 'horror in the face of violence and guilt' but 'the basis of spontaneously just behaviour', respectful of the law (693).[48] The wakeful force of revenge that drove the chain of murders leaves the stage, along with the sleep-upsetting terrors it produced. It is now replaced by an institution that relies on the fear of punishment to watch over everyone's rest. Insofar as it effectively upholds justice, the institution's vigilance contrasts with the ineffective slumber of the bloodthirsty Erinyes in the opening scene.[49] It also replicates the wakefulness of the watchman at the beginning of the trilogy, but with opposite goals. While the sleep-deprived servant is subjected to tyrannical rulers who are getting ready to kill, the 'wakeful sentry of the land' is a collective and impersonal body, whose task is to suppress crime and to shield the citizens' rest under a polity that strikes a middle ground between 'anarchy and despotism' (696).[50]

The power of the law to watch over everyone's sleep sets the moderate democracy idealized in *Eumenides* in stark opposition to despotism in particular, for a despot not only does not care to protect his subjects' rest, but cannot even look after his own. When charged with conspiring against Oedipus' rule, Creon fires back with a question: why would he choose a kingship haunted by continuous fear rather than sleeping in peace, since he already enjoys de facto power and privileges equal to those of the ruler? (Soph. *OT* 584–6)[51] The idea is developed extensively in Xenophon's *Hiero* (6. 7–10), which argues that a tyrant cannot count on the law to keep his sleep safe. Since he himself is the law, his guards have no other restraining force but their loyalty to him. Soldiers on the battlefield sleep better than a tyrant in his palace because they have watchmen who stay awake, fearing for them on account of their own fear of the law. Likewise the citizens of democratic Athens have law-fearing watchmen that protect their nightly rest, guarding them not from outside enemies but from each other.

PART TWO: SLEEPERS ON THE TRAGIC STAGE

Trachiniae

Sleeping figures had stage appeal. They feature not only in *Eumenides* but also in *Trachiniae*, *Heracles*, *Philoctetes* and *Orestes*. Neither the one-day span of tragic plots nor the daytime setting of both plot and performance posed a challenge to the production of sleep scenes, because sleep, unlike sleeplessness, can happen in full daylight, as indeed it does in all the plays. The daytime hour marks it as an eerie phenomenon, laden with tension. What will happen when the sleeper awakes? Will he awake or not? Staged sleep is always a site of uncertainty. It is also caused by extreme predicaments: by the joint attack of fatigue and a god (in *Eumenides*), by paroxysms of unmanageable suffering (in *Trachiniae* and *Philoctetes*) or by madness (in *Heracles* and *Orestes*).

Presumably the earliest play after *Eumenides* to include a sleep scene is Sophocles' *Trachiniae*.[52] A servant has just recounted Deianira's suicide when the dying Heracles, unconscious, appears onstage, carried on a litter by silent escorts (964–70). This entrance is his homecoming, towards the end of a tragedy that has been labeled a '*nostos* play'[53] because its plot, like the *Odyssey*'s, is directed towards the hero's return, which is announced, delayed and finally accomplished after a prolonged absence that has filled his wife's nights with anxiety, Penelope-wise.[54]

Deianira fashions herself as a sleepless Penelope in the opening scene: 'Since being united with Heracles as his chosen bride,[55] I always nurture fear after fear, worrying about him. One night brings in distress and another night, in succession, dispels it' (27–30). Unlike Penelope's, however, Deianira's anguish has begun with her marriage. For Heracles, unlike Odysseus, has always been on the road; to be married to him is to lose sleep to fear of losing him.

The young women of the chorus join their voices with hers. In their entrance song they oppose the regular course of the sun, which night 'begets and puts to sleep' (95), to the unsleeping fixity of Deianira's yearning: 'I learn that much-wooed Deianira, longing always like a sorrowful bird, never lulls to rest the longing of her eyes so as to leave them tearless' (103–7). The ever-lamenting bird is probably the nightingale,[56] the same bird to which Penelope compares herself because she weeps in her bed while everyone sleeps (*Od.* 19. 515–21). Deianira pines on a 'husbandless' bed, which agitates her heart (109).

Talking to the still unmarried women of the chorus, the chronically insomniac wife of Heracles describes the life of a married woman as one of sleeplessness: '[when] a woman is called wife instead of maiden, she receives her share of worry in the night, fearing for her husband or children' (148–50). Drawing on her own experiences, Deianira assumes that sleep disturbances are common to all married women, and she singles out night as the privileged setting for a wife's anxieties.[57] The audience will again think of Penelope, who is capable of distracting herself in the daytime but not 'when night comes' (*Od.* 19. 515).

Deianira ends her speech by further emphasizing her sleeplessness. She knows from an oracle that Heracles' labours are fated to end on the present day, yet the thought does not cheer her but causes her to startle from sleep: 'I leap up from sweet slumber from fear, friends. I am in fear, in case I must be left without the best of all men' (175–7). The oracle's vagueness as to how Heracles' labours will end (169–70) keeps Deianira anxiously awake with her own labours (30), and the audience is thus also left in suspense as to the manner in which Heracles' return will be accomplished. Fear is the dominant emotion on the stage when a messenger wearing a wreath suddenly breaks in (178) to bring about a happy reversal – Heracles has made it back alive – that does not last: he is dying.

The discovery that Deianira's robe is burning Heracles alive clarifies the meaning of 'the end of Heracles' labours': they will stop with death, for there can be no labouring after death (829–30). The anxiety shared by characters and audience alike then changes its object: no longer 'will Heracles return alive?' but 'is he still alive'? (806; see 835) This uncertainty frames the sleep scene, and the likeness of sleep and death plays into its unfolding.

The scene is anticipated in the narrative of Deianira's suicide. She went inside the house alone and 'saw her son in the courtyard, spreading a hollow bed to go back to meet his father' (901–2). This foreshadowing of Heracles' entrance in sleep links it to his wife's death, for the bed is central to both episodes. The intervening account of Deianira's suicide puts the bed before the audience's imagination with great insistence:

> I saw her throwing and spreading sheets on Heracles' bed, and when she finished, she [...] sat in the middle of [it] and [...] said: 'o bed and bridal chamber, forever farewell! You will never welcome me again as bedfellow on this bed!'
>
> (915–22)

Deianira behaves like a Homeric lady who makes her husband's bed: but not to retire with him.[58] The standard 'farewell to the marriage bed' of dying heroines acquires a distinctive meaning from this heroine's emphasis, at the beginning of the play, on her sleepless nights on a 'husbandless' bed. The wife is now about to leave it doubly empty. The detail that she 'spreads' sheets on the bed of her death after seeing her son 'spreading' a bed to carry his dying father joins the two beds and intertwines Deianira's death with Heracles'. The pairing of their deaths is reflected in the seamless transition from the evidence of hers to the prospect of his (950–1), before Heracles makes his first and last entrance.

Heracles' entrance marks a *piano*: his escorts advance noiselessly (965–7) and call for silence (974) so as not to arouse the 'wild pain' that possesses him. But Hyllus cannot keep quiet, and his cry ('oh me!') stirs Heracles. The manner of his awakening is evocative of Odysseus' on Scheria, also caused by a cry (*Od.* 6. 117). Heracles' first words, 'Zeus! To what land have I come? Among which mortals do I lie?' (984–5), likewise repeat Odysseus' in that episode and in the parallel scene of awakening on Ithaca: 'Oh me! To what land have I come? Of which mortals?' (*Od.* 6. 119 = 13. 200)[59] Both episodes seem to be behind the tragic scene.[60] Though the cause of Heracles' stirring, a scream, suggests *Odyssey* 6, the conjunction of sleep and homecoming is more closely reminiscent of *Odyssey* 13. Like Odysseus, Heracles is unconscious as he accomplishes his *nostos*.

The allusion to Odysseus' sleep points up Heracles' predicament by inviting comparison with the hero who awakens from 'death'[61] to discover new surroundings or rediscover his homeland. As soon as he opens his eyes, Odysseus seeks to relocate himself in the world. He asks questions that aim to help him understand the environment where he finds himself. Heracles' questions, in contrast, only seem to concern his environment; in fact they are governed by pain so strong as to cut him off completely from it. His mind turns instantly to his pain (985–7), the only object of his awareness.[62] For him the end of sleep does not mark a return to life but the rekindling of a frenzy that 'cannot be charmed' or 'put to sleep' except by Zeus (998–9; 1002). While Odysseus' slumber on Scheria stopped his 'distressful (δυσπόνεος) tiredness' (*Od.* 5. 493), Heracles awakens to the distress (πεπονημένος, 985) of unbearable shafts of pain. While the Homeric hero asks, 'to what land have I come? Of which mortals?' his tragic counterpart adds, 'among which mortals *do I lie*?' He is prostrated and wishes for more rest: 'Let me, let wretched me slumber' (1005). There is no making Heracles' life 'forgetful of toil' (1021) except by sleep. The permanent sleep of death, that is, as he spells out by recasting his wish as a wish for eternal slumber: 'Sweet Hades, oh Zeus of my own blood, put me to sleep, to sleep, destroy the wretched one with a swift death' (1040–3). Heracles reverses the commonplace attribution of 'sweet' to life and light in opposition to gloomy death[63] with a coinage, 'sweet Hades', which also transfers to death the most common Homeric epithet for sleep. Death is sweet because it can relieve him of a pain that sleep cannot cure.

Anaesthetic slumber offers Heracles only a temporary lull, from which he awakens unchanged: he cries out and curses Deianira

(1036) just as he did before losing consciousness (791–3). Like the silence that protects it, sleep has the dramatic function of keeping the audience in suspense, but it does not underscore a transformation in the hero's mental state. Heracles' awakening, far from initiating a process of recognition, 'signifies the surging development of [his] misunderstanding of the truth about himself and his transgression of the bounds of moderation'.[64] His realization that his death was willed by destiny (1159–62) is far removed from the sleep scene and unrelated to it. As we shall see presently, things sit differently for the same hero in Euripides, where he awakens from madness to sobriety and recognition.

Heracles

Euripides' *Heracles* is another *nostos* play, and one in which the protagonist's return, instead of being advanced by the sweetest slumber, like Odysseus' *nostos*, is ruined by an attack of madness that ends in sleep. Heracles plays in a scene structurally similar to the one in *Trachiniae,* but more elaborate. While the audience of Sophocles' tragedy does not know that Heracles will make his entrance unconscious, in Euripides a messenger's speech prepares for the stage appearance of the knocked-out madman by describing how sleep took hold of him: Athena 'hurled a rock against Heracles' chest to stop his murderous frenzy and sank him into slumber. He falls on the ground, knocking his back against a pillar' (1004–7). Tied to it, 'he sleeps, wretched one, not a happy sleep' (1013).

Heracles becomes visible soon thereafter: 'You see those miserable children lying before their wretched father, who sleeps an awful slumber after murdering his sons' (1032–4). His appearance prompts an animated verbal exchange, similar in content to the one in *Trachiniae* ('silence!' 'How can I be quiet?'), but more extended and more mindful of his sleep. The noisy party is the chorus and the silencer Amphitryon: 'Quiet! Won't you let him, relaxed in sleep, forget his sufferings?' (1042–4) 'Don't cry! Don't rouse him from his calm, slumbering rest!' (1048–50) 'Mourn softly! Otherwise he will awaken and break his bonds' (1054–55). 'Silence, let me note his breathing! [...] Does he sleep? Yes, he slumbers, a sleep non-sleep, baneful' (1060–1).

Heracles' unhappy slumber has a divine provenance, like his madness,[65] and it likewise hits him violently. Athena knocks him out with a stone just as she killed the giant Enceladus with one (908).[66] The manner of sleep's coming and its parallel with the onslaught of madness underscores the gods' hostility to Heracles[67] and casts his sleep as the opposite of the restoring slumber in which Athena enfolds her dear Odysseus after he lands on Scheria (5. 491–3). While the location of Odysseus' enveloping sleep is a cosy and windless bush, the location of Heracles' attacking one is a broken pillar, which 'fell' just as he does (1006–7). The contrast between the two heroes' sleep is further enhanced by its opposite relationship to πόνος, 'toil'. Heracles' wretched slumber does not cure a 'distressful (δυσπόνεος) tiredness' (*Od.* 5. 493) caused by a superhuman feat of swimming, but follows the killing of his family, the last πόνος in his career of heroic labours, and the most appalling (1275, 1279).[68] From that πόνος sleep can provide no cure.

Accordingly, Heracles is plunged in a 'sleep non-sleep, baneful', 'not happy', 'awful'.[69] The chorus cannot keep quiet because the blood that surrounds him 'rises' (1052), crying for vengeance, as Clytemnestra 'rises' (*Ag.* 27) from bed to avenge bloodshed that cannot slumber. By hinting at the Aeschylean motif of unsleeping blood,[70] the chorus possibly intimates that Heracles might awaken mad, possessed by the Furies. (The threat actually looms large in his father's words [1074–6].) This suggestion is reinforced by the last description of his state, far from reassuring in spite of its intent. The chorus, attempting to quiet Amphitryon's apprehension that Heracles might stir, unwittingly makes his sleep seem ominous by saying: 'Night holds your son's eyelids' (1071). The audience will think instantly of madness, because the play emphatically couples it with night in the figure of Lyssa, introduced as 'the offspring of Night' (822), the 'unwedded maiden of black Night' (834), 'Night's blood' (844), 'the daughter of Night' (883). The words 'night holds his eyes' will remind the audience of the nocturnal filiation of Madness and breed more fear: will Heracles indeed awaken mad?

This fear is further communicated by Heracles' slow rising from sleep, more suspenseful than in the parallel scene from *Trachiniae*, and by Amphitryon's reactions. He reassures himself that his son is plunged into a calm slumber (1049–50)[71] by checking his breathing (1058) and notes his first stirring with apprehension (1069). The old man is anxious about his own safety. Though he calls for silence to let Heracles 'forget his ills' in sleep (1042–4), he is worried that, should the madman awaken, he would rend his bonds, destroy Thebes, kill his father and shatter the palace (1055–6). As soon as Heracles stirs, Amphitryon seeks a place to hide (1069–70), and shortly thereafter he flees, urging the old men of the chorus to follow him (1081–3). Heracles is left alone on stage.[72] The light is fully on him when he awakens.

Contrary to the bystanders' fear, Heracles awakens sedate, bewildered but lucid. The meter of his monologue conveys his lucidity, for he does not scream in lyric verse as his namesake in *Trachiniae* but speaks in iambics from the start. Sleep has transformed the hero's mental state, preparing him and the audience for the recognition to come.

A comparison with the scene of madness in Sophocles' *Ajax* suggests that Euripides chose to end Heracles' madness in sleep in order to give the recognition greater prominence on the stage. Ajax, like Heracles, is taken on a delusional expedition against 'disastrously inappropriate opponents',[73] in Ajax's case an expedition with mock-epic grandeur, emphatically nocturnal[74] and conducted 'while the whole host sleeps' (Soph. *Aj.* 291), like Priam's journey in the *Iliad* (24. 363). Unlike Heracles, though, Ajax does not lose consciousness at the end of his mad journey. Because he does not sleep, there can be no sustained scene in which he awakens to sanity and realizes his predicament. Sophocles does not focus on the process of recognition but on its aftermath. Ajax regains possession of reason offstage, and learns what he has done offstage as well (305–16). The tragedy that unfolds before the spectators is not concerned with his coming to see the truth but with his rehearsal of it and his inability to cope with it. In contrast, Heracles opens his eyes on stage, and is forced to face his actions before learning how to live with them. The long sleep episode builds up tension towards this culminating scene.

Heracles' recognition is often compared with Agave's in *Bacchae*, for both characters have murdered their children in madness, and both realize this gradually, in the course of excited dialogues with their fathers. Agave, though, moves seamlessly from madness to sanity to realization. She does not imitate Heracles by collapsing into an unconscious slumber before recovering her senses. Perhaps this is because an occurrence of sleep after murderous madness would be at variance with this play's emphasis on the bliss of sleep, which is always and only the gift of Dionysus. Wine drowns our sorrows in an oblivious slumber (278–83), and the marvellous actions performed by the Bacchants when the god is in them receive impulse and energy from a 'composed' and 'life giving' sleep,[75] which belongs with ritualized possession, not blind madness. In *Heracles* there is only blind madness, and sleep is not life giving but sick, fittingly marking the protagonist's tragic turn from insanity to despair.

Philoctetes

In Sophocles' *Philoctetes* the protagonist's deep slumber promotes another reversal: from deception to honesty.[76] Sleep's significance comes to the fore already in the prologue: Philoctetes' cave benefits from a hypnotic breeze (18–9); he is introduced as possibly dozing there (30); his bed warrants mention (33) and his dwelling is 'a house with two doors, consisting of a rocky resting-place' (159–60).[77] This emphasis on Philoctetes' sleep and sleeping arrangements is in line with his need to rest after an attack of pain (766–8). Much-needed slumber, however, has tricked him once, when the Greeks took advantage of it to abandon him as they headed for Troy (271–3). An episode of sleep is the cause of his solitude and imprisonment on Lemnos.

When Neoptolemus promises to take him home, Philoctetes presses him: 'let us leave, for timely (καίριος) haste brings sleep and rest when the toil is over' (637–8). These words are poignant because Philoctetes himself must sleep immediately after his paroxysms, whether or not it is timely. The present day proves this again. For shortly after he speaks these words, he suffers another attack that ends in a deep slumber and prevents a timely departure. He knows he cannot stay awake, just as he cannot avoid the attack, and when he feels the pain quieting he asks Neoptolemus to keep his bow safe while he sleeps, as he always does in that circumstance: 'Slumber seizes me whenever this plague leaves. There is no way it can stop before, but you must let me rest in peace' (766–9).

The scene occurs almost exactly at the play's midpoint. Philoctetes dozes off at the end of the second episode (825–6) and his awakening begins the third (865), while the song in the middle covers the duration of his sleep. The central placement of it throws into high relief its crucial role as an instigator of the plot's reversal. Its pivotal function is also underscored by the stage action, which includes, uniquely in extant tragedy, the gradual coming of slumber.[78] We see Philoctetes about to doze off before we see him unconscious: as Neoptolemus marks, 'sleep, it seems, will seize the man shortly. Look, his head is nodding' (821–2). The imminent onset of slumber shapes the last line of Neoptolemus' description: '[leave] him in peace until he should fall asleep' (ἔκηλον αὐτόν, ὡς ἂν εἰς ὕπνον πέσῃ 826), where ὕπνον and πέσῃ, with the alliteration *p-p*, fall as heavily at the end of the line as sleep is falling on Philoctetes' drooping head. Next the men of the chorus sing a prayer to Hypnos, which is intended to work as a lullaby, rich as it is in soft, hypnotic sounds (827–32),[79] and they take note of Philoctetes' deepening slumber. He first sleeps lightly, a 'sleep non-sleep, sharp sighted' (847–8), then soundly, 'without eyes', a sleep very much like death (856–61). When he is about to awake, Neoptolemus observes that he is raising his head (866), just as he had observed its drooping. The circle is completed.

The scene points up the ambivalence of sleep, as cure and danger. Philoctetes needs unbroken slumber but is afraid of being tricked again (766–72). The men of the chorus ask Hypnos, 'who knows not of pain', to come 'breathing gently' and 'blessed' (828–30) and to keep 'holding before his eyes the light[80] that is spread now' (830–1). Though their prayer expresses genuine pity, their self-interest is stronger:[81] 'Come for us' they say (828); 'Come, come for me, Healer' (832). The datives of interest ('sleep, protect me! I am concerned for myself if you should not come!') betray their thinking.[82] They hail Hypnos openly as a liberator but covertly enlist the god's services to deceive the sleeper, as Hera does in *Iliad* 14.[83] The protection afforded by Philoctetes' slumber should allow Neoptolemus to seize the moment, καιρός (837), and to speak as the moment requires, καίρια (862), exerting the mastery over timeliness that is denied to Philoctetes. The chorus exposes his helplessness: 'The man has no eyes, no helper, he lies stretched in the night – good sleep is fearless [or wards off pain][84] – with no control over hand, foot, anything, like one who lies by Hades' (855–61). The beneficial brightness of a healing slumber has turned into the blackness of death, and sleep's confident abandonment amounts to death's insensitivity. The chorus' comparison of Philoctetes to a dead man is cruelly precise,[85] for sleep indeed risks killing him by robbing him of the bow that provides his sustenance.

Since Philoctetes looks dead,[86] his awakening equals a return to life. The first words he utters, 'o light (φέγγος) that follows sleep' (867), call forth the light of life.[87] This sequence has been compared to the symbolic deaths and rebirths of Odysseus each time he survives an adventure.[88] Another close parallel is Odysseus' home-bringing slumber and his awaking on Ithaca, the last episode of death and rebirth in his journey. His deathlike sleep likewise occurs at the midpoint of the epic and is the hinge around which its action turns, and both Odysseus and Philoctetes discover that they have not been robbed, though both feared that they would be. Philoctetes has not suffered from sleep this time, as he did the first time around, and he evokes that episode (872–3) to express his surprise at his new friend's loyalty. His trust and gratitude cause Neoptolemus' definitive breakdown and his abandonment of his deception.[89]

When Philoctetes awakens, Neoptolemus does not speak words that the chorus would call καίρια, but ends up declaring his true intentions, prefacing the disclosure with the emphatic 'I will hide nothing' (915). The pity that he has felt for a long time (806) takes the shape of a resolution to follow his inclinations. His last words before Philoctetes falls asleep, 'let us leave him in peace', might already have been well meant, for they correspond with the sick man's request: 'You must let me rest in peace'. During the lyric dialogue that accompanies Philoctetes' slumber, Neoptolemus says little. His reticence heralds the coming reversal in his actions.

As in all tragic sleep scenes, one party urges the other to be quiet lest the sleeper awaken. The urgings come from the chorus: 'When you answer me again, speak your words softly, softly, child' (844–6). But Neoptolemus, unlike Hyllus in *Trachiniae* or the chorus in *Heracles*, provokes the hushing not by his cries but by his firm, and presumably loud, rebuttal of the chorus' exhortation to leave with the bow (839–42). He speaks no more until Philoctetes' stirring causes him to ask for silence in turn (865). His aim is not to prevent the sleeper from awakening, as in *Trachiniae* or *Heracles*, but to stop the chorus from urging expedient action (see 862–4). His own minimal participation in the song and his condemnation of the chorus' suggestions convey his distance from the immoral methods he had reluctantly embraced. Philoctetes' sleep, by exposing the sick man's vulnerability, has intensified Neoptolemus' compassion and worked towards his recovery of his Achillean self.

Orestes

In Euripides' *Orestes*, healing slumber quiets the hero's madness, as in *Heracles*. The long sequence starring Orestes unconscious has the sleep scene in that play as its main referent.[90] In both scenes a relative urges the chorus to muffle movements and hush sounds; in both, the relative listens to the sleeper's breathing, and both heroes are disoriented upon awakening. Orestes does not know whence or how he came to be where he is (215). The depictions of sleep's attack in the two plays also share traits: as Heracles 'falls' against a column when he is knocked out, Orestes 'fell' into slumber (151 and 217). Falling conveys the two madmen's exhaustion and betokens the heaviness of their sleep, the working of which is described with the same verb (*Her*. 1043; *Or*. 210).[91]

These parallels throw into stark relief a major difference in sleep's quality: Heracles' is accursed whereas Orestes' is 'the sweetest boon' (159, 186). While Heracles does not even seem to be aware of having been unconscious, acknowledging only his unsteady breathing, Orestes lavishes praise on his restorative slumber as soon as he awakens: 'O sleep's dear spell, helper in my illness, how sweetly did you come to me in my need!' (211–2) While Amphitryon wishes that Heracles could stay asleep to forget his ills (*Her*. 1043–4), Orestes thanks sweet slumber for making him forget his (*Or*. 213). These differences are related to the different nature of the two heroes' madness. Heracles' is a one-time attack to which a heavy sleep puts as violent an end. Hurled against him by a goddess, his baneful unconscious state prepares for a recognition that ruins his life. In contrast, Orestes' sleep, natural and restful, gives him reprieve from a lasting and known madness. In that it relieves him from a chronic illness, it is nearer to Philoctetes'.[92]

Philoctetes, though, looks ahead upon awakening, while Orestes cannot. Both heroes counter worries that they might be dead (see *Or.* 209–10) by stirring immediately after those worries are voiced. But Philoctetes' first word is 'light': the light of life and hope for the life he has not had. Philoctetes is happy to see his friends by him and looks forward to his departure. Orestes' first words are 'sleep's dear spell'. He looks backward, to the oblivious slumber that has left him, and is happy not because he is alive but because he has been drowned in sleep after six days of frenzy.

Those six days are in the prequel of the drama. While Philoctetes and Heracles doze off during the course of the plot, Orestes is already unconscious when the play begins. Together with his identity, the placement of his sleep harks back to *Eumenides*. Some fifty years after the production of that play Euripides echoes and distorts features of its opening scene:[93] the Erinyes' victim is asleep, not the Erinyes; Orestes is tended like a baby, not instructed by a god; whereas Clytemnestra rouses the Erinyes, Electra seeks to keep Orestes asleep; he awakens, soon to be pursued by the Erinyes, who in Aeschylus awaken to pursue him.[94] Euripides' reworking of Aeschylus also showcases one of his own play's thematic kernels: Apollo's reproachable aloofness from the murderer he has unjustly ordered to kill his mother (419–20). In *Eumenides* the Erinyes' sleep comes from Apollo, the protector of Orestes; in *Orestes* the Erinyes spare their target only when his 'wandering frenzy' (327) leaves him. Apollo does not check their pursuit.

Orestes' sleep lasts longer than the Furies' in Aeschylus. While they are shown onstage at the end of the first part of the prologue, which is spoken by the Pythia and serves to prepare the audience for their appearance, Orestes is sleeping onstage from the first word of the prologue, and while they awaken to sing the parodos, Orestes keeps slumbering until the end of the parodos. Spanning over 210 lines, this sleep covers the longest dramatic time in extant tragedy. Is there any point to its duration?

As in the other cases, the sleep scene is designed to build up tension. The length of Orestes' slumber thickens the suspense by allowing a progressive narrowing of focus on him and his unconscious state. Electra draws attention to Orestes as early as line 35. More verbal pointers keep his presence before the spectators' eyes throughout her dialogue with Helen (74, 84, 88, 131), but the first proper mention of his sleep occurs only at the approach of the women of the chorus, which causes Electra to fear lest he awaken: 'Soon they will rouse him, who is at peace, from slumber. And they will make my eyes melt away with tears, when I see him raving' (133–5). During the song that accompanies the chorus' tiptoed dance, Orestes' sleep is forefront. Electra's urgings to hush sounds and lighten steps keep the audience's attention steadily focused on it, until it becomes the almost exclusive subject of the song: 'At last he fell asleep and lies' (149); 'You will ruin me,[95] if you drive sleep, the sweetest boon, from his eyelids' (158–9); 'You see? He stirs under his cloak!–Your outcry broke his slumber!' (165–6); 'I thought he was sleeping' (167); 'He slumbers' (174); 'Night, who give sleep to much-travailed mortals, come!' (176–8); 'Will you grant him the grace of peaceful slumber?' (184–5) And the last remark before Orestes recovers consciousness: 'Watch [...] lest your brother here have died unawares, for I do not like his extreme relaxation'. The first comments on Orestes' sleep, by Electra, suggest that he might awaken mad; the last one, by the chorus, that he might not awaken at all. The cloak that shrouds him (166) keeps the audience in the dark as to his condition.[96]

A third possibility further increases the suspense: Orestes might awaken cured of his madness.[97] In the prologue Electra does not say that Orestes is accustomed to sleep after a paroxysm, but that 'at times, covered in his cloak, when his body finds relief from his illness, he weeps, in possession of reason, and at times he jumps and runs from his bed' (42–5). Her words, 'At last he fell asleep and lies', strengthen the impression that this is the first time that a restful slumber has quieted Orestes' madness: for good?

Orestes' warm praise of sleep and his emphasis on its healing powers push forward the possibility that his madness might indeed be a thing of the past, inviting the audience to go along with Electra's suggestion that he has never experienced the 'sweetest boon' of sleep before and to think that his slumber is not a lull, like Philoctetes', but a definitive cure for his disease. Of course this is not true, for Orestes suffers an attack of madness soon after he awakens. Thus, his lasting sleep has the dramatic function of mystifying the audience.

The protracted scene is also thematically significant. As is often noted, it builds a unity with the celebrated scene of madness that follows it, after which Electra leaves the stage for the first time, ending the first episode. What has happened so far is superfluous for the unfolding of the plot. Orestes' unconscious state, his attack of madness and Helen's brief appearance do not feed into the action proper, which begins with Menelaus' entrance and the second episode. The preceding sequence forms an independent whole, the purpose of which is to isolate Orestes and Electra in their mutual love and show the intimacy of their affection.[98] Front stage is the focal point of her nurturing love: his bed, where her movements, gestures, words and worries are directed. She has lost sleep to watch over him: 'And I, sleepless, sit near a wretched corpse' (83). She does not abandon her post (93), raises him from bed to lay him down again, and again raises him. After his attack of madness, he returns her care by urging her to rest from her ever-wakeful watch: 'Lie down and give slumber to your sleepless eyes, take food and wash your body' (302–3). She reluctantly agrees and exits.

Orestes' exhortation effects a departure that is necessary to redistribute the actors.[99] Sending someone off to sleep is a handy way of changing the cast of characters, as we know from the *Odyssey*. Orestes' words, however, are not just expedient: they have a deeper meaning, for they show how much he cares for his only friend. And on the point of leaving, she demonstrates a like affection by asking him to lie down and stay in bed (311–3). A focus on sleep marks out the independent whole that begins with Orestes slumbering under Electra's watchful eye and ends with Electra sent off to rest by the caring Orestes and urging him to stay in bed. The role of sleep as crystallizer of the intense bond between brother and sister is thus reflected in the dramatic movement.[100]

Cyclops

In Euripides' satyr drama, the sleeping Cyclops is not on stage, but he is repeatedly brought before the imagination of the audience. Euripides' Odysseus shows that he has read the *Odyssey*, as it were, when he imagines that the Cyclops, 'relaxed in sleep, soon [...] will thrust pieces of flesh out of his shameless mouth' (592). As one critic puts it, 'the *prediction* derives from the *description* at *Od*. 9. 372–4'.[101] Another signal of the *Odyssey*'s influence is the added emphasis on the potency of the wine that causes the Cyclops' sleep. While in Homer only the wine is 'unmixed' (205), in the play 'unmixed' modifies the wine (149) as well as the Cyclops' pleasure in drinking it (576) and the slumber it will hopefully cause (602).

To adapt the epic narrative to the stage, Euripides had to change the time of the Cyclops' sleep: not at night, as in Homer, but in the hottest hour (542). This change accords with the dramatic 'one day rule', which compelled the playwright to compress the three days and two nights of the Homeric episode. Euripides did not handle the compression well, for the play begins close to sunset, when the sheep return to their folds, but then the clock turns illogically backwards.[102]

The dramatic medium, however, allows Euripides to enliven the movement of the epic narrative by grafting elements of tragic sleep scenes onto it. His episode shares a major structural feature with them: one party silences another to keep the sleeper from awakening. The hushing voice is Odysseus, and the noisy one the chorus:

> –Silence, by the gods, you beasts! Be quiet, fastening your lips together! I don't allow any of you to breathe, blink or cough, so that the pest might not awaken until the sight of the Cyclops' eye will be rooted out by fire.
> –We are silent, holding our breath with our jaws.
>
> (624–9)

The placement of Odysseus' exhortation in the dramatic sequence suggests Neoptolemus' hushing of the chorus as the closest parallel, for in both instances the call for silence marks the beginning of a new episode. More details single out *Philoctetes* for comparison. Both sleep incidents contain a prayer to Hypnos, and his hoped-for help is couched in similar word patterns, featuring an adjective, a verb (the same) and a dative: 'Come unmixed to the beast (ἄκρατος ἐλθὲ θηρὶ)' (*Cycl.* 602) and 'Come for us, gently breathing (εὐαὴς ἡμῖν ἔλθοις)' (*Phil.* 829). The prayer in the satyr play dispels the ambivalent role of Hypnos in the tragedy by asking the god only to harm the sleeper. Hypnos will not spread any light but is 'the offspring of black Night' (601): a dark force of destruction.[103] Finally, in both plays sleep is described as it comes upon its target.

As noted above, Philoctetes lets his head droop when slumber first seizes him. This emphasis on sleep's gradual arrival, I have suggested, underscores its pivotal role. In the satyr drama the thematic importance of sleep is likewise prefaced by repeated mentions of its coming. Though Odysseus does not point to the Cyclops' drooping head or closing eyes, because the ogre is offstage, he time and again directs the audience's attention to the imminence of his drunken slumber (454, 574, 591–2). These numerous parallels might suggest that Euripides had *Philoctetes* in mind.[104]

Euripides' episode, though, bears strong marks of its ironic author. It spoofs dramatic conventions and counters the audience's expectations by its development. Odysseus enters to tell the satyrs that they should have kept their mouth shut to avoid awakening the monster, that is, they should not have been doing what a chorus normally does when left alone on stage: singing.[105] Furthermore, Odysseus urges the chorus to follow him inside the cave to help with the blinding, playing against the audience's likely assumption that it has already occurred.[106] Though he had made it abundantly clear that he needed the satyrs to proceed, during his absence we are led to discount the prospect of their participation by their song, which sounds like a running commentary on the blinding presumably taking place offstage: '*Soon* he will lose his eyesight by fire; *already* the brand lies carbonized in the embers' (610–5). After this song we expect Odysseus to enter and say 'Blinding accomplished' and the Cyclops to scream and appear soon thereafter (as he does at 663). But the song was a red herring and the Cyclops, unlike any tragic character, keeps sleeping through another episode.

PART THREE: SLEEP AND SLEEPLESSNESS ON A STARRY NIGHT

Iphigenia in Aulis

Some fifty years after *Agamemnon*, Athenians watched another scene of sleeplessness at the beginning of *Iphigenia in Aulis*. The scene's kernel is a dialogue between Agamemnon and the loyal servant with whom he shares his sorrows. The nocturnal setting is clearly marked by a number of pointers in the conversation: Sirius is moving past the Pleiades, which are still in the middle of the sky (6–8); all is silent (9–11) and quiet (14); the watches do not stir (15); Agamemnon has a lamp (34) and has been writing a letter 'at night' (109).[107] These particulars have the dramaturgic function of inculcating into the spectators' minds that the play begins before sunrise, even though their eyes are seeing the sun. *Iphigenia* shows greater attentiveness than *Agamemnon* to visualizing the invisible darkness, suggesting that in the course of the century audiences had grown more resistant to unrealistic scenographies.[108]

Agamemnon acts the sleepless character in a lonely vigil. We have met him in this role already in *Iliad* 10, where helpless despair keeps him awake while the other warriors 'were sleeping all night'. But the tragic Agamemnon's anxiety is set off against the repose not only of other humans ('Why do you move restlessly outside the tent, king Agamemnon? It is still quiet here in Aulis, the walls' watchers are not astir yet' [12–5]), but also of animals and natural elements: 'The birds and the sea make no sound; the silence of the winds holds Euripus here' (9–11). This mention of the stillness of nature intensifies Agamemnon's quandary by further isolating him from his surroundings. In *Iliad* 10 he is not alone: his brother shares his sleeplessness and instantly joins him, unbidden. In *Iphigenia* Agamemnon has no friend in his brother or in any other king. The general nocturnal quiet brings out his lonely agony.

The nocturnal quiet also carries sinister overtones. The calmness of the sea and of the winds is ultimately the reason that Agamemnon cannot sleep, the cause of the detention of the ships and of his own tragedy. And in the middle of the sky shines a harbinger of destruction: Sirius, ominously close to the Pleiades, the Doves (πελειάδες). In the words of one critic, the star 'sounds like a portent of danger [...] its nearness to the Pleiades figuring the threat to the dove-like Iphigenia'.[109] The starry night forebodes the very disaster Agamemnon is trying to prevent by means of the letter, which the servant is summoned to deliver instantly and without stopping: '–Go, hurry your steps, do not yield even a little to old age! –I hurry, king. –Do not sit by the woodland's springs, or give in to slumber's magic!' (140–2) Agamemnon's sleepless planning and his sleep-depriving order will not change the course of events, which are taking shape in the sky over his planning head.

An allusion to another Homeric episode furthers the association between Agamemnon's sleeplessness and his impotence. While he is doing and undoing his writing, he 'pours down a blossoming tear' (θαλερὸν κατὰ δάκρυ χέων, 39–40). This is an epic phrase. We are sent back to the beginning of *Iliad* 9, where Agamemnon also 'pours a tear' (δάκρυ χέων) before addressing the assembled warriors (14). The Homeric incipit, like the tragic one, is nocturnal; both times a distressed Agamemnon summons another party to share his plans; in both cases the plan is one of withdrawal, from the war (in the *Iliad*) or from the sacrifice that will make the war possible (in Euripides). And both plans meet with instant opposition.

Rhesus

Rhesus unfolds entirely at night. This setting disturbed Wilamowitz, who took it as sufficient evidence that the tragedy could not be by Euripides.[110] Recent critics do not share the German scholar's uneasiness, but on the contrary appreciate the ingeniousness with which the playwright has taken advantage of the unusual setting. In addition to being demanded by the received myth of Rhesus' death, the nocturnal sky effectively plays into two of the main themes of the tragedy: the illusory transience of hope, symbolized by flashes of light cloaked in darkness, and the failure of humans to understand reality, to 'see' clearly.[111] Darkness is particularly meaningful for the stage action in the sequence featuring Odysseus, which hinges on the association of night with duplicity.[112]

The dramatist makes every possible effort to remind the audience that it is night. He found an inspiring source for this project in the Homeric episode on which the play is based, the spying mission in *Iliad* 10, which points up its nocturnal setting not only by telling the time ('the third part of the night', 10. 253) but also by exploiting the keenness of hearing, sharper in the dark. Odysseus and Diomedes hear the scream of the heron sent by Athena, which they cannot see (10. 256), and Nestor becomes hopeful that the two are returning when he hears the din of galloping horses (10. 535).[113] The stage, though, allows the imagination less freedom than the narrative medium; hence, *Rhesus* multiplies references to stars, darkness, beds, sleep and the failure to see. These hammer the invisible nocturnal scenario into the spectators' minds.[114]

References to sleep, however, are not mere cues offered to help the audience 'see' the night, but are as significant as night itself, for the patent reason that Rhesus dies in his slumber. This is of course true in Homer's account as well, but the main heroes there are Odysseus and Diomedes, and Rhesus' death occupies only a small portion of the narrative. His sleep and sleeping quarters accordingly receive attention only when Odysseus and Diomedes are on their way to find him (*Il.* 10. 464) and then kill him (471, 474). In the play, by contrast, Rhesus is the tragic protagonist and his death the climax. References to sleep and wakefulness are therefore strewn throughout the action.

While the corresponding sequence in Homer, the section that leads to Rhesus' death, begins with an assembly of the Trojans (*Il.* 10. 299–301), the play opens with a wake-up call, when the watchmen who constitute the chorus rouse Hector. The scene harks back to an episode earlier in *Iliad* 10, the awakening of Nestor by Agamemnon.[115] Hector's sleep allows the watchmen to explain that the Greeks are making fires, which Hector could not have noticed because he was resting in his tent. His relaxed slumber also conveys his assurance. The audience will contrast the Greek leader in the epic, insomniac and despondent, with the Trojan one in the play, who is sleeping soundly like the epic

Nestor. While Agamemnon restlessly worries about the Trojan fires, Hector is unaware of the Greek ones, and when told about them, he overconfidently takes them to mean that the enemy are planning to flee.

Hector proposes a call to arms that will awaken the entire host: 'We must give orders to the army, very quickly, to take hold of their weapons and stop slumbering' (70–1). Aeneas' restraining advice persuades him to drop his plan and instead send a spy, Dolon, to the Greek camp, while the others will enjoy an unbroken slumber: 'But let us allow the army to rest by the shields and sleep' (123–4); 'Go, make the allies sleep. Perhaps the army is astir, hearing of our nocturnal counsel' (138–9). The audience will notice that Hector had suggested a course of action that would have prevented disaster, and will take his decision to send a spy and allow the other warriors to stay asleep as a foreshadowing of the catastrophe to come, an unwitting intimation of the vital – in the literal sense – importance of wakefulness.[116] In Homer there is no such intimation, for the Trojans do not even consider mobilizing the entire army but only sending a spy mission, which allows the allies to keep on sleeping.

When Rhesus enters, Hector accuses him of being late. He fires back: 'I did not slumber in my gilded palace but I know the frozen blasts that press hard on the Thracian sea and the Paeonian country, and I have suffered without sleeping in these military garments' (439–42). His defence puts sleep front stage and proves that the play's emphasis on it is not solely dictated by the need to provide verbal scenographies, for here sleep is in a narrative of past events. Rhesus' self-portrait as an ever wakeful, enduring warrior rings chillingly ironic, because his only action in the play is to be instantly dispatched to rest:[117] forever.

After Rhesus has exited and the play has reached its midpoint, at the waning of night the watchmen sing a song in which, in addition to noting the approach of sunrise, they express their desire to be relieved of their guard duties and of their tiredness: 'Sleep charms my eyes, for it comes sweetest to the eyelids before dawn' (554–6). The watchmen's longing for sweet slumber marks out this song as unusual, for a song describing the coming of dawn typically gives impulse to the resumption of activity.[118] Their somnolence looks ahead, to the play's climax. In the words of one critic, 'our thoughts are on Rhesus, who, as we know from the final lines of the preceding scene, must by now be sleeping most soundly and sweetly, never to awaken from his sleep of death'.[119]

The second part of the play, like the first, starts around Hector's bed. The Trojan leader survives simply because Odysseus does not find him there (574–6). This is another clear projection forward, for Rhesus will die because, unlike Hector, he is found slumbering in his bed. Athena's instructions to Odysseus single out the bed as the locus of action. She does not say 'spare Hector and kill Rhesus' but 'leave Hector's bed' (605–6), and she answers Odysseus' question, 'where are the other's [Rhesus'] sleeping quarters?' with, 'Hector has assigned him sleeping quarters outside the ranks, until night gives place to daylight' (611 and 614–5). In the string of events Athena's role corresponds to Dolon's in the *Iliad*, because both inform Odysseus about Rhesus.[120] But Athena puts emphasis on beds and sleeping arrangements, whereas Dolon only says that the allies are resting (*Il.* 10. 421). The goddess points to Rhesus' bivouac once again when she tells Paris: 'Hector is gone to assign sleeping quarters to the Thracian host' (*Rh.* 662).

Paris also makes his entrance to look for Hector in his bed: 'I call you, general and brother, Hector! Are you sleeping? Shouldn't you wake up?' (642–3) Paris' call repeats the watchmen's at the beginning. The audience will appreciate the detail that the two brothers have switched their traditional roles: while in Homer it is Hector who accuses Paris of sluggishness, now Paris rebukes Hector in a manner reminiscent of the dream that rouses Agamemnon in *Iliad* 2. Except that Hector is not slumbering, but has left to take Rhesus to his bivouac (662). Paris' unnecessary call, delivered in a commanding way uncharacteristic of him, is thus geared to draw the audience's attention to the dangers of sleep, while Hector's bed and his real or imagined slumber signpost the play's development, from the first scene, to the entrance of Odysseus and Diomedes, to that of Paris.

Hector's alleged sleep and his bed are front stage again at the next, climactic turn. After Rhesus' death his charioteer seeks the Trojan chief to break the news and asks: 'Where is Hector resting on his bed under his shield?' (739–40) The charioteer's account of

Rhesus' death expands on the Homeric narrative in many details, including mentions of sleep. Homer's 'they were slumbering, filled with tiredness' (*Il.* 10. 471) is echoed in 'we were slumbering, overcome by weariness' (*Rh.* 763–4). But in Homer there is only one other nondescript reference to the sleep of Rhesus (474), whereas the charioteer lingers over the army's 'heavy and bad sleep' (769) before recounting how he himself awoke with an anxious heart (770), only to doze off again when he felt there was no reason to worry: 'I went back to bed and was slumbering again' (779).

This return to sleep satisfies dramatic needs: it allows the nightmare that Rhesus has in the epic to be transferred to the narrator (780), who has to survive to give his report and cannot be omniscient.[121] But at the same time, the serenity with which he dozes again is yet another thematic pointer that emphasizes sleep's destructiveness. Rhesus does not even awaken once. His undisturbed repose conveys his relaxed overconfidence, a feature he shares, on a grander scale, with Hector, especially the Hector of the play's beginning, who is sleeping, unaware of his surroundings, while his watchmen sound the alarm.

Rhesus' overconfidence makes a tragically ironic appearance in his boastful claim that he needs only 'one day of sunlight' to kill the Greek host (447). Athena endorses his boast by explaining to Odysseus that Rhesus, 'should he survive this night', will indeed destroy the Greek army (600–2). The playwright drew from a tradition that contained this detail,[122] which is not in Homer, and adapted the tragic motif 'if he survives this day' (as in *Ajax*) to Rhesus' original predicament. His sleep on the night that decides whether he will live or die underscores his ignorance of the threads that govern his life.

PART FOUR: COMIC SLEEPERS AND COMIC VIGILS

Aristophanes

The comic playwright's handling of sleep is one way in which he makes fun of tragic and epic poetry. He mocks a large number of treatments of sleep and its disturbances in the two genres. Let us begin with this dialogue between Philocleon and the chorus of

Wasps: '–Who is it that keeps you inside and shuts you in? Speak, for you are talking to friends. –My son. But do not scream (μὴ βοᾶτε). He is there in front, snoozing. Lower your voice!' (334–7) This brief exchange parodies tragic sleep scenes,[123] testifying to their popularity. Aristophanes may be specifically targeting the scene in *Heracles*, as is strongly suggested by a phrase, μὴ βοᾶτε, which appears only there in extant tragedy. The allusion would be quite to the point, for Philocleon's passion for trials amounts to madness.[124]

His passion is also as sleep depriving as a lover's. *Wasps* draws a contrast between Philocleon's son and servants, who contentedly yield to their drowsiness,[125] and Philocleon, whom longing for the courthouse keeps awake: 'This is his love, to judge [...] He takes no sleep at night, not a bit. And if he dozes off for a second, his mind flies there at night, to the clepsydra' (89; 91–3); 'He yells asking for his shoes right after dinner, and when he gets there he sleeps in front of the court,[126] very early, sticking to the pillar like an oyster' (103–5). The lover of trials suffers from a mixture of sleeplessness and disturbed sleep, perhaps even sleepwalking.[127] Glued to the house of his beloved with his mind and body, he waits for dawn, whereas the trial-free lifestyle that his son urges him to embrace would allow him to rest soundly and comfortably for long hours (774–5).

The motif of sleep-chasing longing is caricatured again in *Lysistrata*. To rouse the women's sympathy for her plan, the heroine draws attention to their Penelope-like predicament: 'Don't you long for your children's fathers when they are away at war?' (99–100). To be sure, the sex strike will be taxing for the frustrated women, forced to lie in bed 'without a hard dick' (143), but it will cause their men to return their longing. When Lysistrata's fellows begin to falter, complaining of six sleepless nights of occupation (758–61), she equates their plight with that of their men: 'Perhaps you miss your husbands; but do you think they don't miss you? I know it well, they are spending tough nights (ἀργαλέας νύκτας)' (763–5). And she exhorts the women to be confident and hold on a little longer, for there is an oracle predicting victory.

Lysistrata's speech has a Homeric texture: ἀργαλέος is a markedly epic adjective, appearing as it does some 60 times in

Homer, as opposed to only eight in comedy and none in tragedy. Specifically, Lysistrata mimics Odysseus' address to the Greek warriors in *Iliad* 2, in which he shows appreciation for their distress, caused by a nine-year-long separation from their wives, yet urges them to be enduring and recalls Calchas' favourable prophecy. Lysistrata reworks the speech by stressing the men's desire for their faraway wives and by emphasizing the identical frustration of both. By attributing a longing that upsets sleep to the sexually starved men, she points up the effectiveness of the women's strike.

Lysistrata also mocks another wakeful figure typical of tragedy and epic: the ruler in the grip of anxious deliberation. The play begins with the heroine complaining that the women she has summoned are still dozing (14) while she has forsaken sleep to put together her plan: 'I have turned it this way and that for many wakeful nights' (26–7). Lysistrata is the protagonist of a lonely vigil, and it is her unsleeping thinking, like Zeus' or Oedipus', that launches the plot.

Two more plays feature lonely vigils. The motif clearly appealed to Aristophanes, possibly because its high register and the emotional intensity it conveys offered ready material for comic distortions. Seriousness is mocked and solemnity desecrated in the scene in *Thesmophoriazousae* in which Agathon's servant prays that nature would sleep, so that his master could compose undisturbed: 'May all the races of birds slumber, and the feet of the savage beasts that run in the woods not be loosened' (46–8). The prayer meets with a disrespectful interjection, βομβαλοβομβάξ, from Euripides' kinsman, and with more heavily profane rejoinders as the servant continues (50, 51, 57). Furthermore, nature's slumber would serve as backdrop not for some painful predicament, as in epic or tragic lonely vigils, but for a display of poetic hyper-cleverness (59–62).

Clouds begins with another lonely vigil. It is not dawn yet. Though the rooster has crowed, the day is slow to rise (3–4). The worried Strepsiades tosses and turns, considering how to deal with his debts, while his son Phidippides is deep in sleep, along with the house's servants. In this case the scene draws its comicality not so much from the activity of the wakeful party (Strepsiades is seriously beset by anxiety) as from its background:

instead of a silent night, the sleepers' bodily noises. Strepsiades notes that 'the servants are snoring' (5) and that 'this brave young man here does not stay up at night but farts, wrapped in five blankets' (8–10). Sleep talking crowns the scene, with Phidippides upbraiding a racehorse in his dream (25) and continuing to comment on the race until his father's complaints rouse him, but only briefly (35–8).

As in *Lysistrata*, unsleeping cogitation yields the core plot, prompting Strepsiades to seek out Socrates, from whom he can learn to cheat off his creditors. The plan, however, is not disclosed while Phidippides sleeps or when he awakens the first time, or even after he dozes off again. The first part of the scene revolves around Strepsiades' complaint of insomnia and its causes, and features the sleep-talking episode, while in the second, which begins with Phidippides' second snooze, he gives some background history. Before revealing the plan that he has conceived in his 'nightlong thinking' (75), he announces that he will call his son: 'But first I want to rouse him. How can I do it as gently as possible?' (78–9).

This call marks the launching of the action proper, whereas in the first eighty lines little happens. Strepsiades' vigil and his son's stubborn sleep have the dramatic function of delaying the plot's beginning to allow the spectators to settle down and stop talking. For the playwright needed to rouse the interest of a probably unruly audience before detailing the plot.[128] In *Clouds* the sleep-and-sleeplessness scene provides the entertainment that stirs the audience's attention, which Aristophanes finally summons with Strepsiades' wake-up call to his son.

A similar pattern appears in *Wasps*. Like *Clouds*, *Wasps* begins before sunrise.[129] Two servants are supposed to be on guard duty, but one is snoozing: '–Hey, wretched Xanthias, what is this? – I am teaching myself to end my nightlong watch' (1–2). The tragic figure of the sentinel longing to sleep (as in *Agamemnon* and *Rhesus*) is turned comical by the watchers' lack of vigilance and by the cause for their lethargy: drink. Copious imbibing has changed their watch into a revel, and it eventually compels them to doze off, lulled by the Phrygian Dionysus (9–10).

The sleepy servants spend the first 53 lines of the play shaking each other awake, faintly fighting against sleep's spell, nodding off (6–9),[130] recalling the recent attack of 'drowsy slumber' (11–2) and finally telling each other their dreams and exchanging a few political jokes: in other words, doing and saying nothing that is essentially related to the plot. During this time the audience will have settled down and got ready to listen to the announcement of the subject matter, which suddenly ends the servants' bantering (54). As in *Clouds*, the action proper begins with a movement from sleeping to waking, with Bledycleon shouting to the servants, 'are you dozing?', and them marking, 'he is getting up' (136–7).

Birds likewise exploits sleeping and waking in its opening scenes. Hoopoe is taking a siesta after a good meal when Euelpides and Pithetaerus find his residence (81–2). Awoken by his slave bird, he appears in his impressive apparel. Here the summons has the function of introducing not the core plot but a character crucial for its execution. The awakening call also portrays the life of the birds as one of quiet and leisure, just as life will be in the city that the two heroes are seeking: 'a soft blanket in which to curl up' (122). The birds eat and sleep well.

Hoopoe's wife, Nightingale, is also taking a nap. After hearing the brilliant plan that the two heroes have for a city of birds, Hoopoe rouses her, urging her to sing and convene the other birds: 'Now, my companion, cease from sleep and let out the strains of the sacred songs with which your divine mouth mourns Itys, much wept by you and me' (209–12). Again, this call is not designed to introduce the essentials of the plot; rather, it prepares for the music that is instantly heard off stage, which creates an expectation of the appearance of the birds that compose the chorus. Hoopoe awakens the music and the audience's attention to it, building momentum towards the chorus' climactic entry.

Wake-up calls play a greater role in Aristophanes' comedy than in tragedy, where there are only three,[131] all found in the *Oresteia* and *Rhesus*, in accordance with the thematic prominence of vigilance in those tragedies. This difference might be connected to the comic playwright's more overt effort to focus the audience's attention on the play's development. Though addressed to characters, the calls might have functioned like the written signs that ask modern audiences in movie theatres to turn off their cell phones after the sequence of commercials and previews, which, like the sleep scenes prior to the calls, will have allowed plenty of time to settle down.

The greater number of awakening calls in comedy is also due to register: they are too low level for tragedy, as are natural sleep, eating and drinking. Only the undignified and repulsive Erinyes are awoken onstage, while in the other two cases (Clytemnestra in *Agamemnon* and Hector in *Rhesus*) the call glosses over the homey reality of sleep by keeping it out of view. In contrast, the much smaller corpus of Aristophanic comedy features several snoozers kicked awake before the spectators' eyes.

This happens again in *Thesmophoriazousae*, which exploits sleeping and waking to concentrate the audience's attention on the final scene. The Scythian policeman who is guarding Euripides' kinsman dozes off at some point during the last choral ode, before Euripides makes his appearance in a procuress' dress, along with a hussy and a piper. Music and dance rouse the Scythian: 'What is this booming sound? Revellers (κῶμο) awaken me!' (1176) There follows the hilarious scene of Euripides' planned seduction of him (1172), which ushers the plot to its happy ending, allowing the kinsman to sneak out. Euripides could have rescued him on the sly while the guard was dozing. Instead, the Scythian is shaken out of his torpor to become the spectator, and soon the victim, of the play's last effervescent invention. Can we read in his awakening a metatheatrical reference to the power of comic wit and revelling (κῶμος) to keep the audience riveted to the performance until the play's very end?

Menander

In the remnants of Menander's plays, sleep is scantily represented. Drunken, snoring and farting snoozers are at variance with the sober restraint characteristic of his comedies. There is only one sleeper in them: Cnemon, the cantankerous old man. Sick from falling into a well, incapable even of standing on his feet, he 'slumbers, alone' (*Dys.* 893–5). While he lies helpless on a bed, his servants plan to steal his pots to make him pay for his boorish refusal to lend them any. But they will not just carry off his wares: they will force him to watch the scene and to be watched as he suffers his own demise. After dragging him out of his house and laying him on the ground asleep, one of the servants starts pounding on his door and shouting to musical accompaniment. The noise awakens the crippled man: 'I am done for! Alas!' (911).

The audience will instantly think of tragic episodes in which sleep builds towards a climax. Cnemon is relieving his pain through anaesthetic slumber, like Heracles in *Trachiniae* and, like him, he is carried onstage unconscious, by bearers who take care to walk on tiptoes: '–don't make noise! –I am not making noise!' (908) We are reminded of the muffling of sounds characteristic of all tragic sleep scenes.[132] Cnemon's servants, however, do not mean to protect the sleeper, but to guarantee the success of their revenge. While the healing slumber of a Heracles or an Orestes is watched apprehensively, with the hope that it will last indefinitely, Cnemon's is to last only as long as it allows the servants to set him in full view of his cherished door, to be violated pronto.[133] Unlike any tragic character, he is brutally awoken when his sleep is no longer needed.

Cnemon's slumber is not just instrumental to the servants' revenge; it is also an apt retribution for his constant claim that he could do without his fellow men. While he is unconscious, the self-sufficient misanthrope is at the mercy of others who take advantage of his lack of self-awareness to move him around: 'let us drag him out' (898); 'put him down here' (909). Helpless sleep completes Cnemon's defeat by nullifying his pretensions to self-reliance. He is still 'alone', but the adjective, in the emphatic position at the end of the line (893), connotes no longer autarchy but frailty and exposure.[134]

While Menander does little with sleep, he makes sleeplessness the protagonist of at least two sustained scenes, both in plays that became famous in antiquity.[135] Phidias, the hero of *Phasma*, suffers from chronic insomnia. His pedagogue lectures him:

When you complain of sleeplessness, what's really
Your [problem]? I'll tell you the cause. You stroll
[All round the market], come straight home when [legs]
Are weary, bathe in luxury. Then up you get
And [take a] pleasant [stroll. Your] life itself
[Is] sleep! So, finally, there's nothing wrong with you.
This [sickness] you've described is – well, [a] rather coarse

Expression comes to mind – forgive me, master –
The saying goes, you are so well off you don't
Have anywhere [to shit], I'd have you know![136]

In the servant's assessment, the condition that is upsetting his young master exists only in his imagination. If he is sick, it is from a life of luxury and excessive leisure, with no real, healthy problem ('nowhere to shit'). His insomnia is the outgrowth of waking sleep. The real cause of Phidias' condition, however, seems to have been his encounter with the Apparition that gives the comedy its title. In the play's prequel a woman, upon marrying, left the daughter she had had out of wedlock with foster parents who lived next door. So that she could continue to see her, the woman dug a hole in the wall connecting the two houses and decorated the area with sacred paraphernalia to make it look like a shrine and disguise the real reason for her frequent visits. One day Phidias approached the shrine and 'was startled and terrified by his first sight of the beautiful girl, thinking that he had seen a vision of some spirit'.[137] According to one reading, Phidias developed depression, and with it insomnia.[138] He was apparently cured by the discovery that the girl was real, which caused him to fall in love with her.

On another reading, though, love is not the remedy for but the cause of Phidias' insomnia.[139] The servant, to whom he has not confessed his passion, scolds him for idly imagining a disease that does not exist. But the disease is love. The dialogue gains in effectiveness if it assumes a gap of knowledge between the audience and the servant: while the servant, ignorant both of Phidias' predicament and of literary history, misreads his master's behaviour, the audience would promptly identify in it the typical symptoms of frustrated passion.[140] For love-induced sleeplessness was a familiar motif – familiar, above all, from the comic stage.[141] Plutarch recognizes in it a comic *topos* (*Mor.* 513E).[142]

Insomniac lovers, to be sure, are better represented in Roman comedy than in Greek, on account of the state of our evidence,[143] but Menander put on stage one of the best known of them in antiquity: Thrasonides, the soldier turned lover who opens *Misoumenos* in the middle of a wintry night by confiding his unhappiness to Night Itself:

O Night – for you have the largest share in sex
Of all the gods, and in your shades are spoken
Most words of love and thoughts charged with desire –
Have you seen any other man more racked
With misery? A lover more ill starred?
Now either at my own front door I stand,
Here in the alley, or I saunter up
And down, both ways [?], when I could lie asleep
Till now, when you, O Night, have nearly run
Half course, and clasp my love. She's in there – in
My house, I've got the chance, I want it just
As much as the most ardent lover – yet
I don't. . .I'd rather stand here shivering
Beneath a wintry sky – chatting to you![144]

Thrasonides behaves like the *exclusus amator* of Roman elegiac poetry. He enacts a *paraklausithyron* ('lament beside the closed door of the beloved'), pacing back and forth in front of the house where his girl is sleeping. This *paraklausithyron*, however, is peculiar, for it is not the girl that has shut out Thrasonides, but Thrasonides himself. As we learn subsequently, he had told her that he had to leave urgently in the middle of the night, to see somebody. The story was a lie meant to test her affection. If she loved him, she would beg for him to stay. But she did not, and he had to go. Menander handles a literary commonplace with sophisticated irony by turning the *paraklausithyron* into a self-inflicted accident,[145] and he gives the audience a cue to this novelty by having Thrasonides say that he is standing or walking outside while he could be sleeping with his beloved in his arms. How could the protagonist of a *paraklausithyron* in due form have that cosy option? Something must be amiss.

Menander's irony extends to the insomnia motif, which he highlights with marked emphasis. Thrasonides presents the alternative to his wandering at night as 'sleeping with the beloved', and his slave Getas, drawn on stage by his lament, addresses him with the question, 'why don't you sleep?' Faced with Thrasonides' self-absorption, which prevents him from hearing the question, he rephrases it as 'or are you slumbering? Wait, if you are awake and see me!' (21–2) Getas directs the audience's attention to his master's insomnia yet again when asked whether someone had ordered him to come out: 'Good heavens! No orders came from men asleep!' (26) This stress on Thrasonides' failure to find rest winks at the conventionality of the motif. The playwright's irony testifies to the readiness with which the audience could recognize the commonplace, which was soon to reach beyond literature and become a staple of magical spells.[146] A memorable specimen of the sleepless lover is the Medea of Apollonius' *Argonautica*, to which I now turn.

CHAPTER 4

APOLLONIUS OF RHODES' *ARGONAUTICA*

Skipping sleep

Time and again, as the Argo sails the seas, day turns into night and night into day. Apollonius meticulously records the movement of the sun that accompanies the movement of the Argo, matching the progress of the journey with the course of the day more precisely than the *Odyssey*. Here is a typical sequence:

> They ran past Meliboea [. . .] at dawn they at once saw Homole leaning on the sea and passed it by [. . .] and all night they ran with the blowing wind. And at dawn Athos, the Thracian mountain, appeared to the travellers [. . .] On that day, until darkness came, a very strong wind blew for them, and the sails of the ship were spread. But the wind dropped with the setting of the sun.
>
> (1. 592–5; 600–7)

Sleep, however, does not normally break up the journey as it does in the *Odyssey*.[1] Though Apollonius assumes that the Argonauts rest – in narrating a pause towards the middle of their return journey, he notes that they 'slept as before' (4. 884) – he is not interested in marking routine episodes of nightly sleep. The Argo likes to sail swiftly and continuously, as in the passage quoted above.[2] In another instance, Apollonius pairs the ship's swift travel with an image that suggests stopping for the night and sleeping, creating recherché dissonance. After two days of fast-paced sailing,

> When the sun sank and the star rose that bids the shepherds fold and brings rest to the weary ploughmen, then the wind dropped in the black night, and they furled the sails and took down the long mast, and applied their strength to the well-polished oars, all night and through the day, and another night following that day.
>
> (4. 1629–35)

The time notation 'when the sun sank and the star rose [...] that brings rest to the weary ploughmen' does not introduce a cessation of activity, as readers might expect, but the dropping of the wind and thus more wearying activity, effort at the oars. The wind rests like the shepherds and the ploughmen, but not so the Argonauts, who keep travelling and exerting themselves, that night and another day and night.

Even when the Argo stops, activity continues and often replaces sleep where Homeric narrative would record it. This happens, for example, in the episode of Hylas' disappearance. At the end of another stretch of swift navigation following the movement of the sun (1. 1151: 'at dawn'; 1160: 'toward evening'), the Argonauts reach Cius at the time when a ploughman 'gladly goes to his hut, longing for a meal' (l. 1173). The local inhabitants offer them sheep and wine in plenty, and they get ready to eat:

> Some brought firewood, others collected and brought leaves in abundance to spread beds; others were twirling around sticks to make fire, and others still were mixing wine in bowls and preparing a feast after sacrificing to Apollo of Disembarkation in the night.
>
> (1. 1182–6)

This sequence is geared to create the expectation of a description of feasting followed by sleep. Yet there is no mention of either. Instead, the night is full of activity, with Heracles seeking wood to make an oar, Hylas leaving to fetch water and disappearing in the spring, and then Heracles despairing. We are repeatedly reminded that it is night while all this is happening: around the spring to which Hylas comes, nymphs are celebrating Artemis in dance and song 'at night' (1. 1225); Hylas' beauty is enhanced by the moonlight (1231–2); Heracles is returning to the ship 'through the darkness' (1255) when he finds out that Hylas has vanished. The characters' movements fill the nocturnal scene. There is no break from action all the way till dawn, when the Argonauts depart (1273–5) and soon realize, enlightened by the spreading brightness of the new day, that they have left Heracles behind.[3]

How would Homer have narrated the beginning of this sequence? How would he have switched from the group's preparations for feasting to Heracles' departure? I imagine with something like this: 'The heroes collected leaves for beds, made ready a meal and ate, then lay down. But Heracles left'. The narrator would have had the other Argonauts finish their meal and go to sleep before moving on to Heracles' activity. This manner of shifting concentration from one set of characters to another by putting the first to sleep is recurrent in the *Odyssey*.[4] Apollonius instead leaves the preparations for the meal behind without drawing the curtain on the scene, and seamlessly moves the narrative focus from one active theatre to another (Heracles' departure), to yet another (Hylas' disappearance) and back again (Heracles' return and despair), until dawn 'quickly' comes (1. 1273), and with it more activity.

To be sure, the recurrence of sleep in Homeric narrative transitions is consistent with an arrangement of actions in chronological succession rather than in synchrony: 'Penelope went to sleep, and then Telemachus...' Unlike Homer, Apollonius seeks to convey the simultaneity of actions. So in the Hylas episode, the Argonauts' preparations for dinner, Heracles' departure to seek wood and Hylas' to seek water are imagined to happen at more or less the same time. There is no narrative need to close one episode in order to introduce another. Sleep in one theatre, however, could also be happening simultaneously with activity in another: 'They went to lie down, and while they were resting, Heracles left'. This is not what Apollonius writes.

The un-Homeric scarcity of breaks for sleep is related to Apollonius' avoidance of 'typical scenes'.[5] Sleep scenes are left out more systematically than others, perhaps because even in Homer they tend to be brief (except for a few retiring scenes). In the formulaic sequence 'meal, sleep', the narrative of meal-making and even meal-taking is always the longer element. Accordingly, Apollonius shortens accounts of feasting and sacrificing and leaves out references to sleep. For instance, the meal and the conversation that the Argonauts enjoy with king Lycus are immediately followed by the coming of dawn: 'Thus all day long they amused themselves at the feast, but at dawn they went down to the ship' (2. 811–2). In Homer we would read: 'They prepared a meal, ate and drank to their hearts' content, and when darkness came they slept. But at dawn they went down to the ship'.

Apollonius even seems to advertise his rejection of sleep scenes by turning a sequence that, in Homer, would typically include sleep into one that emphatically excludes it. After their victory over the brute Amycus and his people, the Argonauts 'remained there through the night, healed the cuts of the wounded men and offered sacrifice to the immortals, making ready a big meal. And slumber did not seize (εἷλε) anyone by the mixing bowls and the burning victims' (2. 155–8). Instead of resting, the members of the crew put on wreaths and sing to the lyre of Orpheus until dawn, when they depart.

The aftermath of the Cyclops episode is the main subtext for this narrative: both scenes include a sacrifice and in both the victors sail off at dawn. The Argonauts, though, stay up all night, while Odysseus and his comrades get some rest (*Od.* 9. 559).[6] This difference has a thematic rationale, for Odysseus, unlike the Argonauts, had previously spent two sleepless nights, and the Argonauts, unlike Odysseus, have plenty of reasons to celebrate. But the difference is also one of narrative technique. Apollonius seems to be playing against the formulaic sequence 'evening meal, sleep', by changing it into 'evening meal, no sleep'. Given its context, the phrase 'slumber did not seize anyone' might surprise the reader, whose literary horizon of expectations rather calls for 'they all slumbered'. Though in Homer song and conversation can replace the nightly rest at the end of a meal, when this happens there is no mention of sleep in the negative, only a transition to those activities. Apollonius' manipulation of Homer goes further, for he chooses a verb, εἷλε ('seized'), which his predecessor never uses for sleep.[7]

By cutting out the formulaic repetitions of Homeric epic, and sleep scenes in particular, Apollonius tightens the pace of the journey and its narrative. Mentions of sleep would slow them down, as happens, for instance, in the Homeric account of Telemachus' journey to and from Sparta. Though fast paced, this journey also contains a leisurely pause:

> Telemachus mounted the car, took the reins in his hands and whipped [the horses] to start them, and they [he and Pisistratus] eagerly sped through the plain, and left the steep citadel of Pylus. All day long they shook the yoke they held around the horses' neck. And the sun sank and all the ways grew dark. They went to Pheres, to the house of Diocles [...] There they spent the night, and he gave them gifts of hospitality. But when early-born, rosy-fingered Dawn appeared, they yoked the horses and mounted the inlaid chariot.
>
> (*Od.* 3. 483–92)

The audience relaxes along with the travellers when the sun goes down and they stop for the night. (I imagine that during longer narratives of sleep taking, such as retiring scenes, audience members could get up and fetch a cup of wine.)[8] In contrast, as one critic puts it, 'the reader may never relax with Apollonius at the helm',[9] just as his characters are not regularly said to stop and rest. Sleep does not give rhythm to either activity or the narration of it, but is confined to slow-paced sections of the epic, to major episodes. And in those episodes, as we shall see presently, sleep does not mark endings but momentous beginnings.

Sleep and beginnings

On the eve of their departure from Iolcus the Argonauts sacrifice to Apollo, and Idmon prophesies the happy outcome of the expedition. The heavy drinking that accompanies the feast causes a quarrel to break out between Idmon and the godless Idas. Orpheus sings to pacify the heroes, and there follows a scene in which sleep plays a role:

> He ended, and checked his lyre and his divine voice. But though he had ceased, they still were bending their heads forward, insatiably, with intent ears, quieted by the charm (κηληθμῷ) of the music. Such was the magic of the song he had left in them. Not long afterwards they mixed libations for Zeus, as is customary, poured them in a holy fashion upon the burning tongues, and took thought of sleep in the darkness. But when shining Dawn saw the steep peaks of Pelion with her bright eyes, and the quiet headlands were washed as the sea was ruffled by the wind, then Tiphys awoke. Straightaway he roused his comrades to go onboard and make ready the oars. And the harbour of Pagasae and the Pelian Argo itself uttered a loud cry, eager to leave.
>
> (1. 512–25)

This episode is rich in Homeric allusions. The closest parallel is the narrative of the evening that ends with sleep in Nestor's palace.[10] In both episodes the night's rest is preceded by a ritual libation on the tongues of the sacrificial victims (see *Od.* 3. 332), and one character is singled out as he rises at dawn the next day (Nestor at *Od.* 3. 405). Apollonius reworks the Homeric narrative into a much more condensed account: seven lines from the mixing of the wine to Tiphys' awakening, as opposed to the 73 that cover the same sequence in the *Odyssey*. The shorter narrative de-emphasizes sleep. In Homer, Athena's pronouncement that it is time to go to bed (*Od.* 3. 334) initiates an exchange of speeches, which continues after her departure and ends with a full-scale retiring scene, but Apollonius takes no time to describe the preparations for the night's rest. And sleep happens quickly, 'not long' after Orpheus' song.

This almost instant slumber plays against another Homeric episode: Odysseus' nocturnal storytelling in Scheria. Orpheus' song and Odysseus' narrative have identical effects on their audiences, for both performances, and they alone in extant Greek literature, exert the magical charm called κηληθμός.[11] The Phaeacians, though, cannot get enough of Odysseus' bewitching narrative, and stay up all night to hear it. Apollonius replaces their wakefulness with the Argonauts' immediate sleep.

The replacement is not just a playful move in Apollonius' dialogue with his illustrious predecessor; it is also crafted to highlight the pacifying power of Orpheus' song, whose soothing effects call to mind those of the song that fosters the gods' rest at the end of *Iliad* 1. In Homer, though, sleep does not come to the human leaders.[12] The mention of collective slumber at the opening of *Iliad* 2 is not designed to reflect any harmony achieved in the camp, but to underscore Zeus' isolated sleeplessness, which qualifies even the pacification with which the divine feast ends. By contrast, the music in the *Argonautica* works out a definitive and general appeasement.

Apollonius might be further playing against Homer by replacing the wakeful planning of one individual, which begins the core action in both the *Iliad* and the *Odyssey*, with the sleep of a group. While Zeus' or Telemachus' sleeplessness brings out the secretive nature of their actions as well as the existence of tensions among main parties, the shared slumber that precedes the departure of the Argo reflects the crew's esprit de corps, stronger than any clash of personalities.[13] In this respect the eve of the Argo's departure contrasts also with the eve of the return journey from Troy, as narrated by Nestor in the *Odyssey*. For that night contains a quarrel but no sleep. A dispute breaks out between Agamemnon and Menelaus, the host is divided and they 'spent the night pondering harsh thoughts against each other' (3. 151). In Apollonius' episode, serene repose occupies the place of this angry brooding.

The end of the scene rather recalls another Homeric feast that also includes musical accompaniment and winds down in sleep: the sacrifice and song with which the Achaean envoys to Chryses appease Apollo after returning Chryseis in *Iliad* 1. This narrative is yet another probable subtext for Apollonius'. The prayer and the sacrifice take place a similar number of lines from the beginning of each poem and honour the same god, Apollo;[14] in both episodes, sleep follows the celebration (see *Il.* 1. 475–9) and the Achaean envoys are united in their mission and rest together before leaving, just like the Argonauts.

The two episodes, however, differ in the narrative function of sleep: while in Homer it *ends* an enterprise, in Apollonius it *prepares* for one. In both, to be sure, sleep builds a transition between feasting on one day and leaving on the next. But in Homer it is strongly closural, for it puts the seal on the successful outcome of the expedition. The return journey is brief and uneventful, and it meets with no welcome upon arrival (the envoys do not report but disperse to their tents: *Il.* 1. 487). In stark contrast, sleep in the *Argonautica* introduces the climactic departure for which the narrative has long been whetting the readers' appetites.

As one critic notes, Apollonius' epic keeps postponing its beginning: 'The entire book [1], and especially its first half, has the rhythm of a wild repetition compulsion that asks insistently, "have we begun yet?" and answers with the same insistence, "just one more thing before we can begin".'[15] Readers have been tricked into expecting the Argo to take off a day and at least 200 lines earlier, when Jason announces that everything is ready for departure and urges the crew to leave (1. 332–5).[16] But instead of setting sails right then, he goes on to ask who the leader should be – a surprising question, since we have assumed all along that it would be Jason.[17] After he is elected, he instantly renews his exhortation to leave: 'Let our paths no longer be hindered, as before' (1. 352), but in the same breath he also says he has to wait for his servants, and asks his comrades to build an altar and sacrifice to Apollo, again pushing off the departure. The Argonauts do give their action a forward-looking movement before building the altar, by dragging the ship to sea and assigning rowers to each bench, but that movement is soon stopped by the dispute that breaks out after Idmon's prophecy. Sleep at last wipes away those hindrances to the launching of the ship, preparing for the long-awaited departure.

The scholiasts inform us that in an earlier version of the epic[18] Apollonius did not end the celebrations prior to the departure with evening and rest. The feast was entirely diurnal and consisted solely of a sacrifice to Apollo.[19] The additions of the ritual 'night cap' (the libation on the tongues of the victims) and of sleep function as a *rallentando*, from which the departure receives added impetus. The musical vocabulary is warranted by the narrative, for the launching of the Argo has not only a dazzling gleam (1. 544–6), but also a ringing echo. The harbour and the ship cry loudly, urging the crew to go. The combination of light and sounds gives the Argo a vigorous thrust forward.[20]

The other occurrences of sleep are governed by a similar pattern: rather than ending a leg of the journey, the night's rest propels travellers and readers towards the resumption of it. In this respect the *Argonautica* differs greatly from Homeric epic, especially the *Odyssey,* where sleep marks endings at least as much as beginnings. To be sure, it is never entirely final in Homer either. Though sleep can have the last word in a work of literature (as it cannot in life), the only Greek narrative that exploits this possibility is Plato's *Symposium.*[21] In all the others sleep looks ahead, to the awakening that is narrated next. But in the *Odyssey* a sweet slumber rewards Odysseus' superhuman efforts, such as the slaughter or his journey to Scheria. In those episodes sleep is (also) closural, as it is when Odysseus and his comrades escape from the Cyclops' cave, reunite with their fellows, feast and rest. In several other instances, it is closural at least in the sense that it takes place upon arrival, as soon as the travellers touch the shore. Conversely, in the *Argonautica* this happens only for one leg of the journey.[22] But four others begin shortly or immediately after a night's rest. Apollonius engages with Homer not only by dramatically reducing the instances of sleep but also by changing its function in the narrative sequence.

Another stretch of swift navigation comes to a halt at night. The Argonauts land on an island (1. 953), where they receive hospitality from the local inhabitants, the Doliones (1. 968–9). They share food, drink and conversation in the manner of the *Odyssey*: except that there is no mention of sleep but only of the rising of dawn (1. 985). The Argonauts depart, but contrary winds drive them back to the island, where they are detained for twelve days by fierce winds. Sleep moves to the foreground in the account of the last night of the storm:

> And the following night all the other leaders, overcome by sleep, were taking their rest during the last part of the night. But Acastus and Mopsus [...] were watching over their deep slumber. And over the blond head of Aeson's son flew a halcyon prophesying with high-pitched voice the ceasing of the stormy winds. And Mopsus understood [...]

> He shook Jason who slept wrapped in soft fleeces, and awoke him straightaway.
>
> (1. 1080–91)

The emphasis on the heavy slumber that engulfs the Argonauts rings true to life, for after twelve days of forced detention under the sway of blasting winds, depression and fatigue quite naturally set in.[23] Odysseus' nap on Trinacria might likewise have been caused by idleness and tiring winds (he withdraws to a protected area before dozing off). As far as narrative function, however, the Apollonian sleep episode recalls the one on the night before the initial departure: it restarts the journey at a critical juncture. This time the Argonauts' slumber allows the forced inactivity to end by carrying an omen that provides guidance. At dawn the next day (1. 1151) the wind ceases and they row onwards.

This sleep scene shares another feature with the one that precedes the launching of the Argo: in both, a character rouses the others from slumber. Just as Tiphys awakes all the Argonauts, Mopsus shakes Jason, who then rouses his companions (1. 1114). This slow, progressive awakening builds momentum towards the beginning of the new day. And the wakeful character is never Jason. To start the Argo on its way is the helmsman: the one in charge of the ship, whose orders everyone, including Jason, follows. And to deliver the Argonauts from their imprisonment on the island of the Doliones is a seer, who watches over the head of sleeping Jason. Though the scene singles Jason out as the privileged dedicatee of the omen, he is an unconscious beneficiary of the heavens' favours, which would come to naught if the vigilant seer did not mark them and read them. While the halcyon flies and sings, Jason slumbers in comfort. His inclusion among the sleepers and the emphasis, unique in the epic, on the soft bedding on which he lies point up his gentle and non-martial nature but also his weak presence as leader.[24]

In a third scene Jason is again one of the sleepers, and is not even cast in a privileged role. The episode occurs the second evening of the Argonauts' stay with the seer Phineus. On the previous night he delivers his guiding prophecy, almost until dawn. And the next day, when the sun goes down,

> Quickly they invoked Apollo lord of prophecy and sacrificed by the hearth as the day was just sinking. And the younger fellows prepared a pleasant meal. Having feasted well, they went to sleep, some by the ship's hawsers, others gathered there in the house. And at dawn the Etesian winds were blasting, which blow equally over every land by the command of Zeus.
>
> (2. 493–9)

Apollonius has written this sequence with the Circe episode in mind: like the seer, the sorceress provides guidance to the travellers,[25] and both revelations last all night, with the sun rising as soon as the telling is over in Homer (*Od.* 10. 541; 12. 142) and shortly thereafter in Apollonius (2. 449–50). Circe, though, both times instructs Odysseus alone while his comrades are resting. At dawn he awakens them and shares her commands – but not every detail, for he withholds information that would dampen their courage (*Od.* 12. 223–5). Phineus, on the other hand, delivers his prophecy to all the Argonauts, who stay up all night together (2. 308) and learn the same things. Jason does not know more than his men. This configuration is once again in keeping with the nature of his leadership, weaker than Odysseus', and with the more strongly communal, democratic ethos of the Argonautic enterprise.[26]

A second difference in the treatment of sleep concerns its place in the narrative sequence. On both visits to Circe Odysseus and his crew rest upon arriving on her island (*Od.* 10. 142–3; 12. 7), but the Argonauts do so not on their first night at Phineus', only on their second. While Odysseus departs as soon as the night in which he is given instructions is over, the Argonauts wait one more day, in which not much happens, and go to sleep at the end of that day. As the result of this lingering, sleep looks to their departure, the re-launching of the journey that will put an end to the delay and mark a new beginning. All the more so because Phineus' prophecy harks back to Idmon's, though it guides the Argonauts on their journey in far more detail than Idmon's had done. For readers sensitized to this reference, the Argonauts' sleep naturally conjures up their slumber on the night that precedes the ship's initial launching.

But this time the Argo cannot leave because of the Etesian winds. Apollonius deflates the expectations created by his own narrative use of sleep before a climactic departure. And he deflates those expectations slowly, keeping the readers in suspense as to what will happen. He does not say straightaway 'the winds detained the heroes' but only 'the winds were blasting'; he goes on to tell the story of Cyrene, and only then does he make it explicit that the Argonauts are detained (2. 528–9). The effect of this unexpected and anticlimactic detention is to build up momentum towards the upcoming high point of the journey to Colchis: the passage through the Clashing Rocks.

The last sleep scene on the outward journey occurs at yet another crucial juncture, on the island of Ares, which Phineus marks as an important station, where the Argonauts will meet with 'unspeakable help' (2. 388–9, recalled at 2. 1091–2, upon their landing on the island). The help turns out to come from the band of Phrixus' sons, who have been driven to the island by a storm. At sunrise the rain stops and the two groups meet. Jason explains the purpose of his journey and secures the band's assistance.

> Thus they were speaking to each other in turn until, satisfied again with a feast, they went to sleep. And at dawn, when they awoke, a gentle breeze was blowing. They raised the sails, which billowed in the wind's gusts. And quickly they left behind the island of Ares.
>
> (2. 1226–30)

Sleep again occurs before a departure, not upon landing. Though realistically motivated by the pouring rain and presumably by a lack of shelter,[27] the absence of sleep upon arrival might catch the attention of the reader who is following the narrative with two Homeric subtexts in mind: the episodes of the Cyclops and of Circe.[28] Like Odysseus' landing on those two occasions, the arrival of the sons of Phrixus on Ares' island has an uncanny aura. They are the victims of a storm that darkens the sky at night (2. 1102–5; 2. 1120): Zeus' doing (2. 1098), just as their idea to hold on to a beam when their ship collapses is the gods' doing (2. 1110). Zeus is again behind the stopping of the rain at sunrise

(2. 1120–1). This emphasis on the divine hand directing the journey has counterparts in the two Homeric episodes. Both times Odysseus lands 'guided by a god' (*Od.* 9. 142; 10. 141), the first during a black, moonless night (9. 143–5), as gloomy as the night that forces the sons of Phrixus ashore. Odysseus and his crew, though, rest as soon as they touch soil (9. 150–1; 10. 142–3). By contrast, in Apollonius sleep does not come until the second evening, after the encounter that provides the Argonauts with guides for the last leg of their crossing to Colchis.

'Sleep before departure' is a signature of the outward journey, for it occurs only once on the way back to Greece.[29] This difference seems connected to the rhythm of the narrative. In the account of the journey out, fast-paced stretches of narrative, coinciding with legs of the navigation, alternate with slow-paced ones, coinciding with stops[30] – and sleep, as we have seen, restarts the engine – whereas the account of the return has a generally fast pace. This concentration of sleep scenes along the journey to Colchis could also be related to its orderly trajectory, its directionality,[31] which differentiates it from the chaotic, unpredictable course of the navigation back to Greece. Sleep is a narrative pointer to some major advancement along the mapped route.

Dawn at endings

Consonant with Apollonius' use of sleep to mark beginnings is his use of dawn as an ending. Dawn rises to close each of the two books that narrate the journey to Colchis. Thus, Book 1: 'A strong wind blew, bearing the ship all day and all night. But the wind had dropped completely when dawn rose. They noticed a coastline jutting out into a gulf, very wide to look at, and by rowing they put in at sunrise' (1358–*fin.*). And thus Book 2: 'And on Argus' advice Jason ordered them to draw the ship onshore for anchorage, into a shady marsh. It was near their course, and there they camped in the darkness. And not long thereafter they were pleased to see dawn appear' (1281–*fin.*).[32]

Like sleep before departure, dawn at book endings looks ahead, to the continuation of the journey and of its narrative. Dawn and ending are at odds, and this would be so especially for readers contemporaneous with Apollonius, who would have regulated their lives according to the course of the sun and among whose literary references Homeric epic would have featured prominently. For in Homer dawn is a marker of beginnings. There are only two books that conclude with sunrise, and even in those the morning light is dimmed, as it were. The first is *Odyssey* 2, with the last line following Telemachus' ship as it makes its way 'all night and through dawn'.[33] But the sun does not quite rise until the opening of the next book, when 'leaving the beautiful mere, [it] sprang up to the brazen sky, to shine for the immortals and for mortal men'. The new day brightens with the new book.[34] In the second instance the light of the day that rises as the book draws to a close likewise remains subdued. Dawn appears when Telemachus lands on Ithaca towards the end of *Odyssey* 15 (495–6). The book, though, is not over yet. Its final lines recount Telemachus' arrival at Eumaeus' sty, where the swineherd 'used to sleep'. The reference to sleep, even as a habit, not actual fact, turns off the sunlight. So much so that dawn is mentioned again in the second line of the following book. The repetition is both a narrative tag ('dawn as beginning') and a way of restarting the day that did not quite start at the end of the previous book.

For Apollonius to be reworking formal Homeric book endings, the book divisions must be earlier than Aristarchus (*c.*217–145). This cannot be proven,[35] but we can at least say that in Books 1 and 2 Apollonius reworks Homeric endings at large, whether of books or of major portions of narrative, by replacing nightfall with dawn. The pattern could be meant to point up the orientation of the journey, eastbound. For the Argo sails towards Apollo, moving closer and closer to sunrise.[36] When the travellers reach their most important stops – that is, at the end of each book – they would be looking eastward and the readers would be reminded of the direction of the journey by the presence of dawn.

Whatever the case, the rising of the sun gives the narrative a forward impulse by eliding the break between books. Like chapter endings, book endings are 'a kind of white space',[37] offering readers an opportunity to pause. Sleep is a natural punctuating device because it invites readers to put the book aside and rest along with the characters.[38] Dawn has the opposite effect: it invites readers to stay awake with the characters and turn the page.

The forward thrust is particularly vigorous at the end of Book 2, where the quickness with which dawn comes and the Argonauts' desire for it supersede the sketched movement towards closure initiated when they moor the ship and make camp. This time they reach their destination at night (see also 2. 1260) and perhaps even set out to sleep. But the rising of the sun looks ahead. We think of *Iliad* 8, which ends stretching towards the next day and the next book: 'the horses [...] standing by the chariots, were waiting for Dawn of the beautiful throne' (564–*fin.*). The Homeric ending, though, is nocturnal, and dawn remains in the future, while in Apollonius it materializes before the travellers' expectant eyes in the last line, a line full of light, starting as it does with 'dawn' and closing with its appearing (ἐφαάνθη). The light that shines upon their arrival turns the end of their outward journey into the beginning of their Colchian adventure, towards which they and the readers have been sailing. Dawn rises to conclude the first two books perhaps because the journey they narrate is eastbound, but certainly because the emotional energy of all the participants in them, characters and readers alike, has constantly been projected onward, towards the central and culminating section of the epic, Jason's contest. As we shall see, night falls at the end of the next book, when the contest is over.

Sleepless Medea

Dawn rises again to mark the resolution of the quandary that tortures Medea after she promises to help her sister's sons and betray her father, for love of Jason (3. 823–4). As her love and her urgency to act on it take clearer and clearer shape in her mind, her intensifying anguish is reflected in increasing sleep disorders, which culminate in the fateful night in which she decides to meet Jason and save him. The simile that describes the flaring up of her passion as an 'awakening' (ἀνεγρόμενον) flame that grows 'wondrously great' (3. 294–5) pointedly foreshadows her sleep troubles.

The first of the three monologues in which Medea's love makes itself heard occurs while she is unremarkably awake during the daytime, but her mind is not in a full state of wakefulness. She has dreamlike impressions – of Jason's appearance, his movements, his voice – (3. 453–8) and has run after him 'creeping like a dream' (3. 446–7): following him unsteadily, trying to seize him as dreamers try to seize a vision.[39] Her words run ahead of her awareness of her state. The stranger, she says, could be 'the most prominent' of heroes or 'the worst' (in this telling order); she sends him to his doom yet wishes he could escape and return to his home, and she wants him to know that she would not rejoice in his calamity (3. 464–70).

When Medea speaks to herself again, both the intensity of her passion and her awareness of it have increased.[40] The double escalation is conveyed by the volume of her voice: 'mournful' in the first monologue (3. 463),[41] it is now 'thick' or 'packed' (ἀδινὴ φωνή, 3. 635). In that louder voice she admits to the emotion mounting in her heart (3. 638), though the stirring does not yet have a name, and she decides to banish shame (3. 641) and approach her sister. Sleep disturbances have developed along with her passion and her realization of its force. For the second monologue does not follow the dreamlike fantasies of a waking mind but an actual dream, in which she chooses the stranger over her parents, causing their scream and her own frightened awakening. The vision, fashioned by her love, breaks with sudden force (3. 617) into a bout of daytime sleep: 'But a deep slumber relieved the maiden from her distress, as she leaned back (ἀνακλινθεῖσαν) on the couch' (3. 616–7).

The description of Medea's nap contains a direct allusion to the Homeric episode in which 'Athena had another thought and poured sweet slumber over Icarius' daughter. She leaned back (ἀνακλινθεῖσα) and slept' (*Od.* 18. 187–9), allowing the goddess to beautify her unawares.[42] Apollonius has taken pains to make sure that the reader does not miss the reference, not only by repeating 'she leaned back' but also by reproducing the exact rhythm of the Homeric verse that contains the verb: a sequence of dactyl-spondee-dactyl-dactyl-dactyl-trochee, with a pause in the middle of the third foot, after 'leaning back' – right at the moment when the character has adopted a sleeping position.[43]

Apollonius, however, reworks the Homeric episode in two significant respects. First, he makes his scene the theatre of a purely human drama. While Penelope's slumber is forced on her by Athena and serves to advance her plan, Medea's comes from her own love-induced exhaustion. Sleep, as thick (ἀδινός, 3. 616) as the voice that breaks it (ἀδινή, 3. 635), signals the intensification of her passion and breeds a dream that reveals its intensity to her and pushes her, if not to admit her true motives, at least to act on them.[44]

Second, Apollonius changes the quality of the heroine's sleep and of her experience of it. Penelope's 'sweet slumber', the 'soft κῶμα' that she regrets to relinquish (*Od.* 18. 201), is turned into a much troubled sleep, the carrier of a dream that shakes Medea awake with its loud voice. Apollonius intends the reader to appreciate his reworking of Homer also in this detail, because he moulds the phrase 'and with their scream sleep left her' (τὴν δ' ὕπνος ἅμα κλαγγῇ μεθέηκεν, 3. 632) on the corresponding Homeric phrase 'and sweet sleep left her' (τὴν δὲ γλυκὺς ὕπνος ἀνῆκε, *Od.* 18. 199), which describes Penelope's awakening when her maids come and speak. Penelope is roused by an external noise, Medea by an aggressive voice from within.

This episode opens the book's central section, which ends with Medea's momentous decision.[45] The narrator gives the sleep scene the force of a beginning by leaving Medea behind after her first monologue, 'her mind anguished with cares' (3. 471), and switching to the Argonauts' actions. When he comes back to her, she is napping. Her deep slumber soothes the same cares she was displaying in her first monologue; but the break between the two episodes isolates her sleep from that speech, casting the scene as the beginning of a new act, during which she never leaves the stage.

The second, climactic part of this act begins in reverse, not with Medea's sleep but with her sleeplessness. 'Shame' and 'terrible fear' seize her after her sister departs with her promise of help. The light falls entirely on her, as she is left alone on stage (742) to fight her psychomachy. Her struggle is set off against the deepening quiet of the surroundings:

Νὺξ μὲν ἔπειτ' ἐπὶ γαῖαν ἄγεν κνέφας, οἱ δ' ἐνὶ πόντῳ
ναυτίλοι εἰς Ἑλίκην τε καὶ ἀστέρας Ὠρίωνος
ἔδρακον ἐκ νηῶν, ὕπνοιο δὲ καί τις ὁδίτης

ἤδη καὶ πυλαωρὸς ἐέλδετο, καί τινα παίδων
μητέρα τεθνεώτων ἀδινὸν περὶ κῶμ' ἐκάλυπτεν,
οὐδὲ κυνῶν ὑλακὴ ἔτ' ἀνὰ πτόλιν, οὐ θρόος ἦεν
ἠχήεις, σιγὴ δὲ μελαινομένην ἔχεν ὄρφνην·
ἀλλὰ μάλ' οὐ Μήδειαν ἐπὶ γλυκερὸς λάβεν ὕπνος.
πολλὰ γὰρ Αἰσονίδαο πόθῳ μελεδήματ' ἔγειρεν.

(3. 744–52)

Then night was drawing darkness over the earth. At sea the sailors looked toward Helice and the stars of Orion from their ships. Now the traveller and the doorkeeper longed for sleep, and a deep slumber engulfed the mother whose children were dead. There was no more barking of dogs in the city, no sound of voices. Silence held the blackening darkness. But sweet slumber did not seize Medea at all, for many cares kept her awake in her longing for Jason.

Nightfall marks the beginning of the new episode, un-Homerically. In Homer the coming of darkness does not restart the action but slows it down, preparing for sleep or the interruption of activity.[46] The Homeric episodes parallel in content to Apollonius', the lonely vigils of Zeus, Agamemnon, Achilles and Hermes in the *Iliad*, are not framed by nightfall, which, if mentioned, occurs earlier (*Il.* 1. 605), but by a background of sleepers. By adding the temporal notation, Apollonius further isolates the sleepless character from the general nocturnal quiet.

Poetry other than Homeric epic might have provided Apollonius with models. A picture of cosmic peace opens a celebrated poem by Alcman: 'They sleep, mountain peaks and ravines, headlands and brooks, and all the races of walking creatures that the black earth breeds, the beasts of the mountains and the tribes of bees, and the monsters in the depths of the seething sea, they sleep, too, the races of long-winged birds'.[47] We do not know, however, how the poem continued: with a desperate cry of love, set against the calmness of nature? With the narrative of a nocturnal ritual? With a description of more calmness?[48] In extant poetry, a contrast between the quiet of night and the disquiet of an individual appears for the first time in another much admired fragment, by Sappho: 'The moon has set, and the Pleiades. It is midnight, the hour goes by, and I lie alone'.[49] Two more instances of the motif are the incipit of *Iphigenia in Aulis*[50] and of Theocritus' *Idyll* 2, where the forlorn Simaetha laments that sea and winds are hushed, but not her heart (37–8). Apollonius, however, paints night and sleep descending with original strokes: he does not produce a static picture, like those in the other poems, but a dynamic description, which captures the deepening darkness and with it the spreading of sleep.[51]

The sky is getting darker when the sailors look up to the stars: it is dusk and they are awake and still at sea. It must be later when the traveller and the doorkeeper long for rest, later still when the deepest slumber enwraps the grieving mother and finally the dead of night when not even dogs bark, no sound is heard. Sleep's increasing hold, along with the advance of night, is conveyed by metrical patterns. While the introductory verse has an entirely dactylic rhythm, which renders the regular and continuous descent of darkness, the first mention of slumber coincides with two spondees (ἐκ νηῶν, ὕπν-), suggesting its weight.[52] Its overpowering force is tangibly felt in line 750, when it has fully spread. For the line not only begins with a double spondee (ἠχήεις, σι-) but also has a soothing, monotonous dominance of e-sounds.[53]

To this dynamic description of sleep and silence gradually taking hold of the city, Medea's mounting restlessness responds, in counterpoint.[54] While the nap in which she plunged earlier 'relieved her from her distress' (ἐξ ἀχέων [...] κατελώφεεν, 3, 616), now she would not find 'relief from distress' (οὐ [...] λωφήσειν ἀχέων, 3. 783–4), even if Jason should die. While her daytime nap was ἀδινός (3. 616), the adjective now describes the deep slumber that seizes the bereaved mother, whereas Medea herself cannot sleep. She is worse off than she was a few hours earlier, worse too than a woman whose children are dead. This reference to the grieving mother, in addition to being ominously suggestive of Medea's tragic future,[55] foregrounds her solitude by implying that no god is by her side to help her and lull her to sleep. The mother's heavy slumber might be of divine origin, for κῶμα normally denotes an unnatural loss of consciousness, and in Homer, Apollonius' inspiration here (κῶμ' ἐκάλυπτεν at 3. 748 is Homeric), it always comes from a deity.[56] The gods have deserted Medea and left her alone to wrestle with her sleep-depriving love.[57]

Apollonius adds depth to the traditional motif of love-induced insomnia not only by making Medea's the culmination of a series of gradually worsening sleep disturbances but also by devoting to her condition an extended narrative that allows him to follow the mounting of her passion with great detail. As the hours advance from dusk to black darkness and the living beings go from wakeful to drowsy, from drowsy to dead asleep, so does Medea's anguish develop but it follows a reverse course, causing her to express her despair more and more loudly as the night goes on. At first her suffering is soundless. It has strong physical manifestations – she is shaken, her heart whirls around, tears fall, pain courses through her head – but it remains inside (3. 761), wordless. Soon, though, it takes a voice: 'Then sitting down she was of two minds and spoke' (3. 770). 'Speaking' here is φωνέω, which puts forward the sonorous substance of words. Their volume increases later in the monologue, when Medea imagines out loud, in a string of alliterations that convey her screaming, that 'every city [...] will cry out (πόλις περὶ πᾶσα βοήσει) my doom' (3. 792–3),[58] and, in another phrase packed with sound duplications, that the Colchian women will revile her everywhere (3. 794). Along with the volume of her voice grows her realization of the cause and nature of her suffering. Her readiness to give up her modesty (3. 785) spells out her awareness of her love, which she now calls 'raging passion' (3. 797): she has come a long way from suffering inside from a condition with no name.

The full acknowledgement of her passion instantly pushes Medea to think of death. But suddenly fear prevents her from swallowing the drug, and with her resolve to live begins the scene's last movement. The transition is emphatically marked, by a 'but' (3. 809), the abruptness of Medea's turnaround (*ibid.*) and the silence into which she plunges after feeling the horror of death: 'Speechlessness held her for a long time, and around her appeared all the sweet cares of life' (3. 811–2). Medea's silence introduces the new development, which takes her back to light and life. She now wants the night, which culminated in her resolution to die 'this very night', as she said (3. 799), to be over.[59] To see the sun seems to her sweeter than ever (3. 815–6):

> She longed for the rising dawn to appear quickly, so that she could give him the charms as she had agreed, and meet him face to face. Often she loosened the bolts of her door, watching for the gleam, and welcome to her did the Early-Born shed her light, and everyone began to stir through the city.
>
> (3. 819–24)

The scene that begins with the falling of darkness and sleep ends with the return of light and activity. The new day sets in gradually, as did night and slumber. The eyes that watch dawn's coming, however, are not the poet's but Medea's, who yearns for it and cannot wait. Her emotions and movements are the lenses through which the reader sees the first rays of the sun. By adopting Medea's perspective, Apollonius points up the strong synergy between her desire for dawn and its rising. While the sleep that takes hold of the city contrasts with her unsleeping heart, the return of light matches her return to life.

In the dressing scene that follows, where Medea prepares herself to meet Jason, her recovered taste for life gives rise to a luminosity contest between the new day and her apparel: 'As soon as the maiden saw dawn appearing, she bound her blond tresses with her hands [...] She made her skin shine with nectar-sweet ointment [...] and threw over her divinely beautiful head a veil with a silver gleam' (3. 828–35). Of course, radiance is the goal of every beauty treatment, for light is beauty. But light is also life. Medea continues her rebirth by adding the shimmer of adornment to the light of day she so longed for.

The protracted wakeful night thus ends in a strong movement forward, from darkness to light, from the thought of death to an impulse towards life, from the bedroom to the threshold[60] and finally to the road that will take Medea to Jason. The sleeplessness scene provides an impetus to action that makes it crucial to the development of the plot, for it decides no less than the outcome of the epic's climax.

Medea's restlessness is not just caused by the conflict between her passion and her honour and modesty. She is facing an even harder struggle, since love is forcing her to betray her family to help the man she loves. In terms of plot development her decision is as consequential as those made by sleepless characters in Homeric epic. Though prey to love, Medea is pondering in her heart, like the Homeric Zeus, Agamemnon and Hermes.

The style and diction of this scene indeed demonstrate that Apollonius has the wakeful Agamemnon in mind.[61] Compare, in Homer, 'But sweet slumber was not holding Atreus' son Agamemnon [...] who was pondering many things in his heart' (ἀλλ' οὐκ Ἀτρεΐδην Ἀγαμέμνονα [...]/ ὕπνος ἔχε γλυκερὸς πολλὰ φρεσὶν ὁρμαίνοντα, *Il.* 10. 3–4) and, in Apollonius, 'But sweet slumber did not seize Medea at all, for many cares kept her awake in her longing for Jason' (ἀλλὰ μάλ' οὐ Μήδειαν ἐπὶ γλυκερὸς λάβεν ὕπνος./ πολλὰ γὰρ Αἰσονίδαο πόθῳ μελεδήματ' ἔγειρεν, 3. 751–2).

Both descriptions begin with the same contrasting particle ('but'), followed by a negative ('not'), then with a mention of the sleepless character in the accusative and of 'sweet slumber' in the nominative, with a verb separating noun and adjective (though in reversed order), and finally with 'many' things or cares as the content of both characters' worrying. Among these correspondences, Apollonius' choice of γλυκερός ('sweet') to modify sleep is particularly telling, for it is not his normal practice to borrow Homeric epithets for sleep.[62] In addition, the throbbing of Medea's heart prompts a light simile (3. 756–8), as does the groaning of Agamemnon's (*Il.* 10. 5–10), and both hearts are stirred 'often' (*Il.* 10. 9; Ap. Rhod. 3. 755). Though this kind of transposition of epic language, imagery and motifs from the domain of war to that of love is characteristic of amatory poetry in general,[63] the reference to Agamemnon here has more specific implications: it brings to the fore the deliberative quality of Medea's distress, the outcome of which will be as decisive as the pondering of the epic leader. While Apollonius does not imitate Homer in breaking up the narrative with sleep, he does follow his predecessor in enhancing the momentousness of a development by prefacing it with a sleepless night.

Medea's insomnia is far more consequential than Agamemnon's, for it determines who will win the contest. In this respect it rather recalls Zeus'. Though Medea is forced by Hera to fall in love in order to become instrumental to Jason's victory, she is the one who decides to be cast in that role, choosing as she does to follow the demands of passion.[64] In this respect she is, like the sleepless Zeus, the main deviser of the epic's plot. The comparison between the lovesick heroine and the omnipotent god is not as counterintuitive as it might seem, for the sorceress Medea has powers that allow her to control events in an almost godlike fashion.[65] The plot-devising function of Medea's sleepless night is emphasized by its placement in the epic: almost exactly at the centre of the central book (darkness descends at line 744 in a book of 1,407 lines). The script Medea conceives in that night includes a night without sleep for Jason, to which I now turn.

Wakeful Jason

After Medea and Jason part in the afternoon (3. 1143), the narrative dwells on her elation as she returns to the palace and then on her tearful and speechless anguish (3. 1152–62); afterwards, it leaves her behind to follow him. It is evening when he reaches his comrades. Activity stops: 'rejoicing, they peacefully took it easy[66] at the time when the darkness of night stayed them, but at dawn they sent two men [...] to Aeetes' (3. 1171–4). Apollonius once again refuses to offer a strong caesura, choosing not to break up the narrative by means of sleep; instead, he sketches a scene of meaningless inactivity and instantly replaces the unremarkable night with the resumption of activity along with the rising of the new day.

The day dawns suddenly in the last word of a line (3. 1172), in an un-Homeric fashion.[67] In Homer references to sunrise can end a line, but when this happens the description is more leisurely (it can even fill the entire verse, as in 'but when early-born, rosy-fingered Dawn appeared').[68] I have found only one instance vaguely comparable to the Apollonian line: 'I [Odysseus] lay down content, and there appeared [...] Dawn' (*Od.* 14. 502). As in the *Argonautica*, some kind of rest is followed by the abrupt coming of sunrise at the end of the verse. But in the Homeric passage dawn, exceptionally, does not look to the next day but ends Odysseus' story of a night's activity. After 'Dawn' we put a period. In Apollonius dawn ends a line but begins a new sentence along with a new day, and it introduces a new action that begins in the next line. In that it marks multiple beginnings, it builds momentum after the meaningless night.[69]

This uneventful night after which dawn quickly rises looks to the future, to the eve of the contest, the crucial night which Jason spends performing the ritual that Medea prescribes to him. She instructs him to wait until midnight and bathe in the river 'apart from the others' (3. 1029–31) before proceeding. This time the coming of darkness is in the forefront of the narrative:

> The sun was setting far under the black earth, beyond the furthest mountains of the western Ethiopians, and Night was putting the yoke on her horses. And the heroes made ready their beds by the hawsers. But Jason, as soon as the bright stars of Helice, the Bear, went down, and the sky grew perfectly still (πανεύκηλος) down from the heavens, went to a deserted spot, like a stealthy thief, with everything he needed.
>
> (3. 1191–8)

The description of night falling, and the contrast between the wakeful individual and the world around him, which is growing quiet and preparing for sleep, hark back to the scene of Medea's sleeplessness. The world's deepening calmness is again felt in the rhythm, for the moment when the air becomes completely still, πανεύκηλος, coincides with a spondee in an otherwise dactylic line (1196). The sleeping counterpart to Jason, however, is not an entire city (animals included) as in Medea's case, but the other Argonauts.[70] This difference is related not only to the location of the Argonauts' camp outside the city but also to the nature and purpose of Jason's wakefulness. Whereas the all-inclusive background to Medea's points up the intensity of her pain and passion – everyone is enwrapped in slumber and everything is quiet but her – the frame of Jason's singles him out as the leader who prepares for his mission while his comrades prepare for rest. In other words, the background to Jason's night-time action puts him in the spotlight and underscores his emergence as the main protagonist of the Argonautic enterprise. For the first time he separates himself from his comrades by staying awake.

If we believe Jason, this is not true, for he claims he has been losing sleep since the beginning of the journey. After passing through the Clashing Rocks, the helmsman Tiphys reassures him that the rest of the navigation to Colchis will be easy. Jason objects that danger still lurks. And

> When the day is over, I always spend the night groaning, considering all things, ever since first you gathered for my sake. You talk with ease, being concerned only about your life. I do not have the slightest worry about mine, but fear for this one and that one alike, and for you and the other fellows.
>
> (2. 631–6)

Jason casts himself as a concerned and wakeful leader, following in the footsteps of Agamemnon in *Iliad* 10 and of figures of drama such as Aristophanes' Lysistrata, Aeschylus' Eteocles and Sophocles' Oedipus. The last of these speaks words very similar to Jason's: 'Your suffering touches yourself alone and no one else, whereas my heart groans for the city, myself and you alike. You are not awakening one caught by sleep. Know it well, I have wept much and tried many paths in the wanderings of my mind' (*OT* 62–6).[71]

But is Jason's account of his sleep-deprived nights credible? The speech in which he mentions them presents a notorious critical problem. Its introduction, 'he replied with honeyed words' (2. 621), suggests that it is designed to be effective, not truthful.[72] And the comment that rounds it off, 'thus he said, making trial of the leaders' (2. 638), spells out its goal, which is not to tell the truth but to test the heroes' disposition. Readers will instantly think of Agamemnon's deceptive speech in *Iliad* 2, in which he feigns discouragement in order to test the morale of the army.[73] Both Agamemnon and Jason have been heartened, and both publicly reject or ignore the heartening message. Since Agamemnon is in fact filled with self-confidence, readers might attribute the same quality to Jason and call him a liar.

Further to suggest that Jason is lying is his quick turnaround. When he finishes his speech, his comrades 'shouted with heartening words. And his heart rejoiced at their calling, and he spoke straight among them: "my friends, my courage grows from your valour"' (2. 638–41). As soon as he obtains the crew's support, Jason recovers his good spirits. In retrospect his speech seems geared to elicit confirmation of his leadership from his comrades, to reinforce their solidarity with him and his goals.[74]

It might be objected that Jason's speech is in keeping with his characterization, for depression is very natural to him. What he says about himself is consistent with what we know of him.[75] In fact, the authorial narrative backs his self-presentation by portraying him as anxious and dejected even before the departure: 'Aeson's son was brooding over everything, looking depressed' (1. 460–1). Yet, Jason's self-styling as a wakeful leader worn out by cares finds no backing in the authorial narrative; on the contrary, it is jarringly at odds with what we know of his sleep patterns.

In sharp contrast with Odysseus, Jason is consistently asleep along with his companions, until the night before the contest. During the journey to Colchis he sleeps as soundly as, or even more soundly than his fellows. To begin with, Tiphys, Jason's direct addressee, rouses him and the other Argonauts on the morning of their departure. Their allegedly over-worried leader is not the first to see the sun, and Tiphys must play Odysseus' leading role in comparable scenes of awakening.[76] And again, after twelve days of forced detention on the island of the Doliones, two Argonauts shake Jason out of the cosy bed on which he slumbers under their watchful eye (1. 1080–91, above). This episode blatantly disproves Jason's claim to sleepless worrying. A leader as concerned with everyone's welfare as he claims to be would be expected to show at least some signs of distress under those circumstances! Apollonius writes the scene as a lonely vigil in the Homeric mould: 'All the other leaders, overcome by sleep (δεδμημένοι ὕπνῳ), were taking their rest [...] but Acastus and Mopsus [...] were watching over their deep slumber'. The phrase 'overcome by sleep' suggests that Apollonius is alluding specifically to the lonely vigils of Agamemnon and Hermes (see *Il.* 10. 2 and 24. 678), two exceedingly concerned personages. By drawing attention to those scenes, Apollonius invites the reader to contrast the placidly slumbering Jason with those wakeful Homeric figures.

On the eve of the contest Jason comes closer to the wakeful characters of Homeric epic. He is engaged in a *vigilia in armis*,[77] which connects him with Odysseus and especially Telemachus. Like him, Jason leaves home and mother behind to go through a test of manhood.[78] By comparing him to a thief, Apollonius evokes coming-of-age rituals, which prescribed stealing and wakefulness.[79]

The parallel with Telemachus and Odysseus, however, brings out the peculiar nature of Jason's *vigilia in armis* – and of his heroism. Telemachus thinks of his journey and of his father, who spends his own sleepless night pondering how to pursue his revenge. Neither of them is acting out a script written by an all-knowing helper. Though Telemachus does follow Athena's recommendations in his decision to leave home, the goddess does not tell him how exactly he has to go about every detail of his journey, but only that he has to leave and where and with what purpose he must go. When she again appears to him to speed up his return, he is already awake and absorbed in thought. In contrast, Jason forsakes sleep to implement the detailed instructions given him by an almost divine figure and he knows that they will guarantee his success. His wakeful night is not, like Telemachus', characterized by a growing awareness of his responsibilities, nor is it, like Odysseus', filled with efforts to make decisions and cope with adversity. Instead, it is devoted to a ritual of anointment, of consecration to the goddess of magic under the supervision of Medea the plot deviser, who has herself spent the previous night sleeplessly, in excruciating deliberation. Though Jason's wakefulness singles him out from the other Argonauts, the rationale for it spells out his dependency on Medea for his success.[80]

The appearance of dawn is yet another feature that recalls the scene of Medea's sleeplessness, on account of both its narrative function (in both cases sunrise coincides with the end not only of night but also of nightlong activity) and the manner of its description. Compare: 'welcome to her did the Early-Born shed her light (βάλε φέγγος Ἠριγενής)' (3. 823–4) and 'already Dawn, the early-born (ἠριγενής), rose and shed light (φόως [...] βάλεν) over the snowy Caucasus' (3. 1223–4).[81]

The echo, however, underscores the different ways Jason and Medea relate to the rising of dawn. For Medea it is a return to life, a rebirth. Hence, the sunlight is seen through her eyes and the description of its coming, 'welcome to her', stresses her emotional involvement in it. Medea remains at the centre of the following scene, where dawn shines in her features and garments as she prepares to meet the man she loves. Conversely, dawn does not rise for Jason or through his eyes but 'over the snowy Caucasus'. It marks a switch in narrative focus from Jason's night to Aeetes' morning, as he prepares to watch the contest.

Aeetes dons his armour in a scene that corresponds to Medea's dressing scene. Both take place at sunrise after a night filled with activity, and both put the dazzling shine of the characters' apparel front stage. Aeetes wears a golden helmet 'that gleams like the round light of the sun when it first rises from Ocean' (3. 1229–30). His entrance at dawn and the brightness of his armour, rivalling the sunlight, match not only his solar ancestry,[82] but also the pomp and circumstance of his appearance, like a god (Poseidon) who is going to watch rites in his honour (3. 1240–5). The sun shines for him and through him, whereas Jason disappears with the darkness to which his victory belongs. His stealthy action, like that of a thief clad 'in a dark robe' (3. 1204–5), is incompatible with light. Thus, he exits when night turns into day.

Nessun dorma

The course of the sun measures the progression of Jason's contest: its second half (the killing of the warriors born of the dragon's teeth) begins when three parts of the day have elapsed and 'tired labourers' long to unyoke the oxen (3. 1341–2). The time notation, couched in imagery that fits Jason's work as ploughman and also sets off his heroic tirelessness (3. 1343) against the labourers' fatigue,[83] creates the expectation that his labour will be completed. And in fact it is finished at nightfall, and with nightfall ends the epic's culminating book: 'The day set, and Jason's contest (ἄεθλος) was completed.' The nocturnal ending builds the first strong caesura in the epic and suggests closure. While the first two books conclude with dawn because they look to the contest, the third concludes with night because the contest is over and Jason has won it.

This night, though, brings no rest. Its restlessness should come as no surprise, given that Apollonius generally uses sleep to signpost beginnings rather than endings. The sleepless mood of the night also fits the state of affairs, for it is only technically true that Jason's contest is finished: 'heavy anguish came upon the heart of Aeetes. He went back to the city among the Colchians, pondering how he might quickly oppose them [the Argonauts]' (3. 1404–6). Aeetes' angry brooding qualifies the appeasing quality of nightfall in a manner that conjures up the scene in which Zeus was 'devising evil all night' for the feasting and subsequently sleeping armies at the end of *Iliad* 7.[84] Or: Aeetes' brooding qualifies the closure that sundown brings by intimating future action. While he had promised to surrender the fleece 'on the same day' as the contest (3. 419), the transition from day to night marks neither a happy ending nor any ending at all. Jason does not know this yet. But he is not entitled to rest, because the reader knows it.

We might contrast this state of affairs with Odysseus' unqualified victory, crowned by closural sleep. Odysseus prefaces the beginning of the slaughter by calling attention to his success at stringing the bow: 'Now this decisive contest (ἄεθλος) has been completed' (*Od.* 22. 5). At the end of the slaughter, the second contest,[85] he sleeps at last. Though he has more ἄεθλα to face (23. 248), the one he has just fought is over. Jason also will have more ἄεθλοι to face (1. 442), but the one he has just fought is not quite over. He is not allowed to rest because his victory brings no peace to him – or to anyone. This is highlighted by the general sleeplessness that characterizes the night with which Book 3 ends and Book 4 begins.

The Colchian section of the epic as a whole has a wakeful atmosphere, which both conveys the tensions that oppose the characters and builds up suspense as the final act, the capture of the fleece, draws near. The insomniac mood creates a contrast between Jason's experience and Odysseus' in Scheria, filled with his desire to sleep. As is often noted,[86] Jason's stay in Colchis adapts Odysseus' Phaeacian episode by reversing it in a number of features: the stranger does not meet a good king but a cruel one, does not obtain his help but is set to deadly tasks, and departs not with an official escort and a public blessing but in secrecy.

Furthermore, while Alcinous offers a bed to Odysseus after promising his return, Aeetes dismisses Jason after challenging him in anger.[87] The contrasting treatment of the two heroes is mirrored in their contrasting dispositions towards sleep. Odysseus longs for it because he is tired and relaxed. Sweet slumber is welcome to him. Jason does not rest, or, if he does, his sleep goes unmarked. Of the three nights he passes in Colchis before the contest, one is skipped (Medea's sleeplessness is in the foreground), one is spent doing nothing and instantly replaced by dawn, and one is a *vigilia in armis*. The night after the contest likewise turns out to be wakeful for Jason, as for all the other main players.

The beginning of Book 4 could be titled *Nessun dorma* (*None shall sleep*) after Puccini's famous aria. While Aeetes 'all night long, with the best leaders of his people, was devising utter treachery' against the Argonauts (4. 6–7), Medea, after contemplating suicide, flees to their camp, where they are celebrating and keeping fires lit 'all night long' (4. 68–9). Her second sleepless night is a doublet of her first. Both times she thinks of death and takes out lethal drugs, and both times when she resolves to live she also resolves to leave. The structural and thematic echoing brings out her growing despair and foreshadows her tragedy. On the first night she is still in control of her life and destiny: it is she who shrinks away from the prospect of death, while Hera intervenes only to strengthen her resolve. She longs for dawn, for life, and leaves reborn, bathing in the light of the sun and of her own beauty. The second time Hera writes the entire script by instilling fear in her (4. 11) and causing her to live and flee (4. 22) – in the darkness of night, without any renewal of hope.

Future trouble is vividly portended in the narrative of Medea's arrival at the Argonauts' bivouac. Apollonius is probably alluding again to the end of *Iliad* 7, which features two parties engaged in the same activities as in his episode: the armies, feasting 'all night' like the Argonauts, and Zeus, thundering 'all night [and] devising ills' like Aeetes.[88] Apollonius' language strongly suggests that he is consciously referring to that scene. Compare, in Homer, 'all night long Zeus the planner was planning ills against them' (παννύχιος δέ σφιν κακὰ μήδετο μητίετα Ζεύς) and, in Apollonius, 'all night long he [Aeetes] was planning utter treachery against them' (παννύχιος δόλον αἰπὺν ἐπὶ σφίσι μητιάασκεν). Over the Argonauts' joyful celebrations there looms the ominous thunder of Zeus-Aeetes, who will re-launch the fighting.

The comparison with the end of *Iliad* 7 also emphasizes how consistently Apollonius avoids using sleep as caesura. The Homeric scene, in spite of the threatening developments it portends, winds down in slumber, but Apollonius has Medea break into the theatre of the Argonauts' feast and restart the action with pressing urgency. She cuts their party short with a 'sharp cry' (4. 70), urges them to flee with her 'before he [Aeetes] mounts his swift horses' (4. 86), and hurries with Jason to capture the fleece 'while it is still night' (4. 101). The Argonauts' celebrations end with a sudden awakening to new emergencies.

It is indeed still dark when Medea and Jason arrive at the grove where the fleece is guarded. The description of the hour emphasizes their wakefulness. They reach the spot at the time 'when hunters cast sleep from their eyes, hunters who [...] never slumber all through the night to avoid the light of dawn', lest it efface tracks and scents (4. 109–13).[89] The reference to the hunters' early rising highlights the unsleeping activity of the couple, for neither one has dozed off even a little. It is as if they have awoken again, but from an already wakeful night. Their advance meets the dragon's likewise wakeful watch, the 'sleepless eyes' with which it sees them come (4. 128), and for which both Jason and the readers have long been prepared (2. 406–7; 2. 1209).[90] The monster's awful hissing in turn causes young mothers to get up from fear and to hold their sleeping babies, whose limbs shake at the hiss (4. 136–8).

But the dragon will eventually be plunged into a fatal slumber. Its enduring wakefulness, filled with more fearful movements (4. 141–4), enhances the hypnotic potency of Medea's art. She begins by invoking the god of sleep: 'with a sweet voice she called Hypnos, the highest of the gods, as helper, to charm the monster' (4. 146–7). Medea's invocation recalls Hera's in *Iliad* 14. Both attribute supreme powers to Hypnos[91] and enlist him to extinguish the unsleeping vision of another god or immortal being (Ap. Rhod. 4. 128; *Il.* 14. 236). And just as Zeus, enwrapped in his κῶμα, 'dies',[92] the dragon, in losing its wakefulness, loses the complement to its immortality (2. 1209).[93]

Unlike Hera, however, Medea has in herself the power to lull her victim to sleep. Hera applies lovemaking, for which purpose she borrows Aphrodite's girdle with its 'charms' (*Il.* 14. 215: θελκτήρια); but even so she seeks the extra help of Hypnos. Medea needs no such help because she has charms in her voice and her drugs. In her invocation, the prayer to Hypnos merges with the actual sleep-inducing magic she works on the dragon. The phrase that describes the 'sweet voice' with which she charms (θέλξαι) the monster, ἡδείῃ ἐνοπῇ, has a hypnotizing ring, suggested by the monotonous prevalence of e-sounds.[94] Medea applies her lulling song (4. 150) before the added drug completes the job with its soporific scent (4. 157–9). The ever-wakeful monster falls asleep slowly, step by step. Though made mellow by Medea's voice, it still lifts its head to swallow the pair, until the drug's smell causes its jaws to drop and its coils to stretch out (4. 159–61). Medea's powers elevate her to the status of a semi-divine figure, for they imitate Hermes' when he lulls Argus, another 'ever-wakeful' monster, to sleep by means of a 'hypnotic tune'.[95]

The extended description of slumber taking hold of the dragon functions as counterpoint to both the repeated emphasis on its unremitting watchfulness and the general sleeplessness that pervades this part of the epic. At last, the dragon has closed its eyes, the fleece is in Jason's hands and the readers and characters should be able to rest, at least a little, before the journey home begins. But no: the day dawns as the couple returns to the camp with the fleece (4. 183–4). The rising of the sun at the end of this hectic night connects it to the sleepless nights of Medea and of Jason in Book 3, both of which are likewise followed by the spreading of daylight and the renewal of activity.

The three main nocturnal sequences in Colchis thus share structural and thematic features: one or more characters spend the entire night in either a quandary or an anxious pursuit; as soon as the quandary is resolved or the pursuit successfully completed, dawn brightens, and with its coming, objects take on a shimmer that rivals its light. In the last episode the gleaming object is the fleece, which shines even in the night, like a moonbeam (4. 167–3; see also 125–6), but more dazzlingly at sunrise: 'Dawn was spreading over the earth and they reached the group. And the young men marvelled, seeing the great fleece that shone like the lightning of Zeus' (4. 183–5).

This time, however, luminosity carries danger. Jason hastens the Argonauts' departure, preventing them from celebrating or even lingering. He stops them from touching the fleece, covers it and urges them to leave instantly (4. 190). Even after obtaining the object of their quest, they cannot relax. The lack of a pause is consonant with the prediction, early in the poem, that the return journey would be difficult (1. 441–2). The hastiness of the departure also sets the beginning of the *nostos* in contrast with the long-drawn launching of the outward journey, delayed from one day to the next. In both cases, the ship takes off at dawn, but there it was after a nightlong sleep, while here it is after a night of frenetic activity. The contrasting pace matches the opposite modes of the departure: with glamour on the way out, on the sly on the way back. The night-time hunters seek to avoid the bright light of day for fear of becoming prey.[96]

Revisiting Homeric episodes of sleep

The return journey is geographically haphazard and generally fast paced. As I have suggested, these features combined might explain why it is not punctuated by occurrences of sleep like the ones distributed along the outward journey, which serve to restart it at crucial junctures. There is one exception: after Peleus tells his comrades about Thetis' order to leave the island of Circe and sail to the Wandering Rocks, through which she and her sisters will draw the ship, they all 'stopped their games straightaway, made ready a meal and beds, on which, after dining, they slumbered through the night, as before. But when light-bringing dawn hit the edge of heaven' (4. 882–5), they leave. As on the outward journey, sleep here marks the momentousness of the subsequent departure, this time because of its literary pedigree: the Argonauts are about to follow in the footsteps of Odysseus, with Thetis replacing the Homeric Circe in the role of guide. Their sleep corresponds to that of Odysseus' companions on both nights before leaving Circe's island (though Jason, unlike Odysseus, once again rests like everyone else).

The Argonauts sail past the Sirens and the Wandering Rocks (in lieu of Scylla), and finally come within sight of Trinacria. They approach it when the oxen of the Sun are still at pasture (4. 970–6), and quickly move on (4. 964–5): 'They passed by them in the daytime; and at nightfall they were crossing a great sea gulf, rejoicing, until again Dawn the early-born shed light on them as they fared on' (4. 979–81). In the *Odyssey* it is evening when the island appears to the weary travellers. The cattle are not at pasture but are entering their folds for the night (12. 265). Apollonius marks his engagement with the Homeric episode by repeating several surrounding words. Homer's 'I heard the bellowing of oxen settling in their quarters and the bleating of sheep' (*Od.* 12. 265–6) is echoed in 'at once the bleating of sheep came to them through the air and the bellowing of oxen nearby reached their ears' (Ap. Rhod. 4. 968–9).[97]

The emphatic replacement of evening with day underscores the luckiness of the Argonauts' passage. Odysseus' comrades get in trouble by 'obeying the night' (*Od.* 12. 291), that is, by landing, eating and going to sleep. Apollonius' substitution of uninterrupted sailing for rest, while consistent with the scarcity of sleep breaks in his epic, brings to the fore the ease with which the Argonauts 'repeat' the most difficult portion of Odysseus' wanderings. They avoid Trinacria not because they force themselves to forgo sleep with Odysseus-like stamina (see *Od.* 12. 279–82) but because they reach the island at a time when they do not need to rest, just as they meet with favourable winds and are lifted across the Wandering Rocks. Unlike Odysseus, they enjoy divine protection in the part of their journey contiguous with his, which Hera and her helpers the nymphs stage-manage, steering them away from the dangers faced by Odysseus.[98] The Argo's swift sailing past Trinacria seems to take place under the aegis of the nymphs, who plunge back into the sea right after the passage (4. 966–7).

Again unlike Odysseus, the Argonauts reach the island of the Phaeacians with ease and swiftness. But, yet again unlike Odysseus, they face renewed trouble there. Though Alcinous and his people welcome them with sacrifices, as if they were their children coming home (4. 994–7), the celebrations instantly turn into a call to arms, because the Colchians have pursued them to claim Medea back. As a result, the Argonauts cannot find the tranquility that Odysseus eventually enjoys, and which increases his desire for sleep. Instead of indulging in sweet slumber, Jason and Medea spend another sleepless night while Alcinous and Arete are comfortably ensconced in their marital chamber.

Even after beseeching Arete and the Argonauts (4. 1011–53), Medea fears that she might be surrendered to the Colchians. Darkness descends and with it sleep, but not for her:

> And while she was suffering, upon the host night came, which brings men rest (εὐνήτειρα) from labours, and it lulled (κατευκήλησε) the whole earth. But sleep did not bring the slightest rest to her (τὴν δ' οὔτι μίνυνθά περ εὔνασεν ὕπνος). The heart in her breast was whirling in anguish as when a hard-working woman whirls the spindle at night, and her orphaned children cry all around her. She is a widow, and a tear falls along her cheeks as she considers what dreadful destiny has seized her. In the same way her cheeks were wet. And her heart was oppressed, pierced by sharp pangs.
>
> (4. 1058–67)

Medea is as sleepless as when she fell in love. The world is slumbering all around her, as it was then. Rhythmic features again convey the stilling of the earth: a spondee in εὐνήτειρα, 'rest-bringing', and another in κατευκήλησε, 'lulled'. The recurrence of patterns reminiscent of the previous sleeplessness scene brings Medea's helplessness and despair into bold relief, harking back as it does to the night on which she chose to follow her love and start on the journey that has taken her to the present dreadful predicament. On that earlier night Medea's passion dictates her decision, but the decision is still her own; this time, though, she is not deciding anything. Her sleeplessness has no content except the upheaval of her heart and the flowing of her tears. She is no longer in control of her destiny and that of others, but others are in control of hers. She is not torn between love and home, but is homeless because of her choice to follow her love, a love that she cannot count on. She makes this clear by addressing her supplication first to a 'foreign queen', as she says reproachfully to the Argonauts (4. 1048), then to 'each man in turn' (4. 1030):

not to Jason first, or only.[99] Her betrothed is one of the strangers with whom she is wretchedly wandering (4. 1041). The unspecified theatre of her restless suffering (she seems to be with the heroes, but we are not told) points up her homelessness – she is nowhere – as opposed to the homey setting of the first episode: her room. Her present despair is the consequence of her decision to cross the threshold of her room at the end of that fateful night.

Medea's homeless sleeplessness is further emphasized by the contrast with the cosy marital scene to which the narrator turns his attention right after leaving her anguished heart behind: 'And the pair (τώ) was inside the palace in the city as before, lordly Alcinous and much-revered Arete, his wife, and lying in their bed in the darkness, they were making plans about the maiden' (4. 1068–71).

Alcinous and Arete, united by the dual that begins the narrative, are living according to the routine ('as before') of a married couple, now in bed like every night. Their togetherness and regulated life, with its nightly ritual, underscores Medea's solitude and unregulated life, the life of a wanderer. She is now awake in anguish while the royal couple discusses her fate in a pillow talk. Alcinous pronounces that Medea and Jason will stay together if they have consummated their marriage, then dozes off: 'Thus he spoke, and at once sleep brought him rest (εὔνασεν ὕπνος)' (4. 1110). Apollonius highlights the contrast between Alcinous' serenity and Medea's distress with one of his carefully measured repetitions: the same phrase, εὔνασεν ὕπνος, is used to describe sleep coming to Alcinous and not coming to Medea (4. 1060). Alcinous does not let his tranquility be troubled.[100]

The sequence of these two scenes reworks the Homeric narrative of Odysseus' first night in Scheria.[101] The phrase 'as before' not only highlights the routine of the Phaeacian couple but also hints at the Homeric model, substituting literary for narrative time.[102] At the end of *Odyssey* 7, we might recall, Odysseus is sent to sleep on the porch of Alcinous' palace. The narrative lingers over the pleasure he finds in going to bed, then describes his hosts retiring inside and lying down for the night. Apollonius replaces Odysseus' rest with Medea's sleeplessness, thus building an un-Homeric background for the bedroom scene that ends with Alcinous dozing off. In Homer retiring scenes provide the frame for episodes of individual sleeplessness, but it does not happen the other way around, and the individual who is awake against a background of sleepers normally makes a decision.[103] By reversing the order (the wakeful figure is described first) and the roles of the characters (the one soon-to-sleep makes the decision), Apollonius further brings out the helplessness of Medea, whose unproductive insomnia is superseded by the plot-devising tranquility of the Phaeacian couple that decides her case.

Alcinous and Arete, however, are not in unison, for as soon as he pronounces and dozes off, 'she put the wise word in her heart and straightaway rose' (4. 1111) to send a herald to Jason, urging him to consummate the marriage. While in the *Odyssey* the couple's joint sleep ends the evening action, in the *Argonautica* the wakeful Arete leaves her husband's side to carry out her plan. This spur to further activity that replaces sleep fits with Apollonius' tendency to fill the night with movement and avoid breaks. But Arete's secret action also fosters her wishes, unbeknownst to her husband, and determines the outcome of his judgement. Her choice to take advantage of his sleep qualifies their togetherness or, as Homer would say, their like-mindedness. Marital bliss is so alien to Apollonius' epic[104] that even a harmonious relationship like that of the young Phaeacian couple has its shadows. Alcinous' sudden slumber is a worrying sign in itself, for it seems to substitute for the expected lovemaking.[105]

Alcinous is the only one sleeping. When the herald dispatched by Arete reaches the Argonauts, he finds them 'by the ships, awake with their arms' (4. 1124). This sketched *vigilia in armis* corresponds to Jason's in Book 3; but he does not stand out now. In response to the herald's message we hear the voice of 'each man', whose heart rejoices at the words (4. 1126–7). In Book 3 Jason was the only one awake, but here, the blending of his presence with his comrades' suggests that he has stepped back from his prominent role as leader, and the blending of his voice with theirs puts forward his solidarity with them rather than his passion for his bride-to-be. He is awake with the other Argonauts while she is sleepless alone. The two episodes combined foreshadow Medea's abandonment by Jason, which is also encrypted in the simile that equates her – even before he becomes her husband – with a widow losing sleep to work and sorrow (4. 1062–6 above).

The rising of the new day further stresses Medea's helplessness. The structure and motifs of its narration again hark back to her first sleepless night. Again dawn appears, and with it the streets are filled with noise and the city with movement (4. 1170–4).[106] In the earlier episode, however, dawn rises through and for Medea's eyes, at the end of the night in which she makes her momentous decision, while here the light of day illumines not her movements but Alcinous', as he advances with the Phaeacian chiefs to issue the verdict that will decide her future (4. 1176–81).

CHAPTER 5

THE NOVEL

PART ONE: CHARITON

Sleep and agency

The Greek novels owe much more to Homer than to Apollonius of Rhodes. Though Jason shares traits with novelistic heroes – he is engaged to be married, is often dejected and is extraordinarily handsome – there is almost no evidence that the novelists drew inspiration from the *Argonautica*. The only certain allusion to it is one passage in Chariton's *Callirhoe* in which Chaereas, like Jason, is described as a dazzling star.[1] On the other hand, Chariton quotes Homer obsessively, echoes Homeric phrases and refashions Homeric episodes. Other novelists likewise exploit Homeric epic, though they tend to refer to it more indirectly.[2] They are also indebted to Homer in their treatment of sleep and sleeplessness, as is especially perceptible in the earliest extant novel, *Callirhoe*, and the latest, the *Aethiopica*. At the same time, a great number of influences other than Homer contribute to enrich the sleepscape (if I may) of the ancient novels in specific ways. This final chapter will focus on each novel's distinctive responses to Greek traditions of thinking about sleep, as well as on their shared traits in their exploitation of sleep and wakefulness to construct their plots, themes and characters.

Chariton is fond of initiating momentous events with restless nights. A night 'filled with worries', in which all the involved parties are wakeful, precedes the launching of Mithridates' scheme to help Chaereas recover his wife (4. 4. 4); the transference of Callirhoe from the hands of the pirate Theron to those of Dionysius' servant Leonas is framed by 'a night that seemed long to both, for the one was in a hurry to buy, the other to sell' (1. 13. 6); the tomb robbery that leads to the heroine's kidnapping is decided upon in a sleepless night, when Theron, Odysseus-like, engages in an internal monologue to put together his plan (1. 7. 1–3); and on yet another such night, the same character ponders how to handle his prisoner, who is too beautiful to be sold to a commoner and will make him and his band undesirably conspicuous. After wasting much time,

> When night came he was not able to sleep, but said to himself: 'you are a fool, Theron. You have left silver and gold behind in a solitary place for so many days, as if you were the only robber. Don't you know that there are other pirates sailing the sea? And I am also worried that my own may leave me, and sail away. Certainly you have not enlisted the most upright of men [...] Now', he said, 'you must rest, but when day comes, run to the cutter and throw the woman into the sea [...]' When he dozed off he dreamt he saw locked doors, and decided to wait that day.
>
> (1. 12. 2–5)

The sequence 'sleeplessness followed by a nap with a significant dream' goes back to Homer (in *Odyssey* 4 and 20). A common denominator in the Homeric episodes is that the dreams accord with the sleepers' wishes.[3] In contrast, Theron's vision pushes him to revise his decision to kill Callirhoe and run, telling him that he cannot depart and pursue his plan (the doors are locked). In this respect, the episode calls to mind one in Herodotus (7. 12–8) in which a recurring dream compels Xerxes to adopt a plan he had discarded earlier. Disquieted by the advice of Arbatanus, he spends part of the night in thought and decides not to attack Greece (as Theron decides not to sell Callirhoe). When he falls asleep, however, a handsome man appears to him and urges him to reconsider. He does not, but the vision recurs, and when Arbatanus wears Xerxes' clothes and dozes on his couch, the dream appears to him as well and tells him that the war 'is fated to happen'. The late hour brings Xerxes good judgement (night is called εὐφρόνη, which in antiquity was explained as a coinage from εὖ-φρονεῖν, 'to have good thoughts'),[4] but sleep, which seems to follow from his decision to refrain from war (he is serene and slumbers deeply: καθύπνωσε), harms him by carrying the war-instigating dream. Theron's sleep, which also seems to descend from the tranquility he has reached after making his decision to depart, is similarly harmful to him.

One function of Theron's dream is to avert the foreclosure of the plot via a non-novelistic ending (Callirhoe's death). Another is to undermine his agency, suggesting that he is not entitled to direct the plot as he wishes and revealing that 'Providence' (as it will be called later) is already shaping events against his plans, just as 'fate' was shaping those in Persia against Xerxes' better judgement. While Theron's decision to rob Callirhoe's tomb, the outcome of his sleepless thinking, marks his initial control of the plot, his decision to wait, under the influence of a dream that nullifies his sleepless thinking, foreshadows his exit from the plot as a director, as an active player and soon as a player of any kind. The locked doors ultimately portend his capture and failure to escape.

Callirhoe likewise dreams after prolonged wakefulness at a major turning point. The discovery that she is pregnant by Chaereas causes her to stay up, in deep thought (2. 9. 1): should she abort or raise the child?

> So she was absorbed in such reasoning all night long. For a brief moment sleep came over her. An image of Chaereas stood near her, like him in every way, 'similar in stature and beautiful eyes and voice, and wearing the same clothes' (*Il.* 23. 66–7). He stood and said, 'my wife, I entrust you with our son'. He wanted to say more but Callirhoe leapt up, eager to embrace him. Thinking that her husband had advised her, she decided to raise the child.
>
> (2. 9. 6)

Like Theron, Callirhoe receives an orienting dream. But her heart and mind are in line with it. Though she is undecided, her maternal instinct seems to prevail from the outset. This is made clear by the ordering and length of the speeches with which she weighs her options. In her internal debate the argument for keeping the child has the last word, and it is twice as long as the one in favour of abortion; moreover, it contains a passionate vision of a bright future in which the family is reunited (2. 9. 2–5). In addition, the choice of Patroclus' dream vision as a model for Chaereas' suggests that Callirhoe, like Achilles, is willing to do what the vision tells her. Both dreams shake the dreamer with their requests, but in both cases the request matches the dreamer's dormant or unconscious desire.

The synergy of Callirhoe's dream with her sleepless pondering underscores the fact that she is now seizing control of her life, in contrast to the passivity she has shown so far. Before this scene of internal debate she has had no say in the most momentous events that have befallen her. She does not know who it is she is marrying, then she is 'killed', and when Theron kidnaps and sells her she cannot take any initiative. Though she refuses to give her body to Dionysius, she cannot leave or move on in any other way. And even her success in keeping herself pure greatly depends on Dionysius' unwillingness to force himself on her. Lamentations, prayers, requests and prudent words are her only modes of action.

Sleep twice signifies Callirhoe's passivity. She is not responsible for her first, deep slumber, which is taken for death and evokes to the bystanders the sleep of the abandoned Ariadne (1. 6. 2). The heroine has no active role in her unconscious state (contrast Anthia in Xenophon's novel, who is also the victim of an apparent death but because she tries to kill herself), but it initiates the novel's adventures, in spite of her. And when she sleeps again, her fate has just been decided. Left alone in Leonas' house after he and Theron have concluded the sale, she bemoans her misfortune until a restoring slumber ends her weeping and the first book: 'So was she lamenting when at last sleep came upon her' (ὕπνος ἐπῆλθεν).

There can hardly be any doubt that Chariton is here alluding to, or rather citing, Homer.[5] The phrase rings Homeric. Compare *Od.* 4. 793: 'So was she [Penelope] pondering when [...] sleep came upon her (ἐπήλυθε [...] ὕπνος)' and *Od.* 12. 311: 'While they [Odysseus' comrades] were weeping [...] sleep came upon them (ἐπήλυθε [...] ὕπνος)'.[6] Even the rhythm rings Homeric, for, if we count the last syllable of the preceding word, ἐπράθην ('I was sold'), it is a dactylic hexameter: -θην. τοιαῦτα ὀδυρομένη μόλις ὕπνος ἐπῆλθεν.[7] Chariton often sprinkles his prose with almost-iambic sequences (a debt to New Comedy),[8] but he does not habitually reproduce hexametric patterns. The ending of Book 1 thus stands out as a Homericizing line embedded in his prose.

Specifically, Chariton might be echoing the coming of sleep to Penelope at *Od.* 4. 793, the line that resembles his phrase most closely.[9] The novelistic book ending also resonates with other Homeric episodes in which Penelope, worn out by mourning, rests at last thanks to Athena and in sleeping loses touch with the plot. Like Penelope, Callirhoe is kept out of the action. She calls the room in Leonas' house 'another tomb, in which Theron has locked me up' (1. 14. 6), and this expression of her feelings links the sleep that engulfs her there to the unconscious state that caused her first entombment. She is no more in control of her fate now than she was then. Her slumber conveys her lack of agency.

Callirhoe's sleep in both of these episodes is dreamless. The first time she dreams is when she discovers her pregnancy, and Chaereas' image encourages her impulse to raise their child. From then on, at night she has visions that draw her nearer to what is happening by making her aware of events and shaping her mood and actions. When Chaereas is sold and put in chains, she dreams of him in chains and asks him to come to her (3. 7. 4); shortly thereafter, during a formulaic 'brief nap' following a sleepless night, she sees his ship burnt, as has actually happened, and herself trying to help him (4. 1. 1), and again on the eve of the trial in Babylon (5. 5. 5) she dreams of seeing him, as she indeed does the next day, and of their wedding, which indeed will be celebrated again after their definitive reunion.

I would suggest that the change in the nature of Callirhoe's sleep, from empty to full, from a blank space to a site of activity, occurs when she discovers her pregnancy because only then does she begin to behave like a true agent. The discovery, though framed by a comment on the tyranny of Fortune, 'against whom alone human reasoning is powerless' (2. 8. 3), forces Callirhoe to take her destiny into her own hands. The terms λογισμός and λογίζεσθαι, in the sense of 'reasoning to make a decision', characterize her behaviour only after she finds out her pregnancy (2. 9. 6; 2. 11. 4), whereas earlier, when the same words are (rarely) applied to her, they simply suggest that she is 'trying to understand' what is going on (1. 8. 2; 1. 9. 4), without taking any active role in it. Though she is manipulated into choosing to remarry by Dionysius' servant Plangon, her decision stems from her choice to raise the child and is ultimately her own.[10]

Callirhoe's new role as an active player in conjunction with her pregnancy is also reflected in her unprecedented and repeated wakefulness. She forsakes sleep two nights in a row. On the first she dozes only for the brief moment in which Chaereas' image guides her thoughts, and on the second she stays up, absorbed in her cares after a whole day of pondering: 'She spent that day and night in such reasoning and was persuaded to live not for her sake but for the child's' (2. 11. 4). Her final decision to raise the child and marry Dionysius issues from a whole day and night of thinking.

The transition from Book 2 to Book 3 brings out Callirhoe's enhanced agency by means of parallels and contrasts with the previous book transition. At both junctures a servant (Leonas, Plangon) goes off to Dionysius, both times to bring him a happy message (Leonas that he has bought a beautiful woman for him, Plangon that the beautiful woman wants to marry him), and both times Callirhoe is left behind in her room. But at the end of Book 1 she is slumbering and has decided nothing, while in Book 2 she is awake, having determined her own fate over the course of a sleepless night.[11]

Rewriting Penelope's sweetest slumber

While Callirhoe's first dream orients her action, all the others carry outside happenings into her mind. In Artemidorus' classification they are 'theorematic', visions of objective events external to the dreamer (though Callirhoe's feelings violently break into her dreams).[12] One other character is granted a theorematic dream: the noble and noble-minded Dionysius.[13] Before he meets or even hears of Callirhoe, he tells his servant, who has hurried back to him at night to bring news of the slave he has acquired, that for the first time since the death of his first wife 'I have had a pleasant sleep (ἡδέως κεκοίμημαι), for in my dream I saw her clearly: she was taller and more beautiful, and was with me as if she were really there (ὡς ὕπαρ)'. The servant breaks in: 'You are lucky, sir, both in you dream (ὄναρ) and in reality (ὕπαρ)' (2. 1. 2–3).

This scene is a Homericizing pastiche. The dream harks back to Penelope's vision of Odysseus (in *Odyssey* 20) quite precisely. Both seem real (ὕπαρ) to the dreamers, both come physically close to them and in both the dead or lost spouse has an enhanced appearance. Furthermore, Dionysius' admission that he has rested well for the first time recalls a similar comment made by Penelope in *Odyssey* 23, when she calls her sleep the most pleasant since her husband left. Chariton cues the reader to the reference by ascribing Homeric 'sweetness' to sleep only this one time in the entire novel.

There is a difference, though: Penelope's best slumber is dreamless, while Dionysius' is filled with a wonderful vision. It is actually the vision that causes his sleep to be sweet. This reversal of Penelope's experience, as well as of a more general pattern of thought, according to which the best sleep is dreamless,[14] seems to be related to the more optimistic and sentimental bent of the novelistic character. Penelope is happy while she dreams of Odysseus lying beside her, but upon awakening she hates the vision because it is at variance, or so she thinks, with her harsh reality. She does not let the happy dream spill over into her grim waking world, even if the dream seemed true enough (ὕπαρ). Dionysius, in contrast, is ready to let his blissful vision colour his experience of sleep upon awakening.

Chaereas' rivals, sleepless from love

Dionysius' sweet sleep is soon replaced by love-induced insomnia. A rare specimen of insomnophobia in Greek literature, he knows he will not be able to rest on the night of his fatal encounter with Callirhoe, and so he protracts his drinking to stay awake with his friends. When he breaks up the party, we enter his bedroom, where he still

> Could get no sleep but was entirely in the temple of Aphrodite and remembered everything, her face, her hair, how she turned, how she looked at him, her voice, her

> bearing, her words [...] Then you could see a contest between reason and passion. For, although drowned by desire, he tried to resist like the noble man he was [...] saying to himself: 'Are you not ashamed, Dionysius, the first citizen of Ionia in excellence and reputation [...] of this childish passion?'
>
> (2. 4. 3–4)

Dionysius is the first character in the novel to be shown sleepless because of love. It is true that sleep disturbances do also affect the protagonists after their encounter: 'When night came, it was terrible for both' (1. 1. 8). Chariton, though, does not dwell on their agony, but hurriedly moves on. His choice fits his novel's narrative tempo, fast at the beginning. Chariton treats the onset of love briefly because he wants to get the story going. He is not interested in the preliminaries to the adventures that separate the lovers, only in the adventures themselves. On the other hand, when Dionysius appears on the scene, the adventures are well underway and the narrative pace is slower.[15] The time is ripe for a theatrical display of sleepless torment.

An additional reason Chariton emphasizes the rival's insomnia over that of the protagonists might be the authority of tradition. In Greek literature prior to the novel, sleepless lovers are alone in their suffering. Their passion is and will be either unrequited or much stronger than the sentiment the other feels for them. Medea is sleepless, not Jason; Dido, not Aeneas; the lover in Plato's *Phaedrus* (251e1–2), but not the beloved, not even when he returns his own, paler, affection (255d–e). An epigram by Meleager features a wakeful lover sending a buzzing mosquito to his beloved, with this message: 'He is waiting for you, sleeplessly. But you, forgetful of lovers, slumber'.[16] The contrast between the lover's insomnia and the carefree repose of those who do not love is reproduced in this image of sleeping Eros, indifferent to the restless pain he causes: 'You slumber, you who bring sleepless cares to mortals' (*AP* 16. 211. 1).

The novels change this state of affairs. They attribute lovesick insomnia to both the hero and the heroine, thus highlighting the reciprocity and identity of their passion.[17] Chariton, however, seems to follow the tradition by privileging unloved lovers as the victims of attacks of sleeplessness. Dionysius suffers from one such attack again during his journey to Babylon. Gnawed by jealousy, he regrets having left Miletus, where 'he could have slept holding his beloved in his arms' (4. 7. 7).[18] And the Persian king Artaxerxes spends three nights awake, thinking of Callirhoe.

The sun has long set when Artaxerxes makes his momentous decision to summon Callirhoe to Babylon. Urged in a letter to put Mithridates on trial, since he is purportedly guilty of trying to seduce Dionysius' wife, the king spends the day in consultation with his friends, to no avail. But 'when night came' (4. 6. 6), he decides for the trial.

> And another feeling pushed him to send for the beautiful wife as well. Wine and darkness had been his advisers in his loneliness and reminded him of that part of the letter [which praised the beauty of Dionysius' wife]. He was also goaded by the rumour that a certain Callirhoe was the most beautiful woman in Ionia.
>
> (4. 6. 7)

The decision-making process in this scene reverses the Persian custom of taking counsel first at night, while drunk, and then by day, when sober (Hdt. 1. 133). The reversal makes Artaxerxes' political deliberations susceptible to extra-political motives, fuelled by the influence of counsellors – darkness, wine and solitude – that stimulate erotic imaginings. The scene foreshadows his gradual slide from king to lover, which, as we shall see presently, is mirrored in the content of his sleeplessness.

The eve of a second trial, which will adjudicate whether Chaereas or Dionysius is to be Callirhoe's husband, finds the royal couple entertaining opposite thoughts. The queen is looking forward to the new day as a chance to get rid of the beautiful Callirhoe; but not so the king:

> He stayed awake all night, 'lying now on his side, now on his back, now on his face' (*Il.* 24. 10–1), reflecting with himself, and said: 'the moment for the decision has come [...] Consider what you should do, my soul. Decide with yourself. You have no other counsellor. Eros himself is a

> lover's counsellor. First, answer to yourself: are you Callirhoe's lover or her judge? Don't fool yourself!'
>
> (6. 1. 8–10)

Artaxerxes resembles Dionysius insofar as both offer a theatrical display of sleepless agony. But their performances differ. With Dionysius on stage the spectacle we watch (or rather hear) is a dramatic contest (ἀγών), a psychomachy. The words he utters are those of reason fighting passion and upholding honour and dignity, the words of a 'philosophizing' soul (2. 4. 5) desperately trying to get the better of love. The Persian king makes no such attempt. The detail that his wife is by his side and suspicious of him (6. 1. 6) builds an appropriate frame for his display of adulterous passion. As soon as he enters the stage, his desire comes into full view in the unruly movements of his body. While Dionysius' sleeplessness is, as it were, bodiless, Artaxerxes is exposed as he tosses and turns like Achilles during the insomniac nights in which he longs for Patroclus. Artaxerxes' words do not restore his dignity. Whereas Dionysius vocally rebukes himself for his indulgence in love, Artaxerxes vocally endorses his and gives up his role of judge. Far from enacting an ἀγών between passion and reason, he fills his monologue with imagined voyeuristic pleasures. He addresses his eyes, calling them 'miserable' if they can no longer take delight in the 'most beautiful spectacle' that Helios ever 'saw' (6. 1. 9–10) and measures his passion by his pleasure in seeing Callirhoe: 'You do not admit it, but you love. You will be further convicted when you will see her no more' (6. 1. 10). He thus alleges a dream and postpones the trial, wanting to at least keep the woman in Babylon to be the object of his 'gazing' (6. 1. 12), for the pampering of his eyes.

The next day Artaxerxes confides his passion to his eunuch, who faced with Callirhoe's impregnability, seeks to persuade him to stop his pursuit. He does stop, but only until sunset:

> Again when night came he burnt. Eros reminded him of Callirhoe's eyes, the beauty of her face; he praised her hair, her way of walking, her voice, how she looked when she entered the courtroom, how she stood, her speech, her silence, her embarrassment, her tears. Artaxerxes was

wakeful most of the night and slept only long enough to see Callirhoe even in his dreams.

(6. 7. 1–2)

The opposition between daytime distractions and night-time fixation shapes the king's behaviour. Like Homer and Sophocles, the Greek novelists know that the pains of the heart are sharper at night, when activity stops.[19] The king's resurgence of desire marks a crescendo compared to its display in the first episode of sleeplessness. For then he dwelt only on Callirhoe's 'beauty' (6. 1. 10), with no detail, while now her features, movements, postures, behaviour and voice come alive in his mind one by one. The fantasy prolongs the daydream he had during a hunt, when 'He was seeing Callirhoe alone, though she was not there, and hearing her, though she was not speaking' (6. 4. 5). The imaginary picture that he 'moulded' (ἀναπλάττων) then (6. 4. 7) fills the hours of darkness and fashions a real dream.

No other character in *Callirhoe* is as often described in nocturnal agitation. This privileging of Artaxerxes underscores his double role as king and as lover. As king, he is fitted, even expected, to spend wakeful nights absorbed in thought, in the manner of epic or tragic rulers. To say 'thinking of my people, I cannot sleep' is a mark of good leadership, as the weak leader Jason demonstrates by appealing to the cliché when he seeks to obtain confirmation of his role.[20] Chariton certainly knew the *topos* from earlier literature, first of all from his cherished Homer. Moreover, the dream's reproach to Agamemnon in *Iliad* 2, 'rulers cannot sleep all night', had become something of a proverb by the first centuries AD. The phrase is treated as a maxim in the scholia;[21] it is quoted in the essay *On Homer* attributed to Plutarch (2. 1915–6); it is familiar to the Christian theologian Clement of Alexandria (*Pedagogue* 2. 9. 81. 4) and it appears in a third-century textbook of rhetoric, Hermogenes' *Progymnasmata*, which in an exercise asks the pupil to develop the thesis 'to sleep all night does not become a man who takes care of many things'.[22] Those words were also taken to support the belief that the hours of darkness are the best time to deliberate.[23] Eustathius uses the dictum to shore up his explanation of εὐφρόνη, a post-Homeric epithet of the night, as 'bringing good counsel'.[24]

We first meet Artaxerxes in the grip of a difficult decision, which he is not able to make in the daytime but can make with the help of counsel-bringing night. Though the darkness and the wine instigate a voyeuristic impulse, his decision is still mostly political (4. 6. 6) and summoning Callirhoe is an afterthought. Eroticism plays only a surreptitious role, by enticing the curiosity of a king who is used to having every beautiful thing, women included, at his disposal (6. 3. 4). The second decision he makes in a sleepless night is caused entirely by desire, but still results in a public proclamation in which he issues public orders, as king, while the third is a recantation of his politically wise resolution to stop his pursuit and results in a secretly manoeuvred attempt at seduction. The comparison with Achilles, while eroticizing the epic hero's insomnia,[25] also brings out the purely private and emotional causes of Artaxerxes'.[26]

The three episodes that show Artaxerxes sleepless thus build a sequence in which political responsibility increasingly yields to desire. Dreams participate in revealing this erotic escalation. On the first night Artaxerxes' still openly defensible decision is not influenced by a dream; on the second his erotically motivated actions are covered up by the kind of dream that would be expected of a ruler[27] and on the third his inability to rein in his passion spills over into an erotic dream that extends his sleepless fantasizing. The king turns into a lover, and his night-time quandaries point up this shift in role.

They told stories and made love: but did not sleep

One evening Chaereas, who has successfully fought for the Egyptians and against the Persian king, decides to approach the beautiful, unknown prisoner of war, who turns out to be Callirhoe. After public celebrations of their reunion, the two retire, exchange stories, then 'gladly came to the old rite of the bed', like Odysseus and Penelope (8. 1). The reference to the Homeric couple foregrounds one aspect of the novelistic episode that is often noted: more than just a reunion, it is a second wedding – rather, the true wedding, crowned by lovemaking. The narrative of the nuptials in Syracuse does not cross the threshold of the couple's bedroom. Unlike Xenophon, who devotes an exuberant description to the wedding night and its rituals,[28] Chariton does not go beyond the public ceremony. His choice might once again be related to the initially fast pace of his novel, which runs towards the decisive incident (Callirhoe's 'death'). Nonetheless, by skipping over the wedding night and moving lovemaking to the night of the reunion, Chariton suggests that the wedding only truly happens, or happens 'with more honour' (5. 9. 3), after the trials have been completed.[29]

In one meaningful detail, however, the novelistic duo does not imitate its Homeric model. While in the *Odyssey* the night of love ends in a rewarding, limb-loosening slumber,[30] the novelistic couple is not said to rest. A restorative sleep would have been psychologically and even physically justified for them, in the case of the heroine perhaps even more so than for her epic counterpart.[31] Both Chaereas and Callirhoe have been tried for a long time, up until the very day of their reunion. He has just fought an epic war, she has just borne up with capture and imprisonment and has been so distressed that she has refused to eat. Why don't they fall under Hypnos' spell?

We could invoke narrative reasons for sleep's absence: Chariton might have wished to undercut the finality of the scene of reunion because the couple's dangers are not over. Their threat becomes real on that very night, for the sudden arrival of a soldier causes the couple's bedroom to be opened to let him in (8. 2. 2) – and the action to restart, with pressing urgency. But the *Odyssey* does not end with the end of dangers, either, yet it allows the couple to rest temporarily from their ongoing trials. Chariton could have adhered to his model in this, using the sequence 'sleep followed by a new beginning with renewed dangers'.

The failure of limb-loosening slumber to descend on the novelistic duo highlights not so much the dangers that still loom as the priority of the romantic element. Love has the last word. This is a feature *Callirhoe* shares with the other two novels that describe the protagonists in their passionate intimacy, the *Ephesiaca* and *Daphnis and Chloe,* in neither of which does sleep follow lovemaking. The novels' plotline – two young people falling in love and, after a number of trials, starting a life together – is at variance with marital sleep. No novelistic pair can find happiness in resting side-by-side. None is seasoned enough to imitate Odysseus and Penelope, who, even after twenty years of separation, desire sweet slumber rather than being, like the protagonists of Longus' novel, 'more sleepless than owls'.[32]

More specifically, the absence of sleep from the scene of reunion in *Callirhoe* also contributes to the characterization of Chaereas as a responsible military leader as well as a loving husband. The loving husband, eager to be with his wife, takes care of doing for himself what Athena does for Odysseus: he lengthens the night. While he used to spend all his time on the military ship, busy with many things, after recovering Callirhoe he entrusts everything to his friend and 'without even waiting until evening, he entered the bedroom' (8. 1. 13). But the night he plans to extend is curtailed on the other end: 'It was still night when an Egyptian of high rank landed' (8. 2. 1). He asks where Chaereas is, insisting that he will speak only to him. So his friend opens the door, and 'Chaereas, like a good general, says, "summon him in. War tolerates no delay"' (8. 2. 2). Chariton's hero imitates the historian Xenophon, who, in the flattering self-portrait he draws in the *Anabasis*, is always ready to be approached, at breakfast and dinner, and to be awoken (4. 3. 10). Chaereas is playing two roles: as a happy (at last) lover and husband, he hurries to the bedroom while it is still daylight, but as a capable commander, he is ready to get up before daylight on the happiest night of his life.[33]

PART TWO: XENOPHON OF EPHESUS

Sleepless with love's agonies and joys

Sleeplessness has a more limited presence in the *Ephesiaca* than in *Callirhoe*. Xenophon's characters do not stay awake to make decisions. In one instance the novelist sketches a scene of quandary that might have continued through the night, when Anthia, after killing the would-be rapist Anchialus, 'takes counsel with herself over many things'. What should she do? Commit suicide? But Habrocomes might still be alive. Leave the cave where she is imprisoned? But the journey is impossible. 'So she decided to stay in the cave and bear up with whatever god might choose' (4. 5. 6). The decision amounts to taking no initiative and sleeplessness follows the dilemma rather than containing it: 'That night, then, she waited, without sleep and with much in her thoughts' (4. 6. 1). Anthia's wakefulness is not caused by the urgency she feels to solve her predicament but by her inability to do so.

Love-induced insomnia is more to Xenophon's taste than nightlong pondering. Neither the hero nor the heroine can rest after their fatal encounter: 'When they went to sleep, their misery was complete, and love in both could no longer be contained' (1. 3. 4). We hear first Habrocomes bemoaning his state, then Anthia. The protagonists' sleeplessness is filled not just with words but also with visions: 'So each of them lamented the whole night. They had each other before their eyes, and their souls were moulding (ἀναπλάττοντας) each other's image. When day came...' (1. 5. 1)

Xenophon expands on Chariton's simple phrase 'that night was terrible for both' by dwelling on the two protagonists serially, in keeping with his penchant for narrative doublets.[34] He also modifies Chariton in his distribution of insomnia. Instead of devoting a full narrative to the rivals' and only a passing comment to the protagonists', the *Ephesiaca* lavishes sleepless drama on the protagonists and never attributes sleep disturbances to any rival. The reversal is consonant with a reversal in narrative pace: Xenophon's novel runs almost breathlessly through the core of the adventures but relates their preliminaries very slowly, above all, the encounter between the hero and the heroine.[35] While in Chariton it takes up less than a paragraph, in Xenophon it covers two pages; while in Chariton love flares up casually, at a narrow crossing (1. 1. 6), in Xenophon its ignition is anticipated by the crowd's comments on the protagonists' beauty ('what a wonderful pair they would make!'), by their desire, spurred by those comments, to see each other and by the solemn setting of love's attack, a religious ceremony in which Habrocomes and Anthia parade their beauty and keep looking at each other (1. 3. 1–2). Their nocturnal fantasies prolong the intensity of their first visual contact.

By peeping into the protagonists' bedrooms and showing them not only as they pour out their despair but also as they indulge in visions of each other, Xenophon underscores the sensuality of their mutual attraction. The night-time exposure of their passion agrees with their uninhibited behaviour at their first encounter. The girl is not modestly covered and silent, but makes herself heard and shows as much skin as she can: 'with contempt for maidenly decency, she said something for Habrocomes to hear, and bared the parts of her body she could for Habrocomes to see. He gave himself to the sight and was the captive of the god' (1. 3. 2). The two play their daring act under the public eye, with a 'whole crowd' as witness (1. 3. 1), and when they part, they keep each other's image in mind. Their mutual desire increases all day (1. 3. 4) until night brings more erotic imaginings. Xenophon's hero and heroine have the kind of fantasies that Chariton assigns to the rivals, both in the daylight (*Callirhoe* 6. 4. 5–7, where the same verb ἀναπλάττειν appears) and in their sleepless nights (2. 4. 3; 6. 7. 1).

The strong desire that keeps Anthia and Habrocomes awake is soon shared and satisfied on their wedding night, which both harks back to and reverses the miserable night of their encounter. Habrocomes connects them: 'O most desired night, at last I have you, after so many unhappy nights!' (1. 9. 2) Again, we hear him first (1. 9. 2–3) and then Anthia (1. 9. 4–8), but while he plays a greater role in the lamentation scene, she does on their night of love.[36] The summary phrase that concludes the first episode is echoed and modified in the account of the second: 'they lamented the whole night [...] and when day came', turns into 'the whole night they rivaled each other, both eager to show that they loved the other more. When day came' (1. 9. 9–10. 1). Xenophon's hero and heroine release the erotic tension that filled their first sleepless night (and many more) on another wakeful night, at the end of which they have that unmistakable glow on their faces: 'When day came, they got up much happier, much more cheerful, after giving each other the pleasures they had desired for so long' (1. 10. 1). There is no such image of post-coital contentment in Chariton's more Homericizing novel.[37]

Sleepless while everyone slumbers

Like sleeplessness, sleep plays a smaller role in Xenophon than in Chariton. In both it is primarily a vehicle for dreams, but in Chariton it also comes to end insomniac nights, in Homeric fashion, whether carrying visions or not. When it does carry visions, in Chariton it advances the plot, either by pushing a character's decision in or against the direction it was taking during hours of restless rumination or by causing an involuntary action (as when Callirhoe, sleep talking, calls Chaereas' name aloud, leading Dionysius to discover that she was married before [3. 7. 4]). Sleep in this novel is also an instigator of the plot in the case of Callirhoe's *Scheintod* ('apparent death'), which causes her kidnapping.

In Xenophon, only Anthia's corresponding *Scheintod* elevates sleep to a motor of the action. She is buried, and tomb robbers find her when she has just awoken, and then sell her (3. 6–9). But this plot-advancing sleep replaces an intended death. Anthia is the only novelistic protagonist who commits suicide. To keep herself for Habrocomes when an unwanted marriage is impending, she manages to obtain a drug and drinks it on her wedding night. She sets out to follow the tragic *topos* of 'marriage to death' (as in *Antigone, Hecuba*, and *Iphigenia in Aulis*), without knowing, as the readers do, that death will be replaced by slumber (3. 6. 5) because the drug is not a poison but a hypnotic, fitting to adapt the tragic *topos* to the novelistic rule that the heroine cannot die.[38]

Apart from this episode, sleep has little impact on the novel's development, even as the vehicle for dreams. Dreams can influence mood[39] but do not inspire actions, except in one instance – in which, however, the action instigated by the vision would kill the heroine. Anthia sees herself with Habrocomes in the early days of their love, but another woman appears, also beautiful, and drags him away; as he screams and calls Anthia by name, she awakens (5. 8. 5). Believing the dream to be true, she despairs, thinking that Habrocomes has betrayed their oaths of mutual fidelity, and seeks a means to die.

Anthia' dream is connected to two of Callirhoe's: the one in which she sees Chaereas, in chains, trying to come to her but unable to do so (3. 7. 4), and the one in which she relives the beginnings of their love and the wedding day (5. 5. 5–6).[40] The first vision seems echoed in a phrase found verbatim in both accounts: ὄναρ ἐπέστη, 'a dream stood upon her' (*Ephesiaca* 5. 8. 5; *Callirhoe* 3. 7. 4), while the second is behind the setting of

Anthia's dream in the early days of her love. Though in her vision the chains that appear in Callirhoe's first dream are replaced by another woman (betraying Anthia's obsession with betrayal?), Habrocomes behaves like a prisoner who screams to be freed, as Chaereas does. Anthia's belief that her vision reflects reality also recalls Plangon's conviction that Callirhoe's dream of her wedding day corresponds to reality (*Callirhoe* 5. 5. 7). If Xenophon had this dream in mind, he reversed its purpose: while Callirhoe is heartened by her vision, Anthia's makes her mood take a turn for the worse. The dream, if acted upon, would dispose of the novel's heroine. The one action prompted by it would again be suicide.

Though sleep plays a minor role in the *Ephesiaca,* it is sometimes used in a manner not found in Chariton: to bring the intensity of one party's activity to the fore, providing a backdrop for episodes of sleeplessness or nocturnal action. Two of these episodes involve the flight of a character. Here is the first: 'Then they [Hippothous and his band] slept all night, but Habrocomes was thinking of everything, Anthia, her death, her tomb, her disappearance. No longer able to restrain himself, he pretended he needed something and exited without being seen (for Hippothous' band was lying prostrated by drink), and leaving them all he went to the sea' (3. 10. 4). The second episode further stresses the repose and stillness of the surroundings. Hippothous kills his rival at night, in his sleep, 'and when all was quiet and everyone was resting, I left just as I was, without being seen [...] and travelled the whole night to reach Perinthos, and immediately we boarded a ship [...] and sailed to Asia' (3. 2. 10–1).

These episodes are variations on the lonely vigil motif. The first begins in the same vein as the typical lonely vigil, with everyone slumbering except one person, who is beset by worries. In both narratives the restful background enhances the desperate state of emergency in which the fleeing characters find themselves. In contrast, a third episode with sleep as its background is the happiest in the novel: the protagonists' intimate celebration of their reunion. The scene is configured as an atypical lonely vigil, one in which, as perhaps in no previous Greek specimen, the intense activity of the wakeful party is joyful rather than anguished. The protagonists celebrate together with their newly recovered friends, then all retire, Leucon with Rhode, Hippothous with his boyfriend and Anthia with Habrocomes:

> And when all the others had fallen asleep and there was complete quiet, Anthia, embracing Habrocomes, wept: 'my husband', she said, 'and master, I have found you after much wandering on land and at sea. I have escaped threats of brigands, plots of pirates, insults of pimps, chains, ditches, fetters, poisons and tombs, and I have come to you [. . .] as I was when I was taken from Tyre to Syria. [. . .] And you, Habrocomes, have you stayed chaste? [...]' Thus saying she kept kissing him. [. . .] The whole night they made such protestations to each other and easily persuaded each other, since this was their desire. [. . .] When day came, they embarked.
>
> (5. 14. 1–15. 1)

Structural, thematic and linguistic parallels tie this night to the two earlier sleepless nights experienced by the protagonists. Sleep is forsaken 'the whole night' each time, and each time the new day is said to come, in the same words (the phrase 'the whole night they did this [. . .] and when day came' appears in the last instance as well).[41] The two culminating episodes in the early stages of the plot – the encounter and the wedding – are recalled in the culminating episode at the end.

Xenophon, however, makes the third scene more climactic. While in the first two the protagonists' wakefulness has no background, in the final one it stands out against a landscape of sleepers. The novelist might have had in mind the reunion of Odysseus and Penelope, which is accompanied by a general cessation of activity and by the retiring of Telemachus and of Odysseus' loyal servants (*Od.* 23. 297–9).[42] In Homer, though, sleep does not frame the entire narrative of the couple's reunion, only the portion that follows lovemaking, in which Odysseus and Penelope tell their stories and then doze off in turn. Furthermore, Homer does not enhance the restful atmosphere created by sleep with a statement that 'there was complete quiet'. The added emphasis provided by Xenophon further detaches the wakeful lovers and their words and actions from their soundless surroundings.

Of the extant novelists Xenophon is the only one who stages three full-blown scenes of sleeplessness for his protagonists – one filled with love's pains, one with love's pleasures and one with protestations of love's permanence – to punctuate the main steps in their shared erotic journey. As we shall see in the next section, Achilles Tatius stands diametrically opposed to Xenophon, in that he allots sleepless nights only to his hero, and fills them only with love's pains.

PART THREE: ACHILLES TATIUS

Clitophon's overblown insomnia

Except for its frame, Achilles Tatius' novel is told in the voice of the protagonist, Clitophon.[43] The heroine's feelings at their first encounter remain unknown because the hero chooses not to disclose them, even though he might be aware of them at the time when he is telling his story. In contrast, he offers an inflated narrative of his own experience of love's onslaught, with its attendant sleeplessness. He starts off by giving a full account of the night following his encounter with Leucippe: 'When evening came, the women went to bed first, and soon afterward we did the same. All the others had received enough pleasure from their bellies, but my own feast was all in my eyes: I was filled with the unadulterated vision of the maiden's face, and, sated with it, I left drunk with love. But when I reached the room where I was used to sleeping, I was unable to find sleep' (1. 6. 1–2). Diseases and bodily wounds, he continues, are worse at night because we are at rest and can feel them more intensely. Likewise the wounds of the soul cause more pain when the body does not move. In the daytime ears and eyes are busy with many things that distract us, but 'when stillness binds the body, the soul, alone with itself (καθ'ἑαυτὴν γενομένη), swells with its woe. For all that was lately asleep awakens (ἐξεγείρεται)': pains, worries, fears, fire (1. 6. 2–4).

Clitophon's account of his sleeplessness is affected by his tendency to embellish the experience of the acting character with intellectual flourishes.[44] The alleged woes of the restless lover give the narrator the opportunity for a sententious explanation that does not ring true to the character's raw experience. Clitophon dresses up the commonplace that worries and pains are worse at night by alluding to the Platonic view that the body's slumber empowers the soul to see true reality (*Resp.* 571d–572b). The philosopher claims that sleep, for those who do not overindulge in their appetites but 'awaken (ἐγείρας) their rationality' and 'treat it to beautiful words and thoughts' before bedtime, will allow the soul to be 'pure and alone with itself' (αὐτὸ καθ' αὑτὸ μόνον) and 'apprehend something it does not know'.[45] Clitophon echoes Platonic imagery and language (ἐξεγείρεται, καθ'ἑαυτὴν γενομένη)[46] but distorts Platonic doctrine. He goes to bed filled not with beautiful thoughts but with a vision of the beautiful girl, and he does not awaken his rationality but suffers the awakening of his passion.

When at last Clitophon dozes off, the image of the young woman does not leave him: 'all my dreams were of Leucippe: I talked with her, played with her, ate with her, touched her, and obtained more happiness than in the day. For I kissed her, and the kiss was real' (1. 6. 5). The narrator continues his erudite and playful dialogue with Plato. While the Platonic rational soul will grasp truths during the body's slumber and have dreams that are 'the least lawless' (*Resp.* 571b1–2), the novelistic lover has a dream that is lawless indeed. Finally, love poetry steps in to further glamorize his account: 'As a result [of the dream], when the servant awoke me I scolded him' (1. 6. 5). Clitophon tops off his narrative by hinting at the epigrammatic motif of the lover upbraiding a songbird for awakening him while in the embrace of an erotic dream.[47] The wealthy, urban novelistic hero devolves this unpleasant role to his servant.

Clitophon's insomnia apparently does not abate. Its effects are manifest on his face three days later, when he confides the nature of his love to his cousin Clinias and asks for his help: 'he [Clinias] kissed my face, which showed a lover's sleeplessness, and said, "you love, you really love: your eyes tell the tale"' (1. 7. 3). Before Clinias can offer his advice, however, his beloved Charicles rushes in and breaks into their conversation with the awful news that he will be married off. When he leaves, Clitophon still complains of his insomnia: 'I cannot bear the pain, Clinias. Love in all its power is over me, and drives even sleep from my eyes. I have imaginings of Leucippe everywhere'

(1. 9. 1). Clitophon works mentions of his insomnia into a narrative *entrelacement*, interrupting his confession with the sudden appearance of Charicles and resuming it with intensified pathos after his departure. His complaint of sleeplessness is drawn out by the intervening episode, after which it restarts in a louder voice. The extension and escalation have the effect of amplifying the account of his misery.

But why does Clitophon draw so much attention to his insomnia? His taste for scholarly display might be partly responsible for his lengthy first description of it, but not for his repeated complaints to Clinias. Instead, as Clitophon reports the conversation, he wants the reader to appreciate the ravages caused by his torment. His efforts seem to be aimed at portraying himself as the perfect specimen of the novelistic lover, who outdoes his colleagues in suffering love's pains. Clinias (whose words, of course, could be made up) confirms Clitophon's tale, thus functioning as 'evidence' of its truthfulness and pushing the readers to give credence to it.[48]

At the same time, however, Clitophon's account reveals the erotic proclivities of a young man unabashedly interested in sex, who dreams of touching and kissing the girl he desires on the very first night of his acquaintance with her.[49] No other hero or heroine of a Greek novel has erotic dreams, except for Daphnis and Chloe, who once dream of lying together naked, making up for their daytime shyness (2. 10). But in their case the vision is innocent, because they do not know what sex is and are applying a lesson in love remedies. The erotic dream that prolongs Clitophon's sleepless night, already haunted by Leucippe, rather recalls Artaxerxes' vision in Chariton, which also prolongs a sleepless night haunted by the image of the desired woman. The portrait of a romantic hero's lustful rival thus looms behind the image of Clitophon, whose dream – more daring than Artaxerxes', filled as it is with fondling and kissing – looks ahead to the more advanced overtures that he will soon attempt in his waking hours.

Clitophon's emphasis on his sleeplessness has further implications. To the second-time reader (or to the reader who has reached the end of the novel), it suggests from the outset (or in retrospect) that in this novel the imbalances caused by love, among which is sleeplessness, are *the story*; that there is no satisfying compensation for them.

The day of the reunion ends in a manner atypical of the genre and unsatisfying both for the protagonists and for readers accustomed to more conventional romances: with sleep in a temple. Leucippe retires after reassuring her father about the virginity test she is mandated to take (8. 7. 2–5), and the next day, once her virginity has been proven, the company retires to bed 'in the same way as before' (8. 18. 5). The hero and the heroine obviously have to spend these nights apart, because they are not married and the girl's father is present. But they could have stayed awake in their separate quarters, longing for each other and for their marriage, or at least they did not have to go to sleep 'in the same way as before'. Both episodes are, as in Homer, only caesurae in the action, which resumes with exactly the same words after each night: 'On the following day…' (8. 7. 6; 8. 19. 1) This routine, formulaic rhythm of sleep and activity de-romanticizes the lovers' recovery of each other and substitutes for their wedding night, which is not narrated.

The replacement of the wedding night with a drawn-out reunion that includes two episodes of sleep supports an extreme interpretation of the story's ending: that the marriage turned out to be unhappy.[50] As a matter of fact, Clitophon does not look like a happily married man when he tells his story, but bears the mark of his initiation into love, visible on his face (1. 2. 2). His eyes still 'tell the tale', as they did when he confessed his sleepless love to Clinias (1. 7. 3). His enduring disquiet could explain his choice not to dwell on that special night, which should have repaid him for his loss of sleep, but does not seem to have done so. The prolonged frustration manifested in his allegedly prolonged insomnia found no relief in a night filled with lovemaking.

Hypnotics

Clitophon's erotic dream at the end of his first sleepless night comes true. He manages to kiss and fondle Leucippe and plans to meet later in her bedroom. The operation requires precautions, for her doorkeeper, Gnat (Κώνωψ), is a busybody, true to his name, who buzzes all over to watch the young man's actions closely. To clear the way, Clitophon's conniving servant Satyrus buys a potent sleeping drug, invites Gnat to dinner and pours the drug into his last drink. The doorkeeper is scarcely able to make it to his bedroom, where he 'fell down and lay, sleeping a drugged slumber' (2. 23. 2–3). With Gnat disposed of, Clitophon walks 'on tiptoes' (ἀψοφητί) into Leucippe's room, following a maid. To no avail, for Leucippe's mother Panthea, shaken awake by a frightening dream, bursts in. Clitophon sneaks out just in time.

Drugged sleep furthers the couple's manoeuvres once more. To avoid facing their families, the two decide to elope. When all is ready, Satyrus drugs Panthea with the rest of the potion he had used for Gnat, pouring it into her last drink. She leaves for her room and 'was immediately asleep'. Satyrus proceeds to dispose of Leucippe's chambermaid and the doorman in the same way. And 'when everybody was slumbering', they leave 'on tiptoes' (ἀψοφητί) and reach the harbour, where they hurriedly board a ship about to set sail (2. 31).

Of the extant Greek novels, *Leucippe and Clitophon* is the only one that exploits drugged sleep to remove an obstacle and advance the lovers' plans. When, in Xenophon, Anthia drinks a sleeping potion, she thinks it is a poison and uses it against herself. Two characters in the same novel, Habrocomes and Hippothous, flee unnoticed while everyone rests, but they do not drug people to get their way: in each case, the repose that provides the background for the escape is natural.[51] In Achilles Tatius, by contrast, sleep is artificially induced and individually targeted to allow the lovers to act secretly.[52]

The two episodes made possible (or almost) by drugging opponents underscore Clitophon's cowardliness.[53] In the first he is an anti-Odysseus:[54] he needs his slave even to put his enemy to sleep, and when all is ready and the slave tells him, 'Your Cyclops lies asleep: you prove yourself a good Odysseus!' (2. 23. 3), he enters Leucippe's room 'trembling a double tremor' (2. 23. 3–4). In the second episode Satyrus and Clinias, not Clitophon, organize the flight and take the risks. The servant visits Leucippe, dopes everyone, leads the maiden by the hand (her lover cannot even do that!) and opens the doors, while Clinias arranges for a carriage to wait for them.

Along with pointing up Clitophon's lack of courage, the use of drugs to dispose of an obstacle gives the two scenes a flavour of low literature. Hypnotics put to similar use are a favourite feature of folktales ('guardian magically sent to sleep while girl goes to lover' is an entry in Stith Thompson),[55] beginning with the folktale of Odysseus and the Cyclops. Drunken slumber provides a means of escape also in a mime (preserved in a first-century AD papyrus) in which a Greek girl, Charition, can flee from the clutches of an Indian king because her liberators intoxicate him during a ceremony.[56] To change cultural landscape, drugged sleep used to get the better of an enemy appears in Mozart's *Entführung aus dem Serail*, where the pasha who keeps Constanze as his favourite concubine is knocked out by fortified wine to allow her and her lover to meet, if not to escape. The engineer of the trick is a servant, as in Achilles Tatius.[57]

There is a difference, though, between these episodes and those in *Leucippe and Clitophon*. In folktales and mime, doped sleep not only fosters the organizers' plans but also works towards the expected ending: Odysseus must blind the Cyclops; Charition must escape. This is not the case for the first novelistic scene, in which the drug helps the lovers with a plan – to have sex outside of marriage – that must not come true, for it would steer the novel's plot irremediably away from generic expectations. The trick cannot fully succeed as in the corresponding folk motif 'guardian sent to sleep while girl goes to lover'.

The flight episode does not contravene generic expectations. On the contrary, it initiates the outward journey that is the precondition for and the container of the expected adventures. But the flight also leaves Clitophon and Leucippe unguarded and thus free to have sex, as was their wish. Detailed echoes of the scene in which they attempt to do so set the reader's mind on the possibility that they might make good on their wish. The drug used in the second scheme is what is left of the one used in the first; Panthea drinks it with her 'last cup', as Gnat does with his, in the same words (she κατὰ τῆς κύλικος τῆς τελευταίας, and he κατὰ τῆς τελευταίας κύλικος); both retire and doze off instantly (though we appreciate the writer's more respectful treatment of the lady: she does not 'fall down [...] sleeping a drugged slumber' like the slave but 'is immediately asleep'); both Clitophon entering Leucippe's room and the actors in the escape move 'on tiptoes', and Leucippe is led by Clitophon's servant (2. 31. 3), just as Clitophon in the earlier scene is led by Leucippe's maid (2. 23. 3). The interlocking of the two episodes casts the elopement as the substitute for the failed night of sex, keeping the doors open for sex to be consummated on the road and for the plot to deviate again from generic parameters.

In both episodes, Achilles Tatius sends a dream to counter the lovers' schemes and bring the plot back on the expected track. In the first instance Clitophon and Leucippe cannot carry out their plan because Panthea's nightmare prevents them. In the second they do manage to escape, but a parallel dream forbids lovemaking, against their desire (4. 1. 4; 4. 1. 5). Whether injunctive or predictive, dreams restore generic norms or suggest that those norms must prevail, functioning as antidotes to the lovers' attempts to transgress novelistic protocols with the help of hypnotics.

Sleep, the cure for all illnesses

Leucippe and Clitophon is unique among the extant Greek novels in entrusting characters not only with sleeping potions to remove obstacles, but also with love potions to attract the objects of their desire. Melite seeks to procure a love philter to charm Clitophon, and Gorgias brews such a drug to compel Leucippe. If the narrative is to be an ideal novel, however, these potions must not accomplish their goals; otherwise, the genre's Rule #1, 'I shall love you and only you', would be shattered. The drug would transfer love to new couples, producing plots in which the rivals would succeed at making the hero or the heroine return their affection. Achilles Tatius does not go this far. Just as he counters the protagonists' plans to have sex, he nullifies their rivals' attempts to destroy their attachment through drugs. Melite does not obtain the philter, and Gorgias' potion does not do what it was supposed to do, for Leucippe is given too strong a dose and becomes insane instead of falling in love. (In passing, is Achilles Tatius mocking the Platonic conception of love as madness?)

The narrative of Leucippe's illness contains another type of sleep without parallel in the other novels: sleep artificially induced for healing purposes. The doctor summoned to treat the girl explains to Clitophon that he will give her a hypnotic before administering the therapy: 'We shall make her slumber to quiet the savagery of the crisis, now at its peak. Sleep is the cure for all illnesses' (4. 10. 3). Clitophon sits by her all night, talking to the chains that restrain her. When she awakes, she cries out senseless words. The doctor gives her the second medicine, but to no effect.

'Sleep, the cure for all illnesses': this is a commonplace in Greek culture.[58] The novelistic doctor follows this widespread belief in sleep's healing power, which had also been codified in medical writings since at least the late fifth century.[59] But medicinal slumber this time does not help, for Leucippe awakens as deranged as she was; nor does the second drug help. Is there any point to this medical failure, besides the obvious one of prolonging the suspense by deferring resolution?

Leucippe's sleep eventually does provide the cure. After ten days of madness with no improvement, 'once in her slumber, she uttered these words in her dreams:[60] "It is because of you that I am mad, Gorgias!"' (4. 15. 1) Achilles Tatius causes another dream, with the sleep talking it breeds, to move the action back to its novelistic track by restoring the heroine to sanity and to the hero. Gorgias' servant is eventually found and he promises to heal the girl. Following his instructions, Clitophon drugs her again, and while she slumbers he watches her as he had done the first time around. Verbal repetitions further connect the two scenes. Just as the doctor prescribes sleep 'to quiet the savagery (τὸ ἄγριον) of the crisis', Clitophon prays for the drug to 'overcome that other barbarous and savage (ἄγριον) drug' (4. 17. 1); on the first night, Clitophon asks the sleeping Leucippe, 'are you in your senses (σωφρονεῖς) while you slumber or are even your dreams mad?' (4. 10. 3), and on the second he says, 'your dreams have sense (σωφρονεῖ)' (4. 17. 4). By echoing the previous scene of uncured madness, Clitophon underscores the reversal.

The doctor's failure and the success of the unexpected sleep talking highlight the dominance of Chance, *Tyche*, in this novel. What brings about Leucippe's healing is a random utterance, prompted by no human or divine contrivance. The picture radically changes in *Daphnis and Chloe*, where *Tyche* plays no role in solving the protagonists' predicaments, but the gods do. And they use sleep and dreams as the chief means to reach their goals.

PART FOUR: LONGUS

Chloe's siesta

Daphnis and Chloe are taking a break from their shepherding duties during the hottest hour of the day. He is piping and the flocks are resting in the shade, when Chloe 'dozed off unawares'. Daphnis notices it, stops playing and devotes himself to greedy contemplation of his Sleeping Beauty:

> He looked (ἔβλεπεν) at all of her, insatiably, because he was free from shame, and as he did he softly whispered: 'what eyes are slumbering there, what breath comes from that mouth! Not even apples or pears smell so sweet! But I shrink from kissing her: her kiss bites the heart, and like new honey it drives one mad. I am also afraid that my kiss might wake her. Oh those talkative cicadas, they won't let her sleep with all the noise they make! And those he-goats, banging their horns as they fight! Oh wolves more cowardly than foxes, can't you come to snatch them?
>
> (1. 25)

This scene fits into a cultural landscape rich in images of sleepers. Starting with the Hellenistic period, sleeping figures become much more prominent than they had been in archaic and classical Greece, appearing often in paintings and making their debut in sculpture. New sleepers are pictured: in addition to Ariadne (Figure 5.1) and the maenads, Satyrs, Nymphs, the child Eros (Figure 1.2), Hermaphrodite and Endymion. A variety of settings host their images, including gardens and cemeteries.[61] Epigrammatic poetry and Philostratus' *Imagines* reflect these developments by describing sleeping figures, especially Eros and Ariadne,[62] while the conceit of the lover watching his loved one slumbering appeals to poets and prose writers both Greek and Roman. Longus' vignette, which is part of a narrative that claims to 'counter-write' a painting (*Proem* 2), demonstrates the novelist's keen awareness of contemporary trends in art and literature.

The scene also looks back, to an episode from Plato's *Phaedrus* (259e1–6), which Longus' contemporary readers would easily have recognized because of the dialogue's popularity.[63] Socrates and Phaedrus are conversing under a plane tree, in the midday heat, while the chirruping cicadas tempt them to sleep.[64] Like the two friends in Plato's dialogue, Daphnis and Chloe are starting on a quest. But they are seeking love, not doing philosophy.[65] The different goals of the searchers are also reflected in their different attitudes towards sleep.

Socrates and Phaedrus cannot yield to the temptation of a nap, lest the cicadas consider them like lazy sheep and fail to recommend them to the Muse of their profession. The two must keep conversing so as to produce a countermelody against the cicadas' lulling song. In contrast, Daphnis and Chloe are not conversing to begin with, and they make no effort to stay awake. While he is playing, she slides into sleep without even noticing. The sluggish animals that in Plato constitute the negative

Figure 5.1 *Sleeping Ariadne*, Roman copy of a Hellenistic sculpture (second century BC), Rome, Vatican Museums.

example for the ever-wakeful philosophers reappear in Longus as the resting flocks that lead the way to Chloe's nap.[66]

Rather than imitating the unsleeping philosopher, Chloe resembles the epigrammatic figure of the worn-out lover who wishes to lull his passion to sleep with the help of a talkative insect, as in this poem by Meleager:

> Ringing cicada, drunk with dewy drops, you sing your pastoral song that chatters in the wilderness, and seated on top of the leaves, striking your dark skin with saw-like legs, you make shrill music like the lyre's. But sing, friend, some new merry tune for the nymphs of the trees, strike up a loud sound in response to Pan, that I may escape from love and snatch a midday nap, reclining here beneath the shady plane tree.
>
> (*AP* 7. 196)

Several components of Longus' vignette can be seen in this epigram: the shade (under a 'Platonic' plane tree), the midday hour and the cicada. Both this epigram and a second one, also by Meleager (*AP* 7. 195) and working with the same conceit, share with Longus' novel the additional motif of love-induced insomnia. Just as the lover who calls for the insect's lulling song wishes he could 'snatch a midday nap'; just as he has been suffering, as reads the second poem, 'from the toils of all-sleepless care', Chloe has been almost chronically insomniac since she first felt the pangs of love (1. 14. 4; 1. 22. 3).

It is not an insect, however, that sends Chloe to sleep, as in the wish of the epigrammatic lover, but Daphnis' music. Longus implies this by framing the scene with the lad playing the panpipes rather than with the cicadas chirping in the trees, as in Plato. To be sure, talkative insects used to work their hypnotic charm on Chloe, but that was before she fell in love. 'Who will take care of the chirruping cricket', she says, 'which I toiled much to catch so it could lull me to sleep [...] Now I cannot rest because of Daphnis, and the cricket chirrups in vain' (1. 14. 4). Daphnis' music alone has power, the only music that captivates her ears when she falls in love: 'his panpipes make a beautiful sound, but so do the nightingales. Yet I do not care for those' (1. 14. 2). Marc

Figure 5.2 Marc Chagall, *Midday in Summertime* (1961), lithograph, from *Daphnis and Chloe*.

Chagall, who has illustrated the scene of Chloe's nap in his lithograph *Midday in Summertime* (Figure 5.2), puts the lulling charm of Daphnis' music front stage by drawing him not in the act of looking at Chloe but piping, while she seems to be about to fall asleep, for she is turned slightly sideways. The substitution of

Daphnis' pipes for the chirping cicadas that tempt Socrates and Phaedrus to doze off illustrates the importance of music in Longus' representation of love's development.[67]

Chloe's sleep leads to a separation between the children, assigning them different roles shortly after their first, identical experience of love's onslaught. Before the nap scene they look at each other in the same way. For both, love acts as an eye-opener, causing them to see each other afresh. While at the bath, Daphnis 'appeared beautiful' to Chloe as she 'contemplated' his naked body (1. 13. 2). After the fatal kiss, Daphnis admired Chloe's face 'as if only then for the first time he had acquired eyes, and until then he had been blind' (1. 17. 3).[68] A few lines prior to the nap scene, the children are still enjoying their habitual pleasure of looking at each other:

> When midday came, their eyes were captured. She, seeing (ὁρῶσα) Daphnis naked, was entirely taken by his beauty and melted with love, unable to find fault with any part of him. And he, seeing (ἰδών) her with the fawn skin and the pine wreath as she handed him the pail, thought he saw (ὁρᾶν) one of the Nymphs in the cave.
>
> (1. 24. 1)

Chloe's nap comes shortly after this scene and likewise it takes place at noon, but it reads like a new development against the previous episode. Daphnis and Chloe were accustomed to look at each other in wonder, midday after midday. But one midday she falls asleep, lulled by his music, and their mutual and identical seeing (ὁρᾶν) comes to an end, replaced by his individual and more voluntary act of vision (ἔβλεπεν): it is a 'gaze', that is, 'a way of looking that is intense, focused, and demonstrative of agency'.[69] Daphnis has gazed at Chloe before. Though the children discover each other's beauty with equal eyes, Daphnis behaves, or wants to behave, more actively: 'he wanted to look (βλέπειν) at Chloe, but when he looked (βλέπων) he was filled with blushing' (1. 17. 2).[70] While Chloe slumbers, he can look at her without blushing, and he does so with a gaze that could even be called, following Longus' description of it, 'consumptive', because it rests unchecked and insatiable on the sleeping woman.

Cued by the author's emphasis on Daphnis' unrestrained way of watching Chloe, Longus' readers will instantly be reminded of the familiar image of a sleeper who becomes prey to lustful eyes – or more than just eyes. Sometimes, the lover does not even spend much time watching before rushing into action. In an epigram by Paulus Silentiarius (sixth century AD), for instance, the account of the erotic attack takes precedence over the description of the sleeper, which stops after mentioning the posture conventional for sleeping figures in art:

> One afternoon pretty Menecratis lay outstretched in slumber with her arm twined around her head. Boldly I entered her bed and had to my delight accomplished half the journey of love, when she woke up, and with her white hands set to tearing out all my hair. She struggled till all was over, and then said, her eyes filled with tears: 'Wretch, you have had your will'.[71]

In other instances the gaze becomes prominent. Thus in an epigram by Philodemus:

> Moon of the night, horned moon, friend of all-night festivals, shine! Shine through the cracks of the window and illuminate golden Callistion. For an immortal goddess to spy on the deeds of lovers is no cause for reproach. You bless her and me, I know, Moon. For Endymion also set your soul on fire.
>
> (*AP* 5. 123)

This lover parades a scopophiliac exhibitionism, asking the Moon, whom he imagines to be as voyeuristic as himself, to enter the bedroom and let her light shine, first on his girl, so he can watch her, then on their lovemaking.

Daphnis is as aroused as these lovers, and many more besides. However, he does not make the slightest move towards Chloe. And his gaze, his only 'move', turns out to be far more discreet than Longus announces by calling it insatiable and without shame. Most of Daphnis' soliloquy is occupied with his fear of kissing Chloe and his wish that she keep on sleeping. It is true that the

Figure 5.3 Niccolò Pisano, *An Idyll: Daphnis and Chloe* (*c.*1500), London, The Wallace Collection.

longer she slumbers, the longer he can look at her. His expressed wish, that she should not awaken, hides an unexpressed wish for more undisturbed watching. But his preoccupation with his fear, rather than with her features, saves the girl from the exposure suffered by other sleeping women, who meet with a more expansive gaze. All we are given to see of Chloe through Daphnis' eyes are her own eyes and mouth.

This takes me to a second way Daphnis' gaze turns out to be more modest than is expected. The youth looks only at Chloe's face, countering the titillating expectations raised by Longus' introductory comment: 'he looked at *all* of her'. Later painters have not missed the focus of Daphnis' gaze. So for instance Niccolò Pisano, in *An Idyll: Daphnis and Chloe* (Figure 5.3), points Daphnis' eyes towards the girl's face, while her breasts are exposed only for the pleasure of those viewing the painting. Even more concentrated on her face are the young man's eyes in a work by François Boucher (Figure 5.4), though Chloe's breasts are more lavishly displayed there than in Pisano's painting. Daphnis' contained gaze is consistent with the asymmetrical treatment of the children in the novel: while Chloe repeatedly sees Daphnis naked, he does not see her thus until the very end of Book 1 (32), when for the first time she bathes before his eyes. Until then, Chloe is always wearing something. Even in the narrative of their mutual watching and admiring of each other, which precedes the nap scene, she sees his naked body while he sees her wearing a fawn skin and a wreath.

Daphnis' contained gaze sets Longus' vignette in opposition specifically to this account of Dionysus approaching the sleeping Ariadne:

> See also Ariadne, or rather her slumber. Her breasts here are naked down to her waist. Her neck is bent back and her throat is soft, and her right arm is totally visible while her left hand rests on her tunic to prevent the wind from dishonouring her. How her breath is, Dionysus, and how sweet, whether it smells of apples or grapes, you will tell me when you kiss her.
>
> (Philostratus *Imagines* 1. 15. 3)

This episode is the main mythological inspiration for Longus' scene. The novelist and Philostratus may have worked from a common source.[72] Both stress the care with which the bystanders try not to awaken the sleeper (see *Imagines* 1. 15. 2) and both include smell alongside sight as a sensual stimulus, in both cases the sweet, fruity smell of the woman's breath. Philostratus, however, undresses Ariadne. She is half naked and her body is front stage, while her face does not exist except for her enticing breath, to which Dionysus is lured. To prepare for the erotic contact, Philostratus adds the enticement of touch to those of sight and smell, drawing attention to the softness of Ariadne's skin. Daphnis neither sees nor feels Chloe's skin.

The absence of lustful intent makes Daphnis comparable to sleepwatchers, as Leo Steinberg has called the figures who gaze at sleepers in Picasso's graphic works of the 1930s. Sleepwatchers do not rush to their target but step back, absorbed in thought. A modern critic identifies the seeds of sleepwatching already in Greco-Roman art, in compositions in which a wakeful figure stands in awe and makes no move – not yet – towards the sleeper.[73] Daphnis is likewise frozen in contemplation. The pause that sleepwatching creates, the suspension of action, is filled with his whispered monologue as he watches Chloe.

The reason for Daphnis' inaction, however, is not that the pleasure of contemplation reins in his desire. Rather, he is held back by his ignorance of love and is unable to read his desire, which he calls fear. Fear functions as the restraining force, both allowing Daphnis to keep his naïveté and causing him to abide instinctively by the generic and societal rules that he is required to follow in spite of his ignorance of them.

Daphnis' inability to understand his desire shows that he is still lagging behind Chloe in terms of erotic maturation. She is cast in the vulnerable position of the slumbering prey, but nothing

Figure 5.4 François Boucher, *Daphnis and Chloe* (1743), London, The Wallace Collection.

happens to her, because Daphnis is unable to seize the opportunity afforded to him by her sleep. Conversely, when she awakens, she plays with his desire. After seeing that he took out of her blouse a cicada that had found refuge from a swallow there, she puts the insect back (1. 26). Chloe's gesture suggests that she understands, at least subliminally, what both she and Daphnis are seeking. But he does not seize this second opportunity to reach down to her breast again. Chagall catches Daphnis' naïveté in another lithograph, entitled *The Little Swallow*, in which Daphnis seems to avert his gaze shyly after taking the cicada out of Chloe's blouse.

The swallow, which looks like an innocent pet in Chagall's illustration, is a predator in Longus' novel.[74] Its failure to seize the insect which Chloe's breast shelters thus foreshadows the gentle, non-predatory manner of her own erotic initiation. The swallow's defeat suggests that Daphnis, who does nothing to Chloe in the sleep scene, owing to his fearful ignorance, will abstain even when his ignorance is cured. His restraint finds a doubling in the restraint of the normally lustful god Pan, which is also announced in the sleep scene.

References to Pan crowd the episode. The choice of midday for Chloe's nap sets it in a landscape frequented by the god, who likes to make his appearances at noon and to doze in his pastoral haunts during the 'immobile hour', as Plato calls midday (*Phdr.* 242a4–5).[75] Chloe's siesta may suggest Pan's own. Its Pan-like aura is enhanced by Daphnis' behaviour as soon as she falls asleep, for he stops playing, as if obeying the injunction of Theocritus' goatherd that one should not pipe at noon lest Pan awaken:

> We're not allowed to pipe at midday, shepherd – not allowed.
> We are afraid of Pan. It's then that he rests, you know,
> Tired from the hunt: he is tetchy at this hour,
> And his lip is always curled in sour displeasure.[76]

Another feature of the scene conjures up Pan: the hypnotic power of Daphnis' music. Two epigrams (*AP* 16. 12 and 13), purportedly inspired by a statue of Pan, represent him as he causes sleep with his piping: 'Come and sit under my pine that murmurs thus sweetly, bending to the soft west wind. And see, too, this fountain that drops honey, beside which, playing on my reeds in solitude, I bring sweet slumber'. And: 'Sit down by this high-foliaged vocal pine that quivers in the constant western breeze, and beside my bubbling stream Pan's pipe shall bring slumber to your charmed eyelids'. Pan lulls those who listen to his pipes to sleep, but when he himself dozes, piping must stop. Daphnis lulls Chloe to sleep with his pipes, but when she slumbers – in a setting evocative of Pan – he stops piping.

This cluster of allusions to Pan heralds his active participation in the plot. Though Longus' novel is 'a dedication to Eros, the Nymphs, and Pan' (*Proem* 3), only Eros and the Nymphs have intervened so far, taking concerted action in dreams (1. 7–8). Daphnis has invoked Pan in a beauty contest, but only as a self-serving comparison (1. 16. 3). It is towards the end of Book 1 that the god makes himself increasingly felt. The noon hour is the setting not only of Chloe's nap, but also, immediately before that episode, of the children's game of watching each other, and in the midday light Chloe is wearing a wreath of pine, a tree sacred to Pan, which Daphnis kisses and wears in turn, thus moving it to the forefront of the narrative (1. 24. 2).[77] Immediately after Chloe's siesta, Pan makes his first meaningful appearance as an object of song, along with Pitys, a nymph he loved (1. 27. 2). The singer is a female cowherd who wears a pine wreath, like Chloe, and sits under a pine tree. Three sequences in close succession – the children watching each other, Chloe napping and the herdswoman singing – are thus sprinkled with references to Pan.

In addition to foreshadowing Pan's entry, the episode of Chloe's siesta casts him in the role of the protagonists' helper. Longus might have known stories in which Pan looked favourably on those who slept at noon.[78] He might also have known an epigram in which the god and the mythic singer Daphnis appear in a configuration that both calls to mind and reverses the roles of Daphnis and Chloe in the nap scene:

> You sleep, Daphnis, resting your tired body on the leaf-strewn ground, and your stakes for nets are newly set on the hill. But Pan chases you and with him Priapus, his lovely head bound with saffron-colored ivy. They move

into your cave, of one purpose. But flee, flee, leave slumber's deep stupor.

([Theocritus] *Ep.* 3 = *AP* 9. 338)

While the epigrammatic Daphnis is asleep and the target of Pan's desire, Daphnis' novelistic incarnation is awake and does not move towards the sleeping Chloe. By conjuring up Pan in the figure of the piping Daphnis but converting Pan's behaviour into tame watching, Longus suggests that the god, like the lad, will not lust after Chloe. Pan will not attack her in her slumber or chase her as he does Daphnis in the epigram. He will not behave towards her in the same way he did, as she and we are soon to find out, towards two mythical women, Syrinx and Echo, who rejected his advances and paid with their lives. Chloe, who learns about Pan's erotic proclivities, understandingly protests when Daphnis swears his love by that god (2. 39. 3). How can the harasser of nymphs make good an oath of fidelity? For Chloe he represents lustful infidelity and sexual violence.[79] But the manner and circumstances of her sleep intimate that the rapist of myth will become the couple's protector.[80]

Sleep and Chloe's recoveries

Pan enters the novel in full battle gear to rescue Chloe from the band of Methymnian youths who have kidnapped her. After frightening them with sights and sounds, 'when, around the middle of the day, the chief fell into sleep, not without divine impulse, [he] appeared to him' to demand Chloe's release (2. 26. 5). It is Pan himself who knocks the band's leader out. Sleep's divine provenance is made clear, and the midday hour agrees with Pan's liking for that time of day.[81] The god engulfs his victim in a particularly heavy slumber, as is pointed up by a verb, 'to fall', which describes the attack of sleep on the exhausted Erinyes (Aesch. *Eum.* 68), on Penelope's drunken suitors (Hom. *Od.* 2. 398) and, in the novel, on the drugged doorkeeper Gnat (*Leucippe and Clitophon* 2. 23. 2). Sleep's onslaught carries Pan's epiphany in the form of a threatening dream, which causes the leader to 'leap up (ἀναπηδᾷ) in great agitation' (2. 28. 1).

In spite of the aggressive manner of its coming, however, sleep is beneficial to the Methymnian chief because it breeds a dream that offers guidance to him, guaranteeing a safe end to his journey if he releases Chloe: a dream, in other words, that helps both him and the heroine. Another such dream also visits Daphnis when he despairs over the loss of Chloe, who has just been kidnapped by the band, until an eerie slumber relieves him of his exhaustion: 'While he was so speaking, after all his tears and sorrow, a deep sleep took hold of him' (2. 23. 1). He sees the Nymphs and hears their reassuring words, which cause him to 'leap up (ἀναπηδήσας) from his slumber' (2. 24. 1). The parallels between the two sequences are patent: each time, a character in a predicament suddenly falls into a god-sent sleep and has a guiding dream; both characters 'leap up'; and both sequences herald Chloe's recovery.

These episodes illustrate a characteristic shared by all the novels: whether sent by a god or by nature, sleep never harms deserving characters but it often helps them, while it does harm evil ones: it causes the corrupt rival of Hippothous to be killed (*Ephesiaca* 3. 2. 10–1), Theron, the only true villain in Chariton, to embark on a course of action that turns out to be his ruin, and, as we shall see, the evil-minded Thermouthis (in Heliodorus) to be fatally bitten by a snake. In terms of sleep's consequences for the sleeper, the novels are thus more black and white, or reassuring, than even the *Odyssey*, where sweet slumber harms Odysseus twice and arguably harms Penelope by making it easy for Telemachus to leave on the sly (though his journey is part of a divine scheme favourable to her).[82]

Though shared by all the novels, this function of sleep as a dispenser of poetic justice is manifest especially in *Daphnis and Chloe*. The Methymnian chief, to be sure, is a wicked individual, but he responds to the dream by changing from a bad to a good personage (he releases Chloe), and his slumber with the attendant vision is instrumental in saving the heroine. In yet another episode sleep carries a message that promotes Chloe's interests. When it is discovered that she is the daughter of wealthy parents, Daphnis' father wonders who they are. 'After much thinking [he] was weighed down by a deep slumber' (4. 34. 1), and Eros in a vision tells him how to find them. The episode is cast in a familiar mould: unproductive thinking yields to sleep, which becomes the vehicle for a commanding and revelatory dream.

The two most momentous episodes in Chloe's pre-marital life, her recovery from her kidnappers and her recognition – which is also a recovery, of her identity – are thus initiated by dreams of which the carrier is an unusually deep, god-induced slumber. The activation of sleep and dreams is equally distributed among the deities to whom the novel is dedicated: the Nymphs (acting on Daphnis), Pan (on the leader of the band) and Eros (the main agent in the third dream).[83] The provenance of sleep and dreams, and their directing role at these major junctures, bring to the fore a well-known feature of Longus' novel, namely, that its plot is written by divine rather than human agents.

The gods' commanding presence is further highlighted by the total absence of scenes of productive nocturnal deliberation, such as we find in Chariton. In that novel, as we have seen, characters make consequential decisions during nights of wakeful pondering. If sleep comes at last and guides them by carrying a dream, the dream is either in accordance with the line of action that was already taking shape in the character's mind (so for Callirhoe), or opposed to it (so for Theron). In contrast, Daphnis, his father, and the leader of the band reach no decision whatsoever by themselves, but must fall into a god-sent slumber and have a god-sent dream in order to find directions.[84]

Chronic insomnia

Reassured by the Nymphs about the prospect of recovering Chloe, Daphnis goes home, eats a little and retires: 'But even his sleep was not without tears. He prayed to see the Nymphs again in a dream, he prayed for the day to come quickly [...] That night seemed the longest of all nights' (2. 24. 4).

This episode of nocturnal restlessness is not isolated. On the contrary, Daphnis and Chloe suffer from almost chronic insomnia. Longus adapts the motif of love-induced sleeplessness to fit with the original development of his novel: the discovery of love. Typically, erotic passion flares up at first sight, and the sleep disturbances it causes are filled with the lovers' longing and the painful awareness of their desire, but in *Daphnis and Chloe* things are quite different. The children's love grows from daily companionship, when the time is ripe, and is not immediately known as love, so that they cannot at first understand why they stay up at night. As their erotic awakening progresses, however, their insomnia comes to assume different meanings.

When Chloe first experiences love, and with it sleep troubles, the reason for them is unfathomable to her, but perfectly clear to the readers, who recognize a canonical symptom of erotic passion in literature. Chloe does not even know love's name, as Longus explains right before detailing her symptoms:

> She did not know what she was suffering, being a young girl raised in the country, who had not heard anyone speak love's name. Distress filled her soul, she could not keep her eyes under control, and Daphnis' name was always on her lips. She did not care for food, stayed awake at night, neglected the flock; she would laugh and then cry; fall asleep and then leap up; her face was pale, and then in flames with blushing. Not even a cow when goaded acts as she did.
>
> (1. 13. 5–6)

The mention of Chloe's ignorance, combined with the list of her symptoms, deepens the cultural gap between readers and character. The readers appreciate the literary texture of the list,[85] while the girl whose behaviour is so closely analysed with these literary tools does not know what they mean.[86] Her monologue, which follows the authorial description of her state, with its display of literary knowledge, is a display of ignorance: 'I suffer this, but don't know why' (1. 14).

Daphnis soon falls victim to the same illness. It is true that in his case sleeplessness is not listed among love's symptoms, though he shares others with Chloe (a lack of appetite, pallor, a habit of talking only of or with the other). Longus' goal in omitting sleeplessness, however, seems to be merely to create stylistic variety. For we soon learn that both children have been constantly insomniac, except for one night when extreme fatigue got the better of passion (1. 22. 3).

The two understand the cause of their insomnia after learning about Eros from the old shepherd Philetas. He explains that he loved in his youth, and lists the symptoms as he, the reincarnation of a love poet,[87] would know them:

> I was not mindful of food or drink, nor did I take sleep. My soul was in pain, my heart pounded, my body felt cold; I screamed as if I had been beaten, was quiet as if I were a dead man; I dove in rivers as if I were burning.
>
> (2. 7. 4–5)

As soon as the children return to their homes and meditate upon the lesson, they compare their symptoms with Philetas' list and conclude that they love (2. 8. 1–3). They now know why they keep staying awake at night. Sleep disturbances, though, continue to afflict them for a new reason: their inability to follow Philetas' lesson to its conclusion.

The morning after learning that they love, Daphnis and Chloe run to each other to apply the remedies mentioned by Philetas. They embrace and kiss, but cannot find the audacity to lie together naked, as their teacher had recommended. Their timidity results in sleeplessness, from a mixture of excitement and frustration: 'There followed another night without sleep, in which they thought of what had happened and regretted what they had not done' (2. 9. 2). When they finally doze off, their unfulfilled desire spills over into an erotic dream, in which they not only relive what they had done but also perform what they had not. Their insomnia has grown from an unfathomable symptom of an unknown condition, to a recognizable symptom of a condition that has a name, to the consequence of shyness conflicting with the force of desire.

When winter sets in, there come more nocturnal agonies. While all the peasants enjoy the season's rest, eat regularly and 'sleep long slumbers', Daphnis and Chloe, who remember 'the pleasures they left behind – how they kissed, embraced, ate together – spent sleepless and sorrowful nights, waiting for the season of spring, as a rebirth' (3. 4. 1–2). A variation on the motif of the lonely vigil (everyone rests except the children), this scene marks another development in the meaning of their insomnia, which now betokens not inexplicable turmoil or erotic frustration but longing.[88]

After reuniting with his true father, Daphnis loses sleep again, this time because a rustic has kidnapped Chloe. When her rescuer returns with her, he finds Daphnis' father in a deep slumber, but the young man is 'sleepless and still weeping in the garden' (4. 29. 4). As on the night of Chloe's first kidnapping, Daphnis is beset by anxiety. The contrast between him and his soundly sleeping father underscores the distance that still separates the two: the father does not yet know of his son's love and can rest content with his unexpected recovery of him, while Daphnis experiences yet another attack of love's distress, which proves his passion stronger than the joy of having found his true parents.

Ending with a sleepless night

The wedding night, at last, cures the frustration and inner turmoil that long kept the children from sleeping well. The final paragraph of the novel is devoted to this night:

> Daphnis and Chloe lay together naked, embraced one another and kissed. They were sleepless the whole night even more than owls. Daphnis did to Chloe some of the things Lycaenion had taught him, and then, for the first time, Chloe learned that what had happened in the woods were just shepherds' games.

Longus could have ended with the epilogue that he provides in the previous paragraph, from which we learn that in post-narrative time Daphnis and Chloe had two children and maintained a pastoral lifestyle. Proleptic epilogues are effective ways of offering narrative closure, setting a shift in time scale or orientation and providing elements of *Nachgeschichte* ('post-history') for the major characters.[89] But in this case such an ending would have been unsatisfactory both for the hero and the heroine, who have spent six seasons seeking love's ways, and for the readers, who have read four books following them in their quest. Longus, then, reverts to the present of the wedding night. And it is an emphatically wakeful night, filled with lovemaking, which makes up for the pains that caused the protagonists' insomnia all along their quest.

The children have already spent two nights together before, in sleep.[90] After Chloe escapes from her kidnappers, she, Daphnis and their friends celebrate her recovery with a feast, and 'when night came they slept there in the fields' (2. 31. 2). Improvised slumber likewise follows Chloe's recognition: 'They stayed there and rested' (4. 36. 3). These episodes of casual sleep, which crown the two most momentous episodes in Chloe's unmarried life, are snapshots that look ahead to the most momentous episode in the novel, the wedding night. Longus builds to a climax, moving from the partially happy endings in which Daphnis and Chloe, reunited but not yet married, simply and un-ritualistically sleep in the company of others, to the fully happy ending, which replaces nightlong rest with nightlong sex. Unlike Leucippe and Clitophon, who are only said to sleep in separate quarters when they are reunited, Daphnis and Chloe at last are sleepless with love's pleasures.

PART FIVE: HELIODORUS

Playing Odysseus: the need for sleep, the pleasure of tales

No other Greek novel is as sensitive to the demands of physical and mental exhaustion as the *Aethiopica*. In a fashion that conjures up the *Odyssey*, Heliodorus repeatedly records the characters' need for rest. As soon as he reaches his dwelling, the brigand Thyamis 'went to sleep, weighed down by the fatigue of the journey and beset by pressing worries' (1. 7. 3). The priest Calasiris feels the need to sleep time and again, and his host Nausicles also yields to his tiredness after a journey. Even Theagenes and Chariclea, in spite of their ever-wakeful anxieties, can succumb to a profound slumber.[91] The heroine in particular has a gift for dozing off in the most unexpected places and situations (in a temple, during wedding festivities), after fits of despair.[92]

This novel's characters, however, know a powerful antidote against the natural need for sleep: storytelling. Heliodorus' narrators again follow in the footsteps of Homer's by pitting the excitement of tales against the appeal of sweet slumber. When Theagenes, 'in the first vigil of the night' (1. 8. 1), asks his new friend Cnemon to tell his story, the latter objects: 'This is not the time to introduce a new episode, my misfortunes, into yours. Besides, the rest of the night would not be enough for the telling, and you are in need of sleep and rest after all your toils'. But Theagenes and Chariclea insist, 'thinking that they will find great consolation in a story like their own' (1. 8. 6–9. 1).

Features of this passage hark back to the exchange of tales between Odysseus and Eumaeus: those tales, too, are full of woes, and they drive sleep off and draw the two characters nearer to each other. We might recall their identical, sympathetic responses to each other's stories (*Od.* 14. 361–2; 15. 486–7) and the way Eumaeus prefaces his by asking Odysseus to stay awake and listen.[93] Heliodorus draws on the same sentiments. When Cnemon provisionally ends his narrative, protesting that it would take too long to tell the rest, he and his friends burst into tears. The stirring caused by the stories that replace sleep in Eumaeus' hut escalates in the novel to a mournful concert played by both the speaker and his listeners, who, like Odysseus and Eumaeus, are absorbed in the 'memory' (μνήμῃ) of their misfortunes (1. 18. 1).[94] Chariclea and Theagenes would not have stopped this concert, were it not for the fact that they doze off on account of 'the pleasure of weeping' (*ibid.*).

The novelistic scene, however, differs from the epic one in the way it exploits sleep. While Eumaeus dismisses it and shows himself eager to tell his story, Cnemon calls on it to justify his reluctance to speak. For this detail he had another Homeric model at hand: Odysseus, who likewise invokes the need for sleep to cut his story short (*Od.* 11. 330–2).

Odysseus is also the underlying reference for Cnemon's behaviour earlier in his narrative, when he interrupts himself, claiming that his friends must be tired. After recounting how he was condemned to exile on account of the manoeuvres of his stepmother Demainete, he stops, but not without giving his audience a preview of the story's ending. The evil woman was punished, 'but in which way you will hear another time. Now you must sleep. The night is far advanced and you badly need to rest' (1. 14. 2). Theagenes, though, presses him: 'You will make us even more miserable, if you leave the wicked Demainete unpunished in your story' (*ibid.*).

Cnemon breaks off after piquing the audience's curiosity to hear the rest. Likewise, Odysseus prefaces his interruption by suggesting that there is more to his story (*Od.* 11. 328–30). We note, however, that Cnemon both times appeals to his listeners' tiredness, Odysseus to his own. This difference might suggest that Cnemon is a less confident narrator; that he feels he does not hold the audience under his spell. Odysseus thinks he can decide when to break off his narrative on the basis of his own needs, and this even though he is a guest, whereas Cnemon, overtly at least, shows himself considerate of his new friends' needs.

The power of stories to drive away sleep becomes a leitmotif in the Odysseus-like narrative delivered by Calasiris. When he stops, after recounting how Theagenes kissed Chariclea's hand, Cnemon wants to hear more. But he rejoins: 'Not only are you insatiable of stories, Cnemon, but you are also immune to sleep. Only a small part of the night is left and you resist, wide awake, and are not worn out by the dragging length of my story' (4. 4. 2). Cnemon replies: 'I disagree with Homer, father, when he says that there is satiety in everything, including love, whereas to my judgement there is never a surfeit of it, whether one is engaged in its pleasures or listening to stories of it'.

A reader conversant with Homer will remember that one of the pleasures in the passage targeted by Cnemon is slumber: 'There is satiety in everything, even in sleep, love, sweet song and the excellent dance' (*Il.* 13. 636–7). While in Homer sleep and love are on equal footing, for Cnemon the joy of love, whether experienced firsthand or as a story, surpasses that of sweet slumber and even chases it away. Calasiris' listener pays a compliment to the love story that he is hearing – and we are reading – by suggesting with both his words and his behaviour that *Theagenes and Chariclea* is more compelling than the most needed rest.[95]

Calasiris shrewdly calls for sleep after narrating a climactic episode. Though Cnemon draws a deep breath ('you saved me with that kiss!' 4. 4. 2), he is bound to remain awake because the tale stops at an exciting moment. The narrator's strategic pause matches his prior emphasis, with another pause, on the atmosphere of ritual solemnity that he creates to take the narrative to new heights after recounting the preliminaries to the protagonists' first meeting. The escalation is framed by nightfall. Calasiris tells his story in the daylight, up to the narrative of the procession that leads to the encounter. He wishes to stop there. But, since Cnemon is 'insatiable [...] of good stories', they will light a lamp, make the last libation and then leisurely spend the night in storytelling (3. 4. 11). The nocturnal setting enhances the increasing interest of the story, which will replace sleep from now on.

Calasiris calls for slumber again when his narrative reaches another culminating point, the beginning of his sea journey with the young couple: 'Let us stop the story here and snatch a little nap' (5. 1. 3). Even his sleep-proof listener must be tired, he maintains, and in any case he himself is weighed down by age, 'and the remembrance of my sorrows weakens my mind and lulls it to rest' (*ibid.*). The old man is worn out by his own storytelling. When he first met Cnemon, he was restless, overeager to tell his tale (2. 21. 6). The long performance filled with sorrowful memories has worked as a lullaby. Cnemon, though, does not hear him. Outdoing Alcinous, who is ready to stay up 'until dawn' to listen to Odysseus (*Od.* 11. 375–6), he says he would listen to Calasiris 'many nights and many more days' (5. 1. 4). With this hyperbole, Heliodorus advertizes his novel's charm, superior even to the *Odyssey*'s.

But Cnemon this time yields because he has heard noises in the house. Enter Nausicles, the host. His arrival causes sleep to be postponed again, and almost provides a new story to take its place, for the drowsy Calasiris now wants to hear how his friend's mission went. It is Nausicles' turn to put forward his need to go to bed. He only tells his guests that he has found the woman he was seeking, then he retires: 'I must relieve the tiredness caused by the journey and my worries with a little rest' (5. 1. 7). Like Cnemon, Nausicles both hints at the happy ending of his story and calls on sleep. His move has the effect of tickling the readers' curiosity about his venture, when they have just finished reading a great part of the novel's main plot, including two culminating episodes (the protagonists' encounter and the discovery of Chariclea's origins). Instead of going to sleep with Nausicles and Calasiris at the end of the latter's narrative, the readers are compelled to stay awake, waiting for Nausicles'.

Sleep and sleeplessness during 'epic' journeys

In a manner that again conjures up Homer, but also Apollonius, Heliodorus notes the passing of the day more carefully than the other novelists. He also exploits the coming of dawn and night as narrative markers of beginnings and endings. The first day starts with dawn rising, in the first sentence of the novel, and ends with a mention of sunset (1. 7. 1) and night (1. 8. 1). The first book begins with dawn and ends with dusk. The novel as a whole opens at sunrise and closes at night, creating a unique counterpoint. Time notations also follow the course of journeys and give them a sense of rhythm.[96]

Among the journeys carefully timed by travellers and narrator alike is a day-and-a-half-long flight with Cnemon as its main protagonist. He will manage to lose the unwanted Thermouthis along the way without him noticing, and then reunite with the pair in a village on the Nile about a hundred stadia (eleven miles) away (2. 18. 5). The journey starts at dawn, is interrupted by night and resumed the next day. It is eventide, epically 'the time when the oxen are unyoked' (2. 19. 6), when Cnemon alleges stomach troubles and stays behind for a bit before catching up with his companion; he does this several times, until the other no longer pays attention and Cnemon disappears for good. His disappearance coincides with nightfall. Thermouthis reaches the top of a hill and stops, waiting for Cnemon, but eventually he cannot stay awake, and he dies in his sleep: 'a last, brazen (χάλκεον) slumber, from a viper's bite [...], an end worthy of his life' (2. 20. 2).

Thermouthis' deadly sleep brings out his dimwittedness. He does not follow Cnemon's actions and suspects nothing. He is likewise plunged into an almost deathlike slumber earlier, when the others are putting together a plan against him (2. 18. 1). He dozes off without even noticing it (2. 14. 5). The long, sound sleep that holds him contrasts with the catnap of the others, above all Chariclea, who is soon awoken by a dream (2. 16. 2), and it is in keeping with the lack of alertness that soon kills him. His death casts him as a mock epic hero. It is a 'brazen slumber', like the death of Homeric warriors (*Il.* 11. 241), but he is unarmed, fights only in his mind (when he fantasizes about attacking

Cnemon, Theagenes and Chariclea) and is killed not by a hero, but by a snake, because of his own wickedness.[97] The causal relationship between Thermouthis' wickedness and the mode of his death underscores the optimistic teleology of this novel and of the genre at large, which, as we have seen, affects also the treatment of sleep.

Though Cnemon succeeds in leaving Thermouthis behind, he does not come across as a more heroic traveller than his companion. This is demonstrated by his inability both to exert himself with travelling and to sleep soundly at the end of the journey, even when he is safe. After tricking Thermouthis, he runs until darkness halts him. He hides in the place where he happens to stop, covering himself with as many leaves as he can (2. 20. 3). This gesture imitates that of Odysseus, who likewise covers himself with leaves after landing on Scheria.[98] But Odysseus falls into a deep, 'boundless' slumber. In contrast, Cnemon sleeps little and badly, for fear of being chased by Thermouthis:

> He dreamt of running and often turned around to look for a pursuer who was nowhere. He wanted to sleep but prayed that he would not obtain what he wanted, for his dreams were worse than reality, and he seemed ready to curse the night, feeling it was the longest ever.
>
> (2. 20. 4)

A travesty of an epic traveller, Cnemon ends his brief, un-epic journey with a display of restlessness. He cannot even spend one night running, yet he keeps on running in his sleepless or sleeping mind. Later he himself admits to his inability to endure epic journeys (6. 7. 5), and for this reason he is dismissed as an inadequate travelling companion when Chariclea and Calasiris embark on a quest with no foreseeable end (6. 7. 8–9).

Cnemon is sleepless and agitated on another occasion. At the end of Calasiris' storytelling, the company retires but Cnemon cannot rest because he cannot believe that his erstwhile enemy Thisbe is alive and in the house. Though Calasiris urges him to sleep, he leaves his quarters and wanders all over the house until, persuaded that Thisbe is there indeed, he almost falls down and then proceeds to stumble over walls and doors until he finds his room, collapses on his bed and faints (5. 3). In both episodes, Cnemon's nocturnal roaming showcases his fearful anxiousness, a signature trait of his character.

The sound slumber and the wakeful thinking of a wise man

With regard to sleep patterns, the opposite of the cowardly Cnemon is the sage Calasiris. The contrast is brought out in the narrative of the night they spend together at Nausicles' house, for Cnemon's lasting agitation only briefly awakens the older man from his 'deep slumber' (5. 2. 1). After listening to his companion's worries and exhorting him to rest, Calasiris 'smiled a little and dozed off again' (5. 2. 5). His second plunge into sleep rounds off the expression of serenity conveyed by his smile.[99]

Calasiris also happens to stay up all night, but he does so because he is absorbed in productive, if anxious, thoughts. The cause of his wakefulness is his 'cares', φροντίδες. φροντίς is never behind Cnemon's sleeplessness – he is not weighed down by concerns or responsibilities, but is shaken by his nerves – while Calasiris loses sleep only to problem solving. His own storytelling is capable of lulling his cares to rest (2. 21. 2), but when they beset him, he keeps thinking about the future. He goes three nights without sleep, trying to figure out what the gods have in store for the protagonists. On the first, he 'turns the thought of the young pair round and round' and 'hunts' (3. 11. 4) for the meaning of the last line of an oracle concerning them. Instructed by Apollo and Artemis to take them to Egypt, he cannot find rest on the following night because he does not know how to arrange the journey or which road to travel (3. 15. 3). On the third night he is still perplexed, though has made some progress: 'I was again sleepless, considering which direction we should take to pass unnoticed, wondering which land the god was taking the young pair to. I only knew that our flight had to be carried out by sea, gathering this from the oracle' (4. 4. 5).

The deliberative thrust of Calasiris' insomnia brings out his role as the mastermind of the main plotline. He does not, however, invent it from scratch during his wakeful nights, like the Homeric Zeus, but instead seeks, with prophetic wisdom, to find it encoded in the greater scheme of things by studying messages from heaven. His unsleeping mind is involved in two tasks: trying to understand the script of destiny and making decisions in accordance with it.

Sleeping on the last journey: Calasiris' death in context

Calasiris' wisdom is mirrored in the manner of his death: during a peaceful slumber. Happy to have recovered his children in Memphis, his native city, he indulges in a festive dinner in the temple of Isis, after which he prays to the gods and tells his sons that they will not see him again, then goes to sleep. His sons stay awake by his side, and at the crack of dawn he is found dead, perhaps because of the emotional shock he received from finding his children or because he prayed for death (7. 11. 4).

Calasiris' last sleep conveys his tranquility and mitigates the harshness of death by playing up its identification with sleep, which by the time of Heliodorus had long been commonplace in literature, philosophy and religious belief. Sleeplike death already has a kindly quality in the *Iliad*. It is true that death there is 'brazen slumber' and does not lay the warriors softly to rest, as happens in Hesiod to the aged prophet Calchas, whom 'the sleep of death enshrouded',[100] or in Apollonius' epic to Tiphys, whose gentle, sleep-bringing death, from a short illness, inspired Virgil to entrust Somnus himself with the death of Palinurus.[101] But even if death in the *Iliad* always strikes violently, it shares enveloping properties with sweet slumber: it comes as a cloud, a cover. Additionally, Thanatos can be a helper and work together with Hypnos to transport a dead warrior safely to his homeland.[102]

A hint of the consoling messages that death's kinship with sleep could bring is traceable in the *Odyssey*, in Penelope's prayer for a death as soft as her deep slumber (18. 201–5) and especially in the description of Odysseus' home-carrying sleep, which pairs likeness to death with extreme sweetness. The pairing could easily be taken to mean that death is the most pleasant rest. Plato's Socrates thinks along these lines when he suggests that death might be a deep, dreamless sleep,[103] in which case there would be much to be gained from dying. The sentiment that animates John

Donne's famous lines: 'From rest and sleep, which but thy pictures be / Much pleasure; then from thee much more must flow' (*Death, be not proud*, 5–6), is already given voice by Plato's character.

Plutarch reworks Socrates' suggestion, joining it with the Homeric image of Odysseus' sweet, deathlike slumber, which he takes as evidence of death's gentleness:

> If death is a sleep, and there is nothing evil in the state of those who sleep, it is evident that there is likewise nothing evil in the state of those who are dead. But what need is there even to maintain that the deepest sleep is indeed the sweetest? For the fact is of itself patent to all men, and Homer bears witness by saying, regarding it: 'Slumber the deepest and sweetest, and nearest to death in its semblance'.[104]

Plutarch and Socrates exploit death's equivalence with sleep only to claim that death is not frightening. But the identification could bring further help: it could also suggest that death is not the end. In Orphic and Pythagorean thought, the soul detaches itself from the body during sleep, and even travels outside of it.[105] This conception of a soul freed from its mortal fetters could naturally foster hopes of immortality, as it did for Xenophon's Cyrus, who on the point of death expressed confidence that the soul lives on because it unties itself from the body during sleep and 'looks toward the future' (*Cyr.* 8. 7. 21–2). The Orphics, followed by Plato, recommended this disembodiment of the soul as a practice, an 'exercise of death', which the god of sleep himself affords to us: 'Hypnos [...] you offer an exercise of death and keep the souls safe, for you are the brother of Oblivion and Death'.[106] The Homeric kinsman of death becomes a protector of souls. In this capacity Hypnos can even take on Hermes' responsibility as the tutelary deity of souls, guiding them in their last journey and laying them to rest (Plut. *Mor.* 758B).[107]

Plato's discussion of wakefulness in the *Timaeus* could lend further support to conceptions of sleep as the road to the soul's true life, for he argues that while we are awake, that is, while our bodily senses are active, we cannot distinguish the 'unsleeping and truly existing substance' (52b–c).[108] Plotinus stretched this to mean: it is only when we are in a state of perennial slumber that we can see true reality. The sleep of death opens the eyes of the soul.[109]

At the time when Plotinus and Heliodorus were writing, efforts to dispel the fear of death by collapsing it with sleep – whether to stress death's gentleness or the soul's immortality – had long spread outside of philosophy and literature. The reassuring identification underlies the practice, popular in the early centuries AD, of decorating sarcophagi with sleeping figures. It also accounts for the proliferation, from the Hellenistic period onwards, of sepulchral verses such as: 'She sleeps here the slumber that is apportioned to all' (*AP* 7. 459); 'Therimachus sleeps the long slumber under the oak' (*AP* 7. 173); 'Say that Popilia is asleep, sir; for it would be wrong for the good to die. Rather, they slumber sweetly'.[110]

As this sampling suggests, there is some oscillation in these conceptions between the belief that we all go to sleep when we die and the belief that it is only good people who do so. The blessed men of the Golden Age die 'as if conquered by slumber' (Hes. *Op.* 116). Lore about individual wise men often grants them such blissful deaths, as in an epitaph for Bias of Priene, one of the Seven Sages: 'He made a speech on behalf of a friend and then rested in a boy's arms and kept sleeping a long sleep' (*AP* 7. 91).[111] Other sleepers-unto-death include Diogenes the Cynic, who told a doctor that worried to see him dozing when he was on the point of death: 'There is nothing wrong. One brother anticipates the other'[112] and Cleobis and Biton, the virtuous youths of Argos who improvised themselves as horses to carry their mother to the temple of Hera, and then died there in their sleep after feasting, in fulfilment of their mother's prayer (Hdt. 1. 31).

Calasiris closely imitates Cleobis and Biton. He also dies in a temple, where his two children have transported him (7. 8. 4–5); he also dies after feasting and also (perhaps) in fulfilment of a prayer, his own.[113] The roles, though, are reversed. While in Herodotus the gentlest death rewards the children who have carried their mother, in Heliodorus the treat goes to the old man who has been carried by the children he found and saved at the end of a strenuous journey.

Whether the sleep that engulfs the homecoming Calasiris is Neoplatonically intended to usher his soul to its true home is debatable. Our interpretive choice will depend on how seriously we take Heliodorus' philosophical apparatus.[114] Whatever the case, however, Calasiris' repose, filled with the knowledge of death's coming, seems fashioned after the sleep of philosophical heroes facing imminent death, such as Socrates awaiting execution at the beginning of Plato's *Crito* or Cato the Younger preparing for suicide at the end of Plutarch's *Life* devoted to him. Just as the two philosophers sleep, in a way towards death, while their assistants and friends worriedly and restlessly remain awake beside them, the novelistic priest rests soundly on his last journey while his children keep watch all night long.

Calasiris' serene foreknowledge of his death invites one final comparison, perhaps the most fitting: with Oedipus. Two old men, two wanderers, find a home to die at the end of their peregrinations. Both dying men are tended by their two children (the two girls in Oedipus' case); both are preparing for their final departure, Calasiris by praying, Oedipus by bathing, pouring libations and donning fresh clothes; both share their knowledge of their coming death with their children. And when Calasiris dies in his sleep, we remember that Oedipus leaves, without a groan, to sleep the 'perennial slumber' that the chorus wishes for him (Soph. *OC* 1578) right before the messenger enters and narrates his death.

In order to understand Calasiris' death within its cultural context, we have been spurred to outline the essentials of the long history of death's identification with sleep in Greek thought. But we shall also read the episode from within the novel, recalling Thermouthis' death and contrasting the different meanings of sleep on those two occasions: in one case it is an enfeebling condition, in the other it is something dignified and decisive. While Thermouthis' sleep-unto-death is a diminutive mockery of mythical deaths in sleep, such as those of Rhesus and Alcyoneus, Calasiris' knowing slumber is the crowning event of a life of wisdom.

Sleeplessness and love: modest and immodest ways

Like Calasiris, Chariclea is beset by φροντίδες ('cares') on two insomniac nights (5. 34. 2; 6. 14. 2). The parallel underscores her spiritual kinship with her second adoptive father, as does the fact that they are sometimes simultaneously unable to sleep: as Calasiris relates, 'She went home and spent a night like the others, or even harder, and I was sleepless again' (4. 4. 5).[115] The anxiety that drives their parallel insomnia, though, has different causes. Calasiris is trying to read the script of heaven; Chariclea is of course prey to love. The morning after her encounter with Theagenes, Charicles, her first adoptive father, tells Calasiris that she has spent the whole night without sleep (3. 18. 2). And she has more such nights (4. 4. 5).

Eventually a doctor is summoned, and in diagnosing Chariclea's lovesickness he lists insomnia as one of its standard symptoms (4. 7. 7). But, as it seems, it is one that troubles the heroine much more than the hero. Whereas her sleeplessness is long lasting and attracts much attention, his is not described. It might be foreshadowed by his restless demeanour at the banquet he sets up after their encounter (3. 10. 4) and inferred from the way he shakes Calasiris out of bed at the crack of dawn (3. 16. 1), but there is no explicit mention of it.

The emphasis on Chariclea's insomnia, in addition to being consistent with her role as the true protagonist of the novel, fits her gender and character. Theagenes and Chariclea respond quite differently to the onslaught of love. He tries to fight it on the first evening, but he rushes to Calasiris before daybreak, seeking his help. Though shying away from overt disclosure, he confesses his agony and begs the priest to save his life (3. 17. 1–3). Intriguingly his symptoms are at their strongest on that evening, before his love is confessed (3. 10. 4); then they become unnoticeable. Hers, in contrast, endure and worsen because she suppresses her love for days on end in silence – and 'silence nurtures sickness' (4. 5. 7).

We are reminded of Chariton's protagonists. The night after their encounter 'was terrible for both', to be sure, but the heroine fared worse 'because of her silence, for she was ashamed of being discovered' (1. 1. 8). However, Callirhoe is almost instantly healed by her unexpected marriage to the man she loves, whereas Chariclea's condition becomes more serious because, uniquely in the novels, she mounts a true assault on her love, beyond the initial resistance caused by shame. Her spirited opposition to her passion conjures up Euripides' Phaedra, whose disease likewise worsens with her silence and upsets her nights, 'the long hours of the night' that she spends thinking how human lives are ruined (*Hipp*. 375–6).[116] Chariclea's insomnia is prolonged and intensified by the unyielding conflict between her swelling desire on the one hand and her modesty and adherence to the cult of virginity on the other.

Like Chariclea, the Persian princess Arsace is prey to lovesick sleeplessness because of Theagenes; but modesty is not the hallmark of her behaviour. Accordingly, her insomniac night is filled with undignified movements that display her passion. She throws herself on her bed, where she cannot sleep; she lies voiceless, 'ceaselessly tossing from side to side', sighing continuously; she sits up straight, falls down, takes off some of her clothes, falls on her bed again; she calls a servant for no reason and sends her away with no order. Her passion is becoming madness (7. 9)

Arsace's agitation is offered as a spectacle. We enter her private quarters and watch her restless body. The description of her state recalls that of Artaxerxes', who likewise tosses and turns in his bed, sleepless because of his desire for Callirhoe. Both lovers are described with reference to the insomniac Achilles. But with a difference: Chariton keeps Artaxerxes' undignified behaviour within bounds by limiting the description of his restlessness to the Homeric citation (6. 1. 8), whereas Heliodorus expands on a paraphrase of it ('ceaselessly tossing from side to side'[117]) by adding gestures and movements – falling, taking off clothes – that belong only to the lovesick woman, not to Achilles.

This close-up of Arsace's insomniac dishevelment is the retribution she deserves. For her passion grew from feasting her eyes on Theagenes, insatiably, to the point that he himself noticed: 'He recalled how she had stared at him with such intensity and lack of modesty, never taking her eyes off him' (7. 12. 7). Theagenes was 'a spectacle' for her.[118] Now she pays for her shameless gazing by becoming herself the object of the readers' gaze in her shameless, sleepless night. There is even a lamp to illuminate the scene, a lamp 'sharing in the fire of her love' (7. 9. 4) and thus enhancing and exposing, like a stage light, her unladylike behaviour.

Wakefulness and sleep as narrative signposts

Calasiris dies in his slumber on the same night that Arsace spends awake. His sleep-unto-death ends a major section of the novel. Chariclea and Calasiris have reached Memphis and succeeded in their searches; celebrations have followed. Together with Arsace's sleeplessness, which heralds new developments, Calasiris' last slumber signposts the transition to a new act. Heliodorus exploits the combination of sleep – in its more closural form, death – and its troubles to signal an important turning point in the plot.

The novelist also makes use of this same combination to advance the plot at another juncture, closer to the beginning of the narrative. After Cnemon finishes his story, Theagenes and Chariclea rest at last, worn out by their tears. At the same time Thyamis awakens, disturbed by a dream that he ponders over until dawn (1. 18. 1–2). This sequence is the only one in the extant novels in which a shift in narrative focus (from the protagonists' weeping to Thyamis' ruminations) is produced by switching sleep and wakefulness from one set of characters to another, *Odyssey*-wise.

Sleep disturbances occur again at the most important junction of the narrative, to advertise its driving force. After Calasiris completes his story, the company makes libations and retires. Calasiris finds Chariclea in a shrine, holding the feet of the holy statue and slumbering deeply, until he gently wakes her and leads her back to the women's quarters. But she cannot find rest: 'she was sleepless, thinking of her cares'.

So ends Book 5. To conclude a book with sleeplessness is a marked narrative choice, for sleeplessness is not closural but forward looking.[119] Remote parallels are the endings of *Iliad* 8, of *Odyssey* 1 and of *Argonautica* 2. Heliodorus, however, enhances the forward momentum of his narrative by beginning the next book with more nocturnal restlessness. We move from the women's quarters to the men's, where Calasiris and Cnemon, eager to start off on their expedition to recover Theagenes, are having a hard time waiting. They find the night too long, though not as long as they thought it would be, 'because the greatest part had been spent in feasting and in stories whose length still left them hungry' (6. 1. 1). Without even waiting for dawn, they go to Nausicles and ask him where Theagenes could be.

All this excitement about the beginning of the new mission rings like Heliodorus' message to the readers: don't go to sleep! Imitate the impatience of Calasiris and Cnemon! Keep reading my story! No matter how long it is, it won't bore you! The characters' annoyance with the night is corrected by their observation that it would have been longer if it had not been filled with engrossing stories. We are sent back to Calasiris' words, teasing Cnemon: 'you are not worn out by the length of my story' (4. 4. 2). As in that episode, the remark is directed to the readers, like other comparable ones about how the pleasure of stories can drive off the need for sleep. But this time the author's intrusion is felt more tangibly because it does not match the speakers' restless mood. How can they, in the same sentence, think that the night is longer than they wished but shorter than it could have been, thanks to the stories heard? The dissonance of the intrusion gives its purpose away. Chariclea's restlessness on the same night adds to this cluster of narrative signals, all of them urging the readers to be as eager as the characters, to turn the page.

This buildup of excitement between Book 5 and Book 6 restarts the plot at its main transition. The narrative has reached midpoint and now shifts from Calasiris' retrospective account to Heliodorus' linear one. Furthermore, the end of Book 5 explains the puzzling scene at the beginning of the novel, thus drawing the circle to a close, while Book 6 begins with a journey forward. Wakefulness and impatience with the night evoke the response the author desires from the readers: we cannot wait to start on this new journey!

It is likely that Heliodorus is playing here with Odysseus' slumber as he is carried to Ithaca, which likewise occurs at the major transition in the narrative, from Part One to Part Two, and likewise in conjunction, or almost, with a change in narrator (from Odysseus to Homer) and narrative style (from retrospective to linear).[120] The replacement of Odysseus' sleep with general sleeplessness might be designed to downplay the caesura and foster narrative continuity, since sleeplessness, unlike sleep, cannot function as a blank space. While the epic transition marks a biographical turning point, a 'before' and an 'after' in the protagonist's life and the kinds of challenges he faces, in the novel there is no change in the nature of the adventures between the first part and the second. Book 6 begins with yet another journey, which the restless night seamlessly ties to the events of the previous day.

The journey is initially unproductive, for Theagenes is nowhere to be found. As a result, Chariclea despairs and cannot sleep, as towards the end of Book 5, but with a dramatic crescendo. This time her troubles are displayed for the reader/spectator rather than summarily reported; and they are cast in the tragic mould. She withdraws to her room where she stages a lamentation on her bed, unbinding her hair and ripping her clothes. At last she dozes off and slumbers until well into the day (6. 8. 3–6. 9. 1). Heliodorus echoes tragic scenes featuring a heroine who kills herself after lamenting on the bridal bed. In the novelistic rewriting, definitive death is replaced with temporary slumber through the exploitation of yet another tragic motif, 'sleep after madness': Chariclea's eyes were 'still swelling and bearing the signs of the delirium that preceded her sleep' (6. 9. 2).

The amplified echoing of the scene in Book 5 suggests a new and more determined beginning within the new beginning. Chariclea's tragic performance occurs shortly after the first attempt to recover Theagenes at the beginning of Part Two, and right before the launching of the second. The cast of characters engaged in the new mission also changes: no longer Cnemon, Calasiris and Nausicles, but Calasiris and Chariclea (6. 7. 2).

The first day of the new journey is again unsuccessful. The travellers are forced to stop for the night at the outskirts of Bessa, where a massacre has just occurred. They settle on a mound among the corpses, and 'Calasiris, who was old and moreover tired from the journey, was fast asleep, but Chariclea stayed awake, occupied by her cares' (6. 14. 2). She witnesses the necromantic ritual performed by an Egyptian woman on the body of her son and awakens Calasiris; they then hear from the corpse that Calasiris can forestall the fratricidal war between his children if he rushes to Memphis to meet them, and that Chariclea will be queen of Ethiopia and spend her life with her beloved (6. 15. 4).

Heliodorus is realistic in opposing the old man's fatigue, somnolence and relative detachment to the sleep-depriving anxiety of the young girl. This contrast is foreshadowed by their arrangements on the mound. While he makes a pillow of her quiver and lies down, she sits on her pouch, her muscles at attention. Her wakefulness, however, also has a narrative function, for it allows her and Calasiris – and us – to find out about their stories' happy endings, in the case of Calasiris' for the first time, and of Chariclea's, for the first time in unambiguous terms. While earlier predictions were vague,[121] now it is spelled out that the heroine will recover her royal estate and spend her life by the hero's side. The novel's ending is announced in full in this scene – and never again.[122] Chariclea's wakefulness sends the same message to the readers as the collective restlessness that ended Part One and began Part Two: this is not the time to fall asleep!

Heliodorus' penchant for inserting episodes of sleeplessness at narrative transitions might have been intended to make his novel a page turner, countering the readers' need for rest. As suggested above,[123] the sleep of characters in extended narratives can function as a device for creating a dramatic pause at the end of a unit, when the readers or the audiences are likely to take a break. This use of sleep is a regular feature of Homeric narrative, especially in the *Odyssey*. The Greek novels as a whole do not adopt this pattern, for sleep in them does not generally invite the readers to put the book down, but instead goads them on by announcing some momentous action via a dream, by substituting for death, or by serving as a background for intense activity.[124] Only Chariton ends a book with sleep using overtly Homeric diction and rhythm; but even in that instance, the action does not halt until dawn but continues through the night.

Heliodorus, however, rejects the Homeric pattern more emphatically than the other novelists, replacing or qualifying closural sleep with sleeplessness at narrative junctures where the reader might be inclined to put the book aside. As soon as Chariclea and Theagenes doze off after listening to Cnemon's story, Thyamis awakens and stays awake all night; as soon as Nausicles and his guests retire at the end of another night of storytelling, Cnemon gets up to perform his comic insomnia scene; and when at last Calasiris concludes his narrative and the novel reaches midpoint, no one goes to sleep.

Heliodorus' tendency to substitute ceaseless activity for the Homeric nocturnal pause is best illustrated by the manner in which he stages the most closural sleep possible: that of death.

Calasiris' last slumber creates a narrative transition to the next act, but there is no true pause because Arsace's sleeplessness, which thematically begins the new act, *precedes* his sleep-unto-death in the narrative. The account of his death is occasioned by the action that Cybele, Arsace's servant, takes as a result of her mistress' insomniac night. She seeks admission to the temple of Isis in order to make offerings to the goddess for Arsace's sake, but is refused entrance because, as she and we learn, Calasiris has just died (7. 11. 1–3). This sequence destabilizes the closure produced by Calasiris' peaceful sleep-unto-death, intimating grim future events and preventing the readers from resting.

The novelist plays with Homeric book endings in the same vein. Six of his own books conclude at night, like several in Homer: but none with sleep. On the contrary, the nights contain high tension and hurried, urgent movement. At the end of Book 1 warring brigands set cabins on fire and rejoin their band; of Book 5, the heroine is sleepless; of Book 4, the couple elopes and is pursued; of Book 7, Cybele's son flees to denounce Arsace to her husband.[125] Of the book endings that are not nocturnal, the majority likewise build forward momentum, looking ahead to the pageant where the lovers will meet (Book 2), to their falling in love (Book 3) and to the happy reversal of their fortune (Book 8).[126] Heliodorus' readers are invited to set the novel aside and go to sleep only at the very end, when the couple is escorted, at night, to the rite of the wedding and the author announces the completion of his work, signing it with his name. Where the endings of Homer's epics take place at an indeterminate time of day[127] and are left somewhat open, Heliodorus chooses an ending that is both specifically nocturnal and strongly closural.[128]

CONCLUSIONS

In the texts I have considered, sleeplessness always has a clear cause. The ancient reader, at least, knows or is expected to know why a character cannot rest. The mind going around and around at night for no apparent reason does not appear in Greek representations of insomnia. Characters are not kept awake by unfocused anxiety or unanalysed unhappiness, as is the young heiress in Chekhov's short story *A Medical Case*. In this tale insomnia is the outgrowth of an undefined and perhaps undefinable discontent, 'the devil who watched at night', a generational malaise: '[...] our parents [...] didn't talk at night, they slept soundly, but we, our generation, sleep badly, are anguished, talk a lot, and keep trying to decide if we are right or not'.[1] We do not find statements like these in Greek literature.

Greek insomniacs, who always know why they cannot sleep, do not ask the god of sweet slumber to put them to rest without explaining what is besetting them, as does the speaking voice in Keats' *To Sleep*. The closest ancient literature gets to the conceit of a mysterious insomnia is in a well-known poem by Statius, in which the narrator complains that he has been sleepless for seven nights in a row without saying why and begs Somnus to come by and touch him with his wand at last: 'Youthful Sleep, gentlest of the gods, by what crime, by what error, did I deserve that I alone, miserably, should be denied your gifts?' (*Silvae* 5. 4. 1–3).[2] Keats was influenced by this poem, which perhaps appealed to the romantic sensibility on account of the unfathomable nature of the speaker's sleeplessness. But in Greek and Roman literature, this construction of insomnia seems exceptional.

Nor would a Greek fictional character agree with F. Scott Fitzgerald's dictum that 'every man's insomnia is as different from his neighbor's as are their daytime hopes and aspirations',[3] for Greek authors not only motivate, but also typify sleeplessness. The ease with which it is explained and classified in fictional texts is in agreement with the way it is understood in medical literature, where it is a symptom, the by-product of an illness, not a condition per se.[4]

In fiction, however, the only illness of which sleeplessness is a symptom is love. Love-induced insomnia can develop from an inner conflict between the invasion of passion and an attempt to hide it or fight it, but also from a more complex predicament, caused not only by opposite psychic forces but by the urgency to do something momentous to follow love's compulsion. This is the case for Medea, who is forced to betray her father by her passion. In her sleepless night she both yields to her love and in the name of it decides the outcome of Jason's contest.

The impelling need to make a difficult decision is a second major cause for insomnia in Greek fiction. This kind of wakefulness is shared by all the genres covered in this study, but in changing proportions and with a changing distribution between male and female characters. The *Iliad* and the *Odyssey* are filled with episodes of sleepless pondering and attribute it only to heroes, while heroines lose sleep only to longing for their husbands. Achilles is the odd one out. Tragedy like Homeric epic contains several male characters (Agamemnon, Oedipus, Eteocles) who are kept awake by their responsibilities, and one heroine (Deianira) chronically insomniac because she misses her husband. Lysistrata bears out this gendered distribution of sleeplessness by pointing out that her fellow women spend troubled nights beset by romantic (or rather sexual) nostalgia, while she herself appropriates the male prerogative of devoting night after night to intense political deliberation.

Apollonius' epic marks a shift in the attribution of the two kinds of insomnia – romantic, as it were, and deliberative – to men and women. To be sure, the victim of love-induced sleeplessness in his epic is the heroine, while the hero spends a night in active preparation for the crucial contest. This distribution seems to reproduce those in earlier epic and drama. But the similarities are deceptive, for Medea's insomnia is highly consequential, whereas all Jason does in his wakeful night is follow her instructions. He never loses sleep to problem-solving. His relative passivity foreshadows the even more passive behaviour of novelistic heroes, which is also reflected in the nature of their sleeplessness. None of them remains awake to make a difficult decision. The male characters absorbed in nightlong deliberations are a helper of the protagonists (Calasiris) and two obstacles (Theron and Artaxerxes). In the extant novels the only protagonist who spends insomniac nights in the grip of a dilemma is a woman, Callirhoe. Conversely, all the heroes lose sleep to love, like the heroines, though in some cases the latter, as maidens, suffer more intensely from their condition.

In addition to mirroring changes in the characterization of heroes and heroines, the privilege accorded to deliberative or alternatively to love-induced sleeplessness is in line with thematic shifts: romantic love is far more important in Apollonius than in Homer and becomes the main subject in the novels. Accordingly, the novels contain many insomniac lovers of both genders, but fewer episodes of wakeful thinking, compared with Homeric epic or drama; consequently, fewer stretches of novelistic narrative are set in motion by the unsleeping mental activity of an individual. Only Chariton, adhering to an epic or tragic mould, repeatedly makes nightlong pondering produce major turns in the plot.[5] Chariton also imitates Homeric epic in some of the ways he uses sleep, most noticeably by ending a book with a scene of slumber.

The placement of sleep within narrative or dramatic sequences has been another key concern of this study. Sleep cannot be The End, because it always looks to awakening. Though it can physically conclude a work of literature and push awakening off to the indefinite future, readers are nonetheless drawn to that imagined future. Located as it is between one waking hour and the next, sleep, even in literature, is ultimately always transitional. Furthermore, Greek authors do not generally end their works with sleep, but rather include awakening in the narrated or staged action.

That said, in the *Odyssey* sleep concludes many narrative units as markedly as, or even more markedly than, it looks to the next episode. It brings rest to characters and audiences alike. In contrast, tragic sleep, which is always caused by dire predicaments and laden with tension, consistently points forward: what will happen to the sleeper and those around him when he awakens? A strong forward orientation is also characteristic of episodes of sleep in the novel, which do not invite the readers to put the book down, and in Apollonius' epic, where they underscore the beginnings of important legs of the journey, but do not crown major efforts. Jason does not rest at the end of his heroic feat, like Odysseus; but he does before the departure of the Argo.

Apollonius of Rhodes also plays off against the *Odyssey* by reducing the influence of the gods in the sleep patterns of humans. To be sure, Hera engineers Medea's love, but the poet does not explicitly attribute her worsening sleep disturbances to the goddess' intervention. The role of the gods in the sleep of humans, which has been another preoccupation of this study, relates to the larger issue of their relationship with them, and to kindred notions of divine and poetic justice. Thus, in the *Iliad* the gods rarely interfere in human sleep, while in the *Odyssey* Athena time and again manipulates sleep and wakefulness to forward the hero's interests and to destroy the suitors. She also seizes control of the plot by putting the human players, especially Penelope, to sleep, relieving them of agency. In tragedy, the gods can help their protégés by wielding sleep against their enemies, as Apollo does with Orestes by knocking the Furies unconscious, but they can also show their hostility to a hero, as when Athena plunges mad Heracles into a dreadful slumber. The novels' landscape is simpler, and bluntly reassuring: whether god-induced or natural, sleep never harms the noble protagonists but destroys evil characters.

The gods themselves yield to sleep, not so much because they need it as because it is a joy. Sleep's pleasantness is a commonplace in Greek fiction, shared by all the genres discussed in this book. But sleep's pleasantness is also its danger. This is another commonplace, which informs a great number of stories in myth and literature. From the *Iliad* to drama to the novels, sleepers, both human and divine, are tricked and defeated, and human ones are killed. These episodes accord with the widespread perception of sweet slumber as an enfeebling condition, which does not befit 'those who hold the scepter', as Homer calls kings and leaders, but rather innocent and helpless children, who know nothing of cares.

The most famous Greek story that hinges upon the dangerous spell of Hypnos is the sack of Troy. Accounts of it build a stark contrast between the Trojans' relaxed abandonment to drunken sleep and the watchful wakefulness of the Greeks hidden in the wooden horse. One extended narrative that puts great emphasis on sleep and wakefulness comes from Quintus of Smyrna, the author of an epic that covers the events between Hector's funeral and the return journeys of the Greek heroes after the fall of Troy. In Quintus' account, 'while slumber everywhere in the city held the Trojans, gorged with wine and food, Sinon lifted the flaming torch and sent the sign of light to the Argives' (13. 21–4). He goes near the wooden horse and speaks softly, but those hidden inside can easily hear him because 'sleep had flown very far away from them, eager as they were to fight' (13. 32–3).

Quintus' epic would offer a rich mine of material for a further investigation of the significance of sleep and sleeplessness in Greek literature, for it abounds in scenes describing both states, and it is influenced as much by Apollonius of Rhodes as by Homer.[6] But I must conclude. And I will do so by focusing on a scene from Quintus that has a famous Homeric counterpart.

After the sack of Troy, the Greeks are in the mood for a nightlong celebration, but tiredness gets the better of them:

> Though eager to feast all night, they stopped, for sleep held them fast against their will. Each was slumbering in his place, but in his tent the son of Atreus was sweetly conversing with his wife of the beautiful locks, for sleep did not fall yet on their eyelids. Cypris fluttered around their hearts to make them remember their old love [. . .] And Helen was the first to speak.
>
> (14. 149–54)

Helen and Menelaus imitate Penelope and Odysseus on the night of their reunion. Quintus alerts the readers to his use of this model with unmistakable verbal pointers: 'old love', literally 'old bed' (παλαιοῦ λέκτρου) repeats the Homeric λεκτροῖο παλαιοῦ (*Od.* 23. 296); sleep 'did not fall' (οὐ [...] ἔπιπτεν) on Quintus' couple as it 'did not fall' (οὐδὲ [...] πῖπτεν) on Penelope (*Od.* 23. 308–9). Quintus, however, reworks the Homeric bedroom scene, adapting it to the mythical personage of Helen, the opposite of the faithful Penelope. In Homer lovemaking precedes the exchange of stories, while in Quintus it is the other way around. The reversal is geared to reestablish the harmony of a couple that has been separated not just by the tragedies of war but by an act of infidelity, which caused those tragedies. Helen exculpates herself, Menelaus forgives her, and at last the two can 'remember the old bed'. They remember it in more expansive terms than Odysseus and Penelope. While lovemaking in Homer is treated with verbal restraint, in Quintus it prompts an exuberant narrative:

> She cast her arms around him, and both at once wept sweetly and let tears flow from their eyes. With joy they lay by each other and their hearts remembered their marriage. When the ivy and the vine are twined together at their stalks, the fury of the wind can no longer sever them. In the same way those two were enlaced, eager for love.
>
> (14. 169–78)

The passion of the couple makes this episode resemble a novelistic love scene. Specifically, the narrative sequence resonates with Xenophon's account of his protagonists' reunion, for both episodes are cast in the rare mould of a 'happy lonely vigil',[7] both vigils are preceded by a party and both are framed by the sleep of the couple's partying companions. What is more, Anthia and Habrocomes, like Helen and Menelaus, spend a portion of the night exchanging speeches that aim, if not to put actual infidelity behind, at least to dispel each other's suspicions of it.

In one telling feature, however, Helen and Menelaus do not imitate a novelistic pair, but stay close to their Homeric models. After their effusions of love, 'kindly sleep came to them, too'

(14. 179). Like Odysseus and Penelope – and unlike the protagonists of the novels – Helen and Menelaus are a seasoned couple, and as such, in spite of years of separation fraught with tensions and strewn with deaths, they can at last find peace in the embrace of sweet slumber.

NOTES

Introduction

1. *Purgatorio* 27. 91–3.
2. *Don Quixote*, Part 1, Chapter 35.
3. Meineke 1839, vol. 4, fr. 1, line 1.
4. See, e.g., Calabi 1984; Brown 1986; Byl 1998; Strobl 2002 and several articles in Dowden and Wiedemann 2003. More references will be given where relevant. Sleep and sleeplessness in modern fictional literatures have also received significant critical attention: see, e.g. Chandler 1955; Pachet 1988; Mabin 1992; Risset 2008; Iranzo *et al.* 2004.
5. See Chapter 1.
6. See Chapter 1.
7. See Chapter 2.
8. See Chapter 5.
9. See Chapters 2 and 5, respectively.
10. I make an exception for comedy, which is treated comprehensively for lack of a sustained presence of sleep and sleeplessness in the development of individual plots.

Chapter 1 The *Iliad*

1. In the *Iliad* only the sleep of death bears a negative epithet, 'brazen' (11. 241). On the *Odyssey*, see Chapter 2.
2. See McAlpine 1987: 122–4.
3. See *Il.* 14. 359, where Hypnos calls 'soft' the unconscious state in which he has unwrapped Zeus.
4. See Dowden 2003: 142–5. The phrase is his.
5. *Il.* 2. 1; 10. 1; 24. 677.

6. Thus the phrase 'They took the boon of sleep' (7. 482; 9. 713). Contrast *Od.* 16. 481 and 19. 427, where the phrase describes undisturbed sleep.
7. Agamemnon: 2. 19–23; Achilles: 23. 62–3 (see 69); 23. 232–5; Priam: 24. 673 (see 683). On Achilles' undisturbed sleep in Books 9 and 24 and on Zeus' in Book 14, see below.
8. *Od.* 3. 404–5 = 4. 306–7 = 8. 1–2. See also 23. 348. Translations are mine unless otherwise stated.
9. *Il.* 7. 282; 7. 293; 8. 502. Night is almost always perceived as the limit to action: see Ferrini 1985: 32.
10. In the *Odyssey* all the assemblies are held in the morning, normally after a good night's sleep. This is true even during Odysseus' perilous journey (9. 170–1; 10. 187–8).
11. *Il.* 8. 502–3; 9. 65–7. See also *Il.* 7. 282 and 293. At *Od.* 12. 291, though, the phrase conveys a desire for sleep.
12. *Il.* 9. 325; *Od.* 19. 340. Achilles might be alluding to fighting, while Odysseus could be referring also to his wanderings.
13. For further discussion, see Chapter 2.
14. On sleep in ancient warfare, see Wiedemann 2003a: XIV. Caesar, he notes, felt he had to report that he allowed the army to rest before reaching Gergovia (*B Gall.* 7. 41. 1). Cyrus in Xenophon's *Cyropaedia* (2. 4. 26–7; 4. 2. 41; 5. 3. 44) is likewise sensitized to the army's need for sleep.
15. The days of actual fighting are four (Taplin 1992: 15–8). I add the two in which the Achaeans and the Trojans bury their dead and the Achaeans build their wall (in Book 7).
16. See note 28 below.
17. When Achilles dozes off (23. 62), Patroclus' ghost instantly awakens him.
18. For further discussion, see Chapter 3.
19. See *CI*, vol. 1, on 1. 475–83. Line 479 ('and far-darting Apollo sent them a favourable wind') in its core is identical with *Od.* 2. 420 ('and grey-eyed Athena sent them a favourable wind'). See also *Od.* 15. 34–5.
20. *Il.* 2. 1–4. For Lévy (1982: 26, n. 44) the phrase 'sweet slumber was not holding Zeus' means 'Zeus never slept'. This reading, though, undermines the sense of peacefulness at the end of the feast. Kirk (*CI*, vol. 1, on 2. 1–2) interprets: 'sleep did not continue to hold' Zeus. On the motif of the lonely vigil, see Leeman 1985; Wöhrli 1995, Chapter 4.
21. See Strobl 2002: 17.
22. *Il.* 10. 40–1; 10. 141–2; 24. 362–3. Night belongs to the gods: see Hes. *Op.* 730, with M. West 1982b, on 10; Moreux 1967: 269; Stanley 1993: 237–40. Interpretations of ἀμβρόσιος vary: see Moreux 1967: 269, n. 184; Dué and Abbott 2010: 254–6.

On other possible meanings of the epithet when applied to sleep, see *CI*, vol. 1, on 2. 19; vol. 3, on 10. 41.

23. *Il.* 1. 173–5. See Taplin 1992: 65.
24. See Stanley 1993: 331.
25. On the symbolism of light and darkness in the *Iliad*, see Schadewaldt 1938: 117; Moreux 1967; Griffin 1980: 162, 170–2; Taplin 1992: 166–7, 191; Constantinidou 2010.
26. See also Latacz 1999: 472–3.
27. So read a scholiast (*Il.* 10. 3–4) and Eustathius (*Il.* 3. 2. 4–5).
28. The comparison is more meaningful if Book 10 originally belonged in the *Iliad*, as some scholars now argue. They point out that the night raid is not un-heroic because ambush is as much a test for heroism as open war (Dué and Abbott 2010, Chapter 2), that the episode and its preparations are a response to the problem of how to find a substitute for Achilles (Heiden 2008: 28) and that Book 10 is essential for the themes developed in Books 8 to 17 (Stanley 1993: 118–28). It is also noted that the μῆτις Nestor comes up with in the counsel in which the Achaeans 'devise a μῆτις together' (10. 197) responds to Achilles' exhortation to them that they should find a 'better μῆτις' (9. 423, with Dué and Abbott 2010: 102–3). At the same time, a possible indication (among others) that Book 10 is a later addition is the dissonance between Agamemnon's despair and the confidence and optimism with which the Greeks go to rest at the end of Book 9: see *CI*, vol. 3, 152 and on 10. 1–4. The contrast structurally repeats the transition from sleep to sleeplessness between Books 1 and 2, but does not seem to be as motivated. Whether Book 10 was added or not, however, ancient commentators invite us to read the two episodes of sleeplessness together by doing the same: they explain Agamemnon's insomnia as the result of the dream's reproach to him in Book 2. See the previous note.
29. See Dowden 2003: 144. Scholars debate the nature of Rhesus' vision. Fenik (1964: 44–52) thinks that in a preexisting myth Rhesus had a nightmare foreboding his death, and that *Iliad* 10 refers to the dream ironically. His hard breathing has been taken to suggest that he is awake (Brillante 1990), but the placement of the vision, over his head, is typical of dreams. See further *CI*, vol. 3, on 10. 496–7.
30. A current trend is to date the Homeric poems later than the second half of the eighth century. See, e.g., Burgess 2006: 153, n. 12.
31. See Dowden 2010.
32. See Hanson and Ober, respectively, in Krentz 2000: 172.
33. In my opinion the *Iliad* does not condemn the raid as the Mahabharata does in a parallel narrative and as Garbutt (2006), along with other scholars, thinks. The villain of the story is Dolon, the greedy spy, whereas the actions of Odysseus and Diomedes are supported by Athena. In addition, the alleged chauvinism of

Book 10, which is one of the arguments raised against its 'authenticity', implies that Odysseus' methods could appear praiseworthy enough to put the Greeks in a good light.

34. See Krentz 2000.
35. See Vidal-Naquet 1986: 113.
36. See also Hdt. 1. 103; 5. 121; 6. 45; 8. 27.
37. See Krentz 2000: 183–99. For Rome, see Wiedemann 2003b: 133–4.
38. Krentz (2000: 177) refers to Thuc. 7. 43–4. See also Hdt. 5. 121.
39. See Dowden 2010.
40. The first story Odysseus tells on Ithaca contains the narrative of a nocturnal ambush (*Od.* 13. 268–70). See also *Od.* 14. 217, 469. Fenik (1964: 13) considers Odysseus' night activity 'a common theme'.
41. Figures of μῆτις move in the night: see Detienne and Vernant 1978: 30–1.
42. *Il.* 21. 35–40, above. Achilles participates in ambushes (*Il.* 1. 227).
43. Hesychius, κ, 4825; Hippoc. *Epid.* 7. 1. 5. 22.
44. See Wiesmann (1972: 7: *Ausschaltung des vollen Bewusstseins*) and Page (in Wiesmann: 6, n. 17), respectively. Barker's reading (2003: 117–22) is closer to Page's, while Meier-Brügger's (1993) to Wiesmann's.
45. See Meier-Brügger 1993: 126.
46. κῶμα can appear alongside ὕπνος, as in *AP* 9. 338. 5–6 (Wiesmann 1972: 10), or even in opposition to ὕπνος (Hippoc. *Epid.* 3. 3. 6. 11).
47. See Barker 2003: 117. Hesychius' explanation links κῶμα and sleep with an etymological wordplay: 'soft κῶμα: gentle κοίμημα' (μ, 152). See also π, 1744; Eust. *Il* 3. 661. 16–7.
48. See Barker 2003: 116.
49. *Od.* 18. 201. See Chapter 2.
50. Hes. *Theog.* 765–6 and Soph. *Aj.* 675–6, respectively. There can hardly be any doubt that Sophocles is alluding to and complementing Hesiod: see ἔχει [...] λάβησιν in Hesiod and οὐδ' [...] λαβὼν ἔχει in Sophocles.
51. See Vermeule 1979: 147.
52. *Il.* 24. 5; *Od.* 9. 373. Stafford (2003: 75) suggests that Hypnos' love for Pasithea (*Il.* 14. 275–6), 'All-Goddess', further enhances his status.
53. See Stafford 1991: 106, 114.
54. See Ramnoux 1959: 105; Vermeule 1979: 145, 154; Vernant 1991: 100 (on Eros). λυσιμελής is a common epithet of Eros in archaic poetry (see, e.g., Hes. *Theog.* 121, 911), though not in Homer. For sleep, see *Od.* 20. 57; 23. 343.
55. Detienne and Vernant (1978: 115) are mistaken in thinking that Hypnos has no power over Zeus. The episode in *Iliad* 14 proves the opposite. Their claim seems based on a misreading of Hypnos' words at *Il.* 14. 247–8, which do not mean 'Zeus [...] I can neither

approach nor send to sleep even if he himself orders me to do so', but 'Zeus [. . .] I could not approach or send to sleep unless he should order me to do so'. See also Meleager in *AP* 5. 174. 3.

56. Note the repetition of 2. 5, which launches Zeus' plan, at 14. 161, when Hera launches hers.
57. The equation of course is not exclusively Greek (or Roman). It is central to the epic of Gilgamesh, for one. Some scholars think that in Greece the idea that death is a kind of sleep spread in the Hellenistic period as a literary convention. So Ogle 1933, followed by McAlpine 1987: 141–4. I rather agree with McNally (1985: 166) and Stafford (2003) that the idea is older and has deeper roots, as suggested by archaic and classical paintings featuring Hypnos and Thanatos (Beazley 1963, s.v. Hypnos; Shapiro 1993: 132–47). The kinship of the two is also well attested in tragedy, where several characters express a wish for perennial sleep: see Aesch. *Ag.* 1450–1; Soph. *Aj.* 832; *OC* 1578; Eur. *Hipp.* 1387–8. See also Soph. *OT* 961; *Ant.* 804–5; 810, and for further discussion, Chapter 5.
58. See also Hes. *Theog.* 756.
59. *Il.* 24. 343 and 13. 435.
60. See Cerutti 1986: 133–4.
61. Schol. Ap. Rhod. 4. 57–8. Theocritus conflates sleep and death beautifully in Endymion's 'unbendable slumber' (*Id.* 3. 48): see Hunter 1999, *ad loc.*
62. See Eur. *Hec.* 473; Plut. *Mor.* 420A; 941E.
63. See Vernant 1991: 46, n. 29. On the duration of this κῶμα, see Brown 1994: 97–8.
64. Though the verb δάμνημι is predicated also of natural sleep, Homer uses the aorist participle only for death or cowardice.
65. So Vermeule 1979: 147.
66. For Taplin (1992: 171) Zeus' description 'comes close to mocking the language of death in battle'.
67. Taplin (1992: 142) calls the reassertion of Zeus' plan 'a kind of resumption, almost a second start'.
68. Procl. *In R.* 1. 133–6, with Dowden 2003: 162.
69. Origen, *C. Cels.* 6. 61–2. See Sissa and Detienne 2000: 125.
70. [Plut.] *De placitis* 881C.
71. See, e.g., *AP* 16. 211, 212. In later Roman art, however, slumbering Eros tends to be humanized: see Dowdle 2013, with further references.
72. Epimenides (DK B 8), with Vernant 1991: 46, n. 29; 146–7.
73. Soph. *Ant.* 605–10. The meaning of παντογήρως ('which makes everything age') is, however, disputed, and the text probably is corrupt.
74. *Il.* 10. 98–9; 10. 471; *Od.* 5. 472; 5. 493; 6. 2; 10. 142–3; 12. 281; 13. 282.

75. Aesch. *Eum.* 68, 79, 127, 133. For further discussion, see Chapter 3.
76. λιμός ('hunger') never explains a god's eating, whereas τέρπειν ('to take delight') does (*Od.* 5. 201. Contrast 5. 165: Calypso will provide food to protect Odysseus from λιμός).
77. Mimnermus, though, primarily has lovemaking in mind.
78. The image of Helios going to bed reappears in Soph. *Trach.* 95, where it is night that 'lays him to rest'.
79. Schol. *Il.* 1. 475, with Ferrini 1985: 22.
80. See McAlpine 1987, Chapter 6.
81. See Vermeule 1979: 147.
82. In Homer gods manipulate the course of day and night (*Il.* 18. 239–40; *Od.* 23. 243), but they do so for the sake of mortals, not for their own use.
83. At the end of *Iliad* 1 Hera supposedly rests but her sleep is not emphasized.
84. See Clay 1989: 103–4.
85. The poet of the *Hymn* used these stories: see Parry 1986: 261–2. For this scholar, in both the *Hymn* and *Iliad* 14 sleep illustrates the danger of sex for a male seduced by an erotic female. The sleep of the two males, however, is not only natural but also comes from outside, from the deities who assert their power over them.
86. Further parallels are in Louden 2006: 99.
87. The scholia explain lines 316–7 thus: 'they will not be able to be together on account of the chains' or 'they will not want to come together again for fear of the chains'. There is no mention of literal sleep.
88. This is the only time in the *Iliad* that πανδαμάτωρ modifies sleep.
89. See Fantuzzi 2012: 197.
90. See Fantuzzi 2012: 198: 'the audience may [...] be left with the impression that if something bad happens to either member of the couple [...], that equilibrium will fade away'.
91. See Wöhrle 1995: 39.
92. The scholiasts (*Il.* 23. 63b) mention Achilles' tiredness to justify his sleep, which would otherwise be undignified: see Scaffai 2004: 57.
93. The dream, nonetheless, accords with Achilles' desire (Kessels 1978: 54; Lévy 1982: 29). Though Patroclus' reproach underscores Achilles' selfish absorption in his suffering (Schein 1984: 155), the burial had already taken priority in his mind (23. 43–53).
94. Menelaus, who says that the memory of Odysseus makes him hate sleep and food, provides a faint parallel (*Od.* 4. 105–6).
95. I have skipped 24. 6–9, which elaborate on Achilles' memory, because editors generally delete them, following Hellenistic scholars. On their objections, see *CI*, vol. 6, on 24. 5–11; Fantuzzi 2012: 211–5.

96. Both Penelope and Achilles display uncompromising behaviour caused by their attachment to another being: see Papadopoulou-Belmehdi 1994: 59–60.
97. See Minchin 1985; Gibson 1996: 459.
98. Eust. *Il.* 4. 973. 15–7.
99. See also Minchin 1985.
100. See Chapter 5.
101. See Minchin 1985; Lynn-George 1988: 230; Taplin 1992: 260; Fernández Contreras 2000: 13.
102. See Minchin 1985: 272.
103. See Lynn-George 1988: 230; Heiden 2008: 35.
104. While in the sequel to 1. 490–2 Thetis responds to Achilles' prayer by supplicating Zeus, Achilles' insomniac despair in Book 24 builds no communication between men and gods.
105. This function of sleeplessness in the narrative is yet another correspondence-in-reverse between the beginning and the end of the epic. Critics have noted a number of them: see, e.g., Macleod 1982a: 16–35; Schein 1984: 31–2.
106. For further discussion, see Chapter 2.
107. See Macleod 1982a: 33.
108. See, however, already 20. 21 (with *CI*, vol. 5, on 20. 20–30; but see Griffin 1980: 183) and 19. 340. On Zeus' increased pity for mortals in Book 24, I follow Macleod 1982a: 14–5; Zanker 1996: 4–7, 147; Heiden 2008: 208. Other scholars do not note a significant change: Burkert 1955: 75–85; Lloyd-Jones 1971, Chapter 1; Griffin 1980, Chapters 5 and 6; Schein 1984: 60–2.
109. See Dué and Abbott 2010: 86–7.
110. See Stanley 1993: 237–40, with further references.
111. I am not suggesting that this line or any Homeric line that resemble another quotes its close parallel (the applicability of this kind of intertextuality to oral poetry in an evolving tradition is questionable: see Nagy 1999: 42; Burgess 2006: 177; Danek 2002: 17), but that audiences at some point in the tradition would connect passages from hearing their resemblance. Here audiences would hear an echo of *Il.* 24. 3 because of the line's relative proximity.
112. See Macleod 1982a: 35; Taplin 1992: 80–2, 216. The 'innermost part' of a house is where married couples retire for the night: see E. West 2010: 26.
113. See Arend 1933: 101–5; Murnaghan 2011: 84; E. West 2010; Purves 2014.
114. Often noted: see, e.g., Fusillo 1997: 213, with further references; Murnaghan 1997.
115. I cannot agree with Moreux's claim (1967: 270) that '*L'Iliade se termine sur une nuit d'apaisement*'.
116. See De Jong 1990: 24.

117. Taplin 1992: 293.
118. *Il.* 24. 401–2, 658, 670. Priam's words, 'on the twelfth day we shall fight, if it is necessary' (24. 667) are more likely to express his inability to make sense of the war (Griffin 1980: 100) than his belief that it could be stopped.
119. On Zeus' plan I follow Murnaghan 1997, though it has been variously read: see Schein 1984: 59; Lynn-George 1988: 39 and 279, n. 29; Nagy 1999: 81; Heiden 2008: 28.

Chapter 2 The *Odyssey*

1. Six (5, 7, 14, 16, 18, 19) versus three in the *Iliad* (1, 7, 9).
2. See Fantuzzi 1988: 129. For this scholar, book divisions coinciding with night and sleep follow the rhapsodes' probable practice of ending episodes with night and sleep.
3. See also *Od.* 7. 188–90; 9. 168–71; 10. 185–8; 13. 17–9; 19. 426–9.
4. The identity (but for one adverb) of *Il.* 2. 50–2 with *Od.* 2. 6–8 invites the comparison.
5. See Austin 1975: 87–8; Ferrari 1983.
6. See Austin 1975: 88, 226, n. 7.
7. *Od.* 1. 12; 5. 224; 8. 183; 13. 91.
8. *Od.* 5. 388; 10. 28; 10. 80; 15. 476; 9. 74; 10. 142.
9. On Aeolus' plot-ending conveyance, see Purves 2010a: 334.
10. The standard phrase is 'I was carried nine days' (7. 253 = 12. 447; 9. 82; 14. 314). Though counting days starting from the nights is common in primitive time reckoning worldwide (Summers-Bremmer 2008: 16, with further references), the phrase 'nights and days' describes 'actions prosecuted beyond normal human endeavour' (Dyer 1974: 31). Odysseus' formula is even more emphatic.
11. *Od.* 10. 77 = 9. 105 = 9. 565 = 10. 133. On the absence of spatial coordinates in the early phase of Odysseus' wanderings, see Hunter 2008: 140.
12. See De Jong 2001: 250, on 10. 1–79.
13. De Jong 2001: 224.
14. The length of Odysseus' sleep caught the imagination of the Italian poet Giovanni Pascoli (1855–1912), who further prolongs it in *Il sonno di Odisseo* to take Odysseus' ship around Ithaca without him knowing. Sleep builds the background for a tour of the island, followed by the readers and the crew but not Odysseus. The evocation of his lasting slumber ends each stanza as a monotone, lulling refrain: 'but his heart, deep in sleep, did not see, did not hear'. The harbour, the sacred olive, his palace appear, but Odysseus' heart, buried in sleep, does not see them; Eumaeus' pigs and his woodwork make noise, but Odysseus' heart, deep in

sleep, does not hear them. He keeps slumbering even after his companions release the winds and the ship is carried back seaward. Then Argus barks, but Odysseus' heart does not hear him; Laertes' fields and garden show in the growing distance and so does Laertes himself, looking at the ship, but Odysseus' heart does not see them. When he awakes, he looks at the land vanishing away and hopes to see and hear the sights and voices that passed by while he was sleeping, but sees only an amorphous black thing in the distance.

15. Arend (1933: 100) finds it significant that κοιμηθήμεν ('we slept') is replaced by κείμεθ' ('we lay down'). Tiredness and sorrow keep the travellers from moving two nights and two days already after the episode of the Cicones (*Od.* 9. 74–5).
16. On this growing distance, see Segal 1994: 34.
17. See also *Od.* 9. 558–9.
18. Arend (1933: 99) notes that this eventful night is described in atypical ways: Odysseus' comrades do not 'take' sleep. But it still comes upon them.
19. Stanford 1996, on 12. 333–4.
20. This is the much-debated Zielinski's rule. I found Fenik's discussion (1974: 61–104) illuminating. Delebecque (1980a) rephrases it as '*la loi des temps morts*' or '*la loi de succession*' (1980b). Both Fenik (76) and Delebecque (78) discuss Odysseus' sleep on Trinacria in light of the rule.
21. See De Jong 2001, on 12. 327–96.
22. See De Jong 2001, on 12. 327–96.
23. On the corporeality of night, see Pârvulescu 1985; of sleep, Eust. *Od.* 1. 233. 42.
24. Even if we discount the book divisions (see above), ἀμφικαλύψας ends a full narrative sequence.
25. See Moreux 1967.
26. See Purves 2010a: 336–7.
27. See also Purves 2010a: 339.
28. 'Boundless slumber' is a unique combination: see De Jong 2001: 185.
29. Stanford 1996, on 7. 288–9.
30. Hainsworth in *CO*, vol. 1, on 7. 288–9.
31. *Od.* 2. 393–5; 4. 795–6; 5. 382–4; 6. 112–5; 18. 187–8; 23. 242–3; 23. 344–8.
32. 'Even sleep is not mindless for a wise man. At least Telemachus pondered in his mind what Athena put before him. He, too, thought that "a man who makes decisions should not sleep all night"' (Eust. *Od.* 1. 76. 2–3).
33. See Marks 2008.
34. When Odysseus says that 'a god' put him pitilessly to sleep on Trinacria, the primary narrator does not back this up, whereas he

does when Odysseus says the same about his beneficial slumber on Scheria (7. 286; see 5. 491).

35. See Vagnone 1987: 95; Fernández Contreras 2000: 12.
36. 'Black evening' occurs only here and at 18. 306. On blackness as a mirror of the suitors' folly, see Van Sickle 1984: 130.
37. On Telemachus' adolescence, see Felson 1994, Chapter 4. Katz (1991: 63–72) shows that Telemachus' fame is bound up with his father's.
38. Van Sickle's contention (1984: 130) that Telemachus is still a child disregards his wakefulness.
39. Significantly, Laertes' recovery of status is heralded by Odysseus' observation that 'you look like one who [...] would sleep comfortably' (24. 254–5). See Murnaghan 2011: 21.
40. Though Menelaus' household is not free of tensions: see Foley 1978: 18.
41. So in 19 instances out of 22. In the other three sleep follows.
42. The only other time that the line 'They threw their hands on the food laid before them' stands alone and is followed by an abrupt move is at 20. 256–7, where the focus shifts from the suitors to Telemachus and Odysseus.
43. On retardation in this episode, see Fenik 1974: 84.
44. Marks (2008: 77) notes that Helen's drug 'suppresses memories associated with other epics so that memories of thematic significance to the *Odyssey* can surface', but also that the drug wears off. Its only partial success could intimate that the stories Helen and Menelaus tell under its influence are still Trojan-War material, not as strongly connected to the plot of the *Odyssey* as the account of Menelaus ambushing Proteus.
45. Segal (1994: 68) thinks that sleep becomes positive for Odysseus only when he reaches Scheria.
46. For Stanford (1996, on 11. 328), Odysseus is eager to leave. See also De Jong 1990.
47. See Eust. *Od.* 1. 422. 22: παροιμιῶδες.
48. *Il.* 9. 658; *Od.* 3. 397; 7. 335; 14. 518–9.
49. Alcinous' emphasis on the night's length could also suggest that it is winter: see Austin 1975, Chapter 5.
50. See Ambühl 2010: 262.
51. See Taplin 1992, Chapter 1.
52. Taplin considers Book 10 spurious.
53. Taplin (1992: 31), who reads Alcinous' comment along these lines, thinks that it would have come at about 4:00 a.m.
54. πρυμνῆς· ἂν δὲ καὶ αὐτὸς ἐβήσετο καὶ κατέλεκτο/ σιγῇ· τοὶ δὲ καθῖζον ἐπὶ κληῖσιν ἕκαστοι/ κόσμῳ, πεῖσμα δ' ἔλυσαν ἀπὸ τρητοῖο λίθοιο.
55. Joannes Doxopatres, *Comm. in Hermogenis* περὶ ἰδεῶν 492. 13–6. There is an oversight: Τυδέος should be Ἀτρέος (*Il.* 2. 23 and 60).

56. See De Jong 2001, on 13. 73–92.
57. See Schol. *Od.* 13. 119; Plut. *Mor.* 27E; Eust. *Od.* 2. 38. 34–40. 36.
58. Likewise Segal (1994: 47) calls Odysseus' sleep 'restorative'.
59. Giovanni Pascoli, in another poem dedicated to Odysseus' journey, is sensitive to this meaning of sleep: '*L'eroe dormiva, e non sapea più nulla/ dei molti affanni che patì nel cuore;/ e dal suo mite sonno era lontano/ il fragor di battaglie e di tempeste*'. ('The hero slept, and no longer knew the many sorrows he had suffered in his heart, but far from his gentle slumber was the din of battles and storms', *Il ritorno* 14–7).
60. For the first point, see Maronitis and Polkas 2007: 160–1; for the second, Taplin 1992: 30–1, and above.
61. See also *Il.* 15. 4.
62. See Dowden 2003: 146; Segal 1994, Chapter 2. Hartog (2001: 21–6) maps the Homeric world into three zones, from the most familiar to the most outlandish.
63. See Segal 1994: 69.
64. See Purves 2010a: 339.
65. *Od.* 13. 74, 80. In later literature νήγρετον is used for death (see, e.g., *AP* 7. 338; 7. 305).
66. See Purves 2010a: 339.
67. See Vernant 1991: 108–9.
68. On sleep and mortality in *Gilgamesh*, see McAlpine 1987: 138–9; Summers-Bremmer 2008: 19–23.
69. Austin 1975: 94; see also 97.
70. See Dyer 1974.
71. See Segal 1994: 15–6.
72. Likewise Telemachus' journey back to Ithaca begins at night and ends at dawn, and the one to Pylus takes all night and ends at dawn. The pattern, though, has exceptions (3. 178; 12. 429; 14. 314–5) and does not apply to land journeys: Telemachus arrives at Menelaus' palace in the evening, and so does Odysseus at Alcinous'.
73. See Fenik 1974: 161–2. A disorientating slumber also plays into Elpenor's death (10. 62–4).
74. In Monteverdi's *Il ritorno d'Ulisse in patria* the disorientating effects of Odysseus' slumber are intensified. His first question is 'Do I still sleep, or am I awake?' (Act 1, Scene 7) and Minerva teases him not for lying but for being still half asleep: 'You slumbered for so long that you still talk of shades and recount dreams' (Scene 8).
75. De Jong (2001, on 14. 524–33) notes that Odysseus' appreciation for Eumaeus' husbandry is stronger than the narrator's at the beginning of the book (14. 2–3). On Eumaeus' sleeping habits, see also 15. 556–7.
76. See Arend 1933: 103.
77. See Edwards 1992, following Arend.

78. Eumaeus, like Alcinous, might be pointing to the duration of winter nights: see Austin 1975 and already Eust. *Od.* 2. 104. 1–2. Delebecque (1980a: 5) thinks that Odysseus returns in autumn.
79. Odysseus' stories 'bewitch' Eumaeus (17. 514).
80. See Stanford 1996, on 15. 395–6.
81. See especially Segal 1994: 24–5, 119–22.
82. This equilibrium is at the core of Homeric poetics: see Macleod 2001. Segal (1994: 27, 119–22 and 165) contrasts Odysseus' involved listening and the Phaeacians' detachment.
83. See Segal 1994: 130.
84. Foley (1978: 15) notes that Odysseus' recovery of his blood relations is relatively fast, whereas he has to renegotiate his social ones. Stories fulfill this function.
85. See also *Od.* 15. 292–4; 17. 148–9.
86. *Od.* 3. 487; 3. 497; 11. 121; 15. 185.
87. The only other case is 15. 471.
88. See De Jong 2001, on 15. 1–8.
89. Rose 1971: 510, quoted by Edwards 1992: 308.
90. See *CO*, vol. 2, on 15. 557; Stanford 1996, on 15. 556–7. ἐνιαύειν means 'to spend the night' rather than strictly 'to sleep'.
91. On Penelope's dissimulation, see Papadopoulou-Belmehdi 1994: 42. The story might have been inspired by the familiar folk motif of 'undoing by night what was done by day': see McCartney 1953. If so, the Greek poet stresses Penelope's cunning and stamina by making her both the daytime doer and the night-time un-doer, whereas in the standard tale the nightly destruction is carried out by devils, giants or witches.
92. See Foley 1978: 10; Katz 1991; Papadopoulou-Belmehdi 1994. Murnaghan (2011, Chapter 4) is more skeptical.
93. Segal (1994: 70) sees in Penelope's sleep 'a sign of her reduced life and the static condition of her world without Odysseus'.
94. Odysseus' *nostos* depends on Penelope's memory as much as it does on his own: see Papadopoulou-Belmehdi 1994.
95. Foley 1978: 10.
96. Hecuba and Andromache do so in Homer. In Apollonius of Rhodes, Alcimede gives Jason a mother's guilt trip over his departure.
97. On κῶμα, see Chapter 1.
98. See De Jong 2001, on 18. 187–99.
99. I think that at this juncture the plot is entirely Athena's. For discussion, see Katz 1991: 78–93; Emlyn-Jones 1984: 10–1.
100. See Stanford 1996, on 13. 187.
101. *Il.* 7. 482; 9. 713. I stress finality in the meaning of 'closure' (following Morgan 1989b: 318), though the term has been the object of a lively debate: see, e.g., Torgovnick 1981; Mortimer 1985 and, for classical literature, the articles in Roberts *et al.* 1997.

102. See Detienne and Vernant 1978: 31.
103. See Gantz 1993: 420. A red-figure cup attributed to the Nicosthenes Painter (around 510) shows Athena to the right of Hypnos, who crouches on the giant's body while Heracles attacks him from the left. Alcyoneus' sleep is not in literature, and is possibly the painter's invention: McNally 1985: 155; Shapiro 1993: 149. Sleep may be implied, however, in the short narrative of Alcyoneus' killing in Pind. *Isthm.* 6. 31 (Hazzikostas 1990: 47–8) or it may have featured in a lost Heracles saga (Shapiro 1993: 148–51). On the episode, see also Stafford 2003: 81–3.
104. See Chapter 4.
105. Apollod. *Bibl.* 2. 41–4. See Gantz 1993: 305–6.
106. *Od.* 4. 400–34. Similarly Heracles is advised to go seek Nereus, but whether he is following instructions when he grabs the sea god in his sleep is not specified (Apollod. *Bibl.* 2. 115).
107. See Murnaghan 2011: 62.
108. Arend (1933: 10) thinks that even *Od.* 9. 151 and 12. 7 do not describe sleep. At *Il.* 11. 723, though, the phrase might imply rest.
109. In the course of the conversation, however, the figure of Odysseus recedes while the stranger gets nearer to Penelope: see Vester 1968: 420–1.
110. See *CO*, vol. 3, 106.
111. Russo in *CO*, vol. 3, on 19. 336–48.
112. Penelope strives to maintain appropriate standards of hospitality: see Foley 1978: 9–10. Slightly differently, Murnaghan (2011, Chapter 3) thinks that Penelope's impulses towards hospitality have been lying dormant during the suitors' occupation, until Odysseus reactivates them.
113. Fenik (1974: 155–7) considers the meeting with Eumaeus a doublet of the conversation between Odysseus and Penelope in Book 19.
114. See also Murnaghan 2011: 84.
115. See Wöhrle 1995: 94.
116. See De Jong 2001, on 20. 1–57.
117. See Russo 1968: 291–2; De Jong 2001, on 20. 1–57. For Fusillo (2008: 151) the monologue is not deliberative.
118. Athena's observation reverses Eumaeus' claim that there is surfeit in sleep (15. 394).
119. See De Jong 2001, on 20. 30–57.
120. Murnaghan (2011: 94) speaks of 'Athena's particularly intrusive interventions in Books 18 and 19'.
121. The Odyssean norm in scenes of μερμηρίζειν is that the human agent decides alone, as earlier in this very scene (20. 10). See Russo 1968: 290.
122. This is 'Jørgensen's law': see De Jong 2001, on 7. 240–97. Marks (2008: 41) notes that in Odysseus' narration the gods play a lesser

role than in the authorial narrative because Odysseus is not omniscient.

123. See also Russo 1982: 12.
124. Athena is disguised as a woman (20. 29), but is recognized as a goddess (37) and reveals that she is one (47).
125. See Brillante 1990.
126. For De Jong (2001, on 15. 1–47) Athena is disguised, while the editors of the *CO* (vol. 2, on 15. 9) think that she is not. In any case she does not name herself.
127. See Russo 1982; Stanford 1996, on 20. 92 ff.; *CO*, vol. 3, on 20. 93–4.
128. See Arist. *Parv. nat.* 462a 10–1, quoted by Russo (1982: 16) in connection with Odysseus' vision. The Erinyes are in a 'twilight state' (Rousseau 1963: 130) when they stir at the beginning of Aeschylus' *Eumenides*. Aelius Aristides records that he had visions of Asclepius while between sleeping and waking (Dodds 1963: 113), and Macrobius (*In Somn.* 1. 3. 7) calls 'apparition' the vision occurring 'in the first cloud of slumber, when we think to be still awake'.
129. Monro in Stanford's phrasing (1996, on 20. 92 ff.). Lévy (1982: 23) calls the vision a '*rêverie éveillée*'.
130. However far we stretch the meaning of the verb (as does *CO*, vol. 3, on 93–4), it denotes a conscious mental process. Amory (1963: 108) minimizes the difference between a true dream and an in-between-state vision, but this fails to account for Odysseus' μερμηρίζειν.
131. Amory 1966: 56 (see also 1963: 104), followed by Russo 1982.
132. See Emlyn-Jones 1984; Murnaghan 2011: 101–2.
133. See Doods 1963: 106 (on Penelope's first dream); Emlyn-Jones 1984: 4. Harris (2009: 50) calls Penelope's second dream of Odysseus plainly 'erotic'. παρέδραθεν ('he lay by [me]', 20. 88) has sexual connotations (the only other instance in Homer is *Il.* 14. 163).
134. See Lévy 1982: 30–1.
135. See Emlyn-Jones 1984: 5.
136. See Papadopoulou-Belmehdi 1994: 136.
137. See Lévy 1982: 30–1.
138. See Lévy 1982: 30.
139. De Jong (2001: 407) notes that the *Odyssey* slows down towards the end, with days 39 (17. 1 to 20. 90) and 40 (20. 90 to 23. 341). Day 33, however, or rather night 33, when Odysseus narrates his adventures, is even longer (2,834 lines): see Delebecque 1980a: 7.
140. ἐγρόμεναι (20. 123). The other variant is ἀγρόμεναι ('assembled'). Editors are divided: the Oxford Classical Text prints ἀγρόμεναι, the Teubner ἐγρόμεναι.
141. So is Antinous' request to bring the best goats on the morrow (21. 265–6): see Saïd 1979: 11.

142. An audience will remark the exceptionality of this feast, which does not end with the suitors' departure: see Saïd 1979: 12.
143. *Od.* 3. 342; 3. 395; 7. 184; 7. 228; 18. 427.
144. An attentive audience will take the two episodes together because the expression 'accompaniments of a feast' occurs nowhere else. The substitution of 'dance' with 'lyre' or rather φόρμιγξ foreshadows the suitors' killing, for Odysseus handling the bow has just been compared to a competent musician handling a φόρμιγξ (21. 406).
145. Van Sickle (1984: 130) notes the ironic point of this invitation.
146. See *Od.* 18. 201–5; 20. 57–90.
147. See Hölscher 1991: 392; De Jong 2001, on 23. 16–9.
148. See De Jong 2001, on 21. 350–8; Hölscher 1991: 391. Telemachus' intervention (21. 350) responds to the same narrative need, for Penelope would not willingly have left the halls where her remarriage was being decided: see Vester 1968: 430.
149. Hölscher calls this sleep '*Ein episches Hilfsmotiv*' (1991: 391).
150. *Ap.* 40d–e, summarized. See also Plat. *Resp.* 571c–572b, with van der Eijk 2003; Plut. *Mor.* 686B. In Roman literature, see Plaut. *Rud.* 593–5.
151. In the formulaic ὕπνον ἡδύν, noun and adjective are never separate.
152. See Murnaghan 2011: 32; Foley 1978.
153. Austin 1975: 141.
154. Foley 1978: 17. On the simile, see also Purves 2010b: 91.
155. See Segal 1994: 70.
156. Hölscher (1991) relates Penelope's sleep to her misjudgement of the situation.
157. See E. West 2010: 23.
158. Upon disclosing his identity, Odysseus promised to the two loyal servants that, in case of victory, 'you both will be friends and brothers of Telemachus' (21. 215–6). In sleeping in the same place as he, they are already acting like his brothers.
159. See *CO*, vol. 3, on 23. 241–6 (the editors also defend the lines' authenticity).
160. See *AP* 5. 172, 223, 583; Ov. *Am.* 1. 13. Already Sappho developed the motif, according to Libanius (12. 99. 5): 'Nothing stopped Sappho of Lesbos from praying that the night be doubled for her'.
161. In Plautus' *Amphitryon* the night is lengthened so that Jupiter can have *voluptatem* with Alcmena (114). He leaves in a hurry before dawn, though Alcmena says that he was feeling drowsy and that they went to sleep (806–7). In Lucian, Hermes asks Helios to stay away for three days so that Zeus can enjoy Alcmena's company (*Dial. D.* 14). Ovid (*Am.* 1. 13), in cursing dawn for its hasty rising, names sleep as one of the perks of night, but in a general statement (7). Propertius (2. 15) recounts the delights of love in the course of a night in which no sleep is allowed (7–8). In several of Chaucer's

tales (starting with *Troilus and Criseyde*) the lovers are 'busy' with love at night and exhausted in the morning: see Scattergood 1987.

162. See Maronitis 2004: 58.
163. See Felson 1994: 62.
164. In the second Eurynome also participates. The pair of maids is symbolic of the couple's reunion: see Karydas 1998: 50.
165. See Purves 2010b: 76.

Chapter 3 Drama

1. Arist. *Poet.* 1448b12–20, with Fantuzzi 1990: 19–20. For comedy, see Van Steen 2011.
2. For further discussion, see Fantuzzi 1990. On night scenes in drama, see also Donelan 2014 (though it is unfortunate that this author does not know Fantuzzi's article).
3. See Mace 2002 and 2004. My analysis is indebted to this scholar's, but I do not agree with all her conclusions.
4. Mace 2002 and 2004.
5. κοιμώμενος (2) here does not mean 'sleeping': see Fraenkel 1950 and Denniston-Page 1957, *ad loc. Contra*: Mace 2002: 38.
6. On the meaning of this Aeschylean coinage, see Fraenkel 1950 and Denniston-Page 1957, *ad loc.*
7. See De Romilly 1958: 13, n. 4. *Contra*: Mace 2002: 39, n. 13.
8. Mace 2002: 40.
9. Most editors print ἔν θ' ὕπνῳ (Page, Mazon, Thomson), not ἄνθ' ὕπνου ('instead of sleep') as defended by Fraenkel (1950, *ad loc.*, followed by Mace 2002: 42) and printed by Denniston-Page 1957.
10. στάζει may also suggest the oozing of a wound (Fraenkel 1950, *ad loc.*; Mazon 1983, *ad loc.*), but I agree with Fraenkel that the idea of constant dripping is preferable.
11. Schol. *Ag.* 180a. Modern readings of the passage widely differ: see Mace 2002: 42–3.
12. ἀπαλλαχθέντες ('having got rid') harks back to the watcher's hope for ἀπαλλαγὴ πόνων, and δρόσων ('dews') to his complaint of an ἔνδροσον bed (12): see Mace 2002: 46, n. 52.
13. Eur. *Hec.* 916–38; Verg. *Aen.* 2. 250–67; Petron. *Sat.* 89. 54–66; Quint. Smyrn. 12. 45; 13. 26–43, 122–32; Apollod. *Epit.* 5. 19a–21a. To my knowledge, the only other narrative of the night after the sack is in Quintus of Smyrna: see Conclusions.
14. ἐγρηγορός is a generally accepted emendation for ἐγρήγορον. Fraenkel (1950, *ad loc.*) rejects it, based on the strain that the required meaning would put on the 'if', which would have to be concessive (even if calamity has not yet hit). A concessive reading, however, does not seem necessary. Mazon (1983) translates: *'s'il ne s'est pas déjà trahi par des coups immédiats'*.

15. See Mazon 1983, *ad. loc.* Mace (2002: 47) spots also a foreshadowing of Aegisthus' revenge and of Orestes'.
16. The ambivalence is noted by Denniston-Page 1957, *ad loc.*
17. The adjective refers only to him in the play (see also 1303).
18. The contrasting experiences are poignantly brought out in the stichomythia at 538–50.
19. See Mace 2002: 49.
20. See Garner 1990: 37.
21. See Rousseau 1963: 111–2.
22. See McClure 1997: 125.
23. *Agamemnon* is pervaded by 'a fear of naming fear', as Goldhill (1984: 52) puts it. See also Montiglio 2000: 212.
24. *Ag.* 36–9; 97–9; 253; 548; 1025–34, with Thalmann 1985.
25. The translation of this intricate passage follows Pattoni 2009: 4, to which I refer for discussion of the dream.
26. See Rousseau 1963: 104–13.
27. See Rousseau 1963: 121; Mace 2004: 40.
28. See Mace 2004: 43, n. 19.
29. Mace (2004: 45) thinks that Hermes seizes Scylla and that her death adumbrates Clytemnestra's. This would be neat, but it seems more natural to refer the pronoun μιν to Nisos.
30. The suitors are concerned with their sleep, not Odysseus', for they do not practise hospitality. But otherwise the sequence is similar. See Chapter 2.
31. Mace 2004: 47.
32. See Garner 1990: 39.
33. *Il.* 22. 502–4. See Chapter 1.
34. Simon. 38. 21–2 (Page 1962) and Eur. *Tro.* 1188, respectively. A touching modern rendering of the motif is Frances Cornford's *Mother to Child Asleep*, where the child's slumber makes his mother think of his sailing through life alone when she will be no more.
35. See Rousseau 1963: 124. Differently Mace 2004: 47.
36. See Sommerstein 1989, on 64–93. *Contra*: Taplin (1977: 365–74), who thinks that the Erinyes become visible only when they awaken (140).
37. On the origin of the Erinyes' sleep I follow the scholia on 94a and b. See also Sommerstein 1989, on 67; Jouanna 1981: 53, n. 10.
38. Mace 2004: 50.
39. So Patroclus appearing to Achilles, a dream that the Erinyes' imitates closely: see Sommerstein 1989, on 94–9.
40. Lines 104–5 ('In sleep the mind shines with eyes, while in the day the lot of mortals is to have no vision') explicitly equate the Erinyes with humans, though the lines are likely interpolated: see Thomson 1966, on 104–6; Lévy 1981: 146; Sommerstein 1989, on 104–5.
41. See Sommerstein 1989, on 64–93.

42. See also Mace 2004: 52.
43. See Buxton 1982: 109–14.
44. See Macleod 1982b: 135.
45. The terms for 'charm' in all the instances quoted here are derived from the verb θέλγειν. On θέλγειν as an effect of persuasion, see Buxton 1982: 108–11. The manner of Athena's action does not suggest that 'The idea that "sleep" can metaphorically signal a permanent neutralization of retaliatory μένος is flawed' (Mace 2004: 53), for the metaphor is effectively employed to foster the permanent lulling of the Erinyes' rage. Athena uses κοιμάω, 'put to sleep', not σβέννυμι, 'put out'. The Erinyes' admission of being under her charm amounts to recognizing that their anger is going to sleep also because θέλγειν is hypnotic (Hom. *Il.* 24. 343; *Od.* 5. 47; 24. 3; Pind. *Pyth.* 1. 21; Eur. *IA* 140; Ap. Rhod. 4. 147). For the Erinyes to lull their anger to rest, however, the methods employed had to change from violence to persuasion and the target had to be reduced from anger at large to its pernicious applications: on the last point, see Mace 2004: 55–6.
46. See Mace 2004: 54.
47. On the ideological implications of the ambiguity encoded in ἀστῶν φόβος (691), fear 'for' or 'of' the citizens, see Sommerstein 1989, on 690–2.
48. The citation is from Macleod 1982b: 135. De Romilly (1958: 112) calls this fear '*la bonne crainte*'. Macleod (1982b: 129) compares the Areopagus to the Hindu *Laws of Manu* (vii 18): 'Punishment rules all the people, Punishment alone protects them, Punishment is awake while they sleep'.
49. See Macleod 1982b: 129.
50. See also Macleod 1982b: 129.
51. On the commonplace of the tyrant's fear, see Lanza 1977: 45–9.
52. The date of *Trachiniae* is unknown, but is certainly earlier than *Orestes* and *Philoctetes* and probably *Heracles*: see Easterling 1982: 19–23. Dieterich (1891) contends that Sophocles borrowed the sleep scene from *Heracles*, where it would be more organically integrated into the dramatic development. Whether we agree with this judgement or not, the dating does not seem to fit and the assumption that the model is by definition superior to the imitation is questionable.
53. Taplin 1977: 84, 124–5. See further Fowler 1999: 162–5; Davidson 2003.
54. See Davidson 2003: 520. Garner (1990: 100–2) spots numerous allusions to the *Odyssey*, but not to Penelope's insomnia.
55. Easterling's translation (1982).
56. The scholion suggests either the nightingale or the halcyon, but the former is typically associated with a woman's unceasing lament in Greek poetry, including Sophocles': see, e.g., *El.* 107, 92–3.

57. See Easterling 1982, on 149–50.
58. See Easterling 1982, on 915–6.
59. Davidson (2003: 522) further notes that Hyllus' cry replicates Odysseus' (Ὤ μοι ἐγώ).
60. Commentators tend to privilege *Od.* 6: so Easterling 1982, on 984–5; Davidson 2003: 522. But see Reinhardt 1979: 246, n. 21.
61. See Chapter 2.
62. See Biggs 1966: 228.
63. See, e.g., Eur. *Alc.* 690; *IA* 1218; Ap. Rhod. 3. 815, where the contrast with Hades is explicit (810).
64. Reinhardt 1979: 57.
65. See Hartigan 1987: 127. Heracles' madness, though, stems also from his violent nature: so Papadopoulou 2005.
66. See Bond 1981, on 1004.
67. See Burnett 1971: 171.
68. See Willink 1988: 87–8; Papadopoulou 2005: 79.
69. Line 1061 is corrupt. I follow Diggle's Oxford Classical Text. Willink's proposal (1988) to emend ὕπνον with πόνον is ingenious, but his main objection to ὕπνον ὀλόμενον, namely that the adjective would make little sense, does not seem compelling: Bond (1981, *ad loc.*) takes ὀλόμενον to mean 'accursed' or 'pestilential'. In addition, sleep is ruinous because it translates Heracles to sanity and with it to thoughts of death.
70. Picked up also at Soph. *El.* 41–2, which Bond (1981) cites in connection with *Her.* 1052.
71. Bond (1981, on 1049) thinks that ὑπνώδεα means 'sleep bound', but Amphitryon has just said that Heracles is asleep (1043–4).
72. See Bond 1981, on 1089–145. For Willink (1986, on 140–207) the men of the chorus remain in the orchestra. The fact that Amphitryon asks, 'Old men, shall I go near him?' (1109) before reentering supports this view. If they are onstage, the question creates a link with the offstage, as often happens in drama. But their answer, 'I also will come with you', speaks strongly in favour of their absence, unless we imagine them to be far removed from Heracles, which is not much different from being absent altogether.
73. Garner 1990: 115.
74. Soph. *Aj.* 21, 47, 141, 209, 217.
75. Eur. *Bacch.* 683–6, 692 (θαλερός). Dodds (1944) translates the adjective 'in its flower', 'deep'. But 'refreshing' or 'vitalizing', which he mentions as possible alternatives, better accord with the supernatural vitality displayed by the Bacchants upon awakening.
76. Critics are divided over the exact circumstance that triggers Neoptolemus' change. Reinhardt (1979: 181) considers Philoctetes' awakening the decisive factor, while Whitman (1951: 176) reads in Neoptolemus' condemnation of deception during the sick man's

sleep (842) his 'first moment of conscious moral action'. Schein (2013, on 839–42) criticizes this view, though he concedes that Neoptolemus 'might be represented as having mixed feelings' at this point. For Austin (2011: 103, 122) he is already in a moral quandary at 639–40. More references are in Fulkerson 2013: 69. Whatever the case, the sleep scene marks the point after which Neoptolemus acts honestly.

77. The translation of line 160 is Schein's (2013).
78. See Jouanna 1981: 55.
79. A prevalence of vowels, and especially long vowels, marks the invocation's beginning (827–31). Waern (1960: 4) lists the song among Greek literary lullabies, though euphonic sound patterns are generally typical of paeans (Schein 2013: 249).
80. αἴγλαν (literally 'divine luminosity') has given critics trouble, for it seems at odds with sleep. Jebb translates 'dream light' (2004, *ad loc.*) while Webster (1970, *ad loc.*) notes that Aigla is Asclepius' daughter and glosses: 'the gleam of serenity which the god of healing brings'. See also Austin 2011: 126; Schein 2013, *ad loc.*
81. See Schein 2003: 95.
82. See Webster 1970, on 833; Jouanna 1981: 57; Ussher 2001, on 829.
83. See Jones 1949; Garner 1990: 148.
84. ἀδεής, 'fearless', is a possible emendation of the transmitted ἀλεής, which primarily means 'protecting from danger' (and secondarily 'from the cold'): see Jouanna 1981: 57.
85. See Jouanna 1981: 62.
86. See also *Phil.* 882–5.
87. To stay within Sophocles, see *Aj.* 859; *Ant.* 808; *Trach.* 1144.
88. See Schein 2012: 432.
89. See Reinhardt 1979: 182.
90. This is generally noted.
91. See further Willink 1986, on 140–207 and 210; Garner 1990: 149.
92. See Jouanna 1981: 56–7.
93. See Zeitlin 1980: 55. On the likelihood that Euripides has the *Oresteia* in mind, see also Wright 2008: 79–80.
94. See Zeitlin 1980: 55.
95. For the translation of ὀλεῖς, see Willink 1986, *ad loc.*
96. See Willink 1986, on 208–10.
97. A sane Orestes would clash with the received myth, but so does the entire plot of the play until the end.
98. See Burnett 1971: 184, 195–6.
99. The actor who plays Electra must play Menelaus or Tyndareus in the next episode.
100. See also Burnett 1971: 198.
101. Seaford 1984, on 591–2.
102. See P. Arnott 1961: 168–9.

103. Ussher (1978, on 599–602) reads the darkness of death into 'black Night'. Blackness is also consonant with the blinding that sleep allows.
104. This would speak in favour of a late dating of *Cyclops*, as defended especially by Seaford 1982 and 1984: 48–51, followed, e.g., by Garner 1990: 154–7.
105. See Konstan 2001: 8.
106. See Katsouris 1997: 21.
107. The line order in the prologue is a notorious crux. I follow Diggle's numbering for convenience, though the arguments raised by Willink (1971) in favour of an alternative sequence are attractive.
108. See Fantuzzi 1990: 25.
109. Willink 1971: 351.
110. See Walton 2000: 138.
111. So Parry 1964 and Fantuzzi 2006: 152.
112. See Walton 2000.
113. Though Mcleod (1988) correctly notes that the subsequent actions in the Greek camp bespeak fires, the return of Odysseus and Diomedes is heralded by noise only.
114. See Fantuzzi 1990: 27; Donelan 2014: 549.
115. *Rh.* 7–8 and *Il.* 10. 80, with Fantuzzi 2006: 149.
116. See also Fantuzzi 2006: 148.
117. *Rh.* 518. See Liapis 2012: xlix, quoting Burnett: Rhesus does not do much more than 'allow himself to be led away to bed'.
118. More idiosyncratic features of the song are in Liapis 2012: 216.
119. Parry 1964: 293.
120. The goddess, though, has absolute control over the actions of Odysseus and Diomedes: see Fenik 1964: 23–4; Fantuzzi 2006: 159–68.
121. See Liapis 2012: 280.
122. See Fenik 1964.
123. See Jouanna 1981: 54.
124. Beta (1999: 138) suggests the threat of stoning (1491) as a parallel, though stoning madmen was normal practice: see, e.g., Ar. *Av.* 525. If it is parodied in *Wasps*, *Heracles* must be earlier than 422: see Beta 150–1.
125. Bdelycleon is asleep on the roof (68), awakens (136–7), but dozes off again (336–7) until the noise his father makes awakens him again (394). On the servants, see below.
126. 'Sleeps in front of the court' is Sommerstein's translation (1983).
127. Van Steen (2011: 798) suggests that Philocleon acted out the servant's description of his troubled sleep.
128. See Slater 1999: 362.
129. On the thematic importance of night in *Wasps*, see Donelan 2014: 539–40.
130. So Borthwick 1992: 274, commenting on line 8.

131. Paris' call in *Rhesus* does not awaken a sleeper: see above.
132. The wording specifically recalls *Orestes* 137.
133. On the meaning of the violation, see Lowe 1987 and Traill 2001.
134. Contrast the use of 'alone' at 30, 150, 869, and especially 329 and 331, to stress Cnemon's autarchy. The reversal is anticipated by a servant's threat: 'you will lie down alone' (874).
135. Menander must have exploited sleeplessness more than the extant evidence shows. A character in *Kitharistes* (fr. 1 Arnott 1996) talks about nights of 'tossing up and down' (3) because of financial distress, and extends sleep troubles to the rich as well, since life brings pain to all. See also Introduction, n. 3.
136. *Phasma* 9–18. Translation G. Arnott 2000.
137. Donatus *On Terence Eunuchus* 9. 3, in G. Arnott 2000: 408 (his translation).
138. See Turner 1969: 318; G. Arnott 2000: 368 and 385. A reference to Phidias' melancholy is at 57.
139. See Thomas 1979: 196; Barbieri 2001: 5, 7, 9, 53–4, 61, 65.
140. See Koch 1888: 154; Thomas 1979: 196; Barbieri 2001: 54, 61.
141. Barbieri (2001: 65) traces the motif back to Ibycus (fr. 257a Davies 1991). It might have appeared already in Sappho (fr. 168b Voigt 1971).
142. See Thomas 1979: 197.
143. See Plaut. *Cur.* 181–4; *Poen.* 323; Ter. *Eunuchus* 218–21.
144. *Mis.* 1–14. Translation G. Arnott 1996.
145. See Bornmann 1980: 161.
146. In a large number of erotic spells love and sleeplessness are inseparable. The kinship of the two was so keenly felt that it gave rise to a technical term: 'Love spell of attraction through wakefulness'. See Preisendanz 1973, IV. 2943–66, 1496–595, 2441–621, 2708–84, 3272–3; VII. 374–6; VIII. 887–9; XII. 376–96; XXXVI. 147–53; Thomas 1979: 195; Faraone 1999: 26–7; 65–6; 145. This scholar (26, n. 114) points out that insomnia is a component of love spells also in ancient Mesopotamian and Spanish magic.

Chapter 4 Apollonius of Rhodes' *Argonautica*

1. Vagnone (1987) notes that references to eating or sleeping generally become less frequent in epic after Homer.
2. See Harder 1994: 17.
3. The interconnection between the coming of dawn and the Argonauts' discovery of their loss is brought up by the correlatives 'when/then' (ἦμος/τῆμος): 'At the time when dawn shines, rising from the east, and the paths stand out brightly and the dewy plain shines with a resplendent gleam, then they realized' (1. 1280–3). Fantuzzi (1988: 141) notes that this dawn is the most luminous in the epic.
4. See Chapter 2.

5. See Carspecken 1952: 127; Beye 1982: 66; Hunter 1989: 39; Fantuzzi and Hunter 2004: 123; Fantuzzi 2008a. Differently Cairns 1998.
6. See Knight 1995: 133.
7. Apollonius plays with the Homeric vocabulary of sleep also by multiplying instances of the hapax κνώσσω (*Od.* 4. 809): 1. 1083; 1. 1096; 4. 111.
8. See also De Jong 1990: 23.
9. Beye 1982: 66.
10. See Vian 1974, on 1. 518.
11. Together with context, the fact that the term does not appear anywhere else (except in the lexicographers) proves that Apollonius is echoing Homer.
12. See Chapter 1.
13. The communality of the enterprise is announced in the first line: see Fantuzzi and Hunter 2004: 95. See also 1. 336–7; 2. 173.
14. See Knight 1995: 55. The ritual begins at 1. 447 in the *Iliad* and at 1. 411 in the *Argonautica*.
15. Wray 2000: 248.
16. Jason's announcement echoes lines 234–5: the ship is both times ἐπαρτέα (ready). The relatively close repetition is notable because the adjective appears only two more times in the epic, both far apart and in different contexts (2. 1177; 3. 299).
17. See Wray 2000: 250; Clare 2002: 43.
18. Whether this version was a real edition or circulated informally is disputed: see Fantuzzi 1988: 87–95.
19. Schol. 1. 516–8. For extended comparison, see Fantuzzi 1988: 101–4 and 121–4.
20. Cairns (1998: 70) compares the departure from Iolcus with Odysseus' from Calypso, noting that numerous speeches precede both. Sleep is the narrative equivalent of the lovemaking in that episode. In both dawn rises expansively, filling an entire line, right after mention of lovemaking or slumber.
21. See Introduction.
22. Ap. Rhod. 4. 1689–90, where the Argonauts camp for the night. The journey, however, had already been interrupted by the appearance of Talus and his death. Though we might assume that the Argonauts sleep after they are cast on the Libyan shores, Apollonius only says that they sought a resting place, covered their heads, refused to eat and lay down all night and the next day waiting for death (4. 1293–6).
23. To Beye (1982: 99) the winds evoke sirocco.
24. Contrast the hero of Valerius Flaccus, who is wakeful alone on the night prior to the departure (*Argonautica* 1. 295–6).
25. See Knight 1995: 169–76. Tiresias' prophecy is also in the background, but the nocturnal setting of Phineus' privileges Circe as model.

26. Hunter (1993: 24–5) cites 3. 171–5, where Jason shares his plan and asks for approval and counsel, as 'virtually a programmatic rejection of Odyssean behavior'. See also Fantuzzi and Hunter 2004: 128–9.
27. This is the case for Phrixus' sons. The Argonauts arrive earlier.
28. Knight (1995: 133–5; 185) spots the references.
29. See below.
30. See Fusillo 1985: 196–7.
31. See Hunter 2008: 138–40.
32. The last line of Book 2 was added to end Book 1: see Fantuzzi 2008a: 230.
33. Campbell (1983b: 155) thinks that Apollonius has this line in mind.
34. Van Sickle (1984: 131) fails to see this.
35. De Jong (1990: 29–30) thinks that the divisions do predate Aristarchus.
36. See Clare 2002: 164, commenting on Apollo's epiphany at 2. 669–79.
37. De Jong 1990: 23.
38. See Stevick 1970: 45–6, referenced by De Jong 1990: 23.
39. See Vian 1961, on 447.
40. The latter is often noted: see, e.g., Beye 1982: 136.
41. λιγέως as read by Hunter 1989, *ad loc.* The term describes a high-pitched voice.
42. See Hunter 1989: 164. This scholar notes an additional allusion to Penelope's complaint of sleep disturbances at *Od.* 19. 516–7. We could add *Od.* 4. 794 (= 18. 189), which describes the troubled Penelope resting at last, about to find comfort in a dream sent by Athena.
43. Compare, in Homer, εὗδε δ' ἀ/νακλιν/θεῖσα,// λύ/θεν δέ οἱ/ ἅψεα/ πάντα and, in Apollonius, λέκτρῳ ἀ/νακλιν/θεῖσαν.// ἄ/φαρ δέ μιν/ ἠπερο/πῆες.
44. Hunter (1989: 164) thinks that the hand of Hera might be at work in Medea's sleep and dream. This is possible (the use of κατακνώσσουσα for her sleep at 3. 690 could allude to Penelope's sleep at *Od.* 4. 809 [κνώσσουσ'], which is filled by the dream Athena sends her), but is left unspecified.
45. See Hunter 1989, on 616–824.
46. One exception is *Od.* 14. 457, where the coming of night introduces Odysseus' story. Fantuzzi (1988: 125) notes that one of the most common Homeric phrases for nightfall, 'the sun set and all the ways grew dark', normally concludes a narrative unit.
47. Fr. 89 Page 1962. Alcman's poem might be at the origin of the motif: Livrea 1973, on 4. 1058.
48. See Gibson 1996: 460 and Fernández Contreras 2000: 16, both with further references.
49. Fr. 168b Voigt 1971. 'The hour' means 'the time for sleep': see Ferrari 1983.
50. See Chapter 3.

51. See Carrière 1959: 51–3; Beye 1982: 67–8; Campbell 1983a: 49; Fusillo 1985: 292; Hunter 1989, on 744–51.
52. See Carrière 1959: 53; Hunter 1989, on 746.
53. See Carrière 1959: 53. For Campbell (1983a: 49) the passage as a whole 'is designed to exert a hypnotic effect on the reader'.
54. See Fusillo 1985: 292.
55. See Fantuzzi 1988: 145; Hurst 2012: 90.
56. See Chapter 1.
57. See Hunter 1989: 178: 'There is a suggestion that the gods have relieved the mother's suffering with sleep, but there is no divinity to soothe Medea'. Later Hera intervenes to strengthen her decision to live, because it furthers the goddess' plan.
58. See Hunter 1989, *ad loc.*
59. Medea's speech to her sister, in which she states that she will not see dawn if she does not offer her help (3. 728–31) and that at dawn she will go to the temple to give Jason the drugs (737–9), foreshadows the two options with which she struggles in her sleepless night.
60. On the threshold's symbolic meaning, see Daniel-Müller 2012: 110–1.
61. See Hunter 1989: 177. Vian (1961, on 751–72) notes a contamination between *Il.* 10. 3–4 and *Od.* 15. 7–8 (Telemachus sleeplessly thinking of his father). It has also been suggested (Sanz Morales and Laguna Mariscal 2005) that Achilles' insomnia in *Iliad* 24 is behind the description of Medea's, but I share Fantuzzi's skepticism (2012: 235, n. 118). For Achilles comes to no decision whatsoever in his sleepless nights.
62. There is only one other possible borrowing (2. 407: ἥδυμος). Otherwise sleep is un-Homerically ἀδινός ('thick', 'deep', 1. 1083; 3. 616; 3. 748) or without modifiers (1. 518; 2. 157; 4. 159; 4. 1110).
63. See Hunter 1989, on 744–51. The parallel of the light similes is noted by this scholar.
64. See Fantuzzi 2008b; Beye 1982: 142.
65. See Knight 1995: 281; Fantuzzi 2008b; Cariou 2012: 147–8.
66. The text is corrupt, but inactivity is certainly present in it.
67. See Hunter 1989, on 1171–2.
68. Livrea (1973, on 183), in comparing another description of dawn rising in Apollonius (4. 183) with its closest Homeric equivalents (*Il.* 8. 1 = 24. 695; 23. 227), notes that in Homer the description occupies the whole line but not in Apollonius.
69. Other instances of dawn rising abruptly at the end of a line are at 1. 651; 1. 1151; 4. 1622; 4. 1713.
70. To be precise, the Argonauts are about to sleep. Before they do so, Apollonius transfers the narrative to the more active theatre in a manner reminiscent of the Hylas episode.
71. The parallel is in Hunter 1988: 446.

72. See Hunter 1988: 446–7.
73. The reference is noted by all commentators.
74. See Hunter 1988: 445.
75. See Clare 2002: 81; Byre 2002: 41.
76. See above. The closest Homeric equivalent is *Od*. 9. 556–62. See also 10. 546–9.
77. See Fernández Contreras 2000: 19.
78. See Beye 1982: 84 referencing Lawall; Clare 2002: 171. Jason's commanding treatment of Alcimede on the eve of his departure ('be quiet and stay inside the house with the maidservants', 1. 303–4) recalls Telemachus' harshness towards Penelope on the eve of his.
79. See Hunter 1989, on 3. 1191–4, 1197. Vidal-Naquet (1986: 108) considers the Jason of Pindar's *Pythian* 4 an archetypical ephebe. As we shall see, the stealing of the fleece further emphasizes Jason's liminal status.
80. This does not mean, however, that the epic's true protagonist is Medea: see Clauss 1997.
81. Of the eleven instances of dawn in the nominative, there is only one other (4. 981) in which it is 'early born' and 'sheds' (βάλε) light.
82. See Hunter 1989, on 3. 1224.
83. See James 1978: 173; Fantuzzi 1988: 150.
84. See Chapter 1, and, for the parallel, Van Sickle 1984: 131. The end of Book 3 closely echoes *Il*. 7. 465: see Vian 1961, on 1407; Campbell 1983b: 155.
85. Or, better, the continuation of the first: one merges into the other.
86. See Knight 1995: 224–44; Clauss 1997 (among others).
87. See Knight 1995: 230.
88. The comparison is sketched by Fernández Contreras 2000: 19.
89. The time of the feat underscores its initiatory quality: see Hunter 1993: 17. On night-time hunting in coming-of-age rituals, see Vidal-Naquet 1986: 117–22.
90. The brisk dactylic rhythm of a line (2. 407) describing the dragon's watchfulness (οὐ κνέφας ἥδυμος ὕπνος ἀναιδέε δάμναται ὄσσε, 'sweet slumber does not conquer its shameless eyes in the darkness') conveys the failure of sleep to arrest it.
91. See Livrea 1973, on 4. 146.
92. See Chapter 1.
93. The dragon is deathless, whereas in other traditions it dies. Fantuzzi (2008b: 295–6) observes that by replacing the dragon's death with sleep, Apollonius structures the plot so that all the steps leading to the capture of the fleece are under the sign of Medea's magic.
94. The hypnotic force of Medea's voice is already felt in her promise to the Argonauts that she will 'give them the golden fleece, having put [the serpent] to sleep' (4. 87), a heavily spondaic line (δώσω δὲ χρύσειον ἐγὼ δέρος, εὐνήσασα).

95. Bacchyl. 19. 23 and Aesch. *PV* 575, respectively.
96. Fantuzzi (1988: 150) sees in the temporal periphrasis at 4. 109–13 a foreshadowing of the double dimension that characterizes Medea and Jason, both hunters and prey. See also Livrea 1973, on 4. 109.
97. See Knight 1995: 216–9.
98. See Knight 1995: 159; Clare 2002: 139–43.
99. Contrast 4. 352–4, where Medea takes Jason 'apart from his comrades' and supplicates him.
100. See Beye 1982: 155. Alcinous' instant and carefree slumber has suggested a comparison with Theocritus' Amphitryon (*Id.* 24. 35–41 and 63): see Hunter 1993: 161.
101. The reference is noticed by Hunter (1993: 71) and Knight (1995: 251).
102. See Knight 1995: 251.
103. So do Zeus, Hermes and Agamemnon in the *Iliad* and Telemachus in *Odyssey* 1. In *Odyssey* 20 Odysseus also tries to deliberate, but Athena cuts him short (see Chapter 2).
104. The exception is Cyzicus and Cleite, but they are newlyweds who die on their 'honeymoon'.
105. See Hunter 1993: 71.
106. See Fantuzzi 1988: 146.

Chapter 5 The Novel

1. Ap. Rhod. 1. 774; *Callirhoe* 1. 1. 5, with Bowie 2000. Of course, the novelists' failure to cite Apollonius' epic is no definitive proof that they did not use it.
2. Xenophon probably alludes to the *Odyssey* at the beginning and end of his novel (1. 9. 3, 5. 15. 2); Achilles Tatius plays with the episode of the Cyclops (2. 22. 3); Heliodorus fills his novel with allusions to Homer and imitates the *Odyssey*'s narrative patterns. The bibliography on the novels' exploitation of Homer is vast and ever growing: see, e.g., Biraud 1985; Fusillo 1990; Robiano 2000; Hirschberger 2001; Létoublon 2008; Whitmarsh 2011, especially 112–5, 65, 233 (on the *Odyssey*) and, most recently, De Temmerman 2014 (see the entry 'Homer' in his Index).
3. See also Hdt. 2. 141; Xen. *An.* 3. 1. 3; 4. 3. 8.
4. See below.
5. We can assume that this book of Chariton's novel, like several books in Homer, ends with night because it is late when Theron brings Callirhoe to Leonas' hut (1. 14. 5) and because at the beginning of Book 2 the latter leaves 'when it was still night'. Hägg (1971: 29) puts a question mark.
6. See also *Od.* 5. 472. Chariton again uses ὕπνος ἐπῆλθε in another context that introduces a Homeric citation (2. 9. 6). ἐπελθεῖν is predicated of sleep by other authors only scantily: Hdt. 1. 141;

[Arist.] *Pr.* 957a23; Hippoc. *De flatibus* 14. 9 (and nowhere else in the corpus). Neither Plato nor Xenophon uses the verb for sleep.

7. The superfluous αὕτη is deleted by Cobet, followed by Goold 1995 and Reardon 2004. The parallel with 2. 9. 6 (ταῦτα λογιζομένῃ. . .ὕπνος ἐπῆλθε, 'while she was considering these things [. . .] sleep came upon her') strongly supports the deletion.
8. See Cobet 1859: 265–6.
9. Compare τόσσα μιν ὁρμαίνουσαν ἐπήλυθε νήδυμος ὕπνος and τοιαῦτα ὀδυρομένῃ μόλις ὕπνος ἐπῆλθεν.
10. On Plangon's manipulation of Callirhoe, see Egger 1990: 104–8 and De Temmerman 2014: 66–70. Egger, though, goes too far in undermining Callirhoe's agency, considering her entirely a puppet in the hands of the scheming slave. For Daude (2006: 203), Callirhoe's decision is 'perfectly autonomous'. Her actions, however, like those of all the characters in Chariton's novel, must align with the scheme of Fortune in order to succeed (until Book 8, where Aphrodite takes over): see Montiglio 2010.
11. Whitmarsh (2009) discusses features of the book divisions in *Callirhoe*, but not sleep and wakefulness.
12. See Auger 1983: 41–6.
13. See Auger 1983: 43.
14. For further discussion, see Chapter 2.
15. This is illustrated by Hägg's chart (1971: 28–30), which provides the number of lines for individual segments of narrative, measured in days and nights. Days and nights are filled with narrative after Theron has his dream (Hägg's sections 12 to 14) and the greatest number of lines per day/night sequence in the part of the novel Hägg analyses are in the account of Dionysius' two meetings with Callirhoe (sections 19 and 20).
16. *AP* 5. 152. 3–4. See Fernández Contreras 2000: 28.
17. A noticeable exception is the Latin novel *The Story of Apollonius King of Tyre* (17–8), where Apollonius' future bride is in love with him while he is not, and accordingly he sleeps soundly while she remains awake. Comprehensive studies of the motif of love-induced insomnia in Greek literature surprisingly neglect the novels (so Fernández Contreras 2000, Strobl 2002), and sleeplessness does not appear as one of the symptoms of love shared by novels and epigrams in Maehler 1990.
18. Chariton is citing Menander's *Misoumenos*.
19. See also Achilles Tatius, *Leucippe and Clitophon* 1. 6, below; Heliodorus 1. 8. 1.
20. For further discussion, see Chapter 4. The stereotype of the wakeful leader appears also in Plutarch (*Caes.* 69. 8; *Brut.* 36; *Alex.* 32) and in Roman sources, on which see Woodman 1983: 198–9 (on 2. 79. 1); Dowden 2003: 153–4.

21. See, e.g., schol. Aesch. *Sept.* 3b.
22. Hermogenes 4. 4 and 4. 32, quoted by Leeman 1985: 225; Dowden 2003: 142; Scaffai 2004: 55. Scaffai also gives Latin evidence for the popularity of the dictum. See also Eust. *Il.* 1. 227. 7–8; 1. 250. 31; 1. 252. 4; 1. 258. 29–33; 1. 259. 17–20; 2. 129. 7; 3. 2. 4.
23. The belief is already in Phocylides: 'Deliberate at night; at night a man's mind is sharper' (8. 1–2 Diehl 1949).
24. Eust. *Il.* 1. 259. 5; *Od.* 1. 117. 46. Modern scholars prefer a euphemistic explanation ('good minded'): see LSJ, *ad loc.*; Ramnoux 1959: 14; M. West 1982a, on 224.
25. See Sanz Morales and Laguna Mariscal 2003.
26. The Homeric citation also gives Artaxerxes prominence, raising him to the same level of importance as Chaereas and Dionysius: see Fusillo 1990: 37.
27. Hdt. 9. 209. 4, with Harris 2009: 50; Dodds 1963: 109; Auger 1983: 40.
28. See below.
29. Chaereas can fully marry only after proving his manliness (ἀνδρεία) in war: see Lalanne 2006: 90–3.
30. See Chapter 2.
31. Penelope has slept deeply not long before she dozes off again.
32. See below.
33. Egger's contention (1990: 186) that Chaereas' aretalogy 'comes to an end the very minute that he finds his wife again' needs qualification.
34. See Schmeling 1980: 91–3; Ruiz-Montero 1988: 154.
35. With the majority of scholars, I believe that the novel is not an epitome.
36. This highlights Habrocomes' passivity (on which see Lalanne 2006: 159–61; Montiglio 2013: 61–2). Even sexually, the girl is more enterprising!
37. The protagonists' erotic eagerness is implied after their first dispute (1. 3. 7) and explained as the reason for Callirhoe's pregnancy (2. 8. 4). But in the only account of them satisfying their passion, on the night of the reunion, lovemaking is stifled by the Homeric citation.
38. Fusillo (1989: 36) speaks of a '*topos rovesciato*' because the deaths of novelistic heroines always turn out to be false.
39. See 1. 12. 4; 2. 8. 2; 5. 8. 5.
40. See Oikonomou 2010: 67–8.
41. This combination could be added to the index of Xenophon's formulaic expressions compiled by O' Sullivan 1995: 179–87.
42. The *Odyssey* scene is behind the novelistic one according to Capra 2009: 41–2.
43. Though Clitophon's story is reported in turn. The complex narrative stance of this novel impinges on issues of reliability (is

the report accurate? Is Clitophon telling the truth about himself?) and voice (who is speaking?), on which I can only touch briefly here. Interested readers will find an in-depth and updated discussion in De Temmerman 2014, Chapter 3, especially 152–61.

44. See especially Morales 2004: 96–151.
45. See also Pl. *Ti.* 52b–c, discussed below.
46. For the second phrase, see also Pl. *Phd.* 64c6; 64c7; 65c7; 65d1; 67a1; 67c7; 67d1; 79d4.
47. *AP* 5. 237; 9. 286; *Anacreontea* 9, with Fernández Contreras 2000: 30.
48. On Clitophon's care to look good in generic terms, see Brethes 2007: 109–12; Morgan 2007: 107.
49. De Temmerman (2014: 161–76) discusses Clitophon's keenness on non-committal sex, though not the dream.
50. See Repath 2005.
51. See also Xenophon 1. 13. 4; Heliodorus 4. 17. 3; 9. 11. 2 (attacks and flights helped by natural sleep).
52. Natural sleep removes an obstacle at 2. 35. 1: Leucippe is dozing in a corner of the ship while the men engage in a *jeu d'amour*.
53. Often noted: see Lalanne 2006: 168–72; Brethes 2007: 202–12. On another occasion Clitophon escapes while everyone is sleeping naturally (3. 16. 2), but his goal is to kill himself.
54. See De Temmerman 2014: 173–4.
55. Thompson 1955, D 1965 and D 1965. 1.
56. P. Oxy. 413.
57. On these sources, see Questa 1979: 67; Fusillo 1989: 34. The motif is also in Apul. *Met.* 7. 12 and 8. 11, the latter a reenactment (admittedly tragic) of the Cyclops' blinding.
58. The phrase appears in an almost identical form among the *Sententiae* attributed to Menander (783).
59. Hippoc. *Morb.* 2. 22, with Jouanna 1981: 54–5.
60. Or 'these feverish words', depending on whether we adopt Lobeck's emendation ὀνειροπολουμένη or the manuscript reading πυρπολουμένην.
61. See McNally 1985; Hazzikostas 1990.
62. See *Imag.* 1. 15. 3 (below); *AP* 16. 210, 211, 212; 9. 826, 827.
63. See Hunter 1983: 56–7; Morgan 2004, on 1. 25; Repath 2010: 107–8.
64. Longus alludes to Plato by choosing κατανυστάξασα to describe Chloe dozing off. See *Phdr.* 259e3 (νυστάζοντας).
65. See Repath 2010.
66. Though, as Repath (2010: 108) points out, the flocks in Longus do not necessarily sleep.
67. See Montiglio 2012.
68. On the 'first-time' motif in Longos, see De Temmerman 2014: 219, with further references.
69. Morales 2004: 35.

70. Chloe also 'looked at (ἑώρα) Daphnis' (1. 13. 4), but the verb is not βλέπειν.
71. *AP 5. 275,* 1–9. Paton's translation in the Loeb edition.
72. See Morgan 2004, on 1. 25.
73. See Sorabella 2010.
74. In antiquity the swallow and the cicada were considered the prototypical predator and prey: see Morgan 2004, on 1. 26.
75. See Borgeaud 1988: 111; Caillois 1991, Chapter 4. Noon is also the general hour of epiphanies in Longus. The Nymphs like noon, and Eros appears at noon to Philetas. But, as I hope to show, internal and external evidence invites us to read Pan's presence into the nap scene. On Pan's noontime epiphanies, see also Morgan 2004: 154, and Epstein 2002: 32–3. This scholar points out that Lamon's discovery of Daphnis at noon (1. 2. 2) offers a suggestion of a special affinity between the child suckled by a goat and the goat-footed god.
76. *Id.* 1. 15–8. Translation Verity 2002, slightly modified.
77. See already 1. 23. 3, with Morgan 2004.
78. The sources are in Borgeaud 1988: 111.
79. See Borgeaud 1988: 83.
80. On Pan as Daphnis' educator, see Epstein 2002; Lalanne 2006: 191–2.
81. Merkelbach (1962: 209) is mistaken to think that the Methymnian dreams at midnight.
82. For the novelistic victims of *Scheintod* the alternative would have been a real death. Furthermore, in the case of Anthia, deathlike slumber simply substitutes one obstacle (unwanted marriage) with another (capture by tomb robbers).
83. The nymphs, though, initiate this dream, as they do the first one in the novel. They are the main plot writers: see Liviabella Furiani 1999.
84. See also 3. 27, where the nymphs appear to the helpless Daphnis in his sleep and answer his prayer.
85. Love's symptoms appear also in medical literature (for sources, see Hunter 1999: 224) but retain a fictional quality. This is suggested by Plutarch's story of Antiochus, who grew sick from loving his stepmother. When the doctor summoned to diagnose the disease reveals that it is love, he appeals to Sappho, the symptoms' 'inventor', as his source, not to medical knowledge (*Dem.* 38. 2–4).
86. Longus plays a similar game around the symbolic meaning of throwing apples: while the protagonists innocently pelt each other with them, the reader knows that this game has erotic overtones in bucolic poetry: see Goldhill 1995: 5.
87. Philetas' name conjures up the elegiac poet Philitas of Cos.
88. De Temmerman (2014: 214–5) thinks that the emotion 'is not made explicit [...] because the protagonists themselves have not

experience of [it] and so cannot give it a name'. Their desire to see each other, however, is made explicit, even though they might not know that it is called longing ('They prayed and looked for a way to see each other'.)

89. See Torgovnick 1981: 11, referencing the Russian Formalist Boris Eikhenbaum. See also Fusillo 1997: 218–9.
90. On the winter night in Chloe's house they are in separate rooms.
91. 2. 15. 2 (κῶμα).
92. See 5. 34. 1; 6. 9. 1.
93. For further discussion, see Chapter 2.
94. Compare μνωομένω, 'as we remember', at *Od.* 15. 400. Heliodorus' explicit reference, though, is to the women mourning Patroclus overtly, but in fact weeping for themselves.
95. The author comes out in the next sentence: 'And if the story told is that of Chariclea and Theagenes, who would be so insensitive as [...] not to be spellbound'? My reading of Cnemon's behaviour as an audience supports Morgan's positive characterization of him in this role (1989a: 106) rather than Winkler's more negative one (1982: 138–44). The recurrent mentions of sleep as a competitor that loses to storytelling suggest that Heliodorus expects his readers to be as willing to forsake sleep as Cnemon (or Theagenes and Chariclea) and to read the novel on and on. See also below.
96. See, e.g., 5. 1. 1; 5. 18. 1; 5. 23. 2 (with a Homeric allusion); 5. 27. 1. A clever, if frigid, use of a Homeric formula describing the time of day is at 3. 4. 1: Chariclea, appearing from the temple, is like rosy-fingered dawn.
97. There was an asp called *thermouthis*, whose bite was supposed to be fatal only to evil people: see Morgan in Reardon 2008: 392. Perhaps Heliodorus knew a poem by Statyllius Flaccus (first century BC) in which an exhausted traveller cast ashore by a storm plunges into his 'last sleep', bitten by a viper (*AP* 7. 290).
98. See Morgan in Reardon 2008: 393.
99. See Brethes 2007: 185.
100. Hes. fr. 278 Merkelbach-West 1967.
101. Ap. Rhod. 2. 856: Verg. *Aen.* 5. 854–6.
102. *Il.* 16. 454–5, 672–3, with Vermeule 1979: 145. Sarpedon's post-mortem conveyance is, however, exceptional and 'marks the hero's fate as a kindly one' (M. West 1982b, on 116).
103. Plat. *Ap.* 41 (see Chapter 2). I cannot agree with McAlpine (1987: 141) that Socrates rejects this suggestion. He does not pronounce on the nature of death, leaving the options open.
104. *Mor.* 107 D–E (Babbitt's translation in the Loeb edition, slightly modified).
105. See Van der Eijk 2003.

106. *Orph.* 85. 7–8. The same idea appears in a *Sententia* attributed to Menander (782). Sleep is a teacher of death also for Anaxagoras (DK A 34).
107. On the *Orphic Hymn* and the passage from Plutarch, see Boyancé 1928: 98–101. I agree with him that the god *psychopompos* at *Mor.* 758B is not Hermes but Hypnos, 'the offspring of Night'. In statues Hypnos carries the caduceus: see Stafford 2003: 115.
108. See also Plut. *Mor.* 764E-F.
109. For Plotinus, the soul is truly awake only in the other world: see *Enn.* 1. 8. 13, with Dowden 1998: 18.
110. The last epitaph is in Lattimore 1962: 164 (his translation, modified). See also *AP* 7. 451 ('Here Saon, son of Dicon of Acanthos, sleeps a holy slumber. Do not say that good people die'), with Cerutti 1986: 138. In a particularly felicitous epigram playing with the commonplace (*AP* 7. 260), the dead man contentedly looks back at his long life, during which he had the good fortune of lulling many grandchildren to sleep in his arms, until he himself went to 'sleep a sweet slumber'. More such epigrams are in Stafford 2003: 73, n. 7. See also Ogle 1933.
111. According to Valerius Maximus (9. 12. 7), Pindar likewise died while resting on his lover's lap.
112. Plut. *Mor.* 107E–F. Similar words are attributed to Gorgias (DK A 15).
113. Another parallel is the death of Trophonius and Agamedes as reported by Cicero (*Tusc.*1. 114) and Plutarch (*Mor.* 109A).
114. For discussion, see especially Dowden 1996.
115. Calasiris and Chariclea are both also wakeful on the previous night (3. 11. 4; 3. 18. 2).
116. In Euripides, though, sleeplessness is not a symptom of Phaedra's passion, as it is in Seneca (*Phaedra* 368–9). Fantham (1975) thinks that the Roman author borrowed the symptom from Virgil's Dido.
117. Paraphrasing Homer is Heliodorus' practice: see Fusillo 1990.
118. See 7. 6. 1; 7. 8. 6; 7. 9. 2.
119. Longus, who ends his novel with a wakeful night, inserts a strongly closural tag line ('Daphnis did to Chloe...').
120. Bowie (1998: 5, n. 285) argues that Heliodorus' frequent intertextualities with Homer 'persistently invite us to question how like and how unlike the *Odyssey* this story is going to be'. The transition-in-sleeplessness from Book 5 to Book 6 is both like and unlike the corresponding transition-in-sleep in Homer.
121. See 2. 35. 5; 5. 22. 3.
122. The intimations of the future that the protagonists receive two books later (8. 11. 3–5) are not as transparent.
123. See Chapters 2 and 4.
124. Achilles Tatius does exploit sleep as blank space (see above), but in a context, the lovers' reunion, that keeps the readers from dozing off.

125. The nocturnal ending of Book 6, with the death of the Egyptian sorceress, is more closural.
126. These book endings have an 'anticipatory cadence' (Stevick 1970: 44), though the narrator does not explicitly say, 'you will find this out in the next chapter'. A closural ending is that of Book 9, with the conclusion of the war.
127. This is clearly the case in the *Odyssey*. On the *Iliad*, see Chapter 1.
128. Fusillo (1997: 221) thinks that Heliodorus' closural strategy 'perhaps [is] the strongest in ancient literature'. See also Morgan 1989b: 318: 'A classic closed ending; no questions are left to be asked, the text closes because there is nothing more that could be told'.

Conclusions

1. A. Chekhov, *Stories*. Translated by R. Pevear and L. Volokhnosky. New York, Bantam Books 2000: 330.
2. On the insomnia motif in Statius' poem see, e.g., Pomeroy 1986; Gibson 1996.
3. From *Sleeping and Waking* (in *The Crack-Up* [1945]).
4. See Summers-Bremmer 2008: 15; Byl 1998.
5. Calasiris (in Heliodorus) also tries to make decisions during sleepless nights but, as we saw, he seeks to understand and follow the roads of destiny, not to invent a plot.
6. For instance, Quintus begins a great number of books at dawn (2, 3, 6, 7, 8, 9, 14) and ends several at night (1, 5, 6, 7, 8), outdoing even Homer, but he also exploits sleep to prepare for climatic events (Penthesilea's fighting in Book 1, Memnon's in Book 2) by putting an end to the preliminaries, in a manner close to Apollonius'. Also reminiscent of Apollonius are the leisurely descriptions of nightfall that frame several lonely vigils (3. 656–8; 5. 346–50; 10. 256–8; 10. 436–9).
7. On Xenophon, see Chapter 5.

BIBLIOGRAPHY

Ambühl, Annemarie, 'Sleepless Orpheus: Insomnia, Love, Death and Poetry from Antiquity to Contemporary Fiction', in E. Scioli and C. Walde (eds), *Sub imagine somni: Nighttime Phenomena in Greco-Roman Culture* (Pisa, Edizioni ETS, 2010), pp. 259–84.

Amory, Anne, 'The Reunion of Odysseus and Penelope', in C.H. Taylor, Jr. (ed.), *Essays on the Odyssey* (Bloomington, Indiana University Press, 1963), pp. 100–21.

———, 'The Gates of Horn and Ivory', *Yale Classical Studies* 20 (1966), pp. 1–57.

Arend, Walter, *Die typischen Szenen bei Homer* (Berlin, Weidmann, 1933).

Arnott, Peter D., 'The Overworked Playwright: A Study in Euripides' Cyclops', *Greece & Rome* 8 (1961), pp. 164–9.

Arnott, W.G. (ed. and translator), *Menander* (Cambridge, MA, Harvard University Press, 3 vols; vol 1: 1979, vol. 2: 1996, vol. 3: 2000).

Auger, Danielle, 'Rêve, image et récit dans le roman de Chariton', *Ktema* 8 (1983), pp. 39–52.

Austin, Norman, *Archery at the Dark of the Moon: Poetic Problems in Homer's Odyssey* (Berkeley, The University of California Press, 1975).

———, *Sophocles' Philoctetes and the Great Soul Robbery* (Madison, The University of Wisconsin Press, 2011).

Barbieri, Andrea, *Ricerche sul* Phasma *di Menandro* (Bologna, Pàtron editore, 2001).

Barker, Andrew, 'Lullaby for an Eagle (Pindar *Pythian* 1)', in K. Dowden and T. Wiedemann (eds), *Sleep* (Bari, Levante, 2003), pp. 107–24.

Beazley, John D., *Attic Red-Figure Vase-Painters* (Oxford, Oxford University Press, 3 vols, 2003).

Beta, Simone, 'Madness on the Comic Stage: Aristophanes' *Wasps* and Euripides' *Heracles*', *Greek, Roman, and Byzantine Studies* 40 (1999), pp. 135–57.

Beye, Charles, *Epic and Romance in the* Argonautica *of Apollonius*, (Carbondale, Southern Illinois University Press, 1982).

Biggs, Penelope, 'The Disease Theme in Sophocles' *Ajax, Philoctetes, and Trachiniae*', *Classical Philology* 61 (1966), pp. 223–35.
Biraud, Michèle, 'L'hypotexte homérique et les rôles amoureux de Callirhoé dans le roman de Chariton', *Publications de la Faculté de Lettres et Sciences Humaines de Nice* 29 (1985), pp. 21–7.
Bond, G.W., ed., *Euripides: Heracles*, with introduction and commentary (Oxford, Oxford University Press, 1981).
Borgeaud, Philippe, *The Cult of Pan in Ancient Greece*, translated by K. Atlass and J. Redfield (Chicago, The University of Chicago Press, 1988).
Borgogno, Alberto, 'Menandro in Caritone', *Rivista Italiana di Filologia Classica* 99 (1971), pp. 257–63.
Bornmann, F., 'Il prologo del *Misoumenos* di Menandro', *Atene e Roma* 25 (1980), pp. 149–62.
———, 'La Medea di Apollonio Rodio: interpretazione psicologica e interpretazione testuale', in R. Uglione (ed.), *Atti delle giornate di studio su Medea* (Turin 23–24 October 1995), (Turin, Celid, 1997), pp. 47–68.
Borthwick, Kerr E., 'Observations on the Opening Scene of Aristophanes' *Wasps*', *The Classical Quarterly* 42 (1992), pp. 274–8.
Bowie, Ewen, 'Phoenician games in Heliodorus' *Aithiopika*', in R. Hunter (ed.), *Studies in Heliodorus* (Cambridge, Cambridge University Press, 1998), pp. 1–18.
———, 'The Reception of Apollonius in Imperial Greek Literature', in Harder *et al.* (eds), *Apollonius Rhodius* (Leuven, Peeters, 2000), pp. 1–10.
Boyancé, Pierre, 'Le sommeil et l'immortalité', *Mélanges d'archéologie et d'histoire* 45 (1928), pp. 97–105.
Brethes, Romain, *De l'idéalisme au réalisme. Une étude du comique dans le roman grec* (Salerno, helios editrice, 2007).
Brillante, Carlo, 'Scene oniriche nei poemi omerici', *Materiali e discussioni per l'analisi dei testi classici* 29 (1990), pp. 31–45.
Brown, Christopher, 'Heraclitus fr. 49 Marcovich (DK 22 B 21)', *The American Journal of Philology* 107 (1986), pp. 243–5.
———, 'The Big Sleep: Herodas 8. 5', *Zeitschrift für Papyrologie und Epigraphik* 102 (1994), pp. 95–9.
Burgess, Jonathan S., 'Neoanalysis, Orality, and Intertextuality: An Examination of Homeric Motif Transference', *Oral Tradition* 21 (2006), pp. 148–89.
Burkert, Walter, *Zum altgriechischen Mitleidsbegriff* (Inaugural Dissertation, Munich, Mikrokopie, 1955).
Burnett, Anne P., *Catastrophe Survived: Euripides' Plays of Mixed Reversal* (Oxford, Oxford University Press, 1971).
Buxton, R.G.A., *Persuasion in Greek Tragedy: A Study of Peitho* (Cambridge, Cambridge University Press, 1982).
Byl, Simon, 'Sommeil et insomnie dans le Corpus Hippocraticum', *Revue belge de philologie et d'histoire* 76 (1998), pp. 31–6.
Byre, Calvin S., *A Reading of Apollonius Rhodius' Argonautica: The Poetics of Uncertainty* (Lewiston, The Edwin Mellen Press, 2002).
Caillois, Roger, *Les démons de midi* (Paris, Fata morgana, 1991).
Cairns, Francis, 'Orality, Writing and Reoralisation: Some Departures and Arrivals in Homer and Apollonius Rhodius', in H.L.C. Tristram (ed.),

New Methods in the Research of Epic–Neue Methoden der Epenforschung (Tübingen, Gunter Narr, 1998), pp. 63–84.

Calabi, Francesca, 'Gli occhi del sonno', *Materiali e discussioni per l'analisi dei testi classici* 13 (1984), pp. 23–43.

Campbell, Malcolm, *Studies in the Third Book of Apollonius Rhodius' Argonautica* (Hildesheim, Georg Olms Verlag, 1983a).

———, 'Apollonian and Homeric Book Division', *Mnemosyne* 36 (1983b), pp. 154–6.

Capra, Andrea, '"The (Un)happy Romance of Curleo and Liliet". Xenophon of Ephesus, the Cyropaedia and the birth of the "anti-tragic" novel', *Ancient Narrative* 7 (2009), pp. 29–50.

Cariou, Morgane, 'Αὐτὰρ Ἰήσων μνήσατο Μηδείης πολυκερδέος ἐννεσιάων: statut et enjeux des instructions de Médée', *Gaia* 15 (2012), pp. 143–62.

Carrière, Jean, 'En relisant la chant III des *Argonautiques*', *Euphrosyne* 2 (1959), pp. 41–63.

Carspecken, J.F., 'Apollonius and Homer', *Yale Classical Studies* 13 (1952), pp. 133–43.

Cerutti, Maria Vittoria, 'Sonno e passaggio', in U. Bianchi (ed.), *Transition Rites. Cosmic, Social and Individual Order* (Rome, L'Erma di Bretschneider, 1986), pp. 131–41.

Chandler, Simon B., 'Shakespeare and Sleep', *Bulletin of the History of Medicine* 29 (1955), pp. 255–60.

Clare, R.J., *The Path of the Argo: Language, Imagery and Narrative in the* Argonautica *of Apollonius Rhodius* (Cambridge, Cambridge University Press, 2002).

Clauss, James J., 'Conquest of the Mephistophelian Nausicaa: Medea's Role in Apollonius' Redefinition of the Epic Hero', in J.J. Clauss and S.I. Johnston (eds), *Medea: Essays on Medea in Myth, Literature, Philosophy, and Art* (Princeton, Princeton University Press, 1997), pp. 149–77.

Clay, Jenny S., *The Politics of Olympus* (Princeton, Princeton University Press, 1989).

Cobet, C.G., 'Annotationes criticae in Charitonem', *Mnemosyne* 8 (1859), pp. 229–303.

Constantinidou, Soteroula, 'The Light Imagery of Divine Manifestation in Homer', in M. Christopoulos *et al.* (eds), *Light and Darkness in Ancient Greek Myth and Religion* (Lanham, Lexington Books, 2010), pp. 91–109.

Corbato, C., 'Da Menandro a Caritone: Studi sulla genesi del romanzo greco e i suoi rapporti con la commedia nuova', *Quaderni Triestini sul teatro antico* 1 (1968), pp. 4–16.

Crismani, Daria, *Il teatro nel romanzo ellenistico d'amore e di avventure* (Alessandria, Edizioni dell'Orso, 1997).

———, 'La donna velata e altri ricordi di scena tra le pagine del romanzo greco', in M. Guglielmo and E. Bona (eds), *Forme di comunicazione nel mondo antico e metamorfosi del mito: dal teatro al romanzo* (Alessandria, Edizioni dell'Orso, 2003), pp. 235–41.

Danek, Georg, 'Traditional Referentiality and Homeric Intertextuality', in F. Montanari (ed.), *Omero tremila anni dopo* (Rome, Edizioni di storia e letteratura, 2002), pp. 3–19.

Daniel-Müller, Bénédicte, 'Une épopée au féminin? La question des genres dans le livre III des *Argonautiques* d'Apollonios de Rhodes', *Gaia* 15 (2012), pp. 97–120.

Daude, Cécile, 'La rhétorique de Callirhoé', in B. Pouderon and J. Peigney (eds), *Discours et débats dans l'ancien roman* (Lyon, Maison de l'Orient et de la Méditerranée, 2006), pp. 191–216.

Davidson, John, 'Sophocles' *Trachiniae* and the *Odyssey*', *Athenaeum* 91 (2003), pp. 518–23.

Davies, Malcolm (ed.), *Poetarum Melicorum Graecorum Fragmenta: Volume I: Alcman, Stesichorus, Ibycus* (Oxford, Oxford University Press, 1991).

Delebecque, Édouard, *Construction de l'Odyssée* (Paris, Les Belles Lettres, 1980a).

——— 'Les nuits de l'*Odyssée*', *Actes du Xe Congrès* (Toulouse 8–12 avril 1978) (Paris, Les Belles Lettres, 1980b), pp. 113–5.

Denniston, J.D. and Denys Page (eds), *Aeschylus: Agamemnon* (Oxford, Oxford University Press, 1957).

De Jong, Irene J.F., 'Sunsets and Sunrises in Homer and Apollonius of Rhodes: Book-Divisions and Beyond', *Dialogos: Hellenic Studies Review* 3 (1990), pp. 20–35.

———, *A Narratological Commentary on the Odyssey* (Cambridge, Cambridge University Press, 2001).

De Romilly, Jacqueline, *La crainte et l'angoisse dans le théâtre d'Eschyle* (Paris, Les Belles Lettres, 1958).

De Temmerman, Koen, *Crafting Characters: Heroes and Heroines in the Ancient Greek Novel* (Oxford, Oxford University Press, 2014).

Detienne, Marcel and Jean-Pierre Vernant, *Cunning Intelligence in Greek Culture and Society*, translated by J. Lloyd (Sussex, The Harvester Press, 1978).

Diehl, E. (ed.), *Anthologia Lyrica Graeca* (Lipsia, Teubner, 1949).

Dieterich, Albert, 'Schlafscenen auf der Attischen Bühne', *Rheinisches Museum* 46 (1891), pp. 25–46.

Dodds, E.R. (ed.), *Euripides: Bacchae*, with introduction and commentary (Oxford, Oxford University Press, 1944).

———, *The Greeks and the Irrational* (Berkeley, The University of California Press, 1963).

Donelan, Jasper F., 'Some Remarks Concerning Night Scenes on the Classical Greek Stage', *Mnemosyne* 67 (2014), pp. 535–53.

Dowden, Ken, 'Heliodoros: Serious Intentions', *The Classical Quarterly* 46 (1996), pp. 267–85.

———, 'Cupid and Psyche: A Question of the Vision of Apuleius', in M. Zimmerman *et al.* (eds), *Aspects of Apuleius' Golden Ass*, vol. II (Groningen, Egbert Forsten, 1998), pp. 1–22.

———, 'The Value of Sleep: Homer, Plinies, Posidonius & Proclus', in K. Dowden and T. Wiedemann (eds), *Sleep* (Bari, Levante, 2003), pp. 141–63.

———, 'Trojan Night', in M. Christopoulos *et al.* (eds), *Light and Darkness in Ancient Greek Myth and Religion* (Lanham, Lexington Books, 2010), pp. 110–20.

Dowden, Ken and Thomas Wiedemann (eds), *Sleep* (Bari, Levante Editori, 2003).

Dowdle, Elizabeth, 'Sleeping Child with Dog and Grapes', in H. Valladares (ed.), *Archaeology of Daily Life* (Johns Hopkins Archaeological Museum Online, 2013). http://archaeologicalmuseum.jhu.edu/the-collection/object-stories/archaeology-of-daily-life/childhood/sleeping-child-with-dog-and-grapes.

Dué, Casey and Mary Ebbott, *Iliad 10 and the Poetics of Ambush: A Multitext Edition with Essays and Commentary* (Washington, Center for Hellenic Studies, 2010).

Dyer, Robert, 'The Coming of Night in Homer', *Glotta* 52 (1974), pp. 31–6.

Easterling, P.E. (ed.), *Sophocles: Trachiniae* (Cambridge, Cambridge University Press, 1982).

Edwards, Mark, 'Homer and the Oral Tradition: The Type-Scene', *Oral Tradition* 7 (1992), pp. 284–330.

Egger, Brigitte, *Women in the Greek Novel: Constructing the Feminine*, PhD Dissertation (University of California-Irvine, 1990).

Emlyn-Jones, Chris, 'The Reunion of Penelope and Odysseus', *Greece & Rome* 31 (1984), pp. 1–18.

Epstein, Stephen, 'The Education of Daphnis: Goats, Gods, the Birds and the Bees', *Phoenix* 56 (2002), pp. 25–39.

Fantham, Elaine, 'Virgil's Dido and Seneca's Tragic Heroines', *Greece & Rome* 22 (1975), pp. 1–10.

Fantuzzi, Marco, *Ricerche su Apollonio Rodio* (Rome, Edizioni dell'Ateneo, 1988).

———, 'Sulla scenografia dell'ora (e del luogo) nella tragedia greca', *Materiali e discussioni per l'analisi dei testi classici* 24 (1990), pp. 9–30.

———, 'The Myths of Dolon and Rhesus from Homer to the "Homeric/Cyclic" Tragedy *Rhesus*', in F. Montanari and A. Rengakos (eds), *La poésie épique grecque: métamorphoses d'un genre littéraire* (Geneva, Librairie Droz, 2006), pp. 135–82.

———, '"Homeric" Formularity in the *Argonautica* of Apollonius of Rhodes', in T. Papanghelis and A. Rengakos, *A Companion to Apollonius Rhodius* (Leiden, 2008a), pp. 221–42.

———, 'Which Magic? Which Eros? Apollonius' *Argonautica* and the Different Narrative Roles of Medea as a Sorceress in Love', in T. Papanghelis and A. Rengakos (eds), *A Companion to Apollonius Rhodius* (Leiden, 2008b), pp. 287–310.

———, *Achilles in Love: Intertextual Studies* (New York, Oxford University Press, 2012).

Fantuzzi, Marco and Richard Hunter, *Tradition and Innovation in Hellenistic Poetry* (Cambridge, Cambridge University Press, 2004).

Faraone, Christopher, *Ancient Greek Love Magic* (Cambridge, MA, Harvard University Press, 1999).

Felson, Nancy, *Regarding Penelope: From Character to Poetics in Homer's Odyssey* (Princeton, Princeton University Press, 1994).

Fenik, Bernard, *'Iliad X' and the 'Rhesus': The Myth* (Brussels, Collection Latomus LXXIII, 1964).

———, *Studies in the Odyssey* (Wiesbaden, Steiner Verlag, 1974).

Fernández Contreras, María Ángeles, 'El insomnio como motivo literario en la poesía griega y latina', *Habis* 31 (2000), pp. 9–35.

Ferrari, Franco, 'Il tempo del sonno', *Civiltà classica e cristiana* 4 (1983), pp. 329–32.

Ferrini, M.F., 'Espressioni del tempo nell'epica omerica e postomerica', *Giornale Italiano di Filologia* 16 (1985), pp. 15–52.

Foley, Helene, '"Reverse Similes" and Sex Roles in the *Odyssey*', *Arethusa* 11 (1978), pp. 7–25.

Fowler, Robert, 'Three Places of the *Trachiniae*', in J. Griffin (ed.), *Sophocles Revisited: Essays Presented to Sir Hugh Lloyd-Jones* (New York, Oxford University Press, 1999), pp. 161–76.

Fraenkel, Eduard (ed.), *Aeschylus: Agamemnon*, with a commentary (Oxford, Oxford University Press, 3 vols, 1950).

Fulkerson, Laurel, *No Regrets: Remorse in Classical Antiquity* (Oxford, Oxford University Press, 2013).

Fusillo, Massimo, *Il tempo delle Argonautiche: un'analisi del racconto in Apollonio Rodio* (Rome, Edizioni dell'Ateneo, 1985).

———, *Il romanzo greco: polifonia ed eros* (Venice: Marsilio, 1989).

———, 'Il testo nel testo: la citazione nel romanzo greco', *Materiali e discussioni per l'analisi dei testi classici* 25 (1990), pp. 27–48.

———, 'How Novels End: Some Patterns of Closure in Ancient Narrative', in D. Roberts *et al.* (eds), *Classical Closure: Reading the End in Greek and Latin Literature* (Princeton: University Press, 1997), pp. 209–27.

———, 'Apollonius Rhodius as 'Inventor' of the Interior Monologue', in T. Papanghelis and A. Rengakos (eds), *A Companion to Apollonius Rhodius* (Leiden, 2008), pp. 147–66.

Gantz, Timothy, *Early Greek Myth* (Baltimore, The Johns Hopkins University Press, 2 vols, 1993).

Garbutt, Kathleen, 'An Indo-European Night Raid?', *Journal of Indo-European Studies* 34 (2006), pp. 183–200.

Garner, Robert, *From Homer to Tragedy: The Art of Allusion in Greek Poetry* (London, Routledge, 1990).

Gibson, B.J., 'Statius and Insomnia: Allusion and Meaning in *Silvae* 5. 4', *The Classical Quarterly* 46 (1996), pp. 457–68.

Goldhill, Simon, *Language, Sexuality, Narrative: The Oresteia* (Cambridge, Cambridge University Press, 1984).

———, *Foucault's Virginity. Ancient Erotic Fiction and the History of Sexuality* (Cambridge, Cambridge University Press, 1995).

Goold G.P. (ed. and translator), *Chariton: Callirhoe* (Cambridge, MA, Harvard University Press, 1995).

Griffin, Jasper, *Homer on Life and Death* (Oxford, Oxford University Press, 1980).

Hägg, Tomas, *Narrative Techniques in Ancient Greek Romances: Studies of Chariton, Xenophon Ephesius, and Achilles Tatius* (Stockholm, Svenska institutet, 1971).

Harder, M.A., 'Travel Descriptions in the *Argonautica* of Apollonius Rhodius', in Z. von Martels (ed.), *Travel Fact and Travel Fiction* (Leiden, Brill, 1994).

Harris, W.V., *Dreams and Experience in Classical Antiquity* (Cambridge, MA, Harvard University Press, 2009).

Hartigan, Karelisa, 'Euripidean Madness: Heracles and Orestes', *Greece & Rome* 34 (1987), pp. 126–35.

Hartog, François, *Memories of Odysseus: Frontier Tales from Ancient Greece*, translated by J. Lloyd (Chicago, The University of Chicago Press, 2001).

Hazzikostas, Dimitri, *The Sleeping Figure in Greek Art*, PhD Dissertation (Columbia University, 1990).

Heiden, Bruce, *Homer's Cosmic Fabrication: Choice and Design in the Iliad* (New York, Oxford University Press, 2008).

Hirschberger, M., 'Epos und Tragödie in Charitons Kallirhoe: Ein Beitrag zur Intertextualität des Griechischen Romans', *Würzburger Jahrbücher für Altertumswissenschaft* 25 (2001), pp. 157–86.

Hölscher, Uvo, 'Die Erkennungszene im 23. Buch des *Odyssee*', in J. Latacz (ed.), *Homer. Die Dichtung und ihre Deutung* (Darmstadt, Wissenschaftliche Buchgesellschaft, 1991), pp. 388–405.

Hunter, Richard, *A Study of Daphnis and Chloe* (Cambridge, Cambridge University Press, 1983).

———, '"Short on Heroics": Jason in the *Argonautica*', *The Classical Quarterly* 38 (1988), pp. 436–53.

——— (ed.), *Apollonius of Rhodes: Argonautica III* (Cambridge, Cambridge University Press, 1989).

———, *The* Argonautica *of Apollonius: Literary Studies* (Cambridge, Cambridge University Press, 1993).

——— (ed.), *Theocritus: A Selection* (Cambridge, Cambridge University Press, 1999).

———, 'The Poetics of Narrative in the *Argonautica*', in T. Papanghelis and A. Rengakos (eds), *A Companion to Apollonius Rhodius* (Leiden, 2008), pp. 115–46.

Hurst, André, 'Préfigurations de Médée', *Gaia* 15 (2012), pp. 81–96.

Iranzo, Alex, Santamaria J., de Riquer M., 'Sleep and Sleep Disorders in Don Quixote', *Sleep Medicine* 5 (2004), pp. 97–100.

James, Alan, 'Night and Day in Epic Narrative', *Museum Philologum Londiniense* 3 (1978), pp. 153–83.

Jebb, Richard, *Sophocles: Plays. Philoctetes*, ed. P.E. Easterling, introduction by F. Budelmann (London, Bristol Classical Press, 2004).

Jones, D.M., 'The Sleep of Philoctetes', *Classical Review* 63 (1949), pp. 83–5.

Jouanna, Jacques, 'Le sommeil médecin (Sophocle, *Philoctète*, v. 859: ἀλεὴς ὕπνος)', in *Théâtre et spectacles dans l'antiquité* (Actes du Colloque de Strasbourg: Université des sciences humaines de Strasbourg, Leiden, Brill, 1981), pp. 49–62.

Karydas, Helen P., *Eurykleia and Her Successors: Female Figures of Authority in Greek Poetics* (Lanham, Rowman & Littlefield, 1998).

Katsouris, A., 'Euripides' *Cyclops* and Homer's *Odyssey*: An Interpretive Comparison', *Prometheus* 23 (1997), pp. 1–24.

Katz, Marilyn, *Penelope's Renown* (Princeton, Princeton University Press, 1991).

Kessels, A.H.M., *Studies on the Dream in Greek Literature* (Utrecht, HES Publishers, 1978).

Knight, Virginia, *The Renewal of Epic: Responses to Homer in the Argonautica of Apollonius* (Leiden, Brill, 1995).

Koch, Theodorus (ed.), *Comicorum Atticorum Fragmenta* III (Lipsia, Teubner, 1888).

Konstan, David, 'Introduction', in *Euripides: Cyclops*, translated by H. McHugh, with introduction and notes by David Konstan (New York, Oxford University Press, 2001), pp. 3–19.

Krentz, Peter, 'Deception in Archaic and Classical Warfare', in H. van Wees (ed.), *War and Violence in Ancient Greece* (London, Duckworth, 2000), pp. 167–200.

Lalanne, Sophie, *Une éducation grecque: rites de passage et construction des genres dans le roman grec ancien* (Paris, éditions la découverte, 2006).

Lanza, Diego, *Il tiranno e il suo pubblico* (Turin, Einaudi, 1977).

Latacz, Joachim, 'The Development of the Theme in the *Iliad*: The Plan of Action', in I.J.F. de Jong (ed.), *Homer. Critical Assessments* (London, Routledge, 1999), pp. 462–76.

Lattimore, Richard, *Themes in Greek and Latin Epitaphs* (Urbana, University of Illinois Press, 1962).

Leeman, Anton D., 'The Lonely Vigil', in *Form und Sinn: Studien zur römischen Literatur (1954–84)* (Frankfurt, Peter Lang, 1985), pp. 213–30.

Létoublon, Françoise, 'Λύντο γούνατα: d'Homère aux romans grecs', in D. Auger and J. Peigney (eds), *Phileuripidès: Mélanges offerts à François Jouan* (Nanterre, Presses Universitaires de Paris, 2008), pp. 711–24.

Lévy, Edmond, 'Le théâtre et le rêve: le rêve dans le théâtre d'Éschyle', in *Théâtre et spectacles dans l'antiquité* (Actes du Colloque de Strasbourg: Université des sciences humaines de Strasbourg, Leiden, Brill, 1981), pp. 141–68.

———, 'Le rêve homérique', *Ktema* 7 (1982), pp. 25–41.

Liapis, Vayos, *A Commentary on the* Rhesus *Attributed to Euripides* (New York, Oxford University Press, 2012).

Liviabella Furiani, Patrizia, 'La voce degli dei nelle *Pastorali* di Longo', in E. Mirri and F. Valori (eds), *La ricerca di Dio* (Naples, Edizioni Scientifiche Italiane, 1999), pp. 69–102.

Livrea, Enrico, *Apollonii Rhodii Argonauticon liber quartus*, introduzione, testo critico, traduzione e commento (Florence, La nuova Italia, 1973).

Lloyd-Jones, Hugh, *The Justice of Zeus* (Berkeley, The University of California Press, 1971).

Lombardi, Michela, 'La tradizione letteraria delle notazioni temporali nelle '*Egloghe*' di Virgilio', *Quaderni Urbinati di Cultura Classica* 21 (1985), pp. 71–88.

Louden, Bruce, *The* Iliad: *Structure, Myth, and Meaning* (Baltimore, The Johns Hopkins University Press, 2006).

Lowe, Nick, 'Tragic Space and Comic Timing in Menander's *Dyskolos*', *Bulletin of the Institute of Classical Studies* 34 (1987), pp. 126–38.

Lynn-George, Michael, Epos: *Word, Narrative and the* Iliad (Atlantic Highlands, Humanities Press International, 1988).

Mabin, Dominique, *Le sommeil de Marcel Proust* (Paris, Presses Universitaires de France, 1992).

Mace, Sarah, 'Why the *Oresteia*'s Sleeping Dead Won't Lie: Part I: *Agamemnon*', *The Classical Journal* 98 (2002), pp. 35–56.

———, 'Why the *Oresteia*'s Sleeping Dead Won't Lie: Part II: *Choephoroi* and *Eumenides*', *The Classical Journal* 100 (2004), pp. 39–60.

Macleod, C.W. (ed.), *Homer: Iliad Book XXIV* (Cambridge, Cambridge University Press, 1982a).

———, 'Politics and the *Oresteia*', *The Journal of Hellenic Studies* 102 (1982b), pp. 124–44.

———, 'Homer on Poetry and the Poetry of Homer', in Douglas Cairns (ed.), *Oxford Readings in Homer's Iliad* (Oxford, Oxford University Press, 2001), pp. 294–310.

Maehler, Herwig, 'Symptome der Liebe im Roman und in der griechischen Anthologie', *Groningen Colloquia on the Novel* 3 (1990), pp. 1–12.

Mainoldi, Carla, 'Sonno e morte in Grecia antica', in R. Raffaelli (ed.), *Rappresentazioni della morte* (Urbino, QuattroVenti, 1987).

Marks, Jim, *Zeus in the Odyssey* (Washington, Center for Hellenic Studies, 2008).

Maronitis, D.N., *Homeric Megathemes*, translated by D. Connolly (Lanham, Rowman & Littlefield, 2004).

Maronitis, D.N. and L. Polkas, ΑΡΧΑΙΚΗ ΕΠΙΚΗ ΠΟΙΗΣΗ: ΑΠΟ ΤΗΝ *ΙΛΙΑΔΑ* ΣΤΗΝ *ΟΔΥΣΣΕΙΑ* (Thessaloniki, Ινστιτούτο Νεοελληνικών Σπουδών, 2007).

Mazon, Paul (ed. and translator), *Éschyle: Agamemnon. Les Choéphores. Les Euménides* (Paris, Les Belles Lettres, 1983).

Meier-Brügger, Michael, 'Wie ist κῶμα gebildet?', *Museum Helveticum* 50 (1993), p. 126.

Meineke, August (ed.), *Fragmenta Comicorum Graecorum* (Berlin, Reimer, 5 vols, 1839–57.

Merkelbach, Reinhold, *Roman und Mysterium* (Munich, Beck, 1962).

Merkelbach, Reinhold and Martin L. West (eds), *Fragmenta Hesiodea* (Oxford, Oxford University Press, 1967).

Minchin, Elizabeth, 'The Sleeplessness Theme at *Iliad* 24, 1–18', *La Parola del Passato* 40 (1985), pp. 269–75.

McAlpine, Thomas, *Sleep, Divine and Human, in the Old Testament* (Sheffield, Sheffield Academic Press, 1987).

McCartney, Eugene S., 'Undoing by Night Work Done by Day: A Folklore Motif', in G.E. Mylonas and D. Raymond (eds), *Studies Presented to David Moore Robinson on His Seventieth Birthday*, vol. II (Saint Louis, Washington University Press, 1953).

McClure, Laura K., 'Clytemnestra's Binding Spell (*Ag.* 958–74)', *The Classical Journal* 92 (1997), pp. 123–40.

McLeod, W., 'The Bow at Night: An Inappropriate Weapon?', *Phoenix* 42 (1988), pp. 121–5.

McNally, Sheila, 'Ariadne and Others: Images of Sleep in Early Greek and Roman Art', *Classical Antiquity* 4 (1985), pp. 152–92.

Montiglio, Silvia, *Silence in the Land of Logos* (Princeton, Princeton University Press, 2000).

———, '"My Soul, Consider What You Should Do": Psychological Conflicts and Moral Goodness in the Greek Novels', *Ancient Narrative* 8 (2010), pp. 25–58.

———, 'The (Cultural) Harmony of Nature: Music, Love, and Order in *Daphnis and Chloe*', *Transactions and Proceedings of the American Philological Association* 142 (2012), pp. 133–56.

———, *Love and Providence: Recognition in the Ancient Novel* (New York, Oxford University Press, 2013).

Morales, Helen, *Vision and Narrative in Achilles Tatius' Leucippe and Clitophon* (Cambridge, Cambridge University Press, 2004).
Moreux, Bernard, 'La nuit, l'ombre et la mort chez Homère', *Phoenix* 21 (1967), pp. 237–72.
Morgan, John, 'The Story of Knemon in Heliodoros' *AITHIOPIKA*', *The Journal of Hellenic Studies* 109 (1989a), pp. 99–113.
———, 'A Sense of the Ending: The Conclusion of Heliodoros' Aithiopika', *Transactions and Proceedings of the American Philological Association* 119 (1989b), pp. 299–320.
——— (ed.), *Longus: Daphnis and Chloe*, with an introduction, translation, and commentary (Oxford, Aris & Phillips, 2004).
———, 'Kleitophon and Encolpius: Achilleus Tatius as Hidden Author', in Michael Paschalis *et al.* (eds), *The Greek and Roman Novel: Parallel Readings, Ancient Narrative*, Supplement 8 (2007), pp. 105–20.
Morris, Frank, '"Dream Scenes" in Homer: A Study in Variation', *Transactions and Proceedings of the American Philological Association* 113 (1983), pp. 39–54.
Mortimer, Armine Kotin, *La clôture narrative* (Paris, Librairie José Corti, 1985).
Murnaghan, Sheila, 'Equal Honor and Future Glory: The Plan of Zeus in the *Iliad*', in D. Roberts *et al.* (eds), *Classical Closure: Reading the End in Greek and Latin Literature* (Princeton, Princeton University Press, 1997), pp. 23–42.
———, *Disguise and Recognition in the Odyssey*, second edition (Lanham, MA, Rowman and Littlefield, 2011).
Nagy, Gregory, *The Best of the Achaeans*, second edition (Baltimore, The Johns Hopkins University Press, 1999).
Ogle, Marbury, 'The Sleep of Death', *Memoirs of the American Academy in Rome* 11 (1933), pp. 81–117.
Oikonomou, Maria-Elpiniki, 'The Literary Context of Anthia's Dream in Xenophon's *Ephesiaca*', in Konstantin Doulamis (ed.), *Echoing Narratives: Studies of Intertextualities in Greek and Roman Prose Fiction, Ancient Narrative*, Supplement 13 (2010), pp. 49–72.
O'Sullivan, James N., *Xenophon of Ephesus: His Compositional Technique and the Birth of the Novel* (Berlin, De Gruyter, 1995).
Pachet, Pierre, *La force de dormir* (Paris, Gallimard, 1988).
Page, D.L. (ed.), *Poetae Melici Graeci* (Oxford, Oxford University Press, 1962).
Papadopoulou, Thalia, *Heracles and Euripidean Tragedy* (Cambridge, Cambridge University Press, 2005).
Papadopoulou-Belmehdi, Ioanna, *Le chant de Pénélope*, (Paris, Belin, 1994).
Papanghelis, Theodore D. and Antonios Rengakos (eds), *A Companion to Apollonius Rhodius*, second edition (Leiden, Brill, 2008).
Parry, Hugh, 'The Approach of Dawn in the "Rhesus"', *Phoenix* 18 (1964), pp. 283–93.
———, 'The Homeric Hymn to Aphrodite: Erotic "Ananke"', *Phoenix* 40 (1986), pp. 253–64.
Pârvulescu, A., 'Homeric (ἐν) νυκτὸς ἀμολγῷ', *Glotta* 63 (1985), pp. 152–9.

Pattoni, Maria Pia, 'Il motivo del sogno profetico nelle *Coefore* di Eschilo', *Bollettino dei Classici, Accademia Nazionale dei Lincei* 30 (2009), pp. 3–23.

Perry, Ben Edwin, 'Chariton and His Romance from a Literary-Historical Point of View', *American Journal of Philology* 51 (1930), pp. 93–104.

Pomeroy, Arthur J., 'Somnus et Amor: The Play of Statius, "Silvae" 5. 4', *Quaderni Urbinati di Cultura Classica* 24 (1986), pp. 91–7.

Preisendanz, Karl (ed.), *Papyri Graecae Magicae* (Stuttgart, Teubner, 2 vols, 1973).

Purves, Alex, 'Wind and Time in Homeric Epic', *Transactions and Proceedings of the American Philological Association* 140 (2010a), pp. 323–51.

———, *Space and Time in Ancient Greek Narrative* (Cambridge, Cambridge University Press, 2010b).

———, 'Sleeping Outside in Homer's *Odyssey* and W.G. Sebald's *The Emigrants*', in H. Gardner and S. Murnaghan (eds), *Odyssean Identities in Modern Cultures: The Journey Home* (Columbus, Ohio State University Press, 2014), pp. 213–39.

Questa, Cesare, *Il ratto del serraglio: Euripide Plauto Mozart Rossini* (Urbino, QuattroVenti, 1979).

Ramnoux, Clémence, *La nuit et les enfants de la nuit dans la tradition grecque* (Paris, Flammarion, 1959).

Reardon, B.P. (ed.), *Chariton: de Callirhoe Narrationes Amatoriae* (Lipsia, Teubner, 2004).

——— (ed.), *Collected Greek Novels* (Berkeley, The University of California Press, 2008).

Reinhardt, Karl, *Sophocles*, translated by B. Blackwell (New York, Barnes & Noble, 1979).

Repath, Ian, 'Achilles Tatius' *Leucippe and Clitophon*: What Happened Next?', *The Classical Quarterly* 55 (2005), pp. 250–65.

———, 'Platonic Love and Erotic Education in Longus' *Daphnis and Chloe*', in Konstantin Doulamis (ed.), *Echoing Narratives: Studies of Intertextualities in Greek and Roman Prose Fiction, Ancient Narrative*, Supplement 13 (2010), pp. 99–122.

Risset, Jacqueline, *Sleep's Powers*, translated by Jennifer Moxley (New York, Ugly Duckling Presse, 2008).

Roberts, Deborah H., Dunn F.M., Fowler D. (eds), *Classical Closure: Reading the End in Greek and Latin Literature* (Princeton, Princeton University Press, 1997).

Robiano, Patrick, 'La citation poétique dans le roman érotique grec', *Revue des Études Grecques* 102 (2000), pp. 509–29.

Rose, G. P., '*Odyssey* 15. 143–82: A Narrative Inconsistency?', *Transactions and Proceedings of the American Philological Association* 102 (1971), pp. 509–14.

Rousseau, G.S., 'Dream and Vision in Aeschylus' *Oresteia*', *Arion* 2 (1963), pp. 101–36.

Ruiz-Montero, Consuelo, *La Estructura de la Novela Griega: Análisis Functional* (Salamanca, Ediciones Universidad de Salamanca, 1988).

Russo, Joseph A., 'Homer Against His Tradition', *Arion* 7 (1968), pp. 275–95.

———, 'Interview and Aftermath: Dream, Fantasy and Intuition in *Odyssey* 19 and 20', *American Journal of Philology* 103 (1982), pp. 4–18.

Saïd, Suzanne, 'Les crimes des prétendants, la maison d'Ulysse et les festins de l'Odyssée', in *Études de littérature ancienne* (Paris, Presses de l'École normale supérieure, 1979), pp. 9–49.
Sanz Morales, Manuel and Gabriel Laguna Mariscal, 'The Relationship Between Achilles and Patroclus According to Chariton of Aphrodisias', *The Classical Quarterly* 53 (2003), pp. 292–6.
———, 'Was the Relationship Between Achilles and Patroclus Homoerotic? The View of Apollonius Rhodius', *Hermes* 133 (2005), pp. 120–3.
Scaffai, Marco, 'Servio e il sonno di Achille (*ad Aen.* 1, 487 e 2, 542)', *Aufidus* 52 (2004), pp. 51–77.
Scattergood, John, 'The "Bisynesse" of Love in Chaucer's Dawn-Songs', *Essays in Criticism* 37 (1987), pp. 110–20.
Schadewaldt, Wolfgang, *Iliasstudien* (Leipzig, Verlag von S. Hirzel, 1938).
Schein, Seth L., *The Mortal Hero* (Berkeley, The University of California Press, 1984).
———, *Sophokles: Philoktetes*, translation with notes, introduction and interpretive essay (Newburyport, Focus Publishing, 2003).
———, 'Sophocles and Homer', in Kirk Ormand (ed.), *A Companion to Sophocles* (Malden, Wiley-Blackwell, 2012), pp. 424–39.
——— (ed.), *Sophocles: Philoctetes* (Cambridge, Cambridge University Press, 2013).
Schmeling, Gareth, *Xenophon of Ephesus* (Boston, Twayne, 1980).
Scioli, Emma, 'The Intimacy between Sleep and Death in Book 10 of Statius' *Thebaid*', unpublished conference paper (2013).
Scioli, Emma and Christine Walde (eds), *Sub imagine somni*: *Nighttime Phenomena in Greco-Roman Culture* (Pisa, Edizioni ETS, 2010).
Seaford, Richard, 'The Date of Euripides' Cyclops', *The Journal of Hellenic Studies* 102 (1982), pp. 161–72.
———, *Euripides: Cyclops*, with introduction and commentary (Oxford, Oxford University Press, 1984).
Segal, Charles, *Singers, Heroes, and Gods in the Odyssey* (Ithaca, Cornell University Press, 1994).
Shapiro, H.A., *Personifications in Greek Art* (Zurich, Akanthus, 1993).
Sissa, Giulia and Marcel Detienne, *The Daily Life of the Greek Gods*, translated by J. Lloyd (Stanford, Stanford University Press, 2000).
Slater, Niall W., 'Making the Aristophanic Audience', *American Journal of Philology* 120 (1999), pp. 351–68.
Sommerstein, Alan H. (ed. and translator), *Aristophanes: Wasps* (Warminster, Aris & Phillips, 1983).
———, *Aeschylus' Eumenides* (Cambridge, Cambridge University Press, 1989).
Sorabella, Jean, 'Observing Sleep in Greco-Roman Art', in E. Scioli and C. Walde (eds), *Sub imagine somni: Nighttime Phenomena in Greco-Roman Culture* (Pisa, Edizioni ETS, 2010), pp. 1–32.
Stafford, Emma J., 'Aspects of Sleep in Hellenistic Sculpture', *Bulletin of the Institute of Classical Studies* 38 (1991/93), pp. 105–20.
———, 'Brother, Son, Friend, and Healer: Sleep the God', in K. Dowden and T. Wiedemann (eds), *Sleep* (Bari, Levante, 2003), pp. 71–106.
Stanford, William B., *Homer: Odyssey*, edited with introduction and commentary (London, Duckworth, 2 vols, 1996).

Stanley, Keith, *The Shield of Homer: Narrative Structure in the Iliad* (Princeton, Princeton University Press, 1993).
Stevick, Philip, *The Chapter in Fiction: Theories of Narrative Division* (Syracuse, Syracuse University Press, 1970).
Strobl, Petra, *Die Macht des Schlafes in der griechisch-römishen Welt* (Hamburg, Verlag Dr. Kovac, 2002).
Summers-Bremmer, Eluned, *Insomnia: A Cultural History* (London, Reaktion Books, 2008).
Taplin, Oliver, *The Stagecraft of Aeschylus* (Oxford, Oxford University Press, 1977).
———, *Homeric Soundings: The Shaping of the* Iliad (Oxford, Oxford University Press, 1992).
Thalmann, W.G., 'Speech and Silence in the *Oresteia* 1: *Agamemnon* 1025–1029' 'Speech and Silence in the *Oresteia* 2', *Phoenix* 39 (1985), pp. 99–118 and 221–37.
Thomas, Richard F., 'New Comedy, Callimachus, and Roman Poetry', *Harvard Studies in Classical Philology* 83 (1979), pp. 179–206.
Thompson, Stith, *Motif-Index of Folk-Literature* (Bloomington, Indiana University Press, 6 vols, 1955).
Thomson, George (ed.), *The Oresteia of Aeschylus* (Amsterdam, Hakkert, 2 vols, 1966).
Torgovnick, Marianna, *Closure in the Novel* (Princeton, Princeton University Press, 1981).
Traill, Ariana, 'Knocking on Knemon's Door: Stagecraft and Symbolism in the "Dyskolos"', *Transactions and Proceedings of the American Philological Association* 131 (2001), pp. 87–108.
Turner, Eric G., 'The *Phasma* of Menander', *Greek, Roman, and Byzantine Studies* 10 (1969), pp. 307–24.
Ussher, R.G. (ed.), *Euripides: Cyclops*, with introduction and commentary (Rome, edizioni dell'ateneo, 1978).
———, *Sophocles: Philoctetes*, with an introduction, translation and commentary (Warminster, Aris & Phillips, second edition, 2001).
Vagnone, G., 'Le scene tipiche del pasto e del sonno in Omero', *Quaderni Urbinati di Cultura Classica* 26 (1987), pp. 91–9.
Van der Eijk, P.J., 'Aristotle on Cognition in Sleep', in K. Dowden and K. Wiedemann (eds), *Sleep* (Bari, Levante, 2003), pp. 25–40.
Van Sickle, John, 'Dawn and Dusk as Motifs of Opening or Closure, in Heroic and Bucolic Epos', *Atti del Convegno mondiale scientifico di studi su Virgilio* Milan, Mondadori, 1 (1984), pp. 125–47.
Van Steen, Gonda, 'An Early Morning Person? Aristophanes and His Star-Studded Comic Prologues: Scenarios of Reception' (in Greek, translated by T. Bouchelos), in Th. G. Pappas and A.G. Markantonatos (eds), *Attic Comedy: Characters and Approaches* (in Greek) (Athens, Gutenberg, 2011), pp. 778–813.
Verity, Anthony (translator), *Theocritus: Idylls*, introduction and notes by Richard Hunter (New York, Oxford University Press, 2002).
Vermeule, Emily, *Aspects of Death in Early Greek Art and Poetry* (Berkeley, The University of California Press, 1979).
Vernant, Jean-Pierre, *Mortals and Immortals: Collected Essays*, ed. Froma I. Zeitlin (Princeton, Princeton University Press, 1991).

Vester, Helmut, 'Das 19. Buch der Odyssee', *Gymnasium* 75 (1968), pp. 417–34.
Vian, Francis (ed.), *Apollonios de Rhodes: Argonautiques chant III* (Paris, Presses Universitaires de France, 1961).
———, *Apollonios de Rhodes: Argonautiques* (Paris, Les Belles Lettres, 1974).
Vidal-Naquet, Pierre, *The Black Hunter*, translated by A. Szegedy-Maszak (Baltimore, The Johns Hopkins University Press, 1986).
Voigt, Eva-Maria (ed.), *Sappho et Alcaeus: Fragmenta* (Amsterdam, Polak & van Gennep, 1971).
Waern, Ingrid, 'Greek Lullabies', *Eranos* 58 (1960), pp. 1–8.
Walton, J. Michael, 'Playing in the Dark: Masks and Euripides' *Rhesus*', *Helios* 27 (2000), pp. 137–47.
Webster, T.B.L. (ed.), *Sophocles: Philoctetes* (Cambridge, Cambridge University Press, 1970).
West, Emily B., 'Marriage, Cosmic Tranquility, and the Homeric Retiring Scene', *Classical World* 104 (2010), pp. 17–28.
West, Martin L. (ed.), *Hesiod: Theogony* (Oxford, Oxford University Press, 1982a).
———, *Hesiod: Works and Days* (Oxford, Oxford University Press, 1982b).
Whitman, Cedric H., *Sophocles: A Study in Heroic Humanism* (Cambridge, MA, Harvard University Press, 1951).
Whitmarsh, Tim, 'Divide and Rule: Segmenting *Callirhoe* and Related Works', in Michael Paschalis *et al.* (eds), *Readers and Writers in the Ancient Novel, Ancient Narrative*, Supplement 12 (2009), pp. 36–50.
Wiedemann, Thomas, 'Introduction', in K. Dowden and T. Wiedemann (eds), *Sleep* (Bari, Levante, 2003a), pp. X–XVIII.
———, 'The Roman Siesta', in K. Dowden and T. Wiedemann (eds), *Sleep* (Bari, Levante, 2003b), pp. 125–40.
Wiesmann, Peter, 'Was heisst κῶμα? Zur Interpretation von Sapphos "Gedicht auf der Scherbe"', *Museum Helveticum* 29 (1972), pp. 1–11.
Wilamowitz-Moellendorff, Ulrich von (ed.), *Herakles* (Berlin, Weidmann, 2 vols, 1985).
Willink, Charles W., 'The Prologue of Iphigenia at Aulis', *The Classical Quarterly* 21 (1971), pp. 343–64.
——— (ed.), *Euripides: Orestes*, with introduction and commentary (Oxford, Oxford University Press, 1986).
———, 'Sleep after Labour in Euripides' *Heracles*', *The Classical Quarterly* 38 (1988), pp. 86–97.
Winkler, John J., 'The Mendacity of Kalasiris and the Narrative Strategy of Heliodoros' *Aithiopika*', *Yale Classical Studies* 27 (1982), pp. 93–158.
Wöhrle, Georg, *Hypnos, der Allbezwinger: Eine Studie zum literarischen Bild des Schlafes in der griechischen Antike* (Stuttgart, Franz Steiner Verlag, 1995).
Woodman, A.J., 'Sleepless Poets: Catullus and Keith', *Greece & Rome* 21 (1974), pp. 51–3.
——— (ed.), *Velleius Paterculus: The Caesarian and Augustan Narrative (2. 41–93)* (Cambridge, Cambridge University Press, 1983).
Wray, David, 'Apollonius' Masterplot: Narrative Strategy in *Argonautica* 1', in M.A. Harder *et al.* (eds), *Apollonius Rhodius* (Leuven, Peeters, 2000), pp. 239–65.

Wright, Matthew, *Euripides: Orestes* (London, Duckworth, 2008).
Zanker, Graham, *The Heart of Achilles: Characterization and Personal Ethics in the Iliad* (Ann Arbor, The University of Michigan Press, 1996).
Zeitlin, Froma I., 'The Closet of Masks: Role-Playing and Myth-Making in the Orestes of Euripides', *Ramus* 9 (1980), pp. 51–77.

INDEX